Classic Walks

MOUNTAIN AND MOORLAND WALKS
IN BRITAIN AND IRELAND

CLASSIC WALKS

COMPILED BY
KEN WILSON AND RICHARD GILBERT

with editorial assistance
from Jim Perrin

maps by Don Sargeant

Diadem Books · London

In the same series:

The Big Walks

Wild Walks

200 Challenging Walks
in Britain and Ireland
(a field guide for all the walks
described in The Big Walks
Classic Walks and Wild Walks)

Other companion titles on aspects
of British mountaineering:

Hard Rock

Classic Rock

Extreme Rock

Cold Climbs

British Library and Cataloguing Data:

Wilson, Ken
    Classic walks: mountain and moorland walks in Britain and Ireland
    1. Great Britain–Description and travel–
    1971–Guide-books
    I. Title   II. Gilbert, Richard. *1937 Nov. 17–*
    914.1′04858 DA650
ISBN 0-906371-11-2

First published in 1982 by Diadem Books Limited, London
Reprinted 1986
Reprinted 1990
Reprinted 1997 (by Bâton Wicks Publications)

All trade enquiries to Cordee
3a De Montfort Street, Leicester LE1 7HD.

Colour separations by Wensum Graphics, Norwich
Production by Chambers Green Limited, Tunbridge Wells, Kent
Printed in Singapore by the Kyodo Printing Company

Frontispiece: Buttermere from
High Crag. *Photo: Stephen Greenwood*

Contents

Preface   vii

Acknowledgements   ix

Scotland

1   **The Cape Wrath Coastal Walk** Sutherland *by Richard Gilbert*   10
2   **Ben Loyal** Sutherland *by Phil Cooper*   13
3   **Conival and Ben More Assynt** Sutherland *by Peter Gillman*   16
4   **A Traverse of Quinag** Sutherland *by Gwen Moffat*   19
5   **Stac Pollaidh – the Perfect Miniature** Ross-shire *by Richard Gilbert*   22
6   **The Clisham Ridge** Isle of Harris, Inverness-shire *by Ian Stephen*   26
7   **Explorations in Trotternish** Isle of Skye, Inverness-shire *by Tom Weir*   29
8   **Sgurr nan Gillean** Isle of Skye, Inverness-shire *by W. A. Poucher*   33
9   **Across the Cuillin by Loch Coruisk** Isle of Skye, Inverness-shire *by Donald Bennet*   39
10 **Slioch** Ross-shire *by Sandy Cousins*   43
11 **Beinn Alligin, the Jewel of Torridon** Ross-shire *by Charles Rose*   46
12 **Spidean Mialach and Gleouraich** Inverness-shire *by Stephen Greenwood*   51
13 **The Saddle of Glen Shiel** Inverness-shire/Ross-shire *by Jo Light*   53
14 **The Lairig Ghru** Inverness-shire/Aberdeenshire *by Adam Watson*   56
15 **The Corrieyairack Pass** Inverness-shire *by Alastair Hetherington*   60
16 **Schiehallion** Perthshire *by Cameron McNeish*   63
17 **A Ben Alder Crossing** Inverness-shire/Perthshire *by Richard Gilbert*   64
18 **A Traverse of Bidean nam Bian** Argyllshire *by Donald Bennet*   69
19 **Buachaille Etive Mor** Argyllshire *by W. H. Murray*   71
20 **Ben Cruachan** Argyllshire *by Richard Gilbert*   74
21 **The Peaks of the Black Mount** Argyllshire *by Richard Gilbert*   76
22 **Ben More of Mull** Isle of Mull, Argyllshire *by Campbell R. Steven*   79
23 **A Day on the Cobbler** Argyllshire *by Sandy Cousins*   81
24 **Ben Vorlich and Stuc a'Chroin** Perthshire *by Roger Smith*   84
25 **Ben Lomond** Stirlingshire *by Tom Weir*   86
26 **Around Glencorse in the Pentlands** Midlothian/Lanarkshire *by Neil Mather*   89
27 **The Round of Loch Enoch** Kircudbright *by Ken Andrew*   92

England and The Isle of Man

28 **Hadrian's Wall** Cumbria/Northumberland *by Richard Gilbert*   96
29 **High Street** Cumbria *by Tom Price*   100
30 **Saddleback by Sharp Edge** Cumbria *by Chris Bonington*   104
31 **The Buttermere Circuit** Cumbria *by Geoffrey Berry*   108
32 **Great Gable** Cumbria *by Tony Greenbank*   112
33 **Helvellyn by Striding Edge** Cumbria *by A. Wainwright*   116
34 **The Coniston Fells** Cumbria *by Harry Griffin*   119
35 **Ward's Stone, Forest of Bowland** Lancashire *by Walt Unsworth*   122
36 **Snaefell and the Manx Hills** Isle of Man *by Michael Hoy and Tim Wilson*   124
37 **Great Whernside and Buckden Pike** North Yorkshire *by Richard Gilbert*   127
38 **Malham Cove and Gordale Scar – a Botanist's Paradise** North Yorkshire *by Oliver Gilbert* 132
39 **Wharfedale – a Taste of the Dales Way** North Yorkshire *by Colin Speakman*   134
40 **Black Hambleton by the Drove Road** North Yorkshire *by Richard Gilbert*   136
41 **The Eastern Edges of the Peak** South Yorkshire/Derbyshire *by Roger Redfern*   138
42 **The Round of Kinder Scout from Edale** Derbyshire *by Roger Redfern*   141
43 **Dovedale from Axe Edge** Derbyshire/Staffordshire *by Phil Cooper*   144

44 **The Western Peak by the Gritstone Trail** Derbyshire/Cheshire *by Rex Bellamy*   148
45 **The Long Mynd and Stiperstones** Shropshire *by Chris Collier*   151
46 **High Dyke** Shropshire/Powys *by Lord Hunt of Llanfair Waterdine*   153
47 **The Malvern Hills** Hereford and Worcester *by Richard Gilbert*   156
48 **The Wye Valley and the Forest of Dean** Hereford and Worcester/Glos. *by Maurice and Marion Teal*   160
49 **The Ancient Footpaths of the Chilterns** Oxfordshire/Buckinghamshire *by Christopher Hall*   163
50 **A Cotswold Classic** Hereford and Worcester/Gloucester *by Mark Richards*   165
51 **The Ridgeway over the Berkshire Downs** Berkshire *by Janet Wedgwood*   168
52 **The Wiltshire Downs** Wiltshire *by Geoffrey Wright*   171
53 **The Mendip Hills** Somerset/Avon *by Robin Atthill*   175
54 **The Dunkery Circuit** Exmoor, Somerset *by Brian Chugg*   178
55 **The Quantocks** Somerset *by David Clemson*   180
56 **A Visit to Cranmere Pool** Dartmoor, Devon *by Hugh Westacott*   183
57 **Lamorna Cove to Pendeen Watch** Cornwall *by Dave Cook*   186
58 **The Dorset Coast and the Purbeck Hills** Dorset *by Eric Newby*   190
59 **High Level from Guildford to Box Hill** Surrey *by Christopher John Wright*   193
60 **The Seven Sisters and the Long Man of Wilmington** Sussex *by Richard Gilbert*   196

Wales

61 **The Clwydian Hills** Clwyd *by Peter and Muriel Wild*   201
62 **The Carnedds by the Cwm Eigiau Horseshoe** Gwynedd *by Rob Collister*   205
63 **The Glyders from Pen-y-Gwryd** Gwynedd *by Showell Styles*   209
64 **Snowdon – Llanberis to Beddgelert** Gwynedd *by Tony Moulam*   213
65 **Snowdon by the Miners' Track** Gwynedd *by David Cox*   218
66 **Cnicht and the Moelwyns** Gwynedd *by Showell Styles*   222
67 **The Pennant Ridges** Gwynedd *by Jim Perrin*   226
68 **Deepest Meirionydd – Arenig Fawr and Rhobell Fawr** Gwynedd *by Jim Perrin*   231
69 **The Migneint and Arenig Fach** Gwynedd *by Harold Drasdo*   234
70 **Cader Idris from the South** Gwynedd *by John Neill*   236
71 **The North Pembroke Coast: St. David's Head to St. Non's Bay** Dyfed *by Jan Morris*   241
72 **The South Pembroke Coast: Stackpole Quay to Freshwater West** Dyfed *by Jim Perrin*   242
73 **The Presely Hills** Dyfed *by Wynford Vaughan Thomas*   246

Ireland

74 **The Aghla–Errigal Horseshoe** Co. Donegal *by Denis Rankin*   249
75 **The Benbulbin Group** Co. Sligo/Co. Leitrim *by Gerry Foley*   252
76 **Mweelrea** Connemara, Co. Mayo *by Tony Whilde*   255
77 **The Glencoaghan Horseshoe of the Twelve Bens** Connemara, Co. Galway *by Joss Lynam*   258
78 **The Galty Ridgewalk** Co. Limerick/Co. Tipperary *by Frank Martindale*   262
79 **Brandon Mountain** Co. Kerry *by Hamish Brown*   267

Index   269

Other Good Walks and Scrambles   271

The Country Code   271

Map Location of the Walks   272

Preface

Following the enthusiastic reception given to *The Big Walks*, Ken Wilson and I decided to collaborate again to produce *Classic Walks* – a book in which we hoped to reflect a wide variety of less demanding walks and scrambles. We also felt that *Classic Walks* would offer a marvellous opportunity to collect into one book essays from the many writers involved in mountain description, and thereby reflect the instincts and stimuli that lead people to take to wild countryside for their recreation. As in the previous book, I have organised the collection of walks and essays, and Ken has dealt with the selection of photos and their presentation.

One of the most frequent reactions to *The Big Walks* was surprise and astonishment that so much superlative mountain scenery existed in the British Isles. The extensive use of colour photography in these books has allowed us to show the mountains and countryside at their most tantalising; we hope they will stir many to accept the challenge and experience the walks at first hand. The tourist can only experience a small share of this and it is essential to become a walker to gain a really profound appreciation of the British countryside.

What exactly is a classic walk? Clearly many of the routes in *The Big Walks* could lay claim to this title. For this second book there were hundreds of routes that came into consideration, and making the final selection has been difficult. For many of us, mountain-walking provides the most elevating experiences of all, both literally and figuratively. For this reason we made excursions over hills and upland country the basic framework of the book. The 79 walks eventually selected fulfil a wide variety of criteria. The differing geological characteristics of our mountains and hills give them great interest – granite, gabbro, quartzite, weathered volcanic lava, limestone, gritstone, sandstone, gneiss, and the rolling chalk downs of southern England are all reflected here, as are more pastoral environments – woods, rivers, fields – where geological character is less assertive. It was therefore interesting, while working on this book, to sample the hills and valleys of the Cotswolds, the Mendips, the Quantocks, and Exmoor, and the downlands of Berkshire, Wiltshire, Sussex, and Dorset. There is an indefinable link between these excursions and the more serious fare of the mountains. Possibly it is just the enjoyment of strenuous exercise in open country; maybe it is the lure of discovery. Many mountaineers and mountain walkers, including Frank Smythe, Geoffrey Winthrop Young, and W. A. Poucher, have underscored this link in their writings and photographs.

The link between the mountains and the dramatic coastal environment is more obvious. Mountains and the sea are closely linked in their appeal, and many mountaineers, H. W. Tilman for example, have turned to sailing in later life. Rock-climbers gain great pleasure from sea-cliff climbing, and walkers too derive a distinctive satisfaction from following switchback routes along a rugged coast. The sea's constant ebb and flow, accompanied by the suck and roar of the breakers, is akin to the buffeting and moaning of the wind and the slow erosion by frost and rain of our mountain peaks. In both cases, we gain a peculiar pleasure from close observation of the forces of nature at work. For these reasons I have included several walks along or near some spectacular stretches of coastline. Eric Newby writes about Dorset, Jim Perrin and Jan Morris describe different aspects of the Pembroke coastline, Dave Cook brings a rock-climber's eye to the dramatic Cornish coast, and Hamish Brown describes the intricacies of Brandon Mountain, which rises directly from the Atlantic – a peak he regards as the finest in Ireland and Great Britain.

For a walk to be *classic* it must be not only of excellent quality, but it must have withstood the test of time. Some of the walks selected have been recognised for centuries, and are reflected in the many historical and literary associations connected with them. The moorlands bristle with tumuli, the Wiltshire Downs boast the incomparable Avebury Stone Circle and Silbury Hill, the Romans recognised the value of the Northumbrian whin sill outcrops for defensive purposes, and the ridge of High Street for rapid communications, General Wade constructed his military road through the Corrieyairack Pass and Scottish drovers took their cattle to the lucrative English markets over Black Hambleton. Literary figures associated with the walks include W. B. Yeats, Mary Webb, the Lakeland poets, and William Langland, who dozed on the Malvern Hills and dreamed of Piers the Plowman.

Turning to the length and character of these walks, I hope that we have redressed the balance against *The Big Walks*. In that book the routes were long and challenging, schedules and miles completed became all-important and the successful completion of the walk was paramount. In this book, although few of the walks can be described as afternoon rambles, in general they are shorter and less serious. The walker will find far more time to enjoy the surroundings, and this more detailed appreciation is reflected by the essayists, who often digress with evident pleasure on the natural or historical aspects of their routes.

In preparing the book, we have both been struck by the quality of some very familiar subjects. The magnificent rock scenery on Great Gable is in no way lessened by popularity. Snowdon, that much-visited old favourite, has merited two more chapters to add to the one in *The Big Walks*. This is not excessive when the size and complexity of the mountain is considered. In terms of scale and interest, Snowdon surpasses all other mountains in England and Wales and can hold its own against the Scottish giants. Many other old favourites are included in the book, which I hope will rekindle past memories for some and provide renewed inspiration for all. Ben Lomond, Stac Pollaidh, Blencathra, Cader Idris, and the splendid and challenging Glencoe peaks of Buachaille Etive Mor and Bidean nam Bian can be climbed time and time again without a hint of staleness. In fact, authors such as Harry Griffin, W. H. Murray, and Showell Styles reflect, in their writing, increased pleasure in their walks (the Coniston Fells, Buachaille Etive Mor, and Cnicht and the Moelwyns) even after a lifetime of familiarity.

We are exceptionally lucky in the British Isles in being able to wander freely among our mountains. With a few exceptions we can pretty well go where we like, when we like. We have none of the tiresome official restrictions often encountered in American national parks, and most landowners are fairly relaxed about walkers crossing their land, providing a few reasonable procedures are observed. Yet how many of these walks will still remain in their present form in 50 years time? The loss of wild countryside to agriculture, forestry, industry, the water-boards, the CEGB, and the Ministry of Defence, is alarming, despite the efforts of national amenity or conservation organisations such as The Ramblers' Association, the Council for the Protection of Rural England, the National Trust, and the Commons, Open Spaces and Footpath Society.

Since 1954, over 20% of Exmoor's moorland has been lost to the plough, and recent research by Dr. Martin Parry, of Birmingham University, has shown a national rate of loss of more than 12,000 acres a year. At this rate the entire area of the country's moorlands will be lost in 30 years. From a detailed study of the Brecon Beacons, Dartmoor, Snowdonia, North York Moors, Yorkshire Dales, Northumberland and the Peak District, Dr. Parry and his team found no slowing-down in the rate of moorland loss; if anything it may be accelerating. The Government's new Countryside Bill, heavily influenced by Farmers' and Landowners' pressure groups, has made little attempt to arrest this trend. I still feel dismay at the appalling intrusions of recent years, exemplified by the Kielder reservoir, the pylons marching across Scotland to Loch Hourn and Skye, the despoliation around Llyn Peris below Snowdon and, possibly still to come, further development of Cairngorm ski-ing facilities and test-drillings for disposal of nuclear waste.

Another problem, still to be resolved, is that created by trail riders, whose machines tear up the turf of our most-prized downland, including the historic Ridgeway, shattering the peace for miles around. A motor-cycle safari was recently organised to the summit of Plynlimon! While we can sympathise with their desire to travel to wild places, the price in damage and disruption is surely unreasonably high.

The amenity organisations can claim some success in getting National and Local Governments to hold a much closer watching brief on environmental matters. Waymarking footpaths and establishing National and Country Parks may not be ideal solutions, but they are far preferable to the disappearance of amenities altogether. Vigilance is always necessary however, particularly in heavily cultivated areas. In his chapter on the Chilterns, Chris Hall (editor of *The Countryman* and sometime director of the CPRE) implores us to stick to the public rights-of-way *across* fields, even if they are planted with crops. The irritation and illogicality wherever paths have been forced into a zig-zag course along the sides of fields kills the sense of free movement that must be protected, particularly in areas lacking large tracts of commonland and moorland. All too often farmers attempt to render rights-of-way unusable. I implore them to have more consideration for the walker. Farmers are heavily subsidised by tax payers, most of whom live in conurbations, and it ill befits them to take inflexible stands on rights-of-way.

Let us strive to keep our wilderness areas. Let them keep their rugged character and their surprises, however challenging the terrain. Yet even amongst ourselves, we cannot agree on a consistent policy. Personally, I rejoice when we remove emergency shelters from the Cairngorm plateau and when the army's bridges on the Camasunary path are swept away, but I despair when we 'approve' the building of a bridge over the Carnoch river in Knoydart. Surely we go to Knoydart because of

the wilderness, the lack of amenities and the added challenge, so why do we destroy that which we purport to treasure?

It is nevertheless essential that walkers exercise responsibility. Many of the walks in this book pass through private estates where the letting of sporting rights can be the only income, so it is helpful for walkers to keep to the paths and avoid disturbing deer and grouse. Whenever possible avoid climbing deer fences and never climb dry stone walls which are so important to the hill farmer. Scrupulous observation of the Country Code must be the paramount ethos of the walker.

Before setting out on these walks, read, and take account of the advice given in the summary and in the text. Don't attempt walks which are beyond your capability; if a rope is advised, be sure to take one with you and use it if the slightest difficulty arises. Several routes involve crossing military firing ranges and it is best to telephone to check that the ranges are open before you set out. The numbers to ring are given in the route descriptions.

As in *The Big Walks* place names are taken from the OS 1:50,000 maps with accents omitted in the case of Gaelic names. In Wales, OS versions have been retained often at variance with current forms. I have also retained the old county names in Scotland in preference to the new regional names which have little meaning except to the bureaucrat.

The times given are for a fit party and do not include stops. Several strong walkers have remarked to me that they found the recommended times given for *The Big Walks* to be slightly on the short side, so allow plenty of safety margin. The times refer to good conditions which are seldom met with in the mountains and I expect this is where the discrepancy lies.

The appendix contains a list of other walks which were considered for inclusion. These are highly recommended and, although space could not be found for a detailed description of them, they should be of interest to the reader.

A Note on Mountain Safety

In the appendix to *The Big Walks* a good deal of space was given to a discussion of mountain safety. This emphasised the need for vigilance whilst walking over some of our great mountain ranges, particularly since the desire to complete the itinerary in the face of approaching bad weather and increasing fatigue, might take precedence over sanity. The principal safety point that emerged was that experience is paramount and this can only be acquired by gradually building up knowledge of the hills in all seasons.

The expeditions covered by *Classic Walks* also require a deep sense of responsibility on behalf of walkers because of the wide diversity of terrain that will be encountered. Whilst a ramble along the Ridgeway or the South Downs can be accomplished by a family party under most conditions in complete safety, the same can certainly not be said for a descent of, say, the West Ridge of Sgurr nan Gillean under snow.

Classic Walks contains some major mountaineering routes which, although manna to devotees of *The Big Walks*, should be treated with the utmost caution by those walkers who are lacking in experience and confidence. Since *Classic Walks* is likely to appeal to a far wider spectrum of the walking public than *The Big Walks*, it is vital that the advice given below is heeded.

Do your homework. Before setting out read carefully the account of the walk in the relevant chapter as well as the walk details. Study the map and guidebook before leaving the shelter of the valley, not on an exposed ridge in a rainstorm. Where possible, seek advice from those who know the route.

Make sure your equipment is effective. Strive to keep warm

and dry. It is dangerous to get wet in the hills because evaporation in the wind causes rapid cooling and the possibility of exposure. Expect the worst and go prepared to deal with every reasonable eventuality.

Take an ice-axe if you think there is even a remote possibility of meeting snow. If you do meet snow, don't leave your ice-axe strapped to the back of your rucksack, have it in your hand. In full winter conditions take crampons as well, they could save hours of step-cutting. It is also important to be fully practised in ice-axe and crampon techniques before embarking on a serious expedition.

Don't be afraid to turn back for home or descend to the valley. Make such decisions in good time; when you first start to drop behind schedule, when the weather first begins to deteriorate, or when you first notice a member of the party is becoming cold, wet and tired. Make sure that you know how to use your map and compass and try to know your exact position at all times.

Before leaving the valley, check your rucksack for waterproof clothing, map, compass, whistle, torch, food, first-aid kit, and rope (if required by the expedition). If you leave your car parked in a mountain area, leave a note behind the windscreen giving your name, route, and estimated time of return. If you are staying at a Youth Hostel or hotel, leave details of your proposed route with someone in authority. If an accident should occur while you are out on the hills, you must know the emergency drill:

a. The International Distress Call is six blasts on a whistle, or six shouts or flashes of a torch. The answering signal is three blasts.

b. Send a fit member of the party to summon help. He should dial 999 and report to the Police, who co-ordinate all mountain rescue services.

For a comprehensive coverage of mountain safety matters, read the two booklets which may be obtained from The British Mountaineering Council, Crawford House, Precinct Centre, Booth Street East, Manchester M13 9RZ.

Mountain and Cave Rescue (87p post free)
Safety on Mountains (67p post free)

Finally, try not to become obsessed with safety details. Adequate precautions are sensible, simple to take, and soon become second nature.

RICHARD GILBERT
Crayke, York, 1982

Acknowledgements

Since starting work on *Classic Walks*, we have been overwhelmed with help and advice from the hill-walking public, eager to contribute to the logical sequel to *The Big Walks*. This has been particularly heartening, since one of our objectives in the book was to increase the number of contributors, thereby reflecting the opinions of a broader spectrum of walkers. *Classic Walks* contains articles by 60 eminent writers, and the variety of their styles in keeping to the same general brief, is fascinating.

On the photographic side, between five and six thousand photographs were submitted for consideration. Over 250 photographs were eventually selected, representing the work of 77 individual photographers, many of whom are leading practitioners in this field. Among those whose photographs have lent the book considerable strength we could perhaps single out Ken Andrew, Tom Parker, Stephen Greenwood, Van Greaves, Peter Wild, Ian Reynolds, Donald Bennet, and Hamish Brown. We have also been struck by the outstandingly consistent quality of the monochrome prints of Leonard and Marjorie Gayton.

We are deeply indebted to the following, and offer our apologies to anyone we have inadvertently omitted from the list. Dave Alcock, John Allen, Ken Andrew, Bruce Atkins, Robin Atthill, Mike Baker, Chris Barber, Mike Bate, Rex Bellamy, Donald Bennet, Geoffrey Berry, Chris Bonington, Malcolm Boyes, Derry Brabbs, Stuart Bramwell, Robert Brotherton, Hamish Brown, Chris Bryan, Ken Bryan, Irvine Butterfield, Brian Chugg, John Cleare, David Clemson, Phillip Clough, R. J. Clow, Chris Collier, Rob Collister, Dave Cook, Phil Cooper, Sandy Cousins, David Cox, Cecil Davies, Derbyshire Countryside Ltd., Tom Dodd, Harold Drasdo, Donal Enwright, June Farringdon, Gerry Foley, Derek Forss, Gordon and Margaret Gadsby, Leonard and Marjorie Gayton, Richard Gibbens, Oliver Gilbert, Peter Gillman, Brian Gilsenan, Van Greaves, Alan Green, Tony Greenbank, Stephen Greenwood, Bill Gregor, Shelagh Gregory, Don Gresswell, Harry Griffin, Chris Hall, David Harvey, Carl Harwood, Alastair Hetherington, Colin Hobday, Andy Hosking, Eric Houlgrave, Michael Hoy, Lord Hunt, Phil Ideson, Bert Jenkins, Trevor Jones, Sean Kelly, Raymond Lea, Jo Light, Joss Lynam, Noel Maguire, Frank Martindale, Neil Mather, Dave Matthews, Cameron McNeish, C. Douglas Milner, Gwen Moffat, Jan Morris, Tony Moulam, W. H. Murray, John Neill, Eric Newby, North Yorkshire Library, Tom Parker, Richard Pearce, Jim Perrin, Picturefolio I.O.M., W. A. Poucher, Steve Poulton, Tom Price, Denis Rankin, Roger Redfern, Ian Reynolds, Kev Reynolds, Mark Richards, Alan Robson, Charles Rose, Sean Rothery, Dick Sale, Don Sargeant, Michael Saunders, Ernest Shepherd, Showell Styles, Patrick Simms, Cathy Simpson, Gerard Simpson, Susan Sims, Barry Smith, Richard Smith, Rod Smith, Roger Smith, Colin Speakman, D. Spence, Ian Stephen, Campbell Steven, Graham Swinerd, Maurice and Marion Teal, Edi Thompson, Clive Tully, Bertram Unne, Walt Unsworth, Wynford Vaughan Thomas, Ken Vickers, A. Wainwright, Adam Watson, Janet Wedgwood, Tom Weir, Pete Wells, West Air Photography, Hugh Westacott, Tony Whilde, Peter and Muriel Wild, Paul Williams, Tim Wilson, R. V. Wilson, Richard Wood, John Woodhouse, Chris Wright, and Geoffrey Wright.

KEN WILSON & RICHARD GILBERT

1 The Cape Wrath Coastal Walk

by Richard Gilbert

Maps O.S. 1:50,000 Sheet 9. Start from Oldshoremore (ref. 203585). Finish at Cape Wrath lighthouse (ref. 259748).
Grading A long and rough walk over trackless hills and cliff-tops. In wet weather river crossings could be troublesome.
Time 8 hours.
Distance 16 miles.
Escape Routes From Sandwood Bay a track leads inland, passing Loch a'Mhuilinn and Loch na Gainimh, to Blairmore.
Telephones Kinlochbervie; Kyle of Durness.
Transport Irregular minibus service between Cape Wrath lighthouse and the Kyle of Durness ferry in summer only. Railway Station at Lairg. Durness–Kinlochbervie–Lairg bus service on weekdays throughout the year. Post-bus service Kinlochbervie to Oldshoremore.
Accommodation Hotels and Bed and Breakfasts at Kinlochbervie and Durness. Cape Wrath Hotel at Kyle of Durness ferry. Youth Hostels at Durness and Tongue.
Guidebooks S.M.T. Guide *The Northern Highlands.*

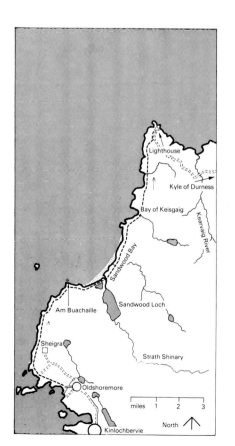

Gale lashed, pounded remorselessly by Atlantic rollers, and virtually uninhabited, the coastline south of Cape Wrath can offer the walker an exhilarating and memorable experience. Here he will find sheer cliffs of grey gneiss, skerries and islets sending the waves into columns of spray with a clap of thunder, wheeling, screaming sea-birds, and wide sandy bays.

Because of poor communications, very careful planning is necessary before embarking on the walk at Oldshoremore. The route which I shall describe ends at Cape Wrath lighthouse, and in summer a minibus plies between the Kyle of Durness and the lighthouse. This links with the passenger ferry over the Kyle at the Cape Wrath Hotel, but the service is not reliable and before setting out it is highly advisable to phone the ferryman, John Muir, at Durness 244, to ascertain the position. If there is no minibus you will have an extra eleven miles to walk to the Kyle, and if you miss the last ferry it is another five miles on top of that. In the winter months the ferry operates on demand, and the walk could satisfactorily be completed in two days with a night spent at the (haunted) bothy beside Sandwood Loch.

Start from the road-end at the walled cemetery at Oldshoremore, and walk along the curve of sand to the rocks on the north side. Climb up the flowery headland at Oldshore Beg, and descend again to another idyllic cove. These early sections of the walk are set in gentle surroundings, and the crofting communities of Droman, Balchrick, and Sheigra extend walls and fences to the coastline. From the higher ground, the sheer cliffs of Handa Island (an RSPB bird sanctuary) can be seen thrusting out into the sea to the south, while inland, the unmistakable outlines of Foinaven, Arkle and Ben Stack are silhouetted against the sky.

As you proceed northwards, hug the coastline whenever possible, at times descending to hidden coves where you will startle the oyster catchers, and at other times traversing round cairned hillocks on heather moorland and eroded peat. Enjoy the diverse bird-life. The fulmar petrels gliding past the red sandstone cliffs, the graceful kittiwakes, shrieking herring gulls, and the superior cormorants, standing aloof in rows on the ledges of the rocky islands.

At Port Mor there is a beach piled high with driftwood and jetsam. A roofless croft stands by the shore, and a stack of rock, bearded with grey lichen, thrusts skyward, topped by an extraordinary ovoid stone covered with bright yellow lichen (*Xanthoria parietina*), like the egg of a giant prehistoric bird. Further on, as you draw level with the island group of Am Balg, one mile out to sea, the cliffs rise to 400ft. and if you peer over the edge, you will see the famous pinnacle of Am Buachaille (the herdsman) rising 220ft. above the waves. It was first climbed in 1967 by Tom Patey, who crossed the boiling gulf between the shore and the base of the stack with the help of two ladders.

Barely have you regained your composure after the remarkable Am Buachaille than, rounding the cliff, one of the most glorious

sights in Britain unfolds before you. Below your feet lies Sandwood Bay, a mile-long sweep of golden sand bounded by rolling dunes and crashing breakers that make you want to shout for joy.

My most recent visit to Sandwood Bay followed a spell of stormy weather, and the roar of the waves was deafening. I stood out on the rocks of one of the two small tidal islands, and watched gannets diving for fish. Gannets, the most beautiful of all sea birds, plummet into the seething waters, their wings folded and their bodies perfectly streamlined at the point of impact, putting an Olympic diver to shame. It was midday in

Above: Walkers head south across Sandwood Bay. Am Buachaille is the distant sea stack.
Photo: Richard Gilbert

Right: Am Buachaille and Sandwood Bay at sunset.
Photo: Phil Cooper

July, yet I enjoyed complete solitude; my footprints on the sand were the first that morning. I could have stayed, mesmerized, for hours, but the lighthouse at Cape Wrath, now clearly visible, looked all of its six miles away and I could not linger. As you climb the loose cliffs out of the bay, you can see behind the dunes to Sandwood Loch and the cottage that is haunted. The ghost takes the form of a shipwrecked mariner, a bearded man dressed in cap, tunic with brass buttons, and seaboots; he has alarmed many travellers who visit this lonely place.

The walking now becomes extremely tough. There is no track, and the narrow sheep-paths contour just above the cliffs in an unnerving way and are best avoided. The grass is coarse, the heather deep, and the peat hagged. No sooner have you climbed up to the top of a high cliff than you must descend again, ford a river, and cross a beach of smooth boulders. I was dive-bombed by huge, evil birds, great skuas (nicknamed bonxies), which will eat young birds and even new-born lambs.

The deep-cut Bay of Keisgaig is bounded by high cliffs. On the south side, a natural arch has been worn through the rocky headland, and a vast split block dominates the north. On the shore is a turf roofed shelter. Approaching Cape Wrath, the coast becomes even more shattered, and the waves of the North Minch, reinforced now by the strong currents of the North Atlantic, boom continuously.

I found Cape Wrath lighthouse to be an anti-climax, and I felt depressed to be looking again on a man-made structure, particularly one set in a natural environment of such grandeur. As I waited for the minibus to Kyle of Durness, the lighthouse keeper regaled me with pride about his charge, and how his beacon light, of a million candle-power, could be seen by a ship 40 miles away through the darkness. I, in turn, told him about my invigorating walk, but wild coastal scenery meant nothing to him; he listened politely but we were poles apart.

2 Ben Loyal

by Phil Cooper

I had decided that in order to explore the Scottish mountains in the detail I wanted, especially those in the remote and wild north and west, the solution was to move north, to live and work closer to them. This I did, and nearly every weekend for three years saw me heading for the hills, in all seasons, often to the Munros, but more and more to the Corbetts. My first hill-climbing visit to the Far North included Ben Hope and Ben Loyal. After the three-seasons walking in England, Wales, and Southern Scotland, where spring sometimes starts in March, I had no concept of the way in which the Northern Scottish winter would turn magically to summer in late May, quite missing spring.

But Ben Loyal, only a Corbett* by a (mountain) hair's breadth of four feet, had laid on a specially rude awakening for me on my mid-March visit.

The Ben could quite reasonably be called Ben Royal, such is its splendour when viewed from the road which runs round the Kyle of Tongue. Its north and west ridges, terminating in rocky precipices, give the mountain a splendour more commonly found in west coast mountains than their lonely cousins in the Far North.

I took the obvious approach, which is also the best, for fine views may be had of the mountain on the whole approach walk. Leaving the Kyle of Tongue road at Ribigill Farm, a track runs down to a shepherd's cottage at Cunside. Directly in front is the northern outpost of Sgor Chaonasaid, whose granite ribs and gullies descend steeply to the moor. Unless you fancy a scramble up them, the best bet is to veer left and make for the grass and heather on the eastern side of the Sgor, where there is a steep pull up to the top. On the Sgor, the sheer force of Scottish March weather really hit me, for it was difficult to stand up straight in the tremendous south-westerly gale, from which I had been sheltered during my ascent. Progress in the face of this blow, whose likes I had not met before, and have only experienced a couple of times since, was made tougher by the frequent hail squalls, which battered me like a shotblast. It had been a mild winter, and there was not much

*Scottish peaks between 2,500ft. and 3,000ft.

snow left at this modest altitude, but quickly the surroundings were transformed by the sudden accumulations of hailstones.

I pressed on with a mitt-clad hand in front of my eyes to Sgor a'Bhatain, and traversed its narrow, rocky crest, quite delightful on a good day, with some trepidation, as the ceaseless gale tried to rip my grasp from the granite. This top may be passed on the east if desired. From here, it was a modest climb up the remaining 200ft. to the OS pillar, marking An Caisteal, the Castle, which is the main summit.

My arrival coincided with a break in the hail, and it became clear enough to reveal the bulk of Ben Hope to the west, and Loch Loyal, some 2,100ft. below, just to the east. A subsequent visit revealed the true splendour of the panorama from this northern sentinel: a day of perfect clarity one September, following several days of heavy rain, which had left the atmosphere crystal clear. Ben Hope now appeared much closer than its six miles, and beyond it, further west and stretching well south, was the magnificent line of northern Corbetts for the connoisseur, those of Reay Forest: Beinn Spionnaidh, Cranstackie, Foinaven, Arkle, Meall Horn, Meallan Liath Coire MhicDhughaill, and Ben Hope. Part of Ben More Assynt, whose summit was still smothered in cloud despite the beautiful weather, could be seen beyond the shoulder of Ben Hee. Another lonely Munro, Ben Klibreck, lay south-east, while the whole eastern arc was filled with the soaking moorlands of east Sutherland and Caithness, speckled with a seeming infinity of silver lochans as far as the eye could see. And – could it be? – a check with the compass and quarter-inch map confirmed it – the cliffs of Hoy in the Orkney Islands far away in the north-east. What a feast for the eye. To the north, the contortions of Britain's north coast could be verified against the map, with the Kyle of Tongue and Loch Eriboll as the most prominent features.

But back to my earlier March visit, when I forced myself on against the gale across a minor top, then headed west and lost a few hundred feet before climbing Sgor a'Chleirich, the mountain's westernmost top. The wind was whipping clouds of snow-

Maps   O.S. 1:50,000 Sheet 10. Start and finish at Ribigill (ref. 582542).
Grading   A fine mountain walk. The summit rocks of Sgor a'Bhatain are exposed but quite straightforward under good conditions.
Time   5–6 hours.
Distance   9 miles.
Escape Routes   None.
Telephone   Tongue.
Transport   Railway Station at Lairg. Bus services Lairg–Altnaharra–Tongue (weekdays) and Tongue–Durness (Mon, Wed, Fri, May–October).
Accommodation   Hotels at Durness, Tongue and Altnaharra. Bed and Breakfasts and Youth Hostels at Durness and Tongue.
Guidebooks   S.M.T. Guide *The Northern Highlands; The Scottish Peaks* by W. A. Poucher (Constable).

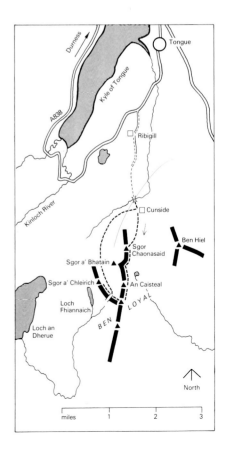

Above: The classic view of Ben Loyal (2,504ft.) – from the north-west, five miles south of Tongue. *Photo: Peter Wild*

white spray from the surface of Loch Fhionnaich far below. The hail seemed to have finished, but on returning to the col below Chleirich, the gale increased even more in its intensity, and I knelt behind a rock eating some chocolate for a few minutes whilst my strength returned.

Leaving the col to the north, I was soon well in the lee, and my cheeks now felt as if they were glowing brightly. It was a rocky but simple enough descent alongside the burn, and the few sheep I met on the way

14

obviously didn't see many walkers here. The burn led me down to the wood of Coille na Cuile, from where it was a straightforward walk directly below the western precipices of An Caisteal, Sgor a'Bhatain, and Sgor Chaonasaid, and back across the moor to Cunside and my base, where I had a most welcome pint mug of tea with a large slice of fruit cake.

3   Conival and Ben More Assynt

by Peter Gillman

Maps   O.S. 1:50,000 Sheet 15. Start and finish at Inchnadamph Hotel (ref. 252217).
Grading   A very rough mountain walk involving steep slopes of sharp quartzite boulders and an exposed rocky ridge.
Time   6–7 hours.
Distance   11 miles.
Escape Routes   There is no refuge to the N, S or E of the range. In difficulties descend from the bealachs between Conival and Beinn an Fhuarain or Conival and Ben More Assynt by the described routes.
Telephones   Inchnadamph.
Transport   Daily bus service, Sutherland Transport, from Lairg (railhead) to Lochinver via Inchnadamph. Infrequent service (summer only) Ullapool to Lochinver.
Accommodation   Inchnadamph Hotel. Hotels, Guest Houses and Bed and Breakfasts in Lochinver (13 miles). Youth Hostels at Achmelvich, Durness and Ullapool.
Guidebooks S.M.T. Guide *The Northern Highlands.*

As a journalist, I have been fortunate enough to visit the World's five continents. But my favourite landscape anywhere remains Scotland's far north-west. Each time I return, and head beyond Ullapool, the sight of the sandstone hills between road and coast, lying like sleeping giants among the sombre lochs, brings an unrivalled thrill of recognition. Suilven, Canisp, Quinag, are names that now convey pleasure in recollection and anticipation as rich as any life can offer.

To begin with, I did not venture into the territory east of the coast road. But my eyes were often drawn to a ridge of white rock among a group of peaks parallel to Suilven, so brilliant that at first I thought it must be snow. When I eventually inquired further, I found it was part of a range containing two main summits, Conival (3,234ft.) and Ben More Assynt (3,272ft.). Poucher ignores them; the SMT guide tells you that the traverse of the ridge 'should not be treated lightly', and instructs you to start at the Inchnadamph hotel.

We were six, and as usual, on an indolent summer holiday based at a cottage on the shore of Loch Broom, we set off late. We parked at the hotel around noon on an overcast day, and followed the path that starts through the house of the Inchnadamph estate. The path follows the course of the River Traligill as it winds down Glean-Dubh, but then turns away towards some caves to the south (the point is marked by a Nature Conservancy sign). We stayed with the river for perhaps a mile and half before striking out right, across Conival's heathery lower slopes. The recommended route lay due north, towards a striking rock amphitheatre divided by a waterfall. Not for the first time in our group, a dispute over the route took place. Four of the party, including my sons Danny and Seth, wanted to make a bold approach, taking Conival direct via a stony gully issuing from the summit. My wife, Leni, and I declared that we were following our original plan, and headed for the ridge to the right of the amphitheatre. The four rebels went their own way.

Neither route proved ideal. Leni and I were soon labouring over heavy scree, with only the occasional mossy oasis for relief.

When we at last reached the crest of the ridge, the way ahead was straightforward. We later learned from *cognoscenti* that we should have headed for the lowest point of the amphitheatre, to gain the ridge from there. The others were already at the summit when we arrived. Their gully had proved painfully loose, but they had found some pleasant scrambling on the rocks to the right, to emerge satisfyingly close to the broad summit cairn. The familiar coastal peaks were well below us now, Quinag and Canisp brooding beneath dark clouds, and Loch Assynt a gash in the landscape between. The clouds moved sternly towards us, occasionally brushing us as they passed over Conival. To the east, the ridge to Ben More Assynt that had beckoned from afar was at last revealed. It seemed to be composed almost entirely of shattered, white rock, as it dipped and swung for a mile to the slightly higher far peak. The SMT guide warned that 'extreme care' was needed in poor visibility, but for the time being it was clear.

The ridge dropped abruptly at first, and then gradually regained its height, with some occasional mild scrambling. Although slender in places, with long views north over the watery Assynt hinterland, it was perfectly safe. There was a final wasteland of flat stones to cross before we climbed the symmetrical cone of Ben More Assynt's summit. We could have continued along the ridge, which now dropped in several sharp steps to the south-east. But given our late start, we decided to retrace our steps towards Conival in search of a place to descend the main ridge to the south. Halfway along was a scree slope, that looked as though it might give a good scree run. The appearance was deceptive: the stones were too firm and consolidated, and we had to pick our way laboriously down. At the foot of the slope, our perspective had utterly changed. We were now in a magnificent corrie formed by the arms of the ridge curving around us, with the clouds that now broke over its crest and drifted down its flanks, conferring grandeur on an Alpine scale. As we drank from a shallow, mossy pool, the clouds suddenly

Right: A view up Gleann Dubh to Conival (3,234ft.).
Photo: Stephen Greenwood

Above and left: Two views of the summit ridges of Ben More Assynt – from the south (above) and from the west ridge that links the mountain with Conival (left).
Photos: Stephen Greenwood

swept lower to envelop us completely.

Inchnadamph lay to the north-west; we took a compass bearing and headed south-west at first, to pass the southern spur of Conival. We emerged from the clouds to find ourselves within 100ft. of a herd of deer, which departed like sprinters from their starting blocks. We dropped steeply down to the bealach between Conival and the peak of Breabag to the south, a marvellous cleft between steep walls disappearing far above. We crossed the watershed, and picked up the first trickle of one of the Traligill's tributaries. From there it was a straight-forward tramp back to the road, and the welcoming bar of the Inchnadamph hotel, which we reached at 8 p.m. It had been a thoroughly worthwhile day, we concluded; and resolved in future to pay more attention to the north-west's less fashionable peaks.

4   A Traverse of Quinag

by Gwen Moffat

Queenaig, Sir Archibald Geikie called it in *Victoria Regnante*, and aptly, for although the name's more Gaelic now, Quinag is a royal mountain, whether seen from Lochinver as a three-mile wall with a scalloped crest, or across Loch a'Chairn Bhain, when twin ridges end in beetling buttresses above the Drumbeg road.

There is no mountain to equal it in Sutherland, not even Suilven, that startling protuberance above a waste of moor. Quinag is a massif in miniature, and for over a decade I had wanted to walk the crest of that castellated ridge.

It was Easter Saturday and, the only guest at the inn, I sat at breakfast and glowered at puddles pitted by rain. The clouds were high, which was bad; it meant I had no excuse not to go. I hate getting wet; I dislike cold; I maintain that wind is dangerous, and that it's pointless to walk on strange mountains (except as a navigation exercise) if you can't see anything. I crave to be a fair weather mountaineer.

It was still raining when I reached the road-end, and the cloud was stuck solid at 2,000ft. Snow showers were forecast. Unhappily, and with difficulty, I dressed inside the car: gaiters, furry hat, and terrible, fluorescent waterproofs, compass, torch, adhesive tape, food – all the paraphernalia you take just so the coroner can't get in that final dig about being ill-equipped and old enough to know better.

A stalkers' track left the road due east of the first top, Spidean Coinich. After a few yards I relinquished it and struck left across slabs of wet quartzite, where I slid like a camel in mud before I got the feel of this nasty new rock.

As moor ran into ridge, the rock became clean and the going easy, a comfortable plod with well-sited cairns looming through the cloud. There was no path, but I had to use the compass only on the last few hundred feet, and then merely to confirm that the cairns were going my way, although it's unlikely a *line* of them would lead me wrong. In this instance there was only one way to go – to the top of Spidean.

I had made two miles from the road and 1,700ft. of rise in an hour and a half without sweating. Now I thought, if only the mist

cleared I could do Quinag in less than the nine hours I had calculated. It was bitterly cold, snowing, but the snow was wet. It wouldn't lie for long.

Ptarmigan walked about among the rocks, blue as feral pigeons; pretty, friendly birds that never seemed worried by the solitary person, yet you seldom see them in company. For that matter, you don't see much of anything in company; you're concentrating too much on the other person. Today I was aware of the first shift in the mist, a sensation of lightness as the ceiling thinned; of improved hearing and clearer sounds; the noise of water rising from an unseen corrie, the click of a dislodged stone, wind beating, soft as wings, against a hidden wall.

There was a matt-grey mass below, without shadow or substance, and in the time that it took to glance at the ground for the next step, the cloud had gone and there was heather, apparently black, a white burn in spate, then pale green turf and golden deer grass sunlit, jagged crags, moisture on bilberries.

The cloud dropped again, but now it was brighter, and I saw my own faint shadow as the sun tried to come through. There was a sense of blue above, windows appeared, with glimpses of unidentified heights across limitless gulfs; then, with a dip and a sway, the clouds parted with infinite ease to reveal whole panoramas: the cliffs of Stoer, Canisp and Suilven, Ben More Assynt covered with new snow. The walking was beautiful. Quinag's snow was melting, leaving aerated sand which consolidated under pressure, interspersed with thick-piled carpets of moss.

Now the cloud was gone completely, and I looked down on Loch Assynt and white flecks of cottages, and a thin road so far away no sound of traffic rose to the top of Quinag. Westward, beyond a fine glen, lay a vast region of lakes and heather, but mostly lakes, with no roads, a few paths on the fringes only, with the odd bit of native birchwood, and who knows how many divers and otters, greenshank and other other delights, in reeds on islands, on crags, among the little knolls that rise a few hundred feet out of this lonely wilderness.

North and north-east was another country

Maps   O.S. 1:50,000 Sheet 15. Start and finish 2 miles N of Skiag Bridge (ref. 232273).

Grading   A fine mountain walk that should present no difficulties in good conditions.

Time   6–7 hours.

Distance   8 miles.

Escape Routes   Easy descents may be made into the two eastern corries from bealachs on the main ridge.

Telephones   Inchnadamph Hotel; Kylesku Ferry; Unapool.

Transport   Daily bus service Kylesku to Skiag Bridge linking with the Lairg to Lochinver bus (Sutherland Transport).

Accommodation   Hotels at Lochinver, Inchnadamph and Kylesku. Youth Hostels at Achmelvich, 3 miles N of Lochinver.

Guidebooks   S.M.T. Guide *The Northern Highlands; The Scottish Peaks* by W. A. Poucher (Constable).

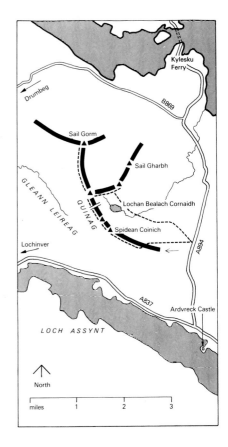

Above: The northern slopes of Quinag from Loch a'Chairn Bhain near the Kylesku Ferry. Sail Gharbh is the prominent spur on the left with Sail Gorm on the right. *Photo: John Allen*

Top right: Looking north over the Quinag tops from the summit of Spidean Coinich. *Photo: Van Greaves*

Bottom right: A gillie with a stag shot by his employer in the Glencanisp Forest south of Quinag – most of the parish of Assynt provides magnificent sport for the stalker. *Photo: Ken Wilson*

where big, black sea lochs cut deep into a hinterland of strong shapes and precipices. Here the killer whales came two months ago, driving up one side of Loch a'Chairn Bhain and down the other; all life disappeared, even the cormorants. And here, they say, the inn is haunted, a beautiful girl threw herself over the highest waterfall, and the ghost of a drowned Dutch sailor still walks in Sandwood Bay. And now, looking down, I saw the sailing ship, *Captain Scott*, stand out for Eddrachillis with sails the colour of burgundy.

From the most northerly top, Sail Gorm, I retraced my steps and went out to the highest summit, which stands on a spur that leaves the main ridge halfway along. From that summit, my line of ascent was revealed to the first top, a truncated cone sporting a broken nose of rock, which I had passed above unsuspecting in the morning's cloud. And from Sail Gharbh, the last top, I looked down plummeting gullies where there should be eagles, but if there were, they were sitting tight today.

I descended to the eastern corrie by way of a slope of red earth and splintered scree, and a deer path under a shattered cliff. It would be a nasty route in mist. Looking back, I thought a better way would be the slopes to the south of the highest point.*

There were deer in the corrie, the same

colour as the dead grass. I dropped down steep heather, and little walls where the holds were padded with wet, black lichen. Then came dry moor and stony pavements, and one clean, grassy place where fox smell hung about – and back to the road, and driving west to Lochinver, and the mountain reflected in all the mirrors like a royal jester. There was no sadness, as there often is when a mountain is no longer strange. For another day I had walked in Sutherland, and after that who could be sad, even though one less mountain in the world was new?

*From the OS pillar marking the 2,653ft. summit of Sail Gharbh the best way of descent is to return down the south-west ridge to the bealach, and then scramble down loose south-facing slopes towards Lochan Bealach Cornaidh. *Editor's Note*

5   Stac Pollaidh – the Perfect Miniature

by Richard Gilbert

Maps O.S. 1:50,000 Sheet 15. Start and finish at the Inverpolly Nature Reserve car park (ref. 108095).
Grading A short walk involving steep slopes of loose rock and some exposed rock scrambling on the summit ridge.
Time 3–4 hours.
Distance 3 miles.
Escape Routes From the bealach marking the lowest point of the ridge easy descents can be made S or N. Many of the gullies descending from the ridge provide possible, but steep, means of descent to lower ground.
Telephones A.A. box at Drumrunie Junction on the A835.
Transport Inverness to Garve Station by the Highland line then bus to Ullapool. Alternatively Inverness to Ullapool direct by bus. Daily minibus service Ullapool to Achiltibuie and (in summer) Ullapool–Inverkirkaig–Lochinver service passes under Stac Pollaidh.
Accommodation Hotels and Bed and Breakfasts at Ullapool, Achiltibuie and Lochinver. Youth Hostels at Ullapool, Achiltibuie and Achmelvich. No camping is allowed in the Inverpolly Nature Reserve.
Guidebooks S.M.T. Guide *The Northern Highlands; The Scottish Peaks* by W. A. Poucher (Constable).

A return to Assynt is, for the mountain lover, akin to a return home. The striking individuality of the peaks is never forgotten, and brings memories flooding back. Suilven stands supreme, the queen of Assynt. Quinag, Canisp, and Cul Mor stake their claims forcefully, but it is Stac Pollaidh, that preposterous little peak rising to 2,009ft. above Loch Lurgainn, which catches the imagination of mountaineer and motorist alike. I always feel like laughing when, driving north from Ullapool, it bursts into view behind the tree-ringed loch at Drumrunie Lodge. It is impudent and mischievous in the way that it dispenses with preliminaries and rises straight out of the moorland, thrusting jagged rocky spikes into the sky like a fossilised stegosaurus. Stac Pollaidh is unique, and a must for the walker. I defy anybody with red blood in his veins to resist the desire to climb to its summit ridge and explore its mysteries for himself.

The base rock of Assynt is grey Lewisian gneiss, formed 1,500 million years ago, but Stac Pollaidh is composed of red sandstone laid down over the gneiss a mere 800 million years ago. Successive ice ages and weathering have worn down the sandstone hills to mere remnants of their former selves. The neighbouring peaks of Quinag and Cul Mor are partially protected by a cap of white quartzite, but this is missing from Stac Pollaidh, hence its spectacular erosion. The feet of man have now replaced natural forces as the principal cause of erosion on popular peaks such as Stac Pollaidh. Although Stac Pollaidh is situated in the Inverpolly Nature Reserve, and conservationists have endeavoured to control the erosion, a broad, black track through the peat makes a sorry scar on the southern slopes. This is particularly evident from the Nature Reserve car park beside Loch Lurgainn.

Stac Pollaidh rises on the south side in three giant steps, with the angle of the face ever-increasing. The quickest route to the summit ridge is to follow the worn path straight up to the screes. However, I don't recommend this way, because Stac Pollaidh is a fairly slight mountain, and we must make the most of it. Consequently, it is best to ascend the main track to the first step, and then follow a narrow, cairned path which makes a rising traverse eastward, passing under the buttresses of the east summit. Once the shoulder has been reached, the path levels off and leads round to the north side of the mountain. The best view now begins to unfold, with the long, primeval shape of Suilven dominating the landscape across Loch Sionascaig and its many satellite lochans, nestling in the scoops of the impervious gneiss. Further east rise successively Cul Beag, Cul Mor, and Canisp. The cairned path soon steepens, and zig-zags up the rough slopes towards the eastern summit. You now have a choice of a scramble up a scree-filled gully which leads directly to the eastern summit, or an easier traverse to gain the summit ridge at its lowest point. This bealach is the meeting point for the paths of ascent from north and south and, being sprinkled with rounded sandstone blocks which provide shelter from the wind, is a popular spot for lunch.

The highest point of Stac Pollaidh lies at the extreme western end of the summit ridge, and it can be reached by a 20-minute scramble. There are many different ways to tackle the summit ridge. The confident climber will keep mainly to the exposed arête, but the walker will prefer to take the sandy path which winds along the south side of the mountain, under the sandstone tiers of the arête, until a narrow bealach is reached. It then crosses the ridge and continues along the north side. The walk is a delight, as the path meanders through gigantic bluffs and pinnacles of rounded, weathered sandstone, crosses the tops of steep gullies, and occasionally holds the airy crest of the ridge itself. As you approach the true summit, you will notice a conspicuous pinnacle of rock rising 30ft. above the screes. This is one of several pinnacles rising on the south side of the ridge, and its ascent is a severe rock climb.

Top right: Stac Pollaidh and Suilven (right) framed by the wind-eroded pinnacles of Sgorr Tuath in the Coigach group. *Photo: Ken Bryan*

Near right: Stac Pollaidh from the east – mirrored in the waters of Lochan Dearg a'Chuil Mhoir below Cul Mor. *Photo: Richard Gibbens*

Far right: The 'mauvais pas' on the summit ridge of Stac Pollaidh. *Photo: Stuart Bramwell*

Above: The summit crags of Stac Pollaidh with Cul Beag and Loch Lurgainn in the background.
Photo: W. A. Poucher

The western tower of Stac Pollaidh, on which is built the summit cairn, can only be reached by negotiating the celebrated *mauvais pas*. This takes the form of an exposed rock step, 15ft. high, on which there are excellent holds, but it needs some respect and a cool head. The inexperienced mountain walker should leave this step alone, since a slip could have disastrous consequences. From the summit you can look over Enard Bay and, further south, the Summer Isles, in the mouth of Loch Broom. The view south, across Loch Lurgainn, is blocked by the complex ridges and outlying peaks of Ben More Coigach, with the steep prow of Sgurr an Fhidhleir (the Fiddler)

particularly prominent. Loch Lurgainn is the perfect Highland loch, with sandy bays, a boat house, and tree-covered islands.

Return with care down the *mauvais pas*, and retrace your footsteps until the path traverses the top of a sandy scree run. Descend this for 300ft. until you meet the lower traverse path on the north side. This path by-passes a tiny lochan under the west end of Stac Pollaidh and then leads you down, guided by cairns, to the car park. After your walk over the perfect miniature peak of Stac Pollaidh, you must agree with Schumacher's axiom that 'small is beautiful'.

Top: The magnificent hinterland of the Inverpolly National Nature Reserve, pitted with lakes surrounding Suilven and Cul Mor – the latter seen here in a view to the east from Stac Pollaidh. *Photo: Tom Parker*

Bottom: The western buttresses of Stac Pollaidh picked out in the evening sun. *Photo: Ken Wilson*

6   The Clisham Ridge

by Ian Stephen

Maps   O.S. 1:50,000 Sheet 14. Start and finish at the Maaruig River bridge, 6 miles N of Tarbert (ref. 174058).
Grading   A rough but easy mountain walk. Needs care in misty weather.
Time   6–7 hours.
Distance   11 miles.
Escape Routes   Beyond Mulla-fo-dheas easy descents may be made E into Glen Scaladale thence to Ardvourlie.
Telephones   Ardvourlie (Vigadale Bay); Maaruig and Ardhasaig.
Transport   Caledonian-MacBrayne's car ferries Uig–Tarbert and Ullapool–Stornoway. Daily bus service Tarbert–Stornoway.
Accommodation   Hotels at Tarbert. Bed and Breakfast available locally. Youth Hostels at Ullapool and Stockinish (Harris).
Guidebooks   S.M.T. Guide *The Islands of Scotland*; *The Hebrides* by W. H. Murray (Heinemann).

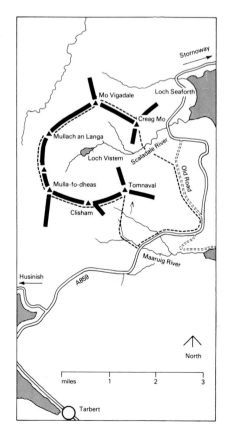

If you are concerned only with heights noted on maps, then there are more rewarding areas for hill walking than the Isle of Harris. Yet, since Lewis and the Uists are mainly flat ground, the jagged Harris hills rise dramatically. From them you look down to steeply cut sea-lochs. It is a landscape closest in spirit to Iceland. There are, however, no surviving glaciers here, but you would not be surprised to stumble across one. The first impression is of grey, lunar rock, but there is much visible colour when your boots take you to the high ground. Clisham is the highest point on the Long Island of Lewis and Harris. You can approach it from the Tarbert side or from the Stornoway road, but it is a long haul up, either way, for any petrol engine. If you are driving, and have not been along the route before, beware of trying to look in all directions at once as well as keeping your eyes on the unpredictable course of thin tarmac ahead. There is a good place to leave the vehicle near the Maaruig River, if you can do so without blocking one of the precious passing places. The Clisham summit is right ahead, and your engine has already coped with some of its 2,622ft.

The peak of Tomnaval (1,805ft.) is now visible on the right flank of Clisham, but your aim must be directed towards the highest point on this group of islands. It is a short, and fairly steep climb, but everyone can make their own zig-zag route at a suitable pace. With patience, there is nothing to stop a family group from making the ascent. The terrain becomes more stark at the higher ground: hardly enough greenery to graze a snail, but the lichens are rich and diverse. It is desert ground to farmers, but productive for potters and weavers, who can see more hues than they could ever dream up for all their patterns and glazes.

Round a shoulder, and the climb levels out. It has taken perhaps an hour and a half or two hours. If the visibility is good, you can't stop looking from round the sharks' teeth rocks to West Loch Tarbert, and then down the less sheer fall to the deep fiord of Loch Seaforth. The time is not so long gone when the whaling boats landed their catches at the whaling station in Loch Tarbert. And at Ard Caol, where Loch Seaforth merges with the Minch currents, there is still a

village with no roads to it – Rainigadale. But that is a different walk.

Now that you have taken coffee, or chocolate, or both, you follow the natural course along the ridge to Mulla-fo-dheas (2,439ft.) – the very spine of Harris. Again, you can be fascinated as you look down to the bare bones of rock at your feet, or you can gaze out and down to the long drop on either side. Legend has it that when the Good Lord finished the job on the sixth day, he scattered all the remaining rubble over the Long Island. This explanation seems quite plausible as you are working your way from rock to rock. Down below are small hill-lochs in either direction, all taking on different shadings every time you look. Clouds are never really still here, so the light is always changing. On the west side, there is a steep glen. Across it is Uisgnaval More, but that is on a separate ridge across the great divide. The grim, overhanging nose of Strone Ulladale, lies much further to the west, and a bit to the north. You are strangely conscious of its presence, over there between the Atlantic end of Loch Resort and the Minch end of Loch Seaforth. This is an area which merits at least another day.

The Clisham horseshoe bends on round. Mullach an Langa (2,012ft.) is a part of it. This is more gentle territory. It is even possible for rough, hill sheep to find enough nourishment here to survive. Loch Langavat is to the north and should be in clear sight. It is well worth looking skywards towards it, for an eagle, and along the high ground for the deer herds. There is no need to lose much height now as you walk on this less severe terrain by Mo Vigadale towards Creag Mo. Here, there is deer grass and moss underfoot, but the ground remains firm and dry. A snaking path is now visible a little to the north. It is part of a well-drained route that goes from Ardvourlie, by the south end of Langavat and then, incredibly, upwards. From Mullach an Langa it looks like a Tibetan mountain path. Its full line is lost to even the sharpest eyes, but it eventually descends through the glens to Meavaig, on the Husinish road.

The present route starts to make its descent. If there is any mist, watch out for the drop. Creag Mo is not nearly as precipitous

as Strone Ulladale, but it is impressive in its own right. It is best to keep well to the south side of this inland cliff, where there is a more gradual way down. Scaladale river is easy to ford. Clisham is seen from another angle, and the green, winding line of the old Clisham road is still discernible. Even now, you can see that it was not for the faint-hearted carter or driver. If the energy is left, you can climb to meet its line, and follow it round to the main road. From there, it is not far to the starting point at the Maaruig river. Or you can ignore that overgrown track, and follow the Scaladale river down the short way to Ardvourlie Bay, and trust in the generosity of car drivers. Now you are back in the modern world. Yet, after Clisham, Stornoway or Tarbert will seem like a metropolis.

Above: The Clisham group from near Ardhasig.
Photo: Stuart Bramwell

Right: A view to the west from near the summit of Clisham. *Photo: Tom Weir*

27

7 Explorations in Trotternish

by Tom Weir

Sgurr Alasdair, highest peak in the rocky Cuillin, takes its name from a native mountaineer and enforcer of law, Sherriff Alexander Nicolson, who was the first man to reach its summit. An advocate of Skye to anyone who would listen, it was he who drew attention to a ridge in the north of the island which he declared would be its grandest promenade – from the peak of Ben Storr, north of Portree, to the Quirang. He wrote of it, but although he made his notable Cuillin ascent in 1873, he did not claim to have made the Trotternish traverse.

Thus it came about that it was an Edinburgh climber who snatched the prize in 1901, on a March day when his native city was beset with mist and bitter east winds, while the Isle of Skye was revelling in calm seas, brilliant sunshine, and cloudless skies. This is what that lucky man, Scott Moncrieff Penney, wrote of his traverse:

It is a fine ridge walk, and the view of the basaltic terraces and cliffs on the east side of the range is unrivalled . . . It is a succession of tops with numerous, although not heavy, dips between. There are seven different dips before Ben Edra, a sharp, imposing top at the north end of the ridge, is reached, and the climbing, including the ascent of the Storr, amounts in all to no more than 4,250ft. With the exception of two easy bealachs, down which a horse might be taken, there did not appear to be any places where a descent towards the east could be comfortably made.

Penney did not have time to complete the traverse, for he had a boat to catch from Staffin, which accounts for a remarkably fast time of four and a half hours from the Storr summit to Beinn Edra. To do the lot you must begin on Beinn a'Chearcaill (1,812ft.), above Loch Fada on the Portree–Staffin road, and follow the Trotternish spine northward to Sgurr Mor, a distance of 19 miles and getting on for 8,000ft. of climbing. Because of the special corrie scenery of the Quirang and the unique pinnacles of the Storr, a more leisurely approach is recommended.

The spine of Trotternish breaks nicely into two classic walks. Climb the Storr via the Old Man, who heads one of the most extraordinary families of pinnacles in the land, and once on top do what Moncrieff Penney did, except you might consider spending the night in Staffin. Next day go up into the inner sanctuary of the Quirang before traversing its summit to Sgurr Mor.

Harold Raeburn, hallowed name in the history of Scottish mountaineering, gave The Storr Rock its first mention in the *Scottish Mountaineering Club Journal*, after a visit in 1898, when he rode a bicycle from Sligachan to Portree and walked an old track to the Old Man in just over two hours. He wrote:

Admirers of the bizarre and the eccentric in rock from would find here a multitude of the most strange-looking rock pinnacles in Scotland, standing up from a green slope below a striking wall of almost vertical rock, seamed with great chimneys of formidable aspect.

The month was September, and a half-gale nearly blew him off the small pinnacle he climbed. He was content just to look with wonder at the drunken lean of the Old Man,

. . . a wonderful obelisk of trap rock, 160ft. high and about 40ft. in diameter. It actually overhangs its base almost the whole way round, so it has the appearance of dangerous instability at close quarters.

One that he named 'The Old Woman' looked a possibility to him, and he considered that some of the chimneys splitting the face of the main cliff might 'go' if properly investigated.

Raeburn was not prepared to assert that the Old Man would never be ascended. But it was 57 years after his pioneering inspection before a climber was bold enough to surmount his overhanging base, traverse left, and force a way up loose and very severe rock to touch the forelock of his leaning brow and sit on his head. Don Whillans was that man, ably supported by Jim Barber and Geoff Sutton. Nor did the Old Man's looseness and severity deter the enterprising party who came eleven years later and attacked it from the Portree side. The confident pair, G. B. Lee and P. Thomson, linked a chain of weakness in the Old Man's crumbling defences, enabling them to top his crown. The chimneys splitting the 500ft. face which Raeburn mentions crumble to the touch and are no use for climbing, but offer marvellous holds for flowers; saxifrages, roseroot, globe

Maps O.S. 1:50,000 Sheet 23. For The Storr and Beinn Edra start from Loch Fada N of Portree (ref. 491495) and finish at Staffin (ref. 482682). For the Quirang start and finish by Loch Langaig (ref. 463709).
Grading The Storr and Beinn Edra traverse is a long and energetic day over rough ground. The Quirang is easy but it can be confusing in mist.
Time The Storr and Beinn Edra traverse 7–8 hours. The Quirang 3 hours.
Distance The Storr and Beinn Edra traverse 16 miles. The Quirang 6 miles.
Escape Routes The Storr – Beinn Edra escarpment can be descended to the E in several places and almost anywhere to the W. Descent from the Quirang area presents no difficulty in clear weather.
Telephones Duntulm; Flodigarry Hotel; Staffin; Elishader; Portree.
Transport Express bus services to Portree and Uig from Glasgow, Edinburgh and Inverness. Weekday bus service from Portree to Staffin and Kilmaluag.
Accommodation A wide variety of accommodation in Portree. Hotels at Duntulm and Flodigarry. Bed and Breakfast at Staffin and Kilmaluag. Youth Hostels at Uig and Broadford.
Guidebooks S.M.T. Guide *The Isle of Skye*; *The Scottish Peaks* by W. A. Poucher (Constable); *The West Highlands of Scotland* by W. H. Murray.

Left: A view south from the north end of the Trotternish ridge, past Quirang (right) to The Storr in the far distance.
Photo: Gordon Gadsby

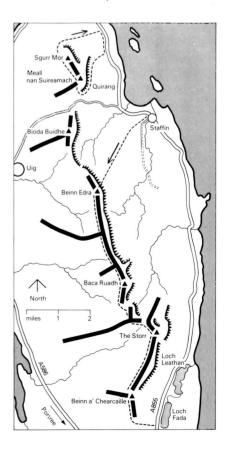

Above: Looking south from the summit of Quirang, past Bioda Buidhe on the right, to Beinn Edra (2,003ft.) the prominent peak on the left. *Photo: Robert Adam*

flowers, orchis, campion; hanging gardens of them.

The Storr is regarded by botanists as the finest volcanic hill of Western Scotland for richness of mountain flora, including a plant peculiar to it, discovered in 1934, *Koenigia islandica*, the Icelandic purslane, which is found from the summit plateau down to 1,300ft., a red-stemmed fleshy-leaved plant only an inch in height and diameter. Look out for it in the red scree soil, where it is most

noticeable.

After visiting the pinnacles, if you traverse to the base of the cliff to hit the north-east shoulder, you will come up to a gap in a north-facing cliff which is the real lodestone of alpine botanists, with whole communities of plants: northern rock cress, moss campion, mossy cyphel, saw-wort, holly fern, alpine saxifrages, and many others. The disintegrating rock and scree favours plants. The geologists tell us that the Storr and the

Quirang are huge masses of tertiary basalt, portions of which have slipped and been eroded to become pinnacles and strange blocks, among hollows now occupied by little lochans. The Gaelic 'Storr' is derived from decayed tooth.

One of my memorable visits there was on an unlikely day of north-westerly gale with the mist scudding and the Old Man sticking his head out from time to time. I bargained for shelter, and got some, under the cliffs, and enjoyed the sight of Raasay and the peaks of Torridon and Applecross heaving their shoulders out of the clouds; but the top was impossible. Staggering about, eyes watering, we had to withdraw. It was worth it, however, for the impression of the western sea, dancing like boiling water in the Force 10 blast. We saw the Outer Isles boat trying to come into Uig at 3 p.m., but it was unable to berth until 10 p.m.

A sparkling June day of light northerly

Top: Looking north to The Storr (2,360ft.) from Loch Fada at the southern end of the Trotternish ridge. *Photo: Ken Andrew*

Bottom: The weird pinnacles of the Quirang. *Photo: Donald Bennet*

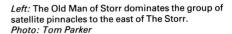

breeze after rain is best for Trotternish; then distance is banished and the step is light. Then, by a mere inclination of the head, the eyes can range west to Barra Head and travel up the 130 miles of the Long Island, sweeping in a glance from the blue range of the lumpy Harris hills east to Suilven, Canisp, Ben More Coigach, and by An Teallach to the other Torridonian giants, Beinn Alligin, Liathach, and Beinn Eighe, merging one with another, top on top. Good things lie immediately below too. Now you can appreciate that Skye is indeed the Winged Isle, Duirinish and Vaternish in parallel to the south-west are separated by Loch Snizort and Loch Dunvegan, with Minginish signposted by the high serrations of the Cuillin. Trotternish is bare and windswept, but its north-west part was known as the granary of Skye, rich in corn, and it has the appeal of a crofting country that is lived in, a green sea-fringe dotted with the white specks of houses. Staffin Bay makes a convenient base for the Quirang.

I think the best approach to this rather secret place is from Loch Langaig, with a climbing path following its north side, leading you up into a hanging valley of weird knolls and imprisoned pools of water; surprising, but nothing to the canyon which opens ahead, with a wall of grey rock on one side and black pinnacles hemming you in on the other. The short turf is riddled with rabbit holes. Then, above you, is the knife-blade of a pinnacle, well-named The Needle, and up you go on steep screes below it, leading between portals of rock into the heart of the 'Pillared Stronghold' which is the meaning of Cuith-raing – the true Gaelic usually Anglicized to Quirang.

Work along the south edge of The Table, and you can drop down the easy gully below The Needle, dizzily poised and unclimbed, whose appearance tells you it is not rock for risking. Keeping your height below The Needle, you can contour south and walk round to the slope leading easily up to the OS pillar at 1,779ft. Now you can have a grand high level walk following the edge of the cliff, looking down on Duntulm Castle as you stride to the final bump of Trotternish, Sgurr Mor (1,460ft.).

8   Sgurr nan Gillean

by W. A. Poucher

When Richard Gilbert sent me a pressing invitation to contribute to *Classic Walks*, my mind drifted back from 90 years by nearly half a century, to the time when I took my son on his first visit to Skye. We left my Surrey home in my first Jag., when the motorways were non-existent, and drove up the Great North Road at speed, as traffic in those days was slight. We were held up for the first time at Dornie, to find about a dozen cars awaiting the rising tide which would enable the ferry to function. An hour later, we left for the Kyle of Lochalsh, where the weather was rapidly deteriorating, and in due course arrived at Glen Brittle. I had reserved the downstairs room at the Lodge, and as the August weather was warm and humid, decided to leave open the window. Imagine my surprise to be awakened about 4 a.m. by a cow licking my face. It had put its head through the open window, and was evidently enjoying my particular fragrance.

Next morning there was no improvement in the weather, with processions of rain clouds sweeping over the nearby hills, but we nevertheless decided to walk up to Coire Lagan, where we found the engirdling cliffs completely hidden. After eating our sandwiches, we walked down to the Lodge soaked to the skin. The wild weather continued, so we packed our bags and drove to Gleneagles, where we found sun and warmth. We played golf in superlative conditions, and I have a special memory of that occasion, as from the furthest tee on the Queen's Course, the immense landscape presented an unforgettable beauty, with the manicured green fairways threading the purple heather as far as the eye could see.

Coming now to *Classic Walks*, and the stupendous peak of Sgurr nan Gillean thrusting its pointed spire of black gabbro rock to the heavens. This peak was only 'discovered' towards the end of the last century, well after the beginnings of Alpine climbing. Essentially a 'climbers' peak, it has just one easy route, the Tourist Route, suitable for the mountain walker. It is as well to bear in mind that the Tourist Route to Sgurr nan Gillean includes three completely different types of terrain. First, there is the crossing of over two miles of moorland from Sligachan to Coire Riabhach; second, there is the collar work

involved in the very rough ascent over scree and boulders to the south-east ridge; and third, the exhilarating climb of 656ft. from the diminutive Sgurr Beag to the lofty summit of Gillean, the last 100ft. of which requires the use of the hands.

Starting from Sligachan on an invigorating morning, you walk up the Carbost road and take the path on the left, which rises to the now-derelict power house. Crossing the burn by a broken-down bridge, you walk along the meandering path, which you hope will be dry. Ahead you can see your peak, but the Pinnacle Ridge is not yet visible, as it faces you end on. On reaching the Allt Dearg Mor, you walk beside it until you reach a cairn marking the crossing of the burn. Make for the dip on the right of Nead na h'Iolaire by a sketchy track, until you reach the cairn overlooking Coire Riabhach. The track is now clearly defined and it rises, encircling the corrie with its glittering lochan below. Here you stop for a moment to admire the splendid view of Blaven, which falls precipitously to Glen Sligachan, together with the indented skyline of Clach Glas, which is a favourite with rock climbers. On turning to the right, you will see the large cairn on the south-east ridge, and may take a direct line for it over the scree and boulders. But it is easier to follow a zig-zag diagonal course for Sgurr Beag, where you will rest awhile to admire the dramatic scene ahead. Gillean rises into the sky like a gigantic cathedral spire, with the Pinnacle Ridge clearly revealed on its right, while on its left the main ridge with its innumerable pinnacles stretches away in the distance.

On your way again, you make for the foot of your peak, and keep to the left of its ridge, overlooking Lota Corrie, where the adhesive gabbro gives a firm grip to your vibrams. Up and up you go, steeper and steeper, until, when nearing the summit, your hands come into play, and you finally step over a small hiatus to stand by the cairn. When you sit down and rest, you may be surprised to find that the slopes of your peak are invisible. You seem to be poised in the sky, which conveys the sense of isolation better than most of the peaks you will eventually climb, and you feel aloof from the turmoil of life far below. On standing up, the first thing to catch your eye

Maps S.M.T. Special map of the Cuillin, about 3 inches to a mile, outline contour; O.S. 1:25,000 Outdoor Leisure Map – The Cuillin and Torridon Hills; O.S. 1:50,000 Sheet 32. Start and finish at Sligachan Hotel (ref. 486298).
Grading A mild rock scramble by the Tourist Route. The descent of the W ridge of Sgurr nan Gillean to Bealach a'Bhasteir (described here) is more serious and a rope should be used for safety.
Time 7 hours.
Distance 9 miles.
Escape Routes In bad weather it is sensible to return down the Tourist Route to Sligachan. From Bealach a'Bhasteir descend N down Coire a'Bhasteir, there is a path but beware of loose rock.
Telephones Sligachan Hotel.
Transport Daily bus service from Kyleakin to Sligachan, Carbost and Portree.
Accommodation Sligachan Hotel. Hotels, Guest Houses, Bed and Breakfasts in Portree (9 miles). Youth Hostels at Glen Brittle, Broadford and Kyle of Lochalsh.
Guidebooks S.M.T. Guide *The Island of Skye; The Scottish Peaks* by W. A. Poucher (Constable); *The Black Cuillin Ridge* by S. P. Bull (S.M.T.)

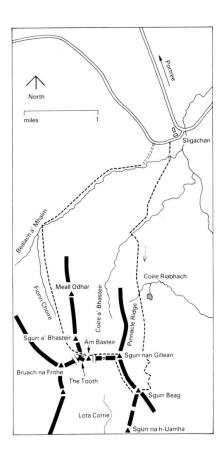

may well be the Pinnacle Ridge, to the north, of which you now have a bird's eye view, and where you can easily pick out the fourth pinnacle, or Knight's Peak, whose traverse is the key to the successful rock climbers' ascent of Gillean. Beyond it you will enjoy the vista of Trotternish, with the Storr dominating the view. To the south you look across Lota Corrie to Druim nan Ramh, and beyond it to Sgurr Alasdair and its satellites, amongst which the lofty ridge of the Dubhs is prominent. To the east, Marsco and Glamaig may charm your eye, and to the right of them Blaven rises finely above the remote stretches of Glen Sligachan. To the west and south, the main ridge forms a semi-circle to merge with Sgurr Alasdair, and you may find it of interest to name the many peaks that deck this famous playground of the rock climber. Having stayed on this peerless summit for perhaps an hour, and enjoyed the wonderful panorama of peak and sea, the decision has to be made as to the route of descent back to Sligachan. I think it would be true to say that the majority of

walkers would elect to return the way they had come, and leave the western ridge to more experienced mountaineers.

On looking down the ridge, its steepness will be apparent, and after passing the adjacent vertical boulder, great care is vital, as a slip might result in a long fall into Lota Corrie. This next section of the west ridge, until the screes are reached at Bealach a'Bhasteir, is potentially dangerous, and a rope should be used for protection by all save experienced rock climbers. The sharp angle continues for about half the height of the ridge, and then you negotiate a safe passage of the innumerable boulders until you pick out below the detached and sensationally poised obelisk now known as the Policeman, but in my early days as the Tooth. It is situated near the bottom of the ridge, and its passing is the crux of the descent to Bealach a'Bhasteir. No wonder the pioneers of long ago paused to speculate on its safety. But in fact the passing of this obstacle is easier than it looks, for you place your hands firmly on top of it, and then swing your body round to

the other side. However, the next section may come as a surprise, because it ends abruptly with a vertical drop. This is usually turned by a 40ft. chimney on the right. And so down to the scree and bealach. Should you be guiding an inexperienced friend down the western ridge, you may have a problem, as, when the sensationally poised Policeman appears below, he may feel unable to tackle it, and the urgent question then arises as to just what to do. But do not worry, an escape

Note: The Policeman collapsed in 1988.

route is near at hand on the right. It is a rake, known as Nicholson's Chimney, and it falls obliquely to the scree and is an easy route down to the bealach.

You are still a very long way from home, but do not go down the stony corrie, as there are two alternatives that afford a more interesting and revealing walk. In any case first traverse below Am Basteir to its Tooth, where the path from Bruach na Frithe descends through Fionn Choire to the Bealach a'Mhaim, and then follows the burn down to Alltdearg House and so to Sligachan. A more interesting route for scramblers is to turn right at the 'Executioner', and walk up to the summit of Sgurr a'Bhasteir, which opens up the classic view of the Pinnacle Ridge. Then scramble down the entertaining north ridge of this peak, and join the path across the moor. When you return to Sligachan, as I have done year after year, Gillean is always there to greet you, and remind you of the walk I have just described from distant and treasured memories.

Top left: A view from the South East Ridge towards Sgurr Beag and Sgurr na h-Uamha. Sgurr na Stri is the prominent peak in the distance. *Photo: Margaret Gadsby*

Bottom left: Climbers and walkers converse on the summit. *Photo: Gordon Gadsby*

Above: Sgurr nan Gillean from Sgurr a'Bhasteir. The Pinnacle Ridge is on the left and the West Ridge links the summit to the col on the right. *Photo: W. A. Poucher*

9 Across the Cuillin by Loch Coruisk

by Donald Bennet

The Cuillin Hills are essentially mountains of the sea. True, most climbers stay at Sligachan or Glen Brittle, and approach the mountains by the ridges and corries around their northern and western perimeter. However, no one would deny that the grandest way to reach the Cuillin is from the seaward side, sailing through the Cuillin Sound into Loch Scavaig, to drop anchor in Loch na Cuilce and scramble ashore at the very foot of the mountains. Unfortunately, this idyllic approach is not for all, but an excellent alternative is the walk from Elgol, round the shore of Loch Scavaig, to Coir' Uisg. Then, having reached the heart of the Cuillin, you will want to continue across the Main Ridge of the mountains, and descend to Sligachan. Provided, of course, that you have a friendly driver to take the car round and meet you.

The first part of this walk, from Elgol to Camasunary, is seldom done, as the start at Kilmarie is shorter and easier. But there can be no finer starting point than Elgol, and the path that clings to the hillside above Loch Scavaig is infinitely preferable to the dreary, bulldozed track westwards from Kilmarie. This path northwards from Elgol crosses the very steep side of Ben Cleat, which is rather more grass and earth than firm rock, so it may be better, particularly if the ground is wet, to climb the extra few hundred feet over the flat summit of this hill, before dropping down to the foot of Glen Scaladal and continuing to Camasunary. The views across Loch Scavaig to the Cuillin from this part of the walk are absolutely superb, provided you can see the mountains, and it is worth waiting for a good day. If that is not being too optimistic for Skye.

At Camasunary there is a beautiful sandy bay, backed by *machair*, but the Cuillin are now hidden behind the steep bulk of Sgurr na Stri, round whose base the walk continues, along a pleasant path between steep hillside and blue loch. Soon the Cuillin are in view again as you come round the Rubha Ban, and half a mile further, the path drops down onto bare rock near the water's edge. The notorious 'Bad Step' is not far ahead.

I suppose that we should be grateful for the 'Bad Step'. It turns an otherwise simple walk into something a little bit more exciting, and makes Loch Coruisk slightly less access-ible, so that to reach it by this route will, for some, be quite an achievement. One Scottish walker of my acquaintance held the 'Bad Step' in such awe that he would strip off, plunge into Loch Scavaig, and swim round the obstacle. That seems rather an extreme evasion, like jumping out of the frying pan into the fire. It is not so extreme as the army's plan, ten years ago, to blast away the entire 'Bad Step' in order to create an easy path. Fortunately they were dissuaded, otherwise the whole hillside might have subsided into the loch. In fact, there is nothing to fear. For about 50ft. the route (for it would hardly be correct to describe it as a path) crosses an easy-angled slab by an open crack, which provides plenty of footholds, while hands on the slab above maintain balance. About 30ft. below the restless sea surges and sucks at the undercut base of the slab. It is a situation to savour, and if you find it too exciting, there is a detour of sorts on the steep hillside above.

Once past the 'Bad Step', the path continues to wend its way among the jumble of huge boulders along the lochside, until it strikes inland through a little valley to reach Loch Coruisk. Now you have reached the threshold, if not quite the heart, of the Cuillin. Before you, Loch Coruisk stretches for a mile and a half towards the innermost corries, its waters reflecting the many moods of mountains and skies. It is the grandest mountain loch in the country.

If the Scavaig River is in flood you may well find the crossing difficult or impossible. It is sometimes easier to go some distance down river to the point where it flows over bare rock, but in really wet weather, you will probably have to stay on the north-east side of Loch Coruisk, and continue along the lochside below the steep crags of the Druim nan Ramh. On the other hand, assuming that you have chosen a good day for this walk, you should have no difficulty in crossing the Scavaig River, and the path to the head of the loch continues, sometimes over whalebacks of dark gabbro, and sometimes through the *glaur* of waterlogged mud, to reach the grassy flats of Coir' Uisg, the watery corrie.

Of the various passes and bealachs over the Cuillin Main Ridge from Coir' Uisg to Glen Brittle, the Bealach na Glaic Mhor is

Maps S.M.T. Special map of the Cuillin, about 3 inches to a mile, outline contour; O.S. 1:25,000 Outdoor Leisure Map – The Cuillin and Torridon Hills; O.S. 1:50,000 Sheet 32. Start from Elgol (ref. 519140). Finish at Sligachan Hotel (ref. 486298).
Grading A serious mountaineering expedition which should not be attempted by the inexperienced.
Time 9 hours.
Distance 17 miles.
Escape Routes None. Note that the Climbing Hut marked on the map beside the Scavaig River is a private hut belonging to the J.M.C.S. When not in use it is securely locked.
Telephones Elgol; Sligachan.
Transport A daily bus service (not Sun.) links Sligachan with Portree, Broadford and Kyleakin with connections to Fort William and Glasgow. Twice-daily service Broadford to Elgol by post-bus on weekdays, once a day on Sat. and no service on Sun.
Accommodation Sligachan Hotel. Hotels, Guest Houses, Bed and Breakfasts in Portree and Broadford. Bed and Breakfasts in Elgol. Youth Hostels at Broadford, Glen Brittle and Kyle of Lochalsh.
Guidebooks S.M.T. Guide *The Island of Skye; The Black Cuillin Ridge* by S. P. Bull (S.M.T.).

Left: The Cuillin Ridge bathed in early-morning sunlight and reflected in the waters of Loch Coruisk. Bealach na Glaic Mhor, the col used in the described route to cross the ridge, is just to the left of the twin-pointed peak (Bidein Druim nan Ramh) on the right. *Photo: Ian Reynolds*

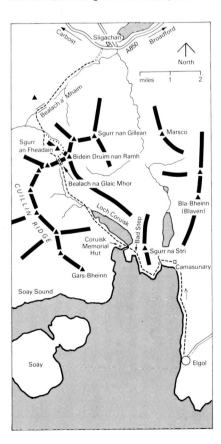

one of the easiest, although in bad weather, particularly low cloud, it may be difficult to decide which of the many streams to follow uphill into the clouds. The best advice that can be offered is to follow the main stream, keeping to the right when in doubt, and climbing the long slope of grass, scree, and finally rock, to the bealach. You can hardly stray too far right, for on that side is the steep wall of the Druim nan Ramh, and if you go too far left, you will find yourself under the cliffs of Sgurr a'Mhadaidh.

The Bealach na Glaic Mhor is a broad col, and from it two descent routes are possible down the craggy north-west slopes to gain the bowl of Coire na Creiche. Directly below the bealach, you can work a way down into Coir a'Mhadaidh. Keep to the right at first, just under the crags of Bidein Druim nan Ramh, before turning steeply downhill on the north side of the slabs which lie immediately below the bealach. Like much route-finding in the misty Cuillin, this can be confusing. An easier descent leads into Coir' a'Tairneilear, traversing north under the crags of Bidein, across the spur of Sgurr an Fheadain, and then down scree into the corrie, where there is a well-cairned route to Coire na Creiche.

By now you will no doubt be thinking that you have had a good day's walk, for although the distance you have come from Elgol may not be very great, possibly nine or ten miles, most of it has been rough going. Now that you are below the rock and screes, and down to the grassy floor of the corrie, your pace will quicken towards the cairn at the top of the Bealach a'Mhaim, and on down the far side to Sligachan. As you stroll down the track, you can reflect that the day's expedition has shown you something of everything in the Cuillin: the sea, Loch Coruisk, the Main Ridge, and finally the north-western moors. Behind you are the pinnacles of Sgurr nan Gillean, and ahead is the sea again. Soon you will arrive at Sligachan, where for over 100 years weary climbers have slaked their thirst.

10   Slioch

by Sandy Cousins

Slioch (3,217ft.) is the most accessible and superbly situated of the mountains of Letterewe Forest. It is a hill to be savoured at various levels. Most walkers tend to make the mistake of heading for the top of a hill, often straight up and down the same route. This is desirable for conservation of the wildlife and flora, but to the thoughtful walker, Slioch has much more to offer. A small, quiet party may be rewarded by a memorable day.

Come in early summer to explore this beautiful and varied hill. From Kinlochewe, we go a short way on the road toward the Heights of Kinlochewe until we cross the river, then we'll walk on the ancient track down the north bank to the southern end of Loch Maree. Passing round the first small bay, we'll pause at the mouth of the burn coming out from Gleann Bianasdail. We could have arrived here by rowing across the loch. (Ask about a boat at the hotels.) The faint ruins here go back to the days when the oak woods were used for smelting, with ore barges plying the loch, and gabbards sailing out to the industrial south; Loch Maree has an interesting history awaiting the enquiring reader. Today, this area is used by the very latest, low-flying jets, and I have often watched them streaking skilfully just above the loch, or through the glens far below me.

For a pleasant walk, Gleann Bianasdail offers a delightful day. The sun is shining, and the burn so clear you can swim under and see the trout in the pools. The path takes you over a bridge, and then easily through the glen to Lochan Fada (Little Long Loch), where you may, as I have, cast flies for the very lively trout, and (sometimes) char. Just the place for a brew-up, and a wander to glimpse the remote hills of Fisherfield. Before leaving Loch Maree, take a look at the escarpment of Beinn a'Mhuinidh, above us. The geologist will recognise the features of Lewisian gneiss, Cambrian, and Torridonian rock. The waterfall near the corner is worth a visit, and the rock wall, over a mile long, offers many steep, clean, exploratory routes for the rock climber.

My line of ascent of Slioch for the day is to follow the Gleann and go up by steep grass and easy slab ledges to Meall Each (Horse Hill). The steep shoulder above then gives us undulating walking on short grass until we are above the dark, green lochan at the saddle. Below us, the southerly aspect of this side of Slioch gives a rich growth on the lower slopes, and plenty of boulders provide cover for the wildlife. If your advance is discreet you may be able to watch the hinds and fawns, the goats and kids, and the miniature delights of the plants and rock crystals. Once, drinking from a burn down there, on raising my head I found I was sharing the spot with a large, sequin-blue dragonfly shimmering inches from me.

Higher on our ridge, there is a sandy pool, offering another dip on a hot day. The high corrie sanctuary on the east side of Slioch lies below us like a meadow. It is often dotted with goats, or deer, and we should avoid disturbing them unnecessarily. The summit view is superb. The islands float on the sparkling Minch. Innumerable ridges and peaks lie west and south, and with map and compass, those unfamiliar with the shapes can identify the famous names. In good visibility, we shall see across Scotland from the Minch to the Moray Firth. Northward lies first the deep trench where the grinding, glacial ice has left Lochan Fada, and then, behind the loch, the rugged hills of Fisherfield and, further away, the glorious hills of Assynt. As I look down the corrie meadow, with its bright green patches, showing mossy springs, I speculate on what a fine ski-run it would make, if we were lucky enough to catch the rather infrequent times of good snow here. But our day is wearing on, so we'll leave the top and take the ridge eastward to Sgurr an Tuill Bhain, then make our way south-east back into Gleann Bianasdail. Here we follow the path to the watershed, and the stepping stones to Lochan Fada.

How grand now to take off boots and freshen up at the sandy shore, with that special, warm, low sunlight of the West Highland evening changing all the greenish colours to glittering gold and blues. As we amble back along the stalkers' path to the Heights of Kinlochewe, and then to the hotel, I shall pause, and turn to look back at the majestic sweep of Slioch, now fading into the dark under its evening cap of mist. I hope you, too, will one day enjoy, as I have often done, these sights and sounds and scents of Slioch.

Maps O.S. 1:25,000 Outdoor Leisure Map – The Cuillin and Torridon Hills; O.S. 1:50,000 Sheet 19. Start and finish at the Kinlochewe Hotel (ref. 028620).
Grading A long mountain walk. Most of the route follows a good path but some rough terrain must be negotiated on Slioch itself.
Time 8 hours.
Distance 18 miles.
Escape Routes None. There is no shelter or available help nearer than Kinlochewe.
Telephones Kinlochewe.
Transport Railway Station at Achnasheen (12 miles). A Kinlochewe–Inverness bus service runs on Tues and Fri.
Accommodation Hotels at Kinlochewe and Loch Maree. Ling Hut in Glen Torridon (S.M.C.) Youth Hostel at Torridon.
Guidebooks S.M.T. Guide *The Northern Highlands; The Scottish Peaks* by W. A. Poucher (Constable).

Left: Slioch from Loch Maree. The described route follows the right skyline to the summit. *Photo: Tom Parker*

Overleaf: A view to the east from the summit of Slioch, past Sgurr an Tuill Bhain. *Photo: Stephen Greenwood*

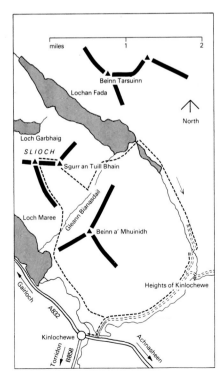

11 Beinn Alligin, the Jewel of Torridon

by Charles Rose

Maps O.S. 1:50,000 Sheet 24; O.S. 1:25,000 Outdoor Leisure Map – The Cuillin and Torridon Hills. Start and finish at the car park near the Coire Mhic Nobuil road bridge (ref. 867577).
Grading A fine traverse of a lofty mountain ridge. Some mild scrambling is necessary. Under full winter conditions the route can become a serious expedition only suitable for the experienced mountaineer.
Time 7 hours.
Distance 9 miles.
Escape Routes From Tom na Gruagaich descend the slopes S.W. to easier ground. The Horns may be by-passed by a traverse path on the S side. In poor visibility it is inadvisable to attempt a descent into Toll a'Mhadaidh.
Telephones Torridon; Inver Alligin.
Transport Daily bus service Kinlochewe to Torridon. Kinlochewe–Inverness service on Tues and Fri. Daily post-bus Torridon–Inver Alligin–Diabaig passes the start of the walk.
Accommodation Hotel, Bed and Breakfast and Youth Hostel in Torridon village. The Ling Hut (S.M.C.) in Glen Torridon.
Guidebooks S.M.T. Guide *The Northern Highlands; The Scottish Peaks* by W. A. Poucher (Constable).

Right: The bastions of the Torridon mountains form a natural mountain reef dominating the country to the south of Loch Maree. In this view over the 'Horns' from Beinn Alligin, Beinn Dearg is in the middle distance with Beinn Eighe beyond. The Fannichs are ranged across the skyline. *Photo: Ken Andrew*

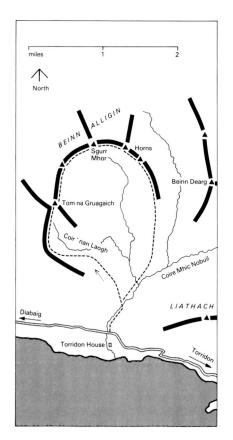

I first saw Beinn Alligin (the jewelled peak) from the spectacular viewpoint on the Balgy Gap road, high above the Ob Gorm Beag along the south shore of Upper Loch Torridon. It was a perfect summer's day, and I was overawed by the monumental serenity of the seemingly immense peaks, floating in pastel shades of maroon and terracotta, the hallmark of Torridonian sandstone, above a dancing, blue sea. I could not decide whether I was surveying one enormous and complex mountain, or as many as three separate hills. In fact, Beinn Alligin is a vast horseshoe ridge, perhaps the most satisfying mountain form for the hill walker, and it encompasses a variety of features that complement one another, to produce the perfect whole. The nearer, massive bulk of Tom na Gruagaich is set against the alpine teeth of the Horns, appearing behind, while the lofty pyramidal summit of Sgurr Mhor towers over the sweeping, saddle-like ridge that curves, almost level, for nearly a mile, linking the two main peaks. On the northern flanks there are huge, precipitous faces, seamed by loose, rocky gullies, while to the west, heathery slopes run at a steady angle from skyline to moorland.

The majority of walkers start their ascent of Beinn Alligin from the car park on the Diabaig road, above Torridon House. A stalking path runs up the east side of Coire Mhic Nobuil, past the splendid waterfall of Eas Rob, and through the romantic Scots pines, haunt of red and roe deer, pine marten, wildcat and otter. A short distance above the tree-line, a small path cuts off to the left, crossing the burn by a neat, wooden bridge. In summer the path deteriorates into a peaty trench, but today it is dry because it is February and night frost has frozen the ground, rendering it firm underfoot. I plod up the steady slope, heading for the mouth of Coir' nan Laogh, which splits the bulk of Tom na Gruagaich. I stop on the first rise to catch my breath and gaze into the awe-inspiring Toll a'Mhadaidh, a huge corrie filled with an unbelievable jumble of blocks, the debris of the rockfall which created the deep cleft which scars Sgurr Mhor almost to the summit. From this point, the Horns provide a theatrical backdrop to the cataclysmic wilderness of Toll a'Mhadaidh.

In summer Coir' nan Laogh is grassy and sheltered, and is a favourite spot for red deer, but today the tiers of vertical sandstone which form the back wall are plastered with snow. The white ribbons threaten to slip into space, and two huge hosepipes of ice mark a permanent watercourse that, in summer, blackens the rock. The left-bounding edge of the corrie makes a clearly-defined ridge. It looks intimidating, but it entails no more than modest scrambling ability and a head for heights. The rock steps are of rounded, horizontal plates of rough Torridonian sandstone. Quite suddenly the scrambling is over, and I find myself on a graceful snow arête, which curves upwards past two small rocky outcrops. On my right, the corniced crest overhangs a sensational drop into a snow gully plunging down into Coir' nan Laogh. I absorb the panoramic view: Skye, South Rona, the Applecross hills, and the beautiful pageantry of Beinn Shieldaig, Beinn Damh, An Ruadh-stac, Maol Chean-dearg, and the Coulin hills, curving round the head of the loch to dominant Liathach.

On the exposed ridge near the summit of Tom na Gruagaich, the wind has swept the snow from the stony ground, and in its place ice crystals have built up on the windward edge of the boulders. In summer, this wind-scoured col is denuded of turf; a text book example of elemental erosion. At the OS pillar, I involuntarily recoil from the adjacent cliff edge and a 1,500ft. drop into Toll a'Mhadaidh. Away to the west, across the Minches, I see the Butt of Lewis, the Harris hills, and the Shiant islands. From the western slopes of Beinn Alligin to the sea sweeps an uninhabited stretch of moorland, studded with jewel-like lochans. I descend a short rock step to the north and pick my way through a tiresome boulder field, rendered treacherous by snow cover, to reach the saddle under Sgurr Mhor. The ridge ahead is clearly defined but steep in places, and I am glad of my ice-axe, since the slope drops away steeply on the left and precipitously on the right. As I pass the huge cleft, I glance down to the rock walls, festooned with icicles.

The summit of Sgurr Mhor is perfect; a narrow ridge with the highest point established by a beautifully constructed dry-stone cairn. The outstanding feature of the view from Sgurr Mhor must surely be the proximity of her strange neighbours, Baos Bheinn, Beinn an Eoin, and Beinn Dearg, which stand as blades of rock rising ethereally from the desolate moorland landscape. The Horns of Alligin look daunting, but they should give no trouble to the wary, and in summer they may be easily by-passed on the right by a useful deer path. The day was drawing to a close as, rather wearily, I scrambled over the rocky crests. Snow had covered the eroded track, which is all too obvious in summer, and I needed to reconnoitre a feasible route. The final, steep, scrambling descent from the lowest of the Horns is marked by a cairn but it is still vilely wet, muddy, and slippery, and needs care. I half-ran, half-stumbled through the heather and peat to regain the stalking path, and darkness was falling as I came down through the pines.

Above: The great 'Gash' that splits the south face of Sgurr Mhor, the highest peak of the Beinn Alligin group. *Photo: Ken Andrew*

12   Spidean Mialach and Gleouraich

by Stephen Greenwood

From the summit of the old road to Cluanie, under a lowering sky, we had first glimpsed the steep, northern crags of Spidean Mialach and Gleouraich, dipping sharply into Glen Loyne. Their dark, mysterious buttresses of rock, rising upwards into the clouds on a late autumn afternoon, excited ideas of an early encounter. In fact, it was almost a year later before this assignation was fulfilled, but we could hardly have dreamt of the quite remarkable conditions under which we were to traverse these two splendid mountains.

The forecast, it is true, had given some slight encouragement to our optimism, but there was little practical evidence to support this as we drove north along Lochy, and turned west towards Tomdoun. Indeed, the all-pervading greyness became perceptibly denser as we approached Loch Quoich, until, along the loch side, we were in genuine Scotch mist. The car was parked some little way short of the point below which the ill-fated Glen Quoich Lodge lies, resting under the raised waters of the Loch. Striking purposefully up a grassy spur, we calculated this would take us to a point immediately west of Loch Fearna. We had no means of knowing when, if at all, there would be any increase in visibility beyond some 50 yards, which was the maximum at that time. But gradually, as we climbed, the sky above became brighter. Clearly something was about to happen. Suddenly the miracle occurred; we burst out from a boiling sea of mist into blazing sun, an azure sky above, with wraiths of swirling vapours spiralling up from the dense mass of cloud below. For the rest of the day, until we dipped again into the pea-soup gloom below, the sun shone beneficently. We had, as planned, emerged onto a knoll immediately to the west of, and just above, Loch Fearna, across whose surface the mists rolled and seethed. Spidean Mialach rose above us, and behind, in the distance, a fantastic backcloth of peaks jutted out of the mist. Away to the south rose the Ben, the Aonachs, and the Grey Corries, whilst to the south-west, Sgurr na Ciche reared up like a Scottish Matterhorn.

We traversed steadily eastwards and upwards towards the summit ridge of Spidean Mialach, something of a grind in truth, though relieved by the astonishing scene below and around us. On reaching the ridge, perhaps half a mile to the east of the summit, we found that, on the north side of the mountain, Glen Loyne too was filled with cloud. Beyond, the whole sequence of the South Cluanie peaks stood ranked, with the Saddle plainly visible beyond their western extremity. The southern flanks of both Spidean Mialach and Gleouraich, being mainly grassy in voluminous folds and hollows, are in marked contrast to the broken, craggy buttresses on the north side, a characteristic that is immediately apparent once the ridge is attained.

The air was still, and lunch on the summit was followed by a spell of genuine sun-bathing, broken by the knowledge that, being October and not June, the time at our disposal was limited. So on westwards we went, to the great dip in the ridge, with the shattered towers of rock on our right falling to hidden depths below, then a descent and corresponding ascent of about 800ft. to take us on to Gleouraich. Gleouraich is deceptive, for the highest point is at the extreme western end of the ridge, and two of our party, having reached the first and lower summit, had to be cajoled from a second spell of sun-bathing to continue to the highest point. We lingered at the top, rejoicing in the rich afternoon glow, and in the certain knowledge that in some three-quarters of an hour we should again be immersed in stygian gloom on the descent.

The Ordnance Survey map shows a stalk-

Maps   O.S. 1:50,000 Sheet 33. Start and finish at Loch Quoich side, 1½ miles E of Quoich Bridge (ref. 033026).
Grading   A rough walk over two splendid West Highland peaks. The north sides of the summit ridges are precipitous and care should be taken in bad weather, to which this area is particularly prone.
Time   5–6 hours.
Distance   9 miles.
Escape Routes   In good conditions the slopes to the S can be descended almost anywhere. An obvious and easy escape route is S from the low bealach (2350ft.) between the two peaks.
Telephones   Tomdoun Hotel; Kinlochhourn.
Transport   On Mon, Wed and Fri a minibus service runs from Invergarry to Kinlochhourn alongside Loch Quoich. Regular bus service from Fort William and Inverness to Invergarry.
Accommodation   Hotels at Invergarry and Tomdoun. Youth Hostel at Loch Lochy.
Guidebooks   S.M.T. Guide *The Western Highlands.*

Left: Spidean Mialach from the slopes of Gleouraich. *Photo: Stephen Greenwood*

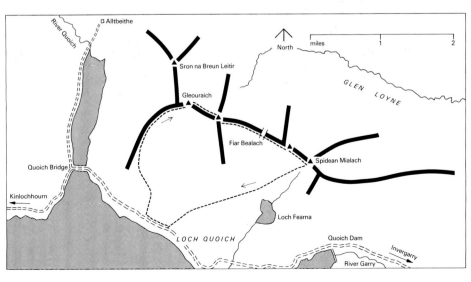

ers' track climbing high onto the western flank of Gleouraich. From the summit cairn we could easily discern the upper reaches of this below us. Reluctantly, at about 4.30 p.m., we tore ourselves away. The upper section of the path, clinging as it does to the western edge of the final spur of Gleouraich, which projects directly south towards Loch Quoich, was sensational. The very steep west flank of this spur disappeared into the boiling mists below. We could have been above a 10,000ft. precipice, such was the feeling of airy suspense. Once the track started to descend, it did so purposefully and rapidly, in a sequence of zig-zags, almost immediately entering the heavy cloud. Astonishingly swiftly, we came down to a region of rushing streams and spreading rhododendrons, a by-product of the once carefully nurtured gardens of the inundated Lodge. A tramp of just over a mile, back east along the road, brought us to our car. The mist was clinging everywhere, to everything, just as we had left it in the morning.

'Aye', said the man in the bar of the Tomdoun Hotel, where we paused to slake our thirst, 'it's been a real gloomy day.' Little did he know . . .

13   The Saddle of Glen Shiel

by Jo Light

You travel in from the east fast and easily along the A87. The watershed between the River Cluanie and the River Shiel is crossed, and then the mountains of the north-west, in their infinite variety, are all there. Towards its western end, the floor of Glen Sheil is relatively wide, flat, and low, but the long ridges, both to the north and south, soar upwards to over 3,000ft. to numerous summits which fling down extremely steep slopes. These are frequently broken by crags, and support rich and varied mountain vegetation, that expresses itself in so many different textures and hues of green, and shades of soft brown and gold, that flare into rust and amber, and include the purple haze of the heather, in the autumn. Suddenly, to the south, tucked behind Sgurr a'Chuilinn, the huge hunched shoulder of Creag nan Damh, and the long spine of Faochag, the graceful line of the slender-pointed summit of the Saddle appears, as it stands back, reticent and finely etched amongst so many giant shapes. Almost immediately, the steep flanks of Biod an Fhithich and the continuing ridge of A'Mhuing, which trend just west of north, cut off the view, and the mountain remains hidden as the head of Loch Duich is approached.

The dominant feature of the Saddle is the narrow, sharp-edged, west-to-east ridge which extends from Spidean Dhomhuill Bhric, to the main summit, then eastwards again to Sgurr nan Forcan, from which it descends very steeply, a few degrees north of east, to the col that separates the head streams of the Allt a'Choire Chaoil and Allt Coire Mhalagain. In its upper section, the northern side of the mountain is very craggy, and the exposed pale grey rock reveals its composition of crystals, that glisten and gleam whenever a shaft of sunlight rests upon the flaky surfaces of the schists. And it displays its structure, which has resulted in the formation of narrow and broad slabs that slant away to the south-east, and are bounded by abrupt edges and also blunt, north-facing buttresses, combining to make a complicated series of slopes. Two main corries, however, can be distinguished: to the west, Coir' Uaine, with its magnificent headwalls that decisively form the crest between the main summit and Spidean

Dhomhuill Bhric, and curve protectively round Loch a'Coir' Uaine. To the east Coire Chaoil is less obvious, because of its width and much lower rim. Between them there is a high, narrow ridge which extends for approximately one mile northwards, from the summit of the Saddle to Sgurr na Creige. This descends in a steep, grassy hillside to the confluence of Allt a'Choire Chaoil and Allt a'Coir' Uaine, becoming the Allt Undalain, which tumbles its waters into the River Shiel at Shiel Bridge. This is the most straightforward route up to the summit of the mountain.

The most beautiful view of the Saddle is from one of the western summits of the Five Sisters, because it is from this vantage point that the elegance of its form is totally revealed. The razor-edged ridges stand out darkly and sharply, and in between there are the much finer, gracefully curving lines that reflect the south-eastward inclination of the schists. The plunging line of the Forcan Ridge, silhouetted against the sky and the distance-faded shapes of the Knoydart hills, provides an enticing challenge to the hill walker well-acquainted with exposed scrambling. There is a choice of routes up to the start of the Forcan Ridge. From the A87 between the Bridge Mhalagain and Achnangart, there is a well-defined track which leads easily up to the gap north of Meall an Odhar. Or you can stroll from the camp site at Shiel Bridge to the lowest of the rocky lumps which marks the start of A'Mhuing, and eventually the final, craggy top of Biod an Fhithich is achieved. This is a personal choice of line, for it involves keeping to the spine and clambering up and over as many of the rocky outcrops as time and the patience of one's companions will allow, but it means that the summit shapes and northern slopes are always visible.

The broad, green back of Meall an Odhar forms the rim of the Coire Chaoil, and provides a gentle approach. A low wall saunters in from the Bealach Coire Mhalagain, and the way ahead becomes very steep. Blocks of parent rock outcrop, and an accumulation of boulders lies scattered in disarray, forcing the path to wind upwards through the piles of frost-shattered rock debris. Soon the outcrops become more continuous, and the

Maps   O.S. 1:50,000 Sheet 33. Start and finish at Shiel Bridge (ref. 935189).
Grading   A fine mountain walk but certain sections of the ridge are rocky and exposed and the route is not recommended for the inexperienced.
Time   7 hours.
Distance   12 miles.
Escape Routes   The Bealach Coire Mhalagain, which leads easily down E into Glen Shiel, is accessible from the lower section of the Forcan Ridge. A descent into Coir' Uaine may be made from several points along the Sgurr Leac nan Each–Sgurr a'Gharg Gharaidh ridge.
Telephones   Shiel Bridge.
Transport   Bus services from Edinburgh to Uig, Glasgow to Portree, and Inverness to Portree, run through Shiel Bridge.
Accommodation   Hotels and Bed and Breakfasts in Shiel Bridge. Cluanie Inn. Youth Hostels at Ratagan and Kyle of Lochalsh.
Guidebooks   S.M.T. Guide *The Western Highlands; The Scottish Peaks* by W. A. Poucher (Constable).

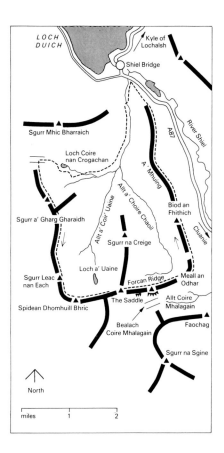

arête beautifully formed. From the jagged and sometimes pinnacled crest, a smooth line of slabs sweeps down to the south-east, and if a less exposed route is preferred, then you can drop down a few feet onto the north-western side, which is more broken. A horizontal section interrupts the vertical line, and provides a crisp balancing exercise but you quickly gain height again by climbing up the series of short scrambling problems, which lead to a definite craggy summit. You can climb down steep rocks directly to the col, or take a well-used by-pass track to the south. This descends steep vegetation, and brings you easily round onto the col. The arête rears up, and once more the crest provides exposed scrambling, whilst an easier line winds away to the right.

The main summit is marked, prosaically, by an OS pillar, but its location demands a lengthy stay, particularly on a fine June day. The eye can travel far in any direction, and rest on distant peaks or race easily along the back of high, ancient masses, carved into distinctive forms dictated by the basic materials present, the time and enormous forces involved, and the elements of erosion that have exerted their influence. Liathach presents its long, lofty spine, and its southern flanks become a continuous wall which ends abruptly to the east, and in a curving tail to the west. Against the western sky, the Black Cuillin Ridge displays magnificently its extent and its wild miscellany of peaks, and to the south there is the grandeur, remoteness, and splendid variety of the

Knoydart mountains, which lead the gaze to the distant shapes of Ben Nevis and Sgurr Thuilm. A pleasant stroll westwards to Spidean Dhomhuill Bhric allows you also to enjoy the ruggedness of the Coir' Uaine, and the true line of the mountain continues on round beyond Sgurr Leac nan Each to Sgurr a'Gharg Gharaidh, down to Loch Coire nan Crogachan. From this col, there is a track which returns to Shiel Bridge, following the beautiful tree- and shrub-lined course of the Allt Undalain. It is possible to descend from a number of places on this continuation ridge, but after discovering the great number of short crags, which offer entertaining problems, the hummocky nature of the final stretch becomes of no consequence.

14 The Lairig Ghru

by Adam Watson

Maps O.S. 1:50,000 Sheets 36 and 43, O.S. 1:25,000 Outdoor Leisure Map – High Tops of the Cairngorms. Start from Coylumbridge (ref. 915106). Finish E of the Linn of Dee (ref. 068898).
Grading A long and rough walk through a remote mountain range. The pass is 2,733ft. above sea level and the crossing can be dangerous in deep winter snow.
Time 8–9 hours.
Distance 19 miles.
Escape Routes None, but in an emergency shelter can be found at the Sinclair Hut and Corrour Bothy.
Telephones Coylumbridge; Derry Lodge; Inverey.
Transport Railway Station at Aviemore. Bus Aviemore to Coylumbridge. Daily bus service from Aberdeen to Braemar.
Accommodation Hotels, Guest Houses and Bed and Breakfasts at Aviemore, Coylumbridge and Braemar. Youth Hostels at Aviemore, Loch Morlich, Inverey and Braemar.
Guidebooks S.M.T. Guide *The Cairngorms; The Cairngorms* by Desmond Nethersole – Thompson and Adam Watson (Melven Press).

Top right: Looking north up the Lairig Ghru from near Devil's Point. The combination of deep snow and mist make the crossing of such a long, high, and remote pass an extremely serious proposition. *Photo: Chris Bryan*

Bottom right: Looking south to Cairn Toul and Devil's Point from the Pools of Dee. *Photo: Robert Adam*

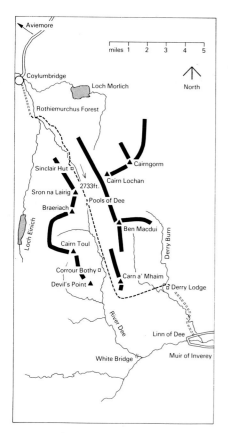

The Lairig Ghru is the finest hill pass in Britain. Cutting right through the middle of the Cairngorms, from Spey to Dee, it offers a wonderful challenge to walkers. From Aviemore, its great V gives you a feeling of mystery. What will it be like in that dark gap? And what lies unseen beyond? Even its name, pronounced Laarig Groo, sounds impressive. Correctly spelt Lairig Dhru, it means the hill pass of the oozing one, after the Dru or Druie stream. But to many local folk and walkers it is often just 'The Lairig', a good name, for this is unquestionably *the* Lairig, best of all the many fine Lairigs in Scotland.

The Lairig Ghru was the ultimate, unattainable challenge to me as a small boy. From Strath Spey, I gazed spell bound at its beauty, and admired those who had walked through it. Since then I have come to know it well at all seasons, night and day. On hard-packed April snow, I once skimmed through it in an effortless few hours on skis. But the Lairig can be dangerous in soft snow and storm, and I remember an exhausting January day when I was reduced to less than a mile an hour, even on skis. Every season has its own beauties and delights, but I prefer the Lairig in spring or early summer, when the rich colour and snowy hills make this walk a special joy.

When I left Coylumbridge before sunrise one April morning, a frost gripped the ancient track through the pines and junipers, but crested tits were already active in the branches, giving that cheery buzzing call so characteristic of the Spey forests. The Lairig's great V became even bigger and nearer, always an exciting prospect. I crossed the Cairngorm Club footbridge, and later turned right at 'Piccadilly', where four paths meet. Then up the soft, needle-covered path to the forest edge, a grand spot to stop. The sun was now out, a smell of resin wafted from the warmed pines, and north, beyond the Spey, I could see the rolling brown hills of Moray. As I carried on towards the Sinclair Hut, a breeze blew off the peaty moor, bringing cool air from the snowy tops. In cattle-droving days, Highlanders repaired the track annually. Now, decades of neglect and treading by many walkers have churned

up this part, and necessitated repairs by other bodies. At the Sinclair Hut, six miles from Coylumbridge, I stood almost in the jaws of the V, and soon the dark crags and red granite screes of Creag an Leth-choin and Sron na Lairig hemmed in both sides. The gradual ascent up the rough path was easy, giving fine views northwards, and to the south, still the great V curved onwards, mysteriously. Soon I strode amongst short arctic-alpine plants, blaeberry, and crowberry, as well as stunted heather on the stony ground. Ptarmigan cocks belched and crackled on the screes, and the hens gave soft

coos like pigeons. The top of the Lairig is a
favourite spot for the hardy ptarmigan. I
thought how marvellously they put into
perspective our own puny attempts at winter
survival.

Here now was the 2,733ft. summit, seven
and a half miles up from Coylumbridge. As
the ground sloped gently towards Deeside,
new hills appeared, with the conical Cairn
Toul, and the Devil's Point, rising dramatically. I trod carefully along boulder fields
to the Pools of Dee, where the last ice
was melting in the warm sun. The Lairig
now became much wider, but bigger slopes

soared steeply to the snowy heights of Ben Macdui and Braeriach. Soon I was looking up west to the Garbh Choire, always an exciting view, with its grand array of wild, high corries. It was still winter up there. Cornices on the snowy peak of Sgor an Lochain Uaine gleamed silvery in the sun, and the shadows on the high snows were a deep blue.

The walk down Glen Dee was a delight, with the Perthshire hills rising as snowy domes far to the south. Near Clach nan Taillear, stone of the tailors, where some Speyside men once died in a snowstorm, meadow pipits fluttered above the heather, pouring out cascades of song. Soon I was opposite the Corrour Bothy, which stands on the west side of Dee beyond a footbridge. Just past here, the path diverged, with right fork heading down Glen Dee. I took the left fork, climbing gently round Carn a'Mhaim. This was a perfect place for a snack, looking past the greens of Glen Geusachan to the slabs of the Devil's Point. The peaty lochans sparkled in the sun. Soon came another view that never fails to welcome; the first gnarled pines of Luibeg. Today, after miles of

heather and snowy tops, their great mushrooms looked an unreal, riotous green. Beyond them, to the north, soared whitecapped Ben Macdui, and away to the east, dark Lochnagar. Around me rose the lower hills of Luibeg, their heathery slopes tinged that plum colour so typical of our Eastern Highlands in spring.

After a night's frost, the Luibeg Burn was low and easily crossed, so I did not have to go to the footbridge upstream. The walk through the old pines was grand. Stags grazed the meadows, and coal tits sang cheerily in the pines. I crossed the Derry Burn by a footbridge just above Derry Lodge, now sixteen miles out from Coylumbridge. The road down Glen Lui led past former farmlands, where many more stags grazed, and oystercatchers piped. At the Black Brig, I stopped for a last view of the Cairngorms. Then down through pine woods to the locked gate at the public road, east of the Linn of Dee. A quick wade in the sparkling, cold water of Lui to cool my feet was just right, before the welcome of a pint at Mar Lodge, a short distance down the road, past some of the finest old pines in Scotland.

15   The Corrieyairack Pass

by Alastair Hetherington

Maps   O.S. 1:50,000 Sheets 34 and 35. Start from Garvamore (ref. 523947). Finish at Fort Augustus (ref. 378092).
Grading   Easy, but can be exposed at the 2,507ft. summit of the pass.
Time   6 hours.
Distance   17 miles.
Escape Routes   None.
Telephones   Garvamore and Fort Augustus.
Transport   Daily post-bus (morning) from Dalwhinnie via Laggan Bridge to Garvamore. On Tues, Thurs and Sat the bus continues to Melgarve. Fort Augustus is well served by Inverness–Fort William buses. Railway Station at Dalwhinnie.
Accommodation   Hotels and Bed and Breakfasts at Laggan Bridge, Dalwhinnie and Fort Augustus. Youth Hostels at Kingussie, Loch Lochy and Loch Ness (Invermoriston).
Guidebooks   S.M.T. Guide *The Central Highlands*; *The Buried Barony* by Alasdair MacGregor (Hale); *The Military Roads of Scotland* by W. Taylor (David and Charles); *The Drove Roads of Scotland* by A. R. B. Haldane (Nelson).

Scenically, the crossing of the Corrieyairack is pleasing, but not in the top class. Historically, it can have few rivals in Scotland. The track follows the line of General Wade's military road, built some 250 years ago, in the summer of 1731, and for much of its length today it still looks not unlike the original. It was built to help subdue the Highlands, but ironically, it was first used in war, by the fresh Jacobite army marching against the Hanoverians in 1745. Cope's failure to stop Prince Charles at the east end of the pass left the way open for his advance to Edinburgh, Manchester, and Derby. Eight months later, in April 1746, it was by Wade's road over the Corrieyairack that the tattered remnants of the Highland army escaped to their glens, after defeat at Culloden.

The walk is good in either direction, but I prefer east to west. That is easier, too, if you depend on public transport. The post-bus will drop you in the morning just short of St. George's bridge, at Garvamore, and you can make the crossing with the light behind you. As you go west, the corrie of the Yairack burn opens up in front of you, with Wade's thirteen horseshoe bends climbing the steepest part. At 2,507ft., at the top of the pass, if lucky with the weather, you will have a tremendous panorama towards Knoydart, Kintail, and the Affric hills; and then there is the long, easy descent past a succession of leafy glades until you arrive by the shores of Loch Ness, at Fort Augustus.

Before setting out, look well at St. George's bridge. Apart from steel reinforcing rods, the fine double arch is just as Wade completed it in 1732, and the scene is almost unchanged, too. A line of pylons, some new forestry, and a road sign are the only evidence of the twentieth century. The hills and the glen are as they were when the redcoats and the Highland army made contact here. For it was close to Garvamore that the scouts of the two sides spotted each other. Charles Edward Stuart had landed in Arisaig, raised his standard at Glenfinnan, and started his march from Loch Lochy. As he climbed the Corrieyairack, word reached him that General Cope, with a Hanoverian force, was marching north from Stirling. Most of Cope's soldiers were untrained, and he was short of food and ammunition. He believed

that unless he reached the crest of the Corrieyairack before the Jacobite rebels, he could be trapped and destroyed there. At Garva he realised that he was too late. He could still have stood and fought, and perhaps ended the rebellion there and then; but he prudently turned north, to Ruthven barracks, near Kingussie. Then, as fast as possible, onwards to take ships from Inverness. The Jacobites had won their first victory, almost bloodlessly. Cope was court-martialled later, with Wade presiding, but was acquitted.

It is hard to realise that when Wade started building, in 1726, there were no roads in the Highlands. Apart from the sea, the only link to Inverness that a wheeled carriage or gun could take was from Aberdeen, keeping clear of the mountains. Wade built first an experimental road from Fort William by Fort Augustus to Fort George (then at Inverness, later moved a few miles east to its present site). Next, in the summers of 1728 to 1730, he built his great north road from Dunkeld to Inverness by Dalwhinnie. Then, while improving the Great Glen route, he built the cross link from Dalwhinnie and Ruthven barracks to Fort Augustus, by Garvamore and the Corrieyairack. So as you cross the Corrieyairack, you are truly walking with history. As you drop down from the summit, you will come to the first trees at the 'Milky Hollow', where Wade, in October 1731, held a great feast with roasted oxen for the 500 men (mostly Highlanders) who had helped build the road; and it was here that Prince Charles, on the march south, lifted his glass and swore not to take off his brogues until he had fought Cope.

The Pass had, of course, been used for centuries before, for it was one of the shortest routes from north to south. William the Lion fought at Garvamore in 1187. From the late fifteenth century, the Corrieyairack was a main droving track for cattle from Skye and the far north, heading for Stirling and the Falkirk tryst. During the bloody and brutal Covenanting wars of the seventeenth century, Montrose used it, once doubling back from Loch Ness up the pass, and then taking his men over the shoulder of Carn Leac (an excellent viewpoint, by the way), and southwards to Glen Roy, to surprise and

overwhelm the Campbell garrison at Inverlochy. He did this in February 1645, with the Corrieyairack under heavy snow. If you cross today, you may still meet great snow-drifts in May. Then you may think of Montrose's men, in bitter February, as they eluded, and then ravaged, the much larger Campbell force. That barbarous conflict played a part in securing the English Parliament's supremacy over the Crown (though Montrose later changed sides, like some others, in those cruel crosscurrents). Again, therefore, as you walk, give humble thanks for the many forces that shaped British democracy.

The pleasure of walking comes first, with history an added spice. Even in bad weather, struggling against the wind, the crossing of the Corrieyairack leaves a warm sense of achievement. But the history is inescapable. On an almost cloudless May night, we slept under the stars beside St. George's bridge. I stirred in the early morning, fell asleep again, and dreamed uneasily of a band of young men, going noisily by with drums and pipes. My superstitious wife was convinced that ghosts of Charles's clansmen had

passed. We were at the top of the Pass, in blazing sun, by 9.30 a.m. Ghosts or no ghosts, it was a good place to be.

Above: At the Speyside start of the Corrieyairack Pass (top), and St. George's bridge. *Photos: Hamish Brown*

16   Schiehallion

by Cameron McNeish

If you were to compile a list of the ten most popular picture postcard views of Scotland, the view of Schiehallion from the road north of Loch Rannoch would surely come amongst them. It is the classic view of the mountain, the distinctive cone shape of the north-east ridge and summit rising high from a foreground of moorland. The perfect cone shape is, in fact, the culmination of a three-mile-long ridge which rears its broad shoulder from the old General Wade road between Aberfeldy and Kinloch Rannoch, and its rocky quartzite summit offers the hill walker views to the north which are unparalleled by any other hill in the Southern Highlands. Schiehallion is, in Gaelic, Sidh Chailleann, the Fairy Hill of the Caledonians. It is an obvious landmark from other hill areas miles away; from Ben Alder, from the Southern Grampians, from Ben Nevis, and from the Glencoe hills, where it stands out like a sentinel above the vast flatness of the Rannoch Moor. 'Like a skerry of the sea', was how Neil Munro, the Scots novelist described it. It is a totally isolated hill, and the hill walker has only one Munro to show for his efforts, but for all that, it offers a good afternoon's walk, either as a 'there and back' effort from Wade's Military Road, or from near Kinloch Rannoch, or, even better, as a traverse of the whole mountain from west to east.

It is best to leave your car a hundred yards or so east of the Braes of Foss farm, about seven miles east of Kinloch Rannoch. A farm gate leads you to a grassy field, over which you must cross to find the well-worn track which runs south, and then south-east, onto the east ridge. The path rises gradually and easily, over soft peat and heather, and then over rocks and quartzy scree, to the summit, 3,547ft. above sea level. The summit comprises large rocks and boulders, and the cairn sits atop a great quartzite block. To the south, the slopes fall away steeply into Gleann Mor, and to the south-west, the Carn Mairg quartet appears as broad, rounded hills connected by broad, rounded ridges.

Two miles east of Kinloch Rannoch, a rough path follows a stream from Tempar to give a shorter, but much tougher, route to the summit by way of the north-west ridge. The steep screes often give a two steps up, one step back, style of ascent, but as you climb higher, so the screes turn to good rock, and the route becomes more interesting. The most enjoyable walk on Schiehallion is a traverse from Tempar to Braes of Foss, linking the above two routes. I recently made this complete traverse as part of a trans-Scotland walk, from Oban to Montrose. Having climbed all the Carn Mairg hills in the morning, the huge bulk of Schiehallion was not often out of our sight, reminding us of the effort it would take to climb it in the afternoon. We approached it from Geal Charn, in the west, and began climbing the steep slopes in temperatures which were well up in the seventies. After our exertions in the morning, with the weight of our 30lb. packs and the heat taking their toll, we expected a struggle, but it was good to get onto the rock and quartzite blocks of Schiehallion after a morning of heather bashing. It felt as though we were on a real mountain. We crossed the summit, and enjoyed the relaxed descent to Braes of Foss, as the bare peat, eroded by countless pairs of boots, was soft underneath, and made a welcome change from the usual knee-jarring descents.

Fine hill as it may be, Schiehallion's chief claim to fame was as an aid in attempting to calculate the density of the earth.* Schiehallion was the mountain chosen for the experiment, because of its almost perfectly conical shape. The major result of the experiment was, in fact, that the earth had a dense core, and not a hollow core as had been thought. Less important then, but more important to us as map users, was the fact that, in the course of the calculations, one Charles Hutton hit upon a method of drawing lines connecting places of equal height, hence the birth of contour lines. Perhaps not many walkers, navigating their way to the summit of Schiehallion on a dark, misty day, appreciate that this is the very hill which gave birth to the basis of the modern maps they are using to calculate their height above sea level.

*In 1774, the Astronomer Royal, Nevil Maskelyne, began working on an experiment first suggested decades before by Isaac Newton. It was thought that a large mass, such as a mountain, would exert its own gravitational pull, and this effect, although small, could well be measurable by hanging a plumb line near the mountain, and finding its angle of deflection from the true vertical. Further, by estimating the mass of the mountain, the whole mass of the Earth could then be calculated, in proportion to the angle of the plumb line.

Maps   O.S. 1:50,000 Sheet 42. Start from Tempar Farm, 2 miles E of Kinloch Rannoch (ref. 687575). Finish at Braes of Foss (ref. 750560).
Grading   A rough but easy mountain walk.
Time   4–5 hours.
Distance   6 miles.
Escape Routes   Schiehallion may be descended almost anywhere.
Telephones   Kinloch Rannoch; Tummel Bridge; Keltneyburn.
Transport   Weekday bus service Pitlochry to Kinloch Rannoch via Tummel Bridge.
Accommodation   Hotels at Kinloch Rannoch and Strathtummel. Bed and Breakfast locally. Youth Hostels at Killin and Garth.
Guidebooks S.M.T. Guide *The Southern Highlands*.

Left: Schiehallion from the north-west from near Kinloch Rannoch. *Photo: Tom Parker*

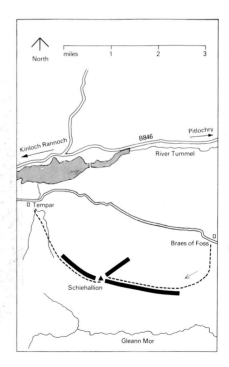

17   A Ben Alder Crossing

by Richard Gilbert

Maps O.S. 1:50,000 Sheet 42. Start from Rannoch Station (ref. 422578). Finish at Corrour Station (ref. 356664).

Grading A two-day expedition over remote mountainous terrain. For the experienced walker only.

Time Two days.

Distance 28 miles from Rannoch Station or 22 miles from Bridge of Gaur.

Escape Routes None. Emergency shelter may be found at Culra Lodge bothy N of Ben Alder and at Corrour Lodge E of Loch Ossian.

Telephones Corrour Station only.

Transport Corrour Station and Rannoch Station are on the West Highland line between Glasgow and Fort William. A post-bus from Kinloch Rannoch meets the morning train at Rannoch Station.

Accommodation Hotels at Rannoch and Bridge of Orchy. Youth Hostel at Loch Ossian (summer only).

Guidebooks S.M.T. Guide *The Central Highlands*.

Top right: Ben Alder from the north-east on the Culra Lodge approach, a view that illustrates the craggy aspect of this side of the mountain. *Photo: Hamish Brown*

Bottom right: Collecting wood for a night at Benalder Cottage. *Photo: Richard Gilbert*

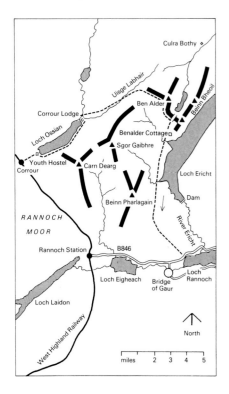

The 8.29 a.m. train from Euston drew in to Bridge of Orchy station bang on time. Gerard and I manoeuvred our bulky rucksacks along the corridor to find an empty compartment. Oblivious to the gleaming landscape, for fresh snow had fallen overnight, the other passengers were rubbing the sleep out of their eyes and fumbling their way to the restaurant car for breakfast. We didn't envy them one little bit for we were bound for Ben Alder, that little-known giant of the Scottish Highlands.

Ben Alder (3,757ft.) stands supreme north-east of Rannoch Moor. It vies with A'Mhaighdean for the privilege of being the most inaccessible Munro, and few are conscious of its existence. The motorist might catch a glimpse of this white-coated monster, glinting in the winter sunshine above Loch Ericht, as he speeds along the Dalwhinnie by-pass on the A9. The rail traveller might glance east, as he rattles across Rannoch Moor on a bed of brushwood, to see a distant mass rising into the clouds, but he will soon return to his crossword, and turn up the heating another notch. The hill walker is attracted to Ben Alder by its size, its remoteness, its grandeur, and its historical associations. It can be climbed from Rannoch, Corrour, Dalwhinnie, or Loch Laggan, and the very energetic walker can even climb it in a day, but the route I have chosen for this article provides a safe, and not too arduous expedition, yet savours the mountain to the full. Two days must be allowed for the conquest of Ben Alder if using Benalder Cottage, near the south end of Loch Ericht, as a launching pad. In addition, the magnificent railway across Rannoch Moor is used to great advantage.

The sky was blue when we disembarked at Rannoch station, but the wind was cruel, and we were glad to be whisked the six miles to Bridge of Gaur by post-bus. The path to Benalder Cottage starts through a plantation, just beyond Rannoch Lodge. It winds over the hills, for much of the way through newly planted forest, before reaching the banks of Loch Ericht near a bridge over the Cam Chriochan burn. We lunched out of the wind in a stand of old pines, and then continued towards Alder Bay. The path

petered out, but we were guided by the vast bulk of Ben Alder ahead, with the Bealach Breabag, our first objective for the following day, clearly visible. Four hours from Bridge of Gaur, we were brewing tea on the broad window ledge in the front room of Benalder Cottage. The view was stimulating, with white horses racing over the loch, and the larches on the hillock across the burn tinged green with the first hint of spring. Although it was late April, the north-facing slopes across the loch were still white with fresh snow, right down to the water's edge.

Benalder Cottage is one of Scotland's most solid and traditional open bothies. Its sits squat beside the Alder Burn, with its slate roof and green door merging into the slopes behind. Known also as McCook's Cabin, after the shepherd who inhabited it for many years, it is said to be haunted. Walkers seeking shelter on stormy nights have reported hearing footsteps pacing up and down, and the sound of heavy furniture being dragged across empty rooms. For years it was rumoured that McCook had hanged himself in the cottage, but this is totally untrue. Yet stories of ghostly happenings continue.

The afternoon passed pleasantly. We collected wood, lit a roaring fire, and buried a large amount of rubbish, left, inexcusably, by previous bothymongers. The sun shone, the views were delectable and we explored the rocky slopes above the cottage for Cluny's Cage, the underground hideout where Bonny Prince Charlie took refuge from Cumberland's troops after Culloden. Try and find it yourself; it is not difficult.

Don't be alarmed by scamperings in the night, it is only mice and they keep behind the wainscot. Rise early, for at the end of the day, you have a train to catch at Corrour. Gerard and I benefited from the (later) winter timetable, and we could afford a leisurely day. Up to the Bealach Breabag, and then across the boulder fields, treacherously covered with fresh powder snow, towards the Ben Alder plateau. Quite suddenly the full glory of the Garbh Choire burst into view. A mile-long curve of broken cliffs fell 1,000ft. to the dark Loch a'Bhealaich Bheithe, while from the corrie floor rose rock buttresses, plastered white

Above: Benalder Cottage. *Photo: Hamish Brown*

Above right: On the Ben Alder plateau, heading towards the summit along the edge of the eastern cliffs. *Photo: Gerard Simpson*

and festooned with icicles from the recent spring blizzard – a savage scene redolent of countless winter days in the Highlands.

Allowing a wide margin for the cornices of the Garbh Choire, we hurried across the bleak plateau to the trig. point at 3,757ft. My mind went back 20 years to my first ascent of Ben Alder, on a high summer day, when I lunched by the cairn and watched a hen ptarmigan usher her brood of chicks to safety under the rocks. But today clouds raced across the pale blue sky, driven by a north-easterly wind, which iced the boulders and nipped our noses and ears. It was not a day to linger, and we made haste for the shelter of the glen. The west ridge of Ben Alder, down which we raced, is gentle and easy-angled right down to the torrent of the Uisge Labhair. Out of the wind we enjoyed lunch and speculated on the tragedy that befell five climbers at New Year, 1951, on this very spot. The party had left Corrour Lodge at 8.30 p.m. bound for Benalder Cottage, only seven miles away, but a ferocious blizzard sprang up, and they were forced to bivouac for the night close to Lochan Allt Glaschoire. In the morning the blizzard raged on, and they turned back for Corrour Lodge, but all except one, a woman, perished in the snow.*

The peat hags and moraines beside the Uisge Labhair are infuriating to cross, but

*For a full account of the accident see *SMCJ* 143 (1952).

we found a distinct path appearing on the north side of the burn as we approached Corrour Lodge. It was warm enough in the sun to stretch out on the smooth granite slabs beside the wooden bridge over the burn, with Loch Ossian, most beautiful of Scottish lochs, shimmering beyond the trees. Take your pick of the tracks north or south of Loch Ossian; they both meet up at the west end near the Youth Hostel. The aroma of wood smoke drifted across the path, and we found the hostel warden in residence. Tom Rigg was spring-cleaning the hostel prior to the opening in mid-May, and he warmly welcomed us with mugs of tea and regaled us with stories of his roving life. Sometime warden, deer stalker, tree-planter, post-master, station-master, a remarkable and worthwhile life for this kind and friendly man.

The sun was slanting across Rannoch Moor, and a large herd of stags moved away up the hill, as our train squealed to a halt at Corrour. With heavy hearts we joined the throng, loth to leave this exquisite and fascinating region.

NOTES ON CLUNY'S CAGE
by Tom Weir

Let's consider how Bonny Prince Charlie got to Cluny's Cage, on Ben Alder. If we take the

starting point as the Dark Mile, at the east end of Loch Arkaig, he had 30 miles to cover. First across the Great Glen, crossed within two miles of Fort Augustus; thence by the Corrieyairack, to reach the head of Glen Roy, then over the shoulder of Creag Meagaidh at 3,000 ft. to slip round Loch Laggan, for Cluny Macpherson's hunting forest.

The night of August 28, 1746 saw Lochgarry and Dr. Cameron guiding the Prince's party, moving fast to get clear of the concentration of enemy troops garrisoned at Fort Augustus, cat-napping when they thought it was safe, and taking very little food, maintaining such a pace that they covered the significant part of the journey in two hard nights. The tired men were not taken to the 'Cage' immediately. They used other hideouts round Ben Alder until September 5, before going to the specially prepared nest of boulders, with a natural upstairs-downstairs arrangement. They slept on the flat slab, roofed and woven round with boughs and moss against the rain. A manuscript in Cluny's Charter Chest describes it.

'The upper floor served for salle à manger and bed chamber while the lower serv'd for a cave to contain liquors and other necessaries, at the back was a proper hearth for cook and baiker, and the face of the mountain had so much the colour and resemblance of smock, no person cou'd discover that there was either fire or habitation in the place.'

The 'Cage' is described as being on the southern spur of Ben Alder, overlooking the loch, on the face of a rocky hill, and openly situated. Well provided with mutton, ham, minched collops, and whisky, Cluny MacPherson had the Prince's comfort in mind, since he might have had to hole-up for the winter here. But on the very day that Charlie arrived at the 'Cage', two French ships were in the Outer Hebrides, and, by a series of extraordinary flukes, traced the Prince to Ben Alder. The messenger, who arrived on September 13 at 1 a.m. set the party moving immediately for Loch nam Uamh, on the Mallaig coast, where the ships awaited. They arrived on the 19th, just six days for some of the hardest walking in Scotland, much of it done under cover of darkness. In five months, from the disaster of Culloden on April 16, Charles had shown that he was no mean walker. Ben Alder was merely the culmination of criss-cross travels on foot from Loch Nevis, through Knoydart, to Glen Cannich, then south again to Loch Arkaig for the final escape march just described. He certainly covered classic country.

Above: At the probable entrance to Cluny's Cage – the hideout used by Bonnie Prince Charlie in 1746 during his escape after Culloden. *Photo: Gerard Simpson*

18   A Traverse of Bidean nam Bian

by Donald Bennet

On one of my earliest visits to Glencoe, Dan Stewart and I left our companions on the JMCS bus, one dark Saturday evening in November, at the Meeting of the Three Waters. Dark clouds scurried across the moon, but its fitful light was enough to show us the way down to the river and over the stepping stones at the Meeting, for there was no footbridge in those days. On the uphill track into the Lost Valley, we stumbled among the huge boulders, the faint beams of our torches barely able to pick out the tenuous path that weaves hither and thither, before emerging at last onto the flat meadow that is the inner sanctuary of this corrie. There we pitched our tent.

The following day we explored the mountain, Bidean nam Bian, climbing the cliffs of Coire nan Lochan and walking the ridges, until winter's early darkness sent us back to our tent. Since that weekend, I have visited Bidean and its satellite peaks many times, in summer and winter, climbing the cliffs and gullies, wandering along the ridges, and sleeping in the corries. Every day has

shown something new about this great mountain, for although you can make its acquaintance at the first visit, it takes many more before you can claim to know all the peaks and corries and their secret places.

Bidean is a mountain which demands our mountaineering respect, as well as our admiration. That November visit many years ago impressed us not only with the beauty, but also the ever present hazards of the mountain, for on our return to the glen long after nightfall we met a sad and silent party in the homeward bus. One of the club had slipped on the icy rocks of Dinner Time Buttress, as he descended after dark, and had fallen to his death above Loch Achtriochtan. Thus we are reminded through tragedy that the mountains call for our ceaseless care and vigilance. Never is this more true than in winter, and on such mountains as Bidean, where snow and ice can transform an easy summer walk or scramble into something very much more serious.

How then should you attempt the impossible – to get to know Bidean in a single

Maps O.S. 1:50,000 Sheet 41; O.S. 1:63,360 Tourist Map – Ben Nevis and Glencoe. Start and finish at Loch Achtriochtan (ref. 139567).
Grading A serious mountaineering expedition involving some exposed rock scrambling. Route finding could be difficult in bad visibility. A rope should be carried by all parties.
Time 6–7 hours.
Distance 9 miles.
Escape Routes From the bealach between Bidean nam Bian and Stob Coire nan Lochan steep descents are possible, N.W. into Coire nam Beith or E into Coire Gabhail.
Telephones At Clachaig Hotel.
Transport The Fort William to Glasgow bus service passes through Glencoe.
Accommodation Clachaig Hotel and Glencoe Hotel. Bed and Breakfast in Glencoe village. Bunk house at Leacantuim. S.M.C. hut at Lagangarbh. Youth Hostel in Glencoe village.
Guidebooks S.M.T. Guide *The Central Highlands; The Scottish Peaks* by W. A. Poucher (Constable).

Left: Leaving the summit of Bidean nam Bian heading east towards Beinn Fhada, with the peaks of the Black Mount in the background. *Photo: Ken Andrew*

Below: Bidean nam Bian and Stob Coire nan Lochan from Beinn Fhada. The described route follows the skyline from right to left. *Photo: Donald Bennet*

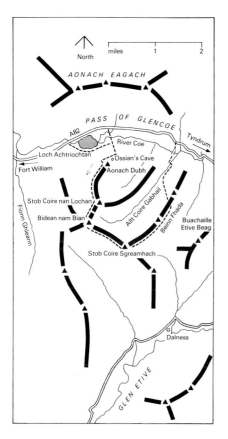

day? You will want to visit as many of the summits as possible, admire the great mountain architecture of the buttresses and gullies, and explore some of the corries. There is one feature of the mountain that is bound to attract your attention as you look up from Glencoe – the huge, dark slit in the north face of Aonach Dubh, known as Ossian's Cave. The romantic, but quite unsubstantiated, association of this cave with the Gaelic poet Ossian, has given it a certain fascination. Rock-climbers would not agree, for the ascent of Ossian's Ladder (the first rock climb done in Glencoe, by the shepherd Neil Marquis in 1868) is an unpleasant climb up vegetatious rock, and the cave itself turns out to be an uncomfortable spot, whose floor of lush grass slopes up steeply to the damp roof. No self-respecting poet, no matter how ascetic, would choose this cave for a contemplative retreat.

There is, however, a good route, hardly a walk but not a difficult scramble, which leads up the north face of Aonach Dubh below Ossian's Cave. This route is in a superb situation, on a steep mountainside in the midst of impressive rock scenery, and it makes an excellent start to the traverse of Bidean. With the qualification that it is only suitable for experienced hillwalkers, and in winter it is likely to be quite a serious expedition. Looking up at the north face of Aonach Dubh from the depths of Glencoe, you will see a deep, slanting gully well to the left (east) of Ossian's Cave. Climb the grassy buttress on the east bank of this gully, until you reach the point where a shelf leads up to the right, towards the Cave, which is not far above. In fact, there are two parallel shelves. The easier route is on the upper one, and a narrow, and in places, exposed, path leads below Ossian's Cave and the impressively steep rock face to its west, where you may see the young tigers of the climbing world testing themselves on some of Glencoe's more frightening climbs.

Scrambling upwards past the great, dark recess of Deep Gash Gully, you come out onto the steep upper slopes of Aonach Dubh as the shelf you have been following peters out, and you can turn up left and climb to the flat summit of the peak. Now the hardest part

of the day's work is done, and you can look forward to some grand ridge walking. South-wards towards Stob Coire nan Lochan, there is the beautiful Coire nan Lochan, with its little lochans backed by the towering buttresses and gullies of the Stob. As you walk up the broad ridge to this peak, keep to the left (provided there is no cornice), and admire the cathedral-like architecture of these buttresses, with their fluted, columnar structure.

From the summit of Stob Coire nan Lochan, the ridge to the highest point of Bidean goes up the edge of the Diamond Buttress, which, with its neighbour the Church Door Buttress, forms the summit of the mountain. The summit, the highest in Argyll, has a great feeling of aloofness, far above the valley of Glencoe, and the surrounding, lesser, peaks. On a clear day, there is a fine panorama, the best feature being the long view down Loch Etive to the distant tops of Ben Cruachan. If you want to include Stob Coire nam Beith in the traverse, it is only a few minutes' walk along the west ridge, but the more interesting continuation is south-eastwards, along the ridge above the Lost Valley, to Stob Coire Sgreamhach, and then north-eastwards along the undulating crest of Beinn Fhada.

The final descent, at the end of the day, should take you down to the Lost Valley, or Coire Gabhail as it is more properly called. It is easy to drop down into this corrie from the second or third col along the Beinn Fhada ridge. The descent is steep, but not difficult, provided you aim for the flat meadow in the lower part of the corrie. (Higher up, the burn flows through a deep and steep-sided gorge.) More than any of the other corries of Bidean, the Lost Valley conveys a feeling of tranquil-ity and solitude. The flat meadow which is its heart is surrounded on three sides by steep ridges, and on the fourth side, where the stream flows silently underground, huge fallen boulders fill the corrie and shut off the outside world. At the end of the day's climbing, it is a place to linger before the descent through the lower gorge to the tar-macadam and traffic of Glencoe. Rest here awhile, stretch out on the grass, and watch the shadows lengthen across the mountain-sides.

19   Buachaille Etive Mor

by W. H. Murray

The Buachaille is my favourite mountain, because so many of my best days have been spent on it, and the firsts impression it made on me has endured. I came to it when new to mountains. I had never seen an Alpine peak, or the Cuillin of Skye. Hence this youthful entry in my diary:

The most vivid part of the day was my first sight of Buachaille Etive Mor, as we approached Glencoe over the Moor of Rannoch. We turned a corner of the road, and the great, shapely bulk, black and intimidating, sprang up on the moor. In the clear morning air, every detail of the enormous, conical cliffs stood out sharp. It looked unclimbable. I had never seen anything like it before, and my breath was taken away from me.

It would have seemed to me then a way-out fantasy, had I imagined that, twelve years later, I should be writing the first rock-climbers' guide to the Buachaille. I went up the easiest way, by its south-east corrie, and felt triumph at the summit. That is the way I would recommend for any walker new to the mountain. He cannot go wrong. At least not to the summit, Stob Dearg. Stob Dearg, the Red Peak, is named from its pink rhyolite. It so dominates the head of Glencoe that the name Buachaille usually refers to it alone, although it is only the highest of four tops, that stretch three miles south and form the west side of Glen Etive. The linking ridge only twice drops below 3,000ft. Apart from its viewpoints, it has this merit: that start and finish can be greatly varied, to give a long walk or a short one, according to time, weather, or personal inclination.

The mountain was named in far-gone days, when cattle-breeding was the Highlands' principal industry, and lower Glen Etive pastured by big herds. Its name means the Big Herdsman of Etive (not the Big Shepherd – the change to sheep came in the late eighteenth century). Close to its west lies the Small Herdsman, Buachaille Etive Beag. It, too, has four tops, but here the summit is the south one, above Dalness. The two mountains lie parallel, divided by the River Coupall, yet linked between their south peaks by a splendid, parabolic saddle called the Lairig Gartain (1,600ft.). The lairig gives a pass from Dalness to Kingshouse. It is thus possible, after traversing the length of Buachaille Etive Mor southwards, to cross the saddle, and return north either over Buachaille Beag, or by the Lairig Gartain, or else by Glen Etive. If you choose the long route, your start is best made from Altnafeadh in Glencoe. Go up by Coire na Tulaich, and allow seven hours. If you choose the shortest route, start two and a half miles down Glen Etive at the bridge below Coire Cloiche Finne (the south-east corrie), come down from Stob na Broige, the south-most top, to Alltchaorunn, and allow five hours for the full round back to starting point.

I deal here with the popular short route. You may think it worth starting from the Glencoe-Glen Etive crossroad, although you may later regret the four-mile walk back on tarmac. The walk south takes you under the great cliffs of Stob Dearg's north-east face, then past its south-east face, until the crags fall away and beyond the long gully of the Chasm. You might now go up anywhere, but the easiest walking is by the normal route into Coire Cloiche Finne, the Bright, Stony Corrie. The name says all – it gets the sun, but has no outstanding features. The upper slopes, leading on to the summit ridge, allow broadening vistas across the moor of Rannoch to the cone of Schiehallion, 30 miles east. The moor scene is the widest and flattest in Scotland, and so bespattered with lochs that you could swim, skate, or canoe most of the way across from Loch Ba to Rannoch Station. A spectacular sight, to be seen from the summit late in the day, is the shadow of Buachaille cast far across the moor, like a gnomon's shadow on a sundial. As the sun moves west, it forms an almost perfect cone.

Northward, you look to Ben Nevis and the Lochaber hills, across the long spine of the Mamore Forest; westward, across the back of Buachaille Etive Beag to the nine tops of Bidean nam Bian. While you are still on the summit, it is worth dropping a few hundred feet (due east magnetic) to see the Crowberry Tower – but not if there is hard snow or ice on the ground, and you have no axe. The Tower's short, inner side is only 40ft., the

Maps   O.S. 1:50,000 Sheet 41; O.S. 1:63,360 Tourist Map – Ben Nevis and Glencoe. Start and finish in Glen Etive (ref. 220520).
Grading   A straightforward mountain walk. Some rough and steep slopes must be negotiated but under good conditions they should not cause trouble.
Time   5 hours.
Distance   7 miles.
Escape Routes   From the bealach E of Stob Coire Altruim (3065ft.) descend easily N to the Lairig Gartain or S to Glen Etive.
Telephones   At junction of A82 with Glen Etive road; Kingshouse Hotel.
Transport   Railway Station at Bridge of Orchy (West Highland line). The Fort William–Glasgow bus service passes through Glencoe.
Accommodation   Hotels at Kingshouse, Clachaig and Glencoe. Bed and Breakfast in Glencoe village. Bunk house at Leacantuim. S.M.C. hut at Lagangarbh. Youth Hostel in Glencoe village.
Guidebooks   S.M.T. Guide *The Central Highlands*; *The Scottish Peaks* by W. A. Poucher (Constable); *West Highland Walks* Volume I by Hamish MacInnes (Hodder and Stoughton).

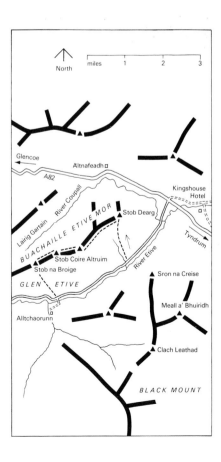

Above: Looking up Glen Etive to the southern end of Buachaille Etive Mor (right) and Buachaille Etive Beag. *Photo: E. A. Shepherd*

Right: The classic view of the East Face of Buachaille Etive Mor from near Kingshouse. The route described by Bill Murray starts from near this point and crosses the moor to ascend the mountain beyond the crags on the left. A slightly more difficult, scrambling, route follows the 'Curved Ridge' which bounds the gully just to the left of the deep summit gully. *Photo: Tom Parker*

outer is the famous Crowberry Ridge of 750ft. To its left, Crowberry Gully plunges into a seemingly bottomless abyss, and to its right an easy gully falls to the top of Curved Ridge. Most rock climbs on the mountain finally converge near the Tower, which, on a good day, is an easy scramble, but that long, outer crest can be transformed in winter beyond summer belief. I have seen its back spiked with shark's fins of translucent ice, or buried in soft snow, or black under verglas.

The walk to the second top goes a mile and a half south-west. The drop to the col is only 400ft. in half a mile of pink scree (in mist steer 270° magnetic). The westward view from the col, at 2,900ft., is better than the summit's; there is a bolder outline to Bidean nam Bian. The ground then lifts only 100ft. in three-quarters of a mile before the last rise of 250ft. to the top. The maps give no height or name to Stob na Doire, 3,250ft. The name, the Peak of the Copse, derives from birch trees low on the Glen Etive flank. The third top lies half a mile west, but the route is markedly angled. If there is mist about, take compass bearings in advance. The col is at 2,600ft. and the top is Stob Coire Altruim, 3,065ft., named Peak of the Nursery Corrie from the corrie opening to its north-west, where hinds gather with their fawns for summer grazing. (The maps again give no name.) The top is buttressed on its north face by a 400ft. mass of rock. Its base can be easily reached from the col. It is undercut below, but a deep chimney gives promise of a route

through. Although I first saw it in 1939, I can remember no record of a climb up it since.

The main ridge now goes half a mile south-west, keeping close to the 3,000 ft. contour, until the last short rise to Stob na Broige, 3,120ft., the Peak of the Shoe. The walk allows splendid views across Glen Etive into the very heart of the Black Mount range. Near the end, you pass the top of the Dalness Chasm. This great gully, which has three forks, falls nearly 2,000ft. towards Alltchaorunn. Its rock is severe. A most interesting way off the mountain, if the members of your party are rock climbers, and carry 200ft. of rope, with spare slings, is to rope down by the central fork. I have found this an experience worth having, for satisfaction of the Tarzan instinct – the lower half is jungle. If you need no such outlet, continue along the ridge to the fourth top. Stob na Broige, as seen from lower Glen Etive, is a blunt cone, linked to the more symmetrical cone of Buachaille Etive Beag by one of the most graceful of Highland saddles. The most eye-catching view from its top is down the length of Loch Etive to the prickly spine of Ben Cruachan. Farther away to its right, across Loch Linnhe, the hills of Mull loom darkly against the light of sky and sea. Close at hand, near the head of Loch Etive, you can see the famous granite slabs of Beinn Trilleachan, facing Ben Starav across the loch.

The descent to Alltchaorunn is a long, steep mile.

20   Ben Cruachan

by Richard Gilbert

Maps O.S. 1:50,000 Sheet 50; O.S. 1:63,360 Tourist Map – Ben Nevis and Glencoe. Start and finish at the Cruachan Dam access road (ref. 115267).
Grading A fine mountaineering route including the traverse of a high and rocky ridge. The summit ridge can become serious in winter when it should be left to experienced parties.
Time 7 hours.
Distance 11 miles.
Escape Routes In good conditions the southern slopes of the summit ridge can be descended to the reservoir.
Telephones Lochawe Hotel; Dalmally; Taynuilt.
Transport Railway Stations at Dalmally and Taynuilt on the Glasgow–Oban line.
Accommodation Hotels, Guest Houses and Bed and Breakfasts in Dalmally. Youth Hostel at Oban.
Guidebooks S.M.T. Guide *The Cental Highlands; The Scottish Peaks* by W. A. Poucher (Constable).

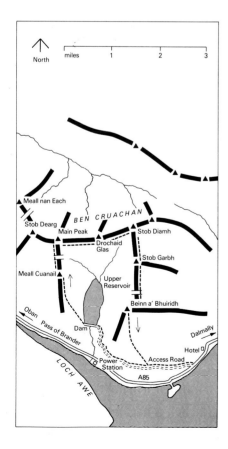

Ben Cruachan, towering to 3,689ft., dominates the rich and spectacular country of Lorn, in mid-Argyll, and the hill walker who traverses the narrow summit ridge of the mountain can enjoy divers pleasures. Although the Hydro-Electric Board's pumped storage scheme has ravished the high, south-facing corrie of the Allt Cruachan, and strewn pylons and high tension cables across the lower slopes of the mountain, the intrusion is offset by the extraordinary, romantic scene laid out below.

Ben Cruachan is most easily ascended from the south, and a car may be conveniently left beside the A85 trunk road running alongside Loch Awe, at the junction with the access road to the Cruachan dam. Even the approach roads to Loch Awe are rewarding: through the deep defile of the Pass of Brander from Oban in the west; through the wild glens of Orchy and Lochy, from the north and east; and alongside the wooded shores of Loch Awe itself, from Inveraray in the south.

As you walk slowly up the access road to the Cruachan dam, at a height of 1,315ft., the view unfolds. The islands of Loch Awe are thickly wooded with deciduous trees, and on my last visit to Cruachan, at the end of October, the leaves were a riot of colour. I could just make out, through the trees, the ruined nunnery on Inishail, and the thirteenth century castle on Fraoch Eilean. A little further to the east, the imposing, grey castle of Kilchurn stood out against the vivid yellow of the oaks. Autumn in the Scottish Highlands is particularly fine. The purple heather is fading, and being replaced by burnished moor grass. In the early morning the bogs are stiff with frost, and there is the excitement of the first permanent snow on the mountain tops. The three-mile walk up to the dam will loosen your muscles, for the going is easy along the metalled road. Be prepared for a shock, though, when you round the shoulder of Beinn a'Bhuiridh, and Cruachan's upper corrie comes into view. The dam, spanning the corrie, is a hideous and brutal construction. Why could not the engineers have given more thought to its appearance, or have attempted some landscaping? In contrast to the dam, the power

station, containing four 100MW turbines, is hidden away in a gigantic cavern blasted out of the mountain. Tourists driving along the side of Loch Awe get the best of both worlds, for not only are they barely conscious of the enormous engineering works beneath the heather clad slopes, but the upper reservoir dam is tucked away in the high corrie, and invisible from below.

Cross the top of the dam, and immediately make your way up the steep, grassy slopes of Meall Cuanail. In misty weather, a fence will guide you to the bealach under the main (3,689ft.) peak of Ben Cruachan. Follow the cairned path through the granite screes and boulder fields to the summit. The views north, up Loch Etive to Glencoe, and beyond to Ben Nevis, are outstanding, while in the east, the graceful cone of Ben Lui is particularly prominent. However, as on all the western peaks of the Scottish mainland, I suspect that your gaze will inevitably be drawn out to the shimmering, blue sea beyond the mouth of Loch Etive. The Firth of Lorne, Mull,

Above: Looking back to the first half of the described route, with Meall Cuanail (left) and the main summit of Ben Cruachan (right), from the slopes of Stob Diamh. *Photo: Ken Andrew*

Colonsay, and Jura; all lie within view.

If time and fitness are on your side, you will want to leave your rucksack on the summit cairn and make the half-mile detour to the western outlier, Stob Dearg (3,611ft.), known as the Taynuilt peak. The main ridge, however, continues due east for one and a half miles to Stob Diamh, passing the subsidiary summit of Drochaid Glas on the way. The ridge is predominantly rocky, and you pick your way across steeply-angled slabs and giant boulders. Friction on the coarse-grained granite is excellent and the traverse, although exposed in places, is not difficult in good conditions. In full winter conditions, though, the ridge can give an exacting climb, and the appropriate equipment, including ropes, must be used. Even in late October I have found the rocks verglassed and requiring great care. These conditions were caused by a sudden anti-cyclone moving across the Highlands after a period of heavy rain, and the clear skies and rapidly falling temperatures produced extensive icing. The north

side of the ridge was white with rime, and the buttresses festooned with icicles.

Drochaid Glas (3,312ft.) has twin summits, and the second of these tops throws out a rocky spur to the north-east. Don't stray along this spur, for it leads down into upper Glen Noe, and thence to Loch Etive. The route to Stob Diamh drops steeply down almost due south, before turning east and levelling out into a well-defined ridge. The path is cairned, but in mist I have experienced some route finding problems here. Once on Stob Diamh, the going is easy, over grassy slopes which give way to more boulders near the top. Descend the broad south ridge over Stob Garbh (3,215ft.) and Beinn a'Bhuiridh (2,941ft.), and drop down to meet the Cruachan dam access road very near to your starting point. If time is pressing, it is simple to strike down the easy slopes west of the bealach under Beinn a'Bhuiridh, to reach the reservoir just north of the Cruachan dam. This saves a further ascent of 500ft.

21 The Peaks of the Black Mount

by Richard Gilbert

Maps O.S. 1:50,000 Sheet 100; O.S. 1:63,360 Tourist Map – Ben Nevis and Glencoe. Start from Kingshouse Hotel (ref. 260547). Finish at Bridge of Orchy Hotel (ref. 299397).
Grading A long mountain traverse involving some mild rock scrambling. Route finding would be very difficult in poor visibility.
Time 8 hours.
Distance 16 miles.
Escape Routes From Bealach Fuar-chathaidh descend S.E. into Coire a' Ba or W into Coire Ghiubhasan thence Glen Etive.
Telephones Inveroran Hotel; Bridge of Orchy; Kingshouse Hotel.
Transport Railway Station at Bridge of Orchy (West Highland line). The Fort William–Glasgow bus service passes through Bridge of Orchy and Kingshouse.
Accommodation Hotels at Bridge of Orchy and Kingshouse. Bed and Breakfasts in Tyndrum and Glencoe. Youth Hostels at Glencoe and Crianlarich.
Guidebooks S.M.T. Guide *The Central Highlands; The Scottish Peaks* by W. A. Poucher (Constable).

Top right: The two highest peaks of the Black Mount – Clachlet (3,602ft.) and Meall a Bhuiridh (3,636ft.) – seen across the lochans of Coire Ba from the main road on Rannoch Moor.
Photo: Tom Parker

Lower right: Buachaille Etive Mor, the Mamores and Ben Nevis from the northern end of the Black Mount. *Photo: Ken Andrew*

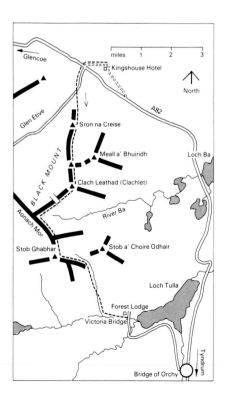

The West Highland Way is now a reality. Scotland's first designated long-distance footpath. The route is defined, the stiles are erected, the Ordnance Survey have printed a special map, and the guide books are published. But many walkers who toil along the Old Military Road between Loch Tulla and Kingshouse must suffer frustrations. They are crossing the Black Mount, yes, but the midges swarm, and the heat rises, and they gaze longingly at the superb range of peaks, within spitting distance of their path on the west side. An alternative traverse of the Black Mount links the hotels of Kingshouse and Bridge of Orchy, by a series of high and broad ridges giving breathtaking views of the Central Highlands. The walk can be taken in either direction, and it can be shortened if necessary. Either way you can look forward to accommodation, a hot meal, and cool beer on reaching your destination. One word of warning. This walk is only for the experienced walker, because it involves some rough scrambling, and the principal summits, Clach Leathad (Clachlet) 3,602ft. and Stob Ghabhar 3,565ft., are exposed to the worst of the weather. In winter conditions it may not be possible to complete the traverse within daylight hours.

Let us start from the Kingshouse hotel, where our first objective is Sron na Creise, the shapely peak dominating the southern aspect between Meall a'Bhuiridh and the gash of Glen Etive. Sron na Creise points its twin summits to the sky, linked by a symmetrically curved ridge like a crescent moon. From the Glen Etive road about half a mile south of Coupall Bridge, strike across the rough moor towards the north ridge of Sron na Creise. This abrupt ridge looks impossibly steep, but, on close acquaintance, you will find plenty of easy steps, ledges, ramps, and scree gullies, which present few difficulties. The rock is sound and, when dry, the friction is excellent. Near the top, a nose of rock forces a detour right before you regain the ridge. A short wall requires the use of the hands, and then you are beside the summit cairn, with Scotland at your feet. There is so much to absorb that I can only indicate a few features. Don't miss the conspicuous deep gully, the Chasm, which makes a 1400ft. Very Severe climb up the east face of

Buachaille Etive Mor; the final pitch, called the Devil's Cauldron, was not climbed until 1931. Away to the south-west rises the sharp-pointed Stob Dearg of Ben Cruachan, and then, swinging north again, you see the Glen Creran hills, Bidean nam Bian, Ben Nevis, the Aonachs, the Grey Corries, and, across the expanse of Rannoch Moor, the huge bulk of Ben Alder.

This northern summit of Sron na Creise marks the end of a broad and undulating ridge which wanders south towards Clachlet. The ridge makes superlative walking, with the views ever changing. The steep corries on the east side hold large patches of snow, while to the west, the gentler slopes descend to delectable hidden glens. The completion of the Munro summits and tops gives one a good knowledge of the Highlands, but it would take a lifetime of exploration to know every nook and cranny of every hill. The narrow south-west ridge of Meall a'Bhuiridh joins our ridge just short of Clachlet's main top. An alternative route for the walker who wishes to avoid the scramble up Sron na Creise would be to climb Meall a'Bhuiridh and traverse across to the 3,506ft. subsidiary summit of Clachlet. But this would subject him to the indignity of having to thread his way up the northern slopes of Meall a'Bhuiridh, through the White Corries' chair-lift system, with its attendant pylons, cables, and drags.

From Clachlet the view east is now clear. The Carn Mairg range, Ben Lawers and the Tarmachans, Ben More and Stob Binnein, the Ben Lui group. I find, though, that the flat expanse of Rannoch Moor commands most of my attention. Rannoch Moor is a unique and magnificent Scottish moor. The average, blinkered motorist driving along the A82 regards the moor as bleak and inhospitable, a moor devoid of merit. He shivers at its barren and featureless wastes, and he accelerates towards Glencoe. But the moor is a fascinating nature reserve and should be treasured by mankind; thankfully areas of it are now owned by the Nature Conservancy. Once covered in pines of the Caledonian forest, sadly only now surviving on the islets of lochs Ba and Laidon, the moor exposes the bare root skeletons, bleached white, and lying starkly above the black peat. Many rare grasses, sedges, and mosses grow on the

Above: Skirting the rim of the eastern cliffs of Clachlet, looking south towards the 'disconcertingly distant' Stob Ghabhar in the centre of the scene. *Photo: Richard Gilbert*

moor, and provide cover for curlew, snipe, dunlin, and greenshank, while black- and red-throated divers visit the lochs.

South of Clachlet, the ground falls away into the vast Coireach a'Ba, and beyond, looking dauntingly distant, is Stob Ghabhar, with its prominent rocky summit rising turret-like above 1,000ft. cliffs. In good conditions, two hours should see you at Stob Ghabhar, but the route involves a long and steep descent to the low Bealach Fuarchathaidh (2,300ft.). The ground is featureless and, in mist, the bealach can be very hard to locate. A small error of compass work would land you in trouble, and I would recommend an inexperienced party to continue beyond Clachlet only in clear weather. An easy descent can be made off Clachlet, by descending the east ridge to the Old Military Road. The ascent from Bealach Fuarchathaidh leads to the long north-west ridge of Stob Ghabhar, known as the Aonach Mor. A vestige of a path appears, and you follow this, over two miles of high and hummocky ridge, to the huge pile of stones marking the summit of Stob Ghabhar. This is another stretch of exhilarating walking on top

of the world.

The Upper Couloir falls away beneath you at the summit, and makes a classic winter climb, where many an epic battle has been fought.* For half a mile from the summit, follow the west ridge, which descends in a smooth curve, giving close-up views of the cliff face. A cairn marks the point where the ridge divides. Both the east and south-east ridges lead down to Glenorchy, but I recommend the east ridge, because it provides a short and spicy scramble along its shattered and exposed crest. This section is known as the Aonach Eagach. Further down the ridge, head off south towards the burn to avoid some cliffs. You will meet a good stalkers' path beside the Allt Toaig, which leads to Loch Tulla. If you have transport waiting at Victoria Bridge, your day is over; if not, you have a further three and a half miles of pleasant walking, firstly through remnants of the old forest, and then beside a river, to the Bridge of Orchy hotel.

*The Upper Couloir of Stob Ghabhar features in several interesting accounts: 'First Ascent' A.E. Maynard (*SMCJ*1897); *Always a Little Further* Alastair Borthwick (Eneas Mackay, 1947); *Tom Weir's Scotland* Tom Weir (Gordon Wright, 1980)

22   Ben More of Mull

by Campbell R. Steven

Lying basking in hot sunshine on one of the beaches of Iona, it is not unusual to notice that, across the Mull, rain-clouds are down on the familiar wedge of Ben More. The only Munro in the islands, apart from those on Skye, has a way of making its own weather, and often enough that is rough indeed. But that is only one small part of the story. When the good days come, and how good they can be, Ben More stands regally alone, and then its upper slopes have their own special attraction, looking out as they do over what is arguably the finest island panorama on the whole of the West Coast of Scotland.

It would be unfair not to make mention of the two approach routes from the road through Glen More, the A849 from Craignure to Fionnphort and Iona, for both are thoroughly enjoyable, without being exactly 'classics'. The ordinary, popular route, starting at or near the B8035 road junction, follows the line of Gleann Dubh, a typically grassy introduction, to the final 1,000ft., which is a rough, scree-cluttered roof, steeply up-tilted, and decidedly tedious in descent. The other line of approach is from the east, starting at the old bridge over the Allt Teanga Brideig, two miles up Glen More. This route is somewhat marred by the extensive scree-slope, a forbidding wilderness of disintegrating basalt, which you face beyond the big cairn at the 1,088ft. spot-height, where the path drops down into the glen leading to Loch Ba.

It may well have been either of these two routes which frightened off the famous French geologist Faujas de Saint Fond, who, in 1784, was one of the earliest visitors to Staffa, and who had excellent intentions about climbing Ben More. He tells how he managed to reach 'a great height', though not the actual summit, and makes the excuse, 'in my journeys among the High Alps I never found so much difficulty as here'. Fortunately, his American friend William Thornton retrieved the party's honour by making his own way to the top. Some 30 years later, another geologist, that early traveller and Munro-bagger Dr John MacCulloch, described Mull as 'a detestable island; trackless and repulsive, rude without beauty, stormy, rainy and dreary'. Obviously, it must have been one of those

bad days, when he did Ben More. But I am sure that neither Saint Fond nor MacCulloch, with all their grumblings, can have sampled what I like to think of as the classic, five-star round. On a fine day, it is a hill walk for the connoisseur which is quite simply not to be missed.

The start is on the north side of Ben More, strictly at sea-level by the shore of Loch na Keal, thus allowing no escape from climbing every one of the 3,169ft. By way of preliminary, the seven miles of road from Salen can make a thoroughly enjoyable cycle ride, a personal recommendation that is all the stronger, as a member of my family is reputed to have accomplished it many years ago on an ancient 'penny-farthing'. Across the introductory moorland, the line of Gleann na Beinne Fhada makes an excellent approach of some two and a half miles. A fine burn, with deep trout pools and little cascades, provides welcome variety in contrast to the grassy uniformity round about. It is particularly encouraging, perhaps, for anyone interested in bird watching, as, after the loch, with its eiders and mergansers, its hoodies and its sandpipers, the moor itself can seem bare territory. The glen leads into a shallow upper corrie, with Beinn Fhada bulking large on the left, and on the right A'Chioch (2,650ft.), the eastern top of Ben More. The face of A'Chioch suggests nothing so much as a crumbling, grey-black ruin, but the peak is shapely, and much the finest approach to the main summit lies over it.

The left-hand crest is easily gained, up a series of grass and scree terraces. Then the real enjoyment of the day begins; steep, but straightforward stairway climbing for some 700ft. to the top of A'Chioch. Nowhere is there any suggestion of difficulty; this is no knife-edge, giving pause for reflection, like some sections of the Aonach Eagach, or the Forcan Ridge of The Saddle. Yet it is pleasantly airy and interesting, reminiscent, perhaps, of the fine ridges of Rhum. Adding remarkably to the enjoyment is the fact that this first section does not come to an end on A'Chioch, but is duplicated on Ben More itself, a similar succession of wall and edge and pinnacle, so that there is, so to speak, a double helping of good things. Yet what,

Maps O.S. 1:50,000 Sheet 48. Start and finish on road B8035 beside Loch na Keal (ref. 507368).
Grading A splendid ridge walk, with interesting steep, but easy, sections on the ascent and a straightforward, gentle descent.
Time 4 hours.
Distance 6 miles.
Escape Routes Alternative descent S from summit to A849.
Telephones Salen; Knock; Balnahard.
Transport Steamer Oban to Craignure. Bus Craignure to Salen (7 miles from the start of the walk).
Accommodation Hotels and Bed and Breakfasts in Tobermory, Craignure and Salen. Youth Hostels in Tobermory and Oban.
Guidebooks S.M.T. Guide *The Islands of Scotland.*

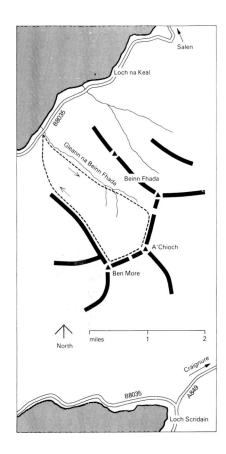

given good weather, makes this ridge climb so unforgettable is the fantastic range of views. The confusion of mainland Munros, and even of the lesser hills on Mull itself, may be difficult to unravel, but out to sea to north and west, identification should not be so troublesome. Skye, Rhum, and the Outer Isles lie on the horizon; behind the unmistakable string of the Treshnish Isles, Tiree and Coll occupy the middle distance, and still nearer is a scattering of islands and islets exciting to the yachtsman or canoist: Staffa and Little Colonsay, the bigger bulk of Ulva, and, immediately below in Loch na Keal, less familiar Eorsa.

It is said that after dark on a fine night, an impressive array of lighthouses may be seen, among them Dubh Hirteach, Skerryvore, Heiskeir, Barra Head, 60 miles away, and even Rudha Mhail, on Islay. Unfortunately, my plan on one visit to Ben More to bed down at the summit was defeated by mist. In compensation, all the way over A'Chioch and up the east ridge, I had enjoyed superb views of the islands, standing out against a flaring sunset, so that, in the gathering darkness, as I made my way down the simple north-west ridge to the moor, I was well content. In the end, my bivouac was near sea-level, beside Gleann na Beinne Fhada. There, with the oystercatchers piping down by the shore, I waged a night-long, losing battle with the midges.

Top: The beautiful profile of Mull's Ben More and A'Chioch rises beyond Loch Scridain.
Photo: Gordon Gadsby

Bottom: Ben More from A'Chioch. *Photo: Roger Redfern*

23   A Day on the Cobbler

by Sandy Cousins

The Cobbler is the daddy of them all. It was the cradle of the outdoor folk, and all the pursuits which are now so popular; hiking (now backpacking), dossing-out (now bivouacking), rock-climbing, and the great camaraderie of those with a love for the outdoors. Many were the lazy plumes of blue woodsmoke that drifted, and sometimes still do drift, from the camp fires at the lochside, the howffs of Succoth and the Cobbler, or from the caves of Glen Loin. Here, the young men from the harsh industrial scene of the 'thirties, who sought outlets for their spirit of self-expression in adventures, found the freedom they wanted around this unique peak.

It is really three peaks, of wild, twisted rock. From the village of Arrochar, by Loch Long, it rises without hesitation from the shore, in continuous, rough slopes to the classic corrie ringed by the famous ridge. The South Peak, Jean, sharp-topped, steep on every side, leans towards the Centre Peak. This, the summit, has the curious summit block which, seen from the lochside, looks like a cobbler bending over his last. The walker may be defeated here, but, with rope protection, a crawl through a hole leads to a ledge, thus taking the careful to the summit. The North Peak, with its huge overhang, like a cobbler's last, gives an easy walk from the col.

But where shall we start? All the approaches are interesting, and the climb starts immediately we leave the road. High up the 'Rest and Be Thankful' road, a straightforward grass climb leads up the back of the Cobbler to the ridge. Lower down, in Glen Croe, various burns give steep, rough routes to the ridge. The traditional route starts from the Ministry of Defence jetty (north), and follows the Buttermilk burn. This is a delightful approach. The path starts almost secretly at the road bridge, by a squeeze through tangled bushes, then weaves under birches by the burn, and up beside the pines, badly damaged by the hurricane that roared into the Clyde valley in the 'seventies. A short section of this path can be very muddy in wet weather. On a hot day, walking up the slabs of the burn adds some fun. As the slope eases, the path rises between fresh pines, which

scent the air. I can remember when they were planted. Suddenly, at the top stile, the jagged Cobbler fills a dramatic skyline, with the crags of Beinn Narnain on the right. Arrival at the dam marks the top of Man's more recent works on the hill. Here, the horizontal track along the aqueduct, taking water to the Loch Sloy dam, offers another popular approach from Succoth. That route starts at the head of the loch. It takes the line made by the mineral railway used for the Sloy scheme. Walkers enter by a path starting at the lay-by.

Crossing the burn at the dam takes us to the route worn by years of Cobbler folk. Erosion has, in fact, improved this route, as the pounding of boots and rain has washed away the mud, and we now walk on the exposed stones and rock. This shows how thin is the soil hereabouts. Close under the crags lie the Narnain Boulders. I remember when one was a well-built howff, without the sorry litter that often mars the spot now. Crossing the burn again, we are almost in the corrie. The path climbs close below the towering North Peak, until we step over the slabs into the great rock amphitheatre. At our elbow rises the famous Recess Route, a rock-climb characteristic of the Cobbler, steep, twisting, and offering the typical holds of this rippling, volcanic rock – secure and sharp in the dry, greasy in the wet. Below, in the lush corrie, walkers may seek and find the grand wee howff, welcome shelter for a brew in wet weather, or in the chilling, snowy days of winter. But keep to the path, and follow the rampart, way up past the almost hidden caves, below the airy overhang, to the col, and the sudden view west to the hills of Argyll. A few yards more, along to the Centre Peak, and the view is superb.

Here, only 30 miles from the industrial Clyde and Glasgow, we are surrounded by Highland country. Eastward is Ben Lomond, in winter clothing looking like a distant Himalayan peak. Below lies Loch Long, where you may see a huge tanker nudging into the terminal at Finnart, and reflect that once the slow swing of Viking oars cut these shimmering waters. Sunlit, far-off waters of, the Firth of Clyde stretch across the horizon, with the silhouette of Arran beckoning. Westward roll the

Maps   O.S. 1:63,360 Tourist Map – Loch Lomond and the Trossachs; O.S. 1:50,000 Sheet 56. Start and finish beside Loch Long (ref. 287040).
Grading   A fine mountain walk in dramatic rock scenery. The walker should only attempt the (easy) ascent of the North Peak. The Centre and South Peaks require some rock climbing expertise and the use of rope.
Time   5 hours.
Distance   5 miles.
Escape Routes   The cols between the rock peaks provide easy ways down into the eastern corrie.
Telephones   Ardgartan; Arrochar.
Transport   Railway Station at Arrochar served by the Glasgow–Oban and Glasgow–Fort William service. Daily bus service Glasgow–Arrochar–Inveraray passes the start of the walk.
Accommodation   Hotels, Guest Houses and Bed and Breakfasts in Arrochar. Youth Hostels at Ardgartan, Inverbeg and Inveraray.
Guidebooks   S.M.T. Guide *The Southern Highlands*; *The Scottish Peaks* by W. A. Poucher (Constable); *Scottish Climbs* Volume 1 by H. MacInnes (Constable).

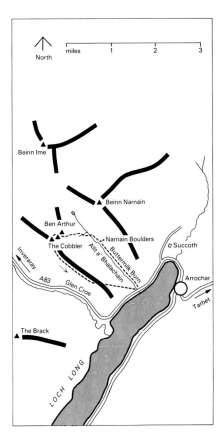

Above: The Cobbler from the Narnain Boulders with (from the right) North Peak, Centre Peak and South Peak. *Photo: Donald Bennet*

Top right: The summit of The Cobbler with Ben Lomond in the background. *Photo: Donald Bennet*

Bottom right: A climber looks down from the summit of North Peak at the Cobbler's small but impressive cliffs. *Photo: Donald Bennet*

countless hills of Argyll. I cannot look north without recalling my walk from Cape Wrath, some years ago, south across miles of peaks unseen from here. How fine it is to stand on this summit, and know so many others await us. How we should cherish this freedom of the hills.

From the summit, the ridge path skirts the sheer wall on its way down to the South Peak col. The ascent of the peak by the normal rock route is a steep scramble, exposed at some points, so roped climbing is advisable.

Farther on, round the corner, the open slope of the peak offers an easier scramble to the top. I always enjoy the walk down, whether following the long spur towards the loch, or crossing the corrie to rejoin the path, and exchange the chat of the day with other Cobbler folk.

The winter hillwalker can find a ridge of exceptional beauty when, standing in the snow-filled corrie, the sparkling cornices and ice-plastered gullies soar against the blue sky. Often the snow in the corrie, sun-

warmed, may belie conditions above, where shadow or wind hardens the winter armour, so that axe and crampons are essential safety gear, together with a standby rope. The round of the peaks presents few problems to the wary, and often the walk down is rewarded with the theatrically-lit, pink sunset on Ben Lomond. But in summer, the early evening shimmer of the birches, and the clear, sweet water of the burn, make me linger on my returning way. I never fail to enjoy a day on the Cobbler.

24 Ben Vorlich and Stuc a'Chroin

by Roger Smith

Maps O.S. 1:50,000 Sheets 51 and 57; O.S. 1:63,360 Tourist Map – Loch Lomond and the Trossachs. Recommended route starts and finishes at Ardvorlich (ref. 632230). Alternative route starts and finishes at Braeleny (ref. 637111).
Grading A fairly simple mountain walk in summer but much more serious in winter conditions.
Time Recommended northern route 5–6 hours. Alternative southern route 6–7 hours.
Distance Northern route 8 miles. Southern route 12 miles.
Escape Routes From the Bealach an Dubh Choirein descend N.W. into Choire Fhuadaraich and Glen Ample or descend S.E. into Gleann an Dubh Choirein.
Telephones Callander; Strathyre; Lochearnhead.
Transport Railway Stations at Stirling and Crianlarich. Stirling–Callander–Lochearnhead–Killin bus service.
Accommodation Hotels, Guest Houses and Bed and Breakfasts at Callander and Lochearnhead. Youth Hostels at Killin and the Trossachs.
Guidebooks S.M.T. Guide *The Southern Highlands*.

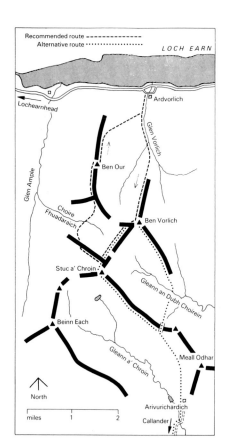

On a clear day, Ben Vorlich and Stuc a'Chroin are the first big hills you see driving north up the motorway towards Stirling. They always lift my heart, for when I see them I know that the real hill country is near. These fine Munros dominate a rather isolated block of hills, south of Loch Earn and east of Strathyre. There is no temptation to link them with other hills, and they have become a favourite day walk for Scottish hillgoers – a classic walk indeed. Access is straightforward: various approaches are possible, two of which I shall describe. My favourite route is the circuit from Ardvorlich, on the south side of Loch Earn, but the Callander route has its appeal also. The only public transport in the area is an infrequent bus service up the A84 between Callander and Lochearnhead, so a car is, regrettably, essential.

Take the A84 from Stirling, or A85 from Lix, to just south of Lochearnhead (good hotel, cafe, filling station), and turn off east at the signpost 'South Loch Earn Road'. This minor road is followed for about three miles to Ardvorlich where a number of small pull-offs by the lochside are available. Here there is a gate, east of the burn, with a sign marked 'To Ben Vorlich: Keep to the Path'. The fine, old house here was formerly a seat of a branch of the Stewart clan, and has a gruesome tale associated with it. In the sixteenth century a Stewart cropped the ears of some MacGregors who were found poaching deer. The MacGregors took revenge. They killed the Stewart, cut his head off, and placed it on the table at Ardvorlich, the mouth stuffed with bread and cheese. The man's wife, who was pregnant, discovered the head, and in her anguish rushed into the hills. This brought on the birth of the baby, a boy who grew up to become Mad Major Stewart of Ardvorlich, a man with a reputation for slaying MacGregors on sight. The glen is peaceful now, and, although you will be unlucky if you do not see sizeable herds of deer on this walk, you are unlikely to be confronted by marauding MacGregors.

To ascend Ben Vorlich, follow the path up the glen for about a mile, and then head straight up the north ridge of the mountain. There is a small, well-defined path which leads all the way to the summit. It is normally an easy climb, with a steep ending, but can be difficult in winter near the top. Fatalities have been known here, and on an icy January day I once had to turn back myself, as the rock was covered with verglas and I had omitted to take crampons. At 3,224ft., Ben Vorlich is a little higher than Stuc a'Chroin, and it has a small summit ridge with an OS pillar at one end, and a cairn at the other. It is one of the tops that people climb at midsummer in the hope of viewing the sunrise. This is an unforgettable experience in the right conditions, but there is room for only a few folk at the summit, so I trust not too many of you will attempt it on the same night.

To reach Stuc a'Chroin, follow the old fence posts west, down rough grass, to a clear bealach. The buttress facing you looks more intimidating than it really is. It gives pleasant scrambling up a scratch of a path (it doesn't really matter if you miss the line), and you pop out at the top onto Stuc's summit plateau. There are three large

cairns, and the highest (3,189ft.) is inevitably the one furthest away from you. In the right conditions, there are splendid views across to the Balquhidder hills, Ben More and Stob Binnein, and north towards the Bridge of Orchy/Tyndrum group. Below your feet is a beautiful little lochan, which might offer a memorable site on a back-packing trip (the whole area is ideal for quiet wandering), and the glens round about, Ample, Vorlich, and Artney, are all well populated with deer. To return to Loch Earnside, work round to the west of the buttress and across the head of Choire Fhuadaraich (a shallow basin, which can be soggy underfoot), and so on to Ben Our, a pleasant, grassy top with wide views over the loch. A steep run off the east side of the hill returns you to the track in Glen Vorlich.

Another favoured approach takes Stuc a'Chroin first, from the south. Leave Callander by the minor road at the southern end of the town, signposted 'Bracklinn Falls'. Follow this road for two and a half miles to the end of the tarmack near Braeleny farmhouse. Walk through the farm, and along the track to Arivurichardich. The long south-east ridge of the Stuc is ahead. Slant up the hill towards the bealach under Meall na h-Iolaire. This is, in fact, the other end of the track which runs up Glen Vorlich from Loch Earnside, and is a very old right of way. Turn left on to the ridge from the bealach, and plod up it all the way to the Stuc's summit, with splendid views of Vorlich across the head of Gleann an Dubh Choirein.

The route across to Vorlich is the reverse of that described earlier, a little care being needed on the descent of the buttress. Leave Vorlich by its broad south-east ridge, which has impressive cliffs on the eastern side for much of its length. At the burn junction, you meet the through track again and follow it up to the bealach, after which you can pick your own way down to Arivurichardich. There is a locked bothy here, but a lean-to can provide shelter if needed. It is, in any case, well worth a pause, to take in the fine scenery of the glen, and a last look back at the bulk of the Stuc, looming over the glenhead.

25   Ben Lomond

by Tom Weir

Maps   O.S. 1:63,360 Tourist Map – Loch Lomond and the Trossachs; O.S. 1:50,000 Sheet 56. Start from Rowardennan (ref. 360982). Finish at Inversnaid Hotel (ref. 338090).
Grading   An easy mountain walk under good conditions.
Time   5–6 hours.
Distance   9 miles.
Escape Routes   From the N ridge an easy descent may be made E to Comer in Gleann Dubh.
Telephones   Rowardennan; Inversnaid.
Transport   Bus service Balloch to Balmaha (6 miles from Rowardennan) or ferry Inverbeg to Rowardennan. Irregular post-bus service Inversnaid to Aberfoyle.
Accommodation   Hotels at Rowardennan and Inversnaid. Youth Hostels at Rowardennan and the Trossachs.
Guidebooks   S.M.T. Guide *The Southern Highlands*.

Top right: Ben Lomond from the north, looking up the secluded corrie above Cailness, noted for its wildlife, but coveted by the North of Scotland Hydro Electric Board as a site for a pumped storage reservoir. *Photo: Tom Weir*

Bottom right: Access to Ben Lomond is inconvenient as the main road runs up the opposite (west) side of Loch Lomond. One novel approach (shown here) is to canoe across the loch and climb the mountain from the south. *Photo: Tom Weir*

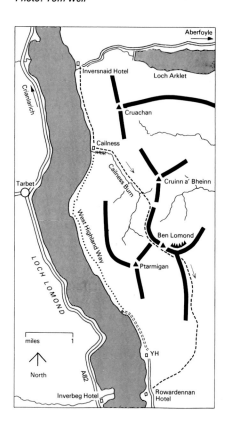

If I had to single out one mountain that has given me more pleasure than any other, at home or abroad, it would have to be Ben Lomond. And I think the same would be true of a lot of men of the 'thirties, who were the first working-class outdoor generation, many of them with a simple ambition – to be a successful tramp. Yes, it was a time of high unemployment and low wages, but electric tramcars took you to the north-western limits of the city, and you were on your way to '. . . the steep, steep sides of Ben Lomond'.

As I left school, the cult of hiking was sweeping Britain. The Scottish Youth Hostels Association had just been formed, offering a bed for a bob a night. Gangs of youths were discovering their own countryside, on foot and by bicycle. A group of tough Glasgow climbers formed themselves into the Ptarmigan Mountaineering Club, a 20-strong bunch who dossed in caves, dispensed with sleeping bags in order to travel light, and never missed a single weekend in years. They were my youthful heroes. Let me try to catch the flavour of one of my own weekends on Ben Lomond at that time. The month is May. It is nearly 2 a.m. and we have been tramping since 10 p.m. It is marvellous at last to spread out our sleeping bags under a sheltering rock on a grassy shelf above the burn, and bliss to be here after the big effort of catching the last bus from Glasgow to Balmaha, with a ten-hour working day behind us.

Wood smoke and the smell of breakfast cooking brings me to consciousness, along with the cheerful notes of bird song. At the fire, my pal Matt is singing a Gaelic song as he turns over the sausages and sizzling chops in the frying pan. I lick my lips, for Matt is a butcher and packs nothing but the best. From our eyrie on the MacGregor shore we feel free as Rob Roy himself, wage-slaves no longer and with hearts as light as the blue sky. We set off along the contouring path that now bears the title of West Highland Way. Below us, oakwoods plunge to the shore, and we walk in a scent of bluebells and rowan blossom. A deep, wooded ravine ahead is the Cailness Gorge, and we leave the shore path to strike up its steep southern edge.

This the Craigroyston shore, banded with rock outcrops and spouting with waterfalls. The climb is uncompromising, but its reward is swift: in 20 minutes we can throw ourselves down and revel in the view that has opened up. There are the three rock prongs of The Cobbler, and the knobbly Arrochar Alps, offering the best rock-climbing within easy reach of Glasgow. Northward, beyond the head of the Loch, stands snow-veined Ben Lui and its neighbours, which dominate Glen Falloch, the route of the West Highland Way to Fort William. We identify the ancient passes which thread west across these hills, the Lairig Arnan and the Dubh Eas, which lead from Loch Lomond through to Loch Fyne; droving routes for cattle and easy booty for the MacGregor and McFarlane clansmen, whose raiding forays persisted long after those of any other clans of the Highlands.

There is plenty of immediate interest in the gorge wall we are following: soaring buzzards, ravens, songs of wood warblers and redstarts, white blobs on the crags that turn out to be hairy wild goats, which share this terrain with the red deer. In just over 1,000ft. we top the last big waterfall, where the big trench gives out into the big basin, which is notable for wild life. Alas, this secret corner of Ben Lomond is coveted by hydro-electric engineers, who see it as an ideal site for a pumped storage reservoir. Their latest published plan for Ben Lomond is to build a wall of concrete and seal the basin, so that water could be pumped into it from a power house on the Loch Lomond shore. To build the reservoir, a road would be driven up to 1,600ft. and pylons would lead northward over the shoulder to link up with the power lines of the Cruachan Pumped Storage Scheme. Conservationists are fighting this proposal, which would breach a superb wilderness which, until now, has been protected by a National Parks Direction Order. But the North of Scotland Hydro Electric Board are adamant that Ben Lomond is the only site that fulfils their requirements.

Our route to the top of the Ben lies immediately above the proposed site of the reservoir, by the twisting north-west ridge. But first we go to the col between Cruinn a'Bheinn and Ben Lomond, to dump our

weekend sacks. Light-footed now, we fairly dance up the airy ridge and suddenly arrive on top of the most southerly Munro in Scotland. As a viewpoint it is unique, Loch Lomond at your feet seeming to stretch to the Clyde and the Antrim coast, with Ailsa Craig and the Arran hills heaving up grandly in the middle distance. Landmark peaks stand out all round, the Paps of Jura, Ben More Mull, Cruachan, Beinn Dorain, Ben Nevis, Ben Lawers, the Crianlarich hills. There was a summit indicator in the time about which I write, but alas it has long since been destroyed by vandals. With the map it is easy to identify the main islands scattered on the greatest breadth of the 27.45 square miles of loch, which is the largest surface area of fresh water in Britain. The broad bit is shallow, but under Ben Lomond the loch is over 600ft. deep, dug out by the last big advance of ice.

The hard schist rocks constricted the moving glacier, but once it got into the softer rocks beyond Ross Point the moving mass could expand, pushing everything before it. The islands, which are the glory of Loch Lomond, are the gritty masses which withstood the passage of the ice.

From the 3,192ft. summit of the Ben, the mountain falls steeply northward, enclosing in its cliff-bound corrie a tiny burn which is the infant River Forth, and the route of our descent once we have collected our sacks. Soon we are enjoying the wildness of this truly Highland corrie, fringed at the top with 300ft. cliffs whose gullies offer good sport for the ice-axe in winter, but whose vegetatious rocks are unsound for enjoyable summer rock-climbing. But an alpine plant hunter will find plenty to delight him in June. Down we go to the farmhouse of Comer to hit the tracks that take us to Aberfoyle, in time to catch the bus which will take us to Glasgow, by 9 p.m., after a busy and very happy 24 hours.

With the opening of the West Highland Way in 1980, the ramblers' right of way paths have been knitted together into a signposted 'Way' from the outskirts of Glasgow at Milngavie, 96 miles to Fort William, with its own 'official' guidebook, complete with maps. Experienced hill men should make the top of the Ben part of their route.

If coming northward from Milngavie, my recommendation is to strike up from Rowardennan, a comfortable three hours to the summit ridge, descending by the north-west ridge and down the Cailness Gorge by the edge I have described to reach the Loch Lomond shore. Down there you will find grand little platforms for wild camping, but if you want a roof over your head you need walk on only another two delightful miles to the Inversnaid Hotel. Ben Lomond, because of its position and shape, is a very special mountain, of many moods. Like Loch Lomond, which carries a busy trunk road to the north, it displays itself with some ostentation. But behind the facade so much is hidden that few folk ever see. In fact, no loch in Scotland is so secret as Loch Lomond, and however much you think you know the Ben, it has a way of surprising you.

26 Around Glencorse in the Pentlands

by Neil Mather

The Pentlands are a chain of old red sandstone hills running north-east to south-west for about 15 miles, from the southern outskirts of Edinburgh to the village of Carnwath in Lanarkshire. At the northerly end, the hills rise abruptly to form a rampart over 1,000ft. above the suburban gardens of Fairmilehead. Generally their south-eastern slopes are much steeper than their north-western, and dominate the A702 road to Biggar and Carlisle for several miles along its northern end. The traveller motoring south through Fife towards the Forth, sees them as a pleasing and shapely backdrop to the two bridges. A glance at the map, however, shows their height to be more modest than their appearance suggests (Scald Law is the highest point at 1,899ft.); also that the contour lines are much closer on the north-easterly hills, and while the south-westerly end is more remote and less frequented, it is largely moorland, and lacks the interest of the northerly part. In all their length, there is only one real glen, Glencorse, or the Logan Glen, a deep, L-shaped trench which contains two reservoirs and some half dozen dwellings in the five and a half miles from its head to its mouth, at Flotterstone, on the A702. All the more attractively-shaped hills flank this glen, and this expedition takes in all these tops, in a circuit from Flotterstone which drops only once below 1,000ft.

Flotterstone is a most attractive spot, and deservedly popular at weekends with local people from the city and the Midlothian towns. There is a pub with restaurant and bar food, and a public car park and information centre, provided by a thoughtful local authority. The road running from here up the glen is closed to motor vehicles, except for access to the water installations and farms. The preferred way round for the walk is anti-clockwise, and interest is maintained by reserving the finest hills till last, to savour them before running down for a drink at the bar; there is very little running water on these hills.

Half a mile up the glen from the car park, a shallow re-entrant drops down from the north, to meet the road by a small wood. This gives convenient access to the lower slopes of Castlelaw Hill via the fort and *souterrain*, which are worth a short detour. Thence, a

path leads north-north-west up the slopes of the hill, and you can follow this for 200 yards, till it is more opportune to make a beeline for the summit. This is War Office land, and is the site of a shooting range, shortly to be developed further, so information as to likely activity should be sought before leaving the car park. I once found myself between two opposing armies, as the hillside erupted with soldiers, firing blanks, with extra realism provided by thunder flashes and smoke bombs. This part of the Pentlands suffers from an army presence, as there are Nissen huts and concrete observation huts liberally scattered over the hillsides. However, as one leaves Castlelaw, 1,595ft., northwards there are fewer reminders, except for the warning flag before the ascent of Allermuir Hill, 1,619ft. Here there is a spectacular view of the city and the firth, and an indicator cairn erected by the National Trust for Scotland, which gives information on more distant hills. A fine little spur runs east from here, to culminate in the craggy Caerketton Hill. We go southwards now, still with fine views, though Capelaw Hill is part of the Dreghorn firing range and is occasionally closed by a red warning flag on its summit. It is then possible to traverse across the southerly slopes till the Bonaly–Flotterstone path is reached, near Bonaly reservoir, and this takes us clear of all army activities.

The next part of the walk, over Harbour and Bell's Hills, is probably the least interesting, as both are rather featureless, though new views are opened up of Harlaw and Threipmuir reservoirs, to the south-west, and of the shapely West Kip, almost due south. Between the two hills is an important crossing point, the path from Currie and Balerno to Glencorse, via the Maiden's Cleuch. After Bell's Hill, the route drops to a boggy hollow, Den's Cleuch, which, at 850ft., is the lowest part of the walk, and dominated by the bulk of Black Hill. As its name indicates, Black Hill (1,644ft.) is a dark mass, its peaty slopes luxuriously heather-clad. While the ascent from Den's Cleuch is not difficult, as there are numerous sheep tracks to follow, the route beyond, to Green Cleuch, is apt to be irksome, on account of the depth of heather and the absence of tracks. In fact, only during Aug-

Maps O.S. 1:50,000 Sheet 66. Start and finish at the A702 S of Edinburgh at Flotterstone (ref. 235630).
Grading A straightforward walk over mainly grassy hills. Watch out for a red flag indicating firing on the Dreghorn range in which case you must take the diversion described in the text.
Time 6 hours.
Distance 13 miles.
Escape Routes Easy descents can be made from the hills to the reservoir access road running through Glen Corse.
Telephones Flotterstone.
Transport Daily bus service (Eastern Scottish) from Edinburgh (St. Andrew's Square) to Dumfries passes through Flotterstone.
Accommodation Penicuik, Loanhead or Edinburgh (6 miles). Youth Hostels at Edinburgh (Eglinton Crescent and Bruntsfield).
Guidebooks *Pentland Walks* by D. G. Moir. (Bartholomew); S.M.T. Guide *The Southern Uplands.*

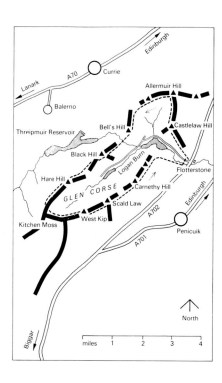

ust, when the heather is in bloom and Black Hill a purple sea, when your boots are covered in pollen and the air is heavy with the fragrance of the flowers, is it worth traversing the summit. A much easier and pleasanter alternative is to flank its northerly slopes, by a series of obvious paths between the 1,000ft. and 1,100ft. contour lines, till Green Cleuch is reached. This gap between Black and Hare Hills is the line of one of the main passes through the northern Pentlands, from Balerno to the Howe at Loganlea, the head of Logan Glen, and thence via the Kirk Road to Penicuik.

We continue our walk by ascending Hare Hill (1,472ft.), another rough, heathery hill, though not so luxuriantly clad as Black Hill. Its summit is marked by a conspicuous cairn, and what appear to be earthworks, but in fact are quarrying remains of much more recent origin. In a further quarter mile, the bridle path from Balerno and Bavelaw to Salterskye and Nine Mile Burn is reached, and followed across the slopes of Kitchen Moss to cross the head of the Logan Burn, at approximately 1,300ft., before climbing gently to the ridge below West Kip.

Walking eastwards along this path one

cannot but be impressed by the outline of West Kip (1,806ft.), which seems far higher than its modest elevation. Its summit, the sharpest and rockiest of the Pentlands, does not boast a cairn, and looks down dramatically on the pastures and farmland of the Eastside Burn, out over the flat Achencorth Moss to the Moorfoot Hills, and beyond to the headwaters of the Tweed. From here back to Flotterstone, a distance of almost four miles, a simple path provides superb going over East Kip, Scald Law, Carnethy Hill, and Turnhouse Hill; a wonderful switchback along the finest tops of the Pentlands. The eye ranges from North Berwick Law and the Bass Rock, marking the entrance to the Forth, across the dark trench of the Logan Glen, with glimpses of its shy reservoirs, to the slopes of Black Hill and Bell's Hill, and over into the distance beyond the Forth, to the Ochils, Ben Ledi, and Ben Vorlich 50 miles away. Between Scald Law and Carnethy Hill is a pass at 1,450ft., which is the line of the Kirk Road. There is a symmetry between these two peaks, with a difference of only nine feet in the height of their summits, and each dropping to a col of around 1,450ft. One *dreich* winter's day, while dropping from the summit of Carnethy, I was surprised to encounter a grey squirrel. Only a little distance from the top, it must have been 1,000ft., and more than a mile, from the nearest tree, but when last seen was running strongly in the right direction. Turnhouse Hill marks the end of the ridge, and also the entrance to the glen. The route swings to the east on steep grass and, passing an outpost of gnarled trees at 1,200ft., heads for, and follows, a moraine ridge between two burns, to cross the Glencorse Burn by a footbridge, 300 yards from the starting point.

27   The Round of Loch Enoch

by Ken Andrew

Maps   O.S. 1:50,000 Sheet 77. Start and finish at Glen Trool car park (ref. 415803).
Grading   A tough walk over remote and rugged hills. In wet weather river crossings could be hazardous.
Time   7 hours.
Distance   14 miles.
Escape Routes   None, but the walk can be shortened by leaving out the ascent of Merrick and returning from Loch Enoch to Glen Trool via the Buchan Burn.
Telephones   Glen Trool and Dukieston.
Transport   Railway Stations at Dumfries and Stranraer. Western S.M.T. buses run between Dumfries and Newton Stewart and the Newton Stewart to Ayr service calls at Glen Trool village.
Accommodation   Hotels at Newton Stewart, 13 miles from Loch Trool. Camp site at Caldons, W end of Loch Trool. Youth Hostels at Minnigaff, Newton Stewart and Kendoon (near Dalry).
Guidebooks   *Galloway Forest Park*, a Forestry Commission Guide (H.M.S.O.); *Romantic Galloway* by John McCulloch (Galloway Publicity Association, Castle Douglas); S.M.T. Guide *The Southern Uplands; The Merrick and the Neighbouring Hills* by J. McBain (Jackson and Sproat).

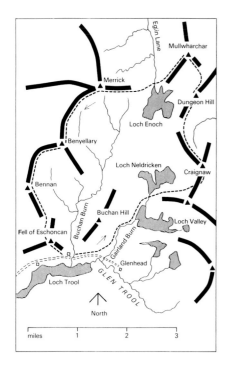

Galloway granite is tucked away from the sight of motorists arriving at the road end in Glen Trool. The steep, sweeping slopes of the glen tempt in half a dozen different directions. But it is the contorted landscape of igneous rock hidden round the corner which offers the greatest challenge to the walker, and draws him back once he has sampled its magic. This walk into the hinterland of Galloway links the three highest granite summits in the Glen Trool and Carrick Forests, with the highest peak in mainland Southern Scotland, and rounds one of the largest and loneliest of upland lochs in Britain.

Glen Trool is a superb little glen, and its elevated car park can draw even the laziest of tourists into the open, to get involved in the action. The monumental Bruce's Stone, nearby, overlooks a scene of astonishing variety, and commemorates the routing of an English force by Robert the Bruce, in a guerilla attack in 1307. The glen is well designed for such revels, with its woodlands and broken slopes. Meadows and hayfields on the valley floor merge with the coarser grasses, heather, and bracken; natural woodlands merge with the newly planted forests; larch merges with pine, and pine with spruce; conifers merge with precipitous slopes, and sheep, cattle, and even goats dot the rugged landscape, which maintains a wide variety of birds and other small creatures.

The routes to Loch Enoch and the uplands of granite lie up the two valleys on the north side of the glen. We take the second one from the car park, but first have to descend, to cross the Buchan Burn by the Earl of Galloway's bridge, on the rough road to Glenhead. Here, on the edge of the natural woodlands of sessile oak, a sign points our way over a stile and up diagonally across the face of Buchan Hill to the Gairland Burn. Height is gained quickly in the great start to the walk, which gives a splendid view backwards to Loch Trool. Then the corner of the hill is turned alongside a drystone dyke, and we enter the valley of the Gairland Burn, which turns out to be a hanging valley, and Glen Trool is soon lost to us below the lip. Now we are on our own, heading deep into the hills and far back in time. Silvan beauty is

replaced by a savage wilderness of glaciated scenery, as the tumbling burn cascades past moraine heaps in its short course from Loch Valley. This loch stretches away to the east, but we take the path along the shorter north-western bank and up the Mid Burn to Loch Neldricken – the next level in this complicated plumbing system.

Just before the loch is reached, a double row of stepping stones leads easily, under normal conditions, across the burn. In a spate, even these massive boulders can be submerged by this formidable stream, and the expedition thwarted. Once the south-

eastern shore of Loch Neldricken is reached, the climb starts in earnest to Craignaw. The direct route is by a grassy gully to the right of the outcrops of the Black Gairy. A shining, white concavity of the grey boiler plates above is a puzzling feature, until the grim story is revealed. This was the collision point of an F111 jet fighter, which flew straight into the hill and exploded, strewing its wreckage far across the hillside. Even the summit cairn, at 2,115ft. has wreckage scattered around it. The summit gives a good view across the lochs of the region, and unravels their step-like topography down to Glen Trool.

To continue northwards from the summit, take the grassy gully on the west side of the start of the north ridge, and go left beneath the cliffs to the north-west ridge. This is an astonishing place, called the Devil's Bowling Green. It is a massive, level, granite platform, littered chaotically with erratic boulders left behind by the melting ice sheets, as though a titanic bowling match had been left unfinished. A tall, well-built cairn marks the Nick of the Dungeon – the col between Craignaw and Dungeon Hill which is our next objective. This is another

Above: Dawn mists clear around Loch Enoch – a view from Merrick. *Photo: Ken Andrew*

Above: The Devil's Bowling Green on Craignaw with Dungeon Hill and Carlin's Cairn in the background. *Photo: Ken Andrew*

Right: At Loch Neldricken looking towards Merrick. *Photo: Ian Reynolds*

hill sculptured by the ice, with granite pavements and slabby outcrops, and perched blocks sitting forlornly awaiting the next Ice Age. It looks across the three lochs of the Dungeon to the dangerous bog called the Silver Flowe. Our route continues to the north-west to our third granite hill, Mullwharchar, passing another crashed aircraft, and two sources of the River Doon, flowing in opposite directions from the col. The remote Mullwharchar became a famous hill in 1976, when the Atomic Energy Authority announced their interest in it as a site for geological research. The locals have no delusions about that research. It is to find a home for nuclear waste, and the result of a public enquiry is awaited at the time of writing.

Enjoy the remote wilderness of Mullwharchar while you can, particularly the rugged eastern face, and the view south from the ridge to Loch Enoch. Return home by this ridge, dropping to the northern shore of Loch Enoch, and crossing the Eglin Lane. This can be a big burn after rain, but if the Mid Burn at Loch Neldricken is fordable, the Eglin Lane should be as well. Loch

Enoch has formed in a granite basin. It is a remarkable sheet of water, and at 1,600ft. above sea level, is one of the largest sheets of water at this height in the country. The silver sand of its beaches was formerly collected for sharpening knives. Now comes a long, relentless pull up to Merrick, which, at 2,764ft., is the highest point on the Scottish mainland south of Ben Lomond. 300ft. below the summit, there is a marked transition from the grey rocks of Loch Enoch to the darker summit shales. The view back to the loch shows it contains several islands, and one of these contains its own little loch.

The hardest work is over on Merrick, and a gentle, grassy descent and short rise leads to Benyellary. The dyke south-west from here leads to the ridge of Bennan, which has some good examples of exfoliation – where hot gases left hollows in the molten rock. Follow the high ground all the way back to Glen Trool, zig-zagging past a short barrier of trees. Finally, on the Fell of Eschoncan, comes a glorious reward for all the hard effort, as Loch Trool spreads itself below you, and a short, steep descent to the east links up with the path to the car park.

28   Hadrian's Wall

by Richard Gilbert

Maps   O.S. 1:50,000 Sheet 86; O.S. 1:31,680 Historical Map of the Roman Wall. Start from Sewing Shields (ref. 810702). Finish at Lanercost Priory (ref. 555638).
Grading   Easy, except for a river crossing at Willowford which, in bad conditions, could mean a three-mile detour.
Time   8–9 hours.
Distance   19 miles.
Escape Routes   The route can be cut short almost anywhere.
Telephones   Sewingshields; Twice Brewed Inn; Greenhead; Gilsland; Banks; Lanercost.
Transport   In the summer months a special bus service runs between Hexham and Haltwhistle via the Roman Wall. The main bus and railway route between Newcastle and Carlisle runs only two or three miles south of the Wall. In term time the school bus will carry members of the public between Housesteads and Greenhead.
Accommodation   Hotels at Chollerford, Wall, Twice Brewed and Lanercost. Bed and Breakfast locally. Youth Hostels at Once Brewed and Acomb (near Hexham).
Guidebooks   *Handbook to the Roman Wall* by Collingwood Bruce (Harold Hill); *Hadrian's Wall* by J. Forde-Johnston (Michael Joseph); *Across Northern Hills* by Geoffrey Berry (Westmorland Gazette); *Hadrian's Wall* by Breeze and Dobson (Allen Lane); *Along Hadrian's Wall* by David Harrison (Pan).

We are extremely fortunate that Hadrian's Wall, by any standards an exceptional historical monument, should also provide a high level walk over some of the finest country to be found anywhere in Britain. I have chosen a 19 mile stretch of the Wall for inclusion in *Classic Walks*, and throughout the journey the Wall itself, or its turf-covered outline, is our constant companion. To obtain the maximum pleasure from the walk it is essential to know a little of the history of the Wall and the reasons for its construction. Guidebooks can be purchased locally at Corbridge, Hexham, or the National Trust office at Housesteads Fort, so I shall give only a short summary.

Towards the end of the first century AD the Romans, under the command of Julius Agricola, conquered the north of England and penetrated deep into Scotland. Yet the northern frontier was ill-defined, and the Romans suffered many set-backs at the hands of raiders. In 122AD Emperor Hadrian visited Britain, and commanded that a wall should be built from the Tyne to the Solway Firth; the wall was to be 10ft. thick and supported by forts, milecastles, and turrets. This wall, with some modifications, was built during the next eight years. The length of the Wall was 80 miles, and the constructed height was about 15ft., but the thickness, originally planned to be 10ft., was reduced to 8ft. As additional protection on the north side, a deep ditch was dug, while on the south side a wider ditch, or *Vallum*, was dug to provide a demarcation zone. Forts housing up to 1,000 soldiers were built at regular intervals just south of the Wall. Smaller milecastles were built every Roman mile (1,620 yards), and turrets at every third of a mile. Rock was quarried locally, and the builders were the Roman legions themselves, with Britons acting as unskilled labourers. Having built the Wall,

the legions returned south and left the defence to a garrison of about 15,000 non-Roman soldiers. Soon after the completion of the Wall, the Romans pushed back their frontiers still further and built a turf wall, the Antonine Wall, between the Forth and Clyde. However, in 181AD the Antonine Wall was destroyed by barbarians, followed in 196AD by Hadrian's Wall itself. In fact, northern England was devastated as far south as York. It was left to Emperor Severus to re-establish control and rebuild Hadrian's Wall. Twice more over the next 200 years the Wall was over-run and finally, towards the end of the fourth century, it was abandoned by the Romans. Over the years many of the carefully-faced stones have been removed from the Wall for buildings and road making but, especially over the wilder sections, it is still in a fair state of preservation.

Enough preamble. Pack your rucksack, lace up your boots, and report to Sewing Shields farm, which sits astride the Wall six miles west of Chollerford on the B6318 Carlisle road. On my last visit, as I shouldered my pack, the clear, bubbling cry of the curlew came over on the wind, an appropriate beginning to my day in the Northumberland National Park, whose emblem is a curlew in flight. The path passes the farm on the north side, and then breaks out of a small copse onto the escarpment of Sewingshields Crags. You are now on the roof of Northumberland, with the view dominated by sky and distant hills. Cross Fell is visible away to the south, Wark Forest rolls away to the north, while below your feet are plunging crags and the blue waters of Broomlee Lough.

One of the most attractive natural features of Northumberland is the whin sill, an intrusion of grey, igneous rock which forms a rough, north-facing escarpment stretching across the high central region. The Wall

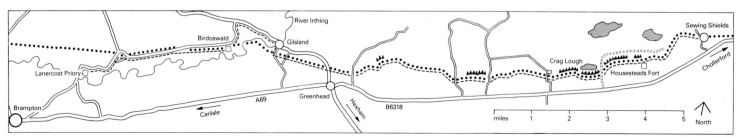

Above: Looking west along Hadrian's Wall from Housesteads. *Photo: Shelagh Gregory*

follows the escarpment edge, which is itself a natural defensive feature, and over these sections the Romans decided that a ditch was unnecessary. Follow the stub of Wall down to Housesteads Fort, the most popular excavation on the Wall and well worth detailed exploration on another occasion, but today you have far to go and must not linger. Skirt the fort to the north, and continue west over Hotbank Crags to Crag Lough and Steel Rigg. This section is the most picturesque and famous of the entire Roman Wall.

Crag Lough, a 100ft. crag of whin sill, partly clothed in vegetation, rises above the lake and is topped by the Wall. Much of my early rock-climbing was learnt at Crag Lough and it has very happy associations. The rock is ideal for the beginner, being clean and sound, and the pillars and buttresses are split by cracks providing an assortment of holds. Long summer evenings on the dry rock, at grips with Hadrian's Buttress or Raven's Tower, while shadows lengthen and swans glide over the lake, can never be forgotten. The delights of Crag Lough were discovered last century by George and Charles Trevelyan and Geoffrey Winthrop Young.

The cliffs of Steel Rigg become lower and more broken as you continue west to the National Trust car park. In summer a mini-bus plies between Housesteads and the Steel Rigg car park, for the convenience of walkers who wish only to sample the famous three-mile stretch of the Wall. The large building half a mile south of here is the Twice Brewed Inn, which houses a good restaurant and the Northumberland National Park Information Centre. West of Steel Rigg, the mass of

tourists and sightseers are left behind and open moorland leads over Winshields, at 1,230ft. the highest point on the Wall. Passing Cawfields Milecastle the switch-back continues as you climb up and away through the largely unkempt and neglected ruin of Great Chesters Fort (Aesica), its mossy and grass-covered walls in pleasant contrast to Housesteads' orderliness. An elevated stretch between Cockmount Hill and Walltown Crags commands a panoramic view north, with moors and forests extending to the Scottish border and beyond. It was here, on my last visit, that I realised the diverse motivating forces that persuade walkers to visit the Roman Wall. Over a short period I passed a party of archaeologists peering through magnifying glasses at inscribed stones, two middle-aged back-

packers walking the Pennine Way in ten-mile stretches, a group of ambling schoolgirls carrying a transistor, which effectively dulled their response to nature, and a fell-runner, with pacer, trying for the Pennine Way record.

Below Walltown Turret you must by-pass a huge quarry and descend to Thirlwall Castle, a spectacular ruin beside the Tipalt Burn. Cross the road and railway line, and circumvent the golf course at Haltwhistle on the north side. The Wall disappears for a mile or two, but you follow the line of the ditch until, near Gilsland Station, you pick up signs to the Poltross Burn Milecastle. Thereafter the Wall passes through the old Vicarage garden in Gilsland and descends to the River Irthing at Willowford. The abutment of the Roman bridge has been excavated, and I was touched for 10p by the farmer's wife for the privilege of access to the site. The River Irthing is not bridged, and when in spate the crossing must not be attempted. In normal conditions the water is about knee-deep, but river crossings always need extreme care, and if in doubt make the three-mile detour through Gilsland. Once across the river, scramble up the steep bank on the other side to Harrow's Scar Milecastle, and a clean stretch of the Wall, carrying several inscriptions, running west to Birdoswald Fort. Before hunting for the inscriptions, be sure to look south down the beautiful valley of the Irthing.

Beyond Birdoswald the Wall runs parallel to, and close beside, the minor road to Banks. It has been excavated for some distance, but thereafter only turrets can be seen. At last the walk is drawing to a close, and at Banks it is convenient to leave the line of the Wall and descend back into the Irthing valley at Lanercost. Stretch out on the lush grass under the sycamores that grow beside the glorious twelfth-century Augustinian Priory and await your transport; or, if energy remains, walk the three miles into Brampton. Lanercost Priory, built mainly of stones filched from the Wall, is 1,000 years more recent than the Roman remains that have been with you all day, yet it makes a fitting end to your historic walk across Northern Britain.

29   High Street

by Tom Price

Maps O.S. 1:50,000 Sheet 90; O.S. 1:63,360 Tourist Map of the Lake District; O.S. 1:25,000 Outdoor Leisure Map – The English Lake District S.E. and N.E. Start from Patterdale (ref. 395161). Finish at Troutbeck (ref. 413028).
Grading A fine mountain walk. No difficulties should be encountered in good conditions.
Time 6 hours.
Distance 12 miles.
Escape Routes From The Knott descend W to Hayeswater and Hartsop. From the Froswick–Ill Bell–Yoke ridge easy descents lead W to lower ground in the Hagg Gill Valley.
Telephones Patterdale; Troutbeck; Hartsop.
Transport Railway Stations at Penrith and Windermere. Bus Penrith–Patterdale. The Windermere–Ambleside–Keswick bus passes through Troutbeck Bridge.
Accommodation Hotels, Guest Houses and Bed and Breakfast establishments abound. Youth Hostels at Patterdale, Ambleside and Windermere.
Guidebooks *The Far Eastern Fells* by A. Wainwright (The Westmorland Gazette); *Across Northern Hills* by Geoffrey Berry (The Westmorland Gazette); *The Lakeland Peaks* by W. A. Poucher (Constable).

My first walk over High Street was after a November weekend spent trapped in the Haweswater Hotel by rain that fell like stair-rods. On the Sunday afternoon we went out, to see what diversion could be wrung from getting wet; whereupon the clouds began to part and the rain stopped. We squelched up Low Kop and High Kop as an extravagant red sunset unfolded, and continued along the whole of the High Street ridge in moonlight, with cloud shadows racing across the hills. We reached Troutbeck at 9.30 p.m. convinced it must be the middle of the night, and addressed ourselves to the problem of getting home.

The old Baddeley guide disparagingly describes the top of High Street as 'a vast sheep-walk'. But to me its high flatness is its attraction; like Grasmoor and Ingleborough, it provides a lofty and inspiring promenade. For many years, until it ceased in 1835, an annual fair day and shepherds' meet was held up there, with horse-racing and other sports, though the original purpose was to sort out strayed sheep. You can imagine what a pleasure it must have been, after months of confinement in the depths of Mardale and Deepdale. Part of the summit area is still shown on the 1:25,000 Ordnance Survey map as Racecourse Hill.

It is the length as well as the breadth of High Street that is striking. The ridge runs straight from Loadpot Hill to Garburn Pass, nine miles unbroken by any considerable dip or col. The Romans in Britain did not usually take their roads so high, but the directness of this line must have been irresistible.

In some respects the best way to *do* High Street would be from Tirril to Troutbeck, since that follows the main ridge and the course of the Roman Road, but a shorter, more classic, and more scenic route is from Patterdale. The start is a few yards along the main road south of Patterdale Church, at a small lay-by. You take a cart-track across the flat floor of the valley and, after passing through some farm buildings, you come abruptly to the steep flank of Place Fell. The path, which soon joins the one from Silver Crag, makes an ascending traverse of the steep slope, heading towards the col between Boardale and Patterdale. Just below the col, however, it trends south, traverses under the

rocky little summit of Angletarn Pikes, and makes a slight descent to Angle Tarn, which is one of the most beautiful of Lakeland tarns. It continues round the side of Satura Crag, across a damp hollow, and up to The Knott. Here you look north into a relatively unvisited tract of fell-country, the last retreat of the red deer of the Lake District. A little further and we reach the summit ridge. Another mile takes us to the OS pillar.

This long and delightful footpath from Patterdale involves some 2,000ft. of ascent, but it is so varied and interesting as to

Above: Heading south along the High Street ridge; Froswick and Ill Bell are the nearest summits in this view from Thornthwaite Crag. *Photo: Richard Gibbens*

minimise the exertion. It traverses steep slopes which, in certain winter conditions, could be a hazard to the unwary, yet it is a gentle path with no punishing gradients. It commands fine views into those impressive crag-bound combes of the Helvellyn range, Deepdale and Dovedale, and down into Pasture Beck and Hayeswater. On the summit it is worthwhile to walk about a little and take a look down into Riggindale, the deep, U-shaped valley in which Hugh Holme took refuge from the vengeance of King John, and lived to found the line of the 'kings' of Mardale, and into Blea Water and Haweswater. But as a viewpoint for a classic Lakeland panorama, Thornthwaite Crag, a mile further on, is pre-eminent. It has been renowned from the early days of hill climbing, when appreciation of views was a major interest, and no doubt that accounts for the exceptionally fine columnar cairn that adorns its summit. Almost every considerable Lakeland hill, from Black Combe to Saddleback, is in sight, not to speak of the plunging depths of Kentmere and Troutbeck. Both Harter Fells are visible,

and Scafell and the Pikes, separated by the remarkable gash of Mickledore. All this, of course, supposes that the weather is fine. In mist, the place to dig out your compass is at the OS pillar on High Street summit, not after you have gone adrift on the 'vast sheep-walk'.

From Thornthwaite Crag, the Roman Road goes down into Hagg Gill, and at one place its course is clearly discernible traversing down the steep fell-side. If you have had enough of the high ground, a pleasing enough finish can be made this way by valley paths and lanes to Troutbeck. There is also a very fine walk over Caudale Head and John Bell's Banner to the top of Kirkstone Pass. But I think the most satisfying continuation is to stick to the ridge over Froswick and Ill

Bell, which are both good rocky summits in their own right, standing high over the precipitous sides of Kentmere. Beyond Ill Bell is Yoke, and beyond Yoke the ridge becomes broad and peaty until the top of Garburn Pass is reached, offering a choice of routes, to Kentmere or Troutbeck. Since Troutbeck is on the road from Kirkstone, it is likely to be the most convenient finishing point. Two more miles on a stony track, and we are dropping into the valley near the squat old church, though from above it is the large caravan park at Limefitt Farm which dominates the scene.

On most hill-walks it matters little from which end you start, but in this case I would recommend doing the walk from north to south, as described, since whereas the section from Patterdale to High Street is enjoyable in either direction, the section from High Street to Troutbeck has excellent southward views, with Windermere winding into the distance like some vast river. But when walked in the opposite direction, it can become a seven-mile-long slog, with Thornthwaite Crag in sight most of the way, and not getting much nearer. High Street has a little of the atmosphere of the Pennines about it, yet it is also a Lake District hill, with its deeply-carved glacial features. For a wayfarer whose sentiment is,

> All I ask is the heaven above
> And the road below me.

There cannot be many better roads than High Street.

Top left: Looking back to Thornthwaite Crag and High Street from Ill Bell. *Photo: Bert Jenkins*

Bottom left: The final slopes of High Street from the north. *Photo: Bert Jenkins*

Above: The old Roman Road leads down the northern slopes of High Street, and continues past The Knott to High Raise on the right, and thence on towards Penrith. The described route joins the Roman Road at The Knott, having ascended the ridge on the left from Patterdale. *Photo: Ken Andrew*

30   Saddleback by Sharp Edge

by Chris Bonington

Maps O.S. 1:50,000 Sheet 90; O.S. 1:63,360 Tourist Map of the Lake District; O.S. 1:25,000 Outdoor Leisure Map – The English Lake District N.E. Start and finish at Mungrisdale (ref. 364305).
Grading Easy except for Sharp Edge, a steep scramble which command respect, particularly in wet weather when the rock is greasy. In winter conditions Sharp Edge should be left to the experienced mountaineer.
Time 6 hours.
Distance 8 miles.
Escape Routes From the summit descend Scales Fell to Scales or continue S.W. along the summit ridge to the slopes of Blease Fell which fall gently S to meet a track just W of Threlkeld.
Telephones Mungrisdale; Scales Inn; Threlkeld.
Transport Railway Station at Penrith. The Keswick to Penrith bus service passes through Threlkeld and Scales, alight at the Mungrisdale road junction, 2 miles from the start of the walk.
Accommodation Inns at Mungrisdale, Scales, Troutbeck and Threlkeld. Bed and Breakfast available locally. Youth Hostel at Keswick.
Guidebooks The Northern Fells by A. Wainwright (The Westmorland Gazette); The Lakeland Peaks by W. A. Poucher (Constable).

It was mid-October and I'd just walked and scrambled up the dramatic ridge of Hallsfell Top to the summit of Blencathra. For a few minutes I had the summit to myself. Great grey clouds were being driven out of the west across the Lakeland fells but between the clouds, arrows of sunlight were able to strike the ground, burnishing the dark, dull green of fell and field into a brilliant emerald. The stream winding up St. John's in the Vale was a sinuous, gilded silver and you could even glimpse the mirrored lake of Derwentwater.

I was alone for only a few minutes and then a little group of walkers, whom I'd overtaken on the way up, reached the summit. One of them obviously recognised me and in passing commented, 'This must be a bit tame after Everest, isn't it?'. I know this might sound corny but I very nearly cried as I tried to tell him how this scene of Lakeland fells, with its infinitely varied tones of colour, light and shade, was as beautiful and as moving as anything anywhere in the world.

Blencathra, or Saddleback as it's also known, is a truly magnificent mountain; the gate tower to the north east Lakes, it stands proud like a gigantic saddle overlooking the main road from Penrith and the M6 into Keswick and west Cumbria. It is good to look at and a wonderful viewpoint. It is a mountain full of surprises and, being near my home, is the one I know best in all the Lake District.

The conventional route of ascent, taking in Sharp Edge, starts from Scales, and after ascending the Edge traverses the mountain and descends to Threlkeld. This has the advantage of focussing in on Sharp Edge during the approach along Scales Fell, but the disadvantage of a two-mile road walk to regain the starting point. There is also a choice of routes taking one of the rocky arêtes on the south side of the mountain and utilising Sharp Edge as a descent. I prefer a different route however, starting and finishing in Mungrisdale, including Sharp Edge, and also boasting some delightfully varied moorland and ridge walking with splendid views. The wide, spacious valley of the River Glenderamackin, that rises above Mungrisdale, is full of intriguing mysteries, for it winds and bends, hiding the peak at its head. There is an old track to follow, up

towards The Tongue, a steep bluff that immediately confronts you as you leave Mungrisdale. You turn this to the south and go up Bannerdale, the track leading to an old mine – if you stick to the path it leads you gently up the southern flank of The Tongue towards the broad col between Bowscale Fell and Bannerdale itself. At the top suddenly everything opens out. Across to the west is the wide upland valley of Skiddaw Forest and the proud sweep of Skiddaw, highest peak of the Northern Fells, whilst to the south the top of Blencathra is now visible, seeming squat and truncated by proximity. If you want to 'bag' an extra peak, it's only a short, easy walk to the top of Bowscale Fell and from its summit, like a giant fan laid out all around it, are the tops of the Northern Fells which I have come to love so much.

But on to our objective. It's easy walking along sinuous little sheep-tracks, weaving their way between beds of heather, across the plateau-ed top of Bannerdale towards the col linking it with Saddleback. From the col you can ascend directly to the summit by the north slope, but a far better route contours the slopes to the south to gain the combe of Scales Tarn, and then makes the final ascent in the grand manner by the graceful arête of Sharp Edge. At first this route doesn't appear very dramatic, the Edge almost lost in the slate and grass slopes on the east side of Tarn Crags but, once again, it is full of surprises. You pull up over a small ridge and there, on the other side, is Scales Tarn, dark and still, cradled between the arms of Sharp Edge and Scales Fell. And Sharp Edge itself suddenly assumes a grander character; a slate-crested ridge mounting the dark flanks above. On a wet day the slate is smooth and slimy with a feeling of exhilarating treachery. There are places where if you slipped you could undoubtedly hurt yourself. In winter, when the rocks are clad with snow or ice, it can become a serious and exciting ridge climb. The difficulties are not prolonged – just a few hundred feet – and then the flying buttress of the ridge is lost in the upper slopes and soon you are on the outlying northern shoulder of Saddleback. A short stroll and you're on the true summit gazing down steep and rocky screes to Threlkeld far below and a full vista of the Lakeland hills stretching

Carrock Fell

Caldbeck

Bonington's route ------------
Conventional route ···············

River Caldew

Bowscale Fell ▲

The Tongue

Mungrisdale

Mungrisdale Common

Bannerdale Crags

River Glenderamackin

Sharp Edge

Scales Tarn

Souther Fell

Saddleback (Blencathra)

Hallsfell Top

Scales Fell

Scales

Penrith

A594

Threlkeld

North

Keswick

miles   1   2

away to the south.

The rest of the walk is very much more gentle but by no means an anti-climax. Once I get onto a ridge I hate abandoning it. There is a sense of airy freedom and so, when I've walked down the broad slopes of Scales Fell to the col at the head of Mousthwaite Comb, instead of dropping back into the valley to the north, I keep to the crest of the hill across the pathless, broken little tops of Souther Fell. This provides an ideal viewpoint to look back to Saddleback. It is also the outer rampart of the Lakeland Fells, its eastern edge marking the boundary between hill and cultivated land. A patchwork of walled fields stretch away to the dark spread of Greystoke Forest. A final steep slope at the end of the ridge leads down into Mungrisdale, where, if I have timed the walk well, the Mill Inn will be open.

Above: Saddleback's distinctive shape is best seen from the south, as in this view from Castlerigg Stone Circle.
Photo: Tom Parker

Near right: Sharp Edge from near Scales Tarn.
Photo: Richard Gilbert

Above right: On the rocky section of Sharp Edge, where a gendarme and an awkward step bar access to the upper face. This photograph, taken several years ago, illustrates the simple equipment and clothing of hill-walkers in the past. *Photo: Tom Parker*

Bottom right: Looking down to Sharp Edge from near the summit of Saddleback.
Photo: Van Greaves

31   The Buttermere Circuit

by Geoffrey Berry

Maps O.S. 1:50,000 Sheets 90 and 89; O.S. 1:63,360 Tourist Map of the Lake District; O.S. 1:25,000 Outdoor Leisure Map – The English Lake District N.W. Start and finish at Buttermere (ref. 176170).
Grading A straightforward but long mountain walk over some of the finest of the Lakeland fells.
Time 7 hours.
Distance 13 miles.
Escape Routes The walk may conveniently be left at the summit of Honister Pass or at Scarth Gap.
Telephones Buttermere; Gatesgarth; Honister Hause.
Transport Railway Stations at Penrith and Whitehaven. Daily bus services, in summer only, from Buttermere to Keswick and Cockermouth. The local Mountain Goat bus services ply over Honister and Newlands passes.
Accommodation Hotels in Buttermere village. Bed and Breakfasts available locally. Youth Hostels at Buttermere, Honister Hause and Longthwaite.
Guidebooks *The Western Fells* and *The North Western Fells* by A. Wainwright (The Westmorland Gazette); *The Lakeland Peaks* by W. A. Poucher (Constable).

This splendid day's walk takes the crest of the fells above one of the loveliest, quietest, and least changed of the lakes of the Lake District. The start must plainly be from Buttermere village, and personally I favour a clockwise direction. I believe that most circular walks are best done clockwise, but this may well be without rational explanation; much must depend on where one prefers the direction of the sun's rays – if any. There is little tarmac to tread in this day's walk, apart from crossing the road at the top of the Honister Pass. There are a few hundred yards of road at the very beginning, when we leave Buttermere towards Newlands Hause. The path to the summit of Robinson goes off near a small lay-by on the right, unsigned and not very noticeably trodden.

The way is upwards from the very start, but there is more variety in the ascent of this rather bulky mountain than may be expected. We round a rocky corner and contour below a dry gully, where the green path is an old sled road, made originally for bringing peat down from Buttermere Moss. The Moss, which we have to cross, is an extensive and marshy depression. Beyond, there is the dry and stony summit dome of the mountain, where the path is marked by a line of cairns. The top (2,470ft.) is a broad, flattish place crossed by ribs of rock, but in the morning light, with the expanses of mountain about us, and with the prospect of a day's elevated tramping before us, it is a

stimulating place. If we have the misfortune to reach the summit in cloud it may well be necessary to take a compass bearing due south, until we pick up the fence, which runs round the head of Little Dale, on Littledale Edge. This is fine walking, with the valleys far below on either hand. We descend to slightly below the 2,000ft. contour, and then climb to the Hindscarth ridge. To bring in Hindscarth summit itself requires a slight diversion of half a mile northwards, but entails only a slight and easy ascent. From the summit, there is the temptation to go a few steps further northwards, descending a little to a pile of stones, from which is revealed the long ridge stretching north-westwards, over High Crags and Scoop End, into Newlands, and further away Derwent Water and the Skiddaw massif.

We go back to our main route and climb the pleasantly narrow, and in places rocky, ridge on to Dale Head. Almost 2,000ft. below on our right, petty cars crawl along the Pass road, below the dark and ominous Honister Crag. On our other hand, the deep bowl of the Newlands Valley, contained on the far side by the steep, heather-dark slopes of Eel Crags, runs from the barren mountain down to a pattern of green pastures. A tall, cylindrical cairn of slate has been carefully constructed on Dale Head summit, and stands at the very edge of the precipitous drop into the Newlands valley. In a mist, it is particularly important to turn right (almost due south) here for the top of the Honister Pass. An old iron fence-post a few yards from the cairn marks the beginning of the descending path, which is then well-cairned, though thankfully not, like many Lakeland paths, over-cairned. If the day is clear, this easy descent gives time and relaxation for the appreciation of the ever-changing views of the central mountains ranged before us, stretching from a glimpse of the Langdale Pikes, by way of Glaramara, Bowfell, Great End, the Scafells, Great Gable, Kirk Fell, Pillar, to the High Stile range, along the latter of which our route goes.

As we come lower, the unspoiled splendour of the mountain scene is marred by man's untidy work about the Honister Pass. Slate-quarrying has gone on here since the middle of the eighteenth century, and there is

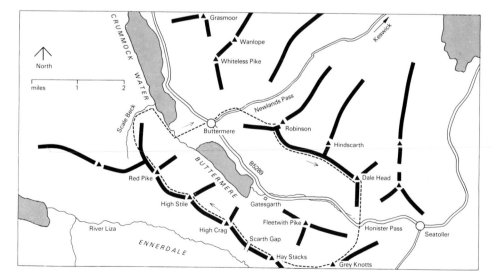

much evidence of this earlier activity carried out with perilous persistence on the cliffs of Honister and Yew Crags. Today quarrying continues on the less exposed southern slopes of Fleetwith. We are soon across the top of the Pass, beyond the slate-cutting sheds, and climbing the rough, stony track which goes by the route of an old ropeway. This direction should be followed on to the crest of the col where it passes over a huge pile of stones, the foundations of the former Drum House. From here, there is a choice of routes to Hay Stacks; either turning southwards to climb onto the slopes of Grey Knotts and curve around the head of Dubs Bottom, or to continue in almost a straight line to Dubs Quarry, now abandoned. This section is one of delightful variety, twisting its way around the craggy head of Warnscale Bottom, edging beneath the rocky face of Little Round How, rising and falling in a terrain of crags, dark gullys, and lichen-patterned boulders. We pass close to the foot of Blackbeck Tarn, set in a rocky amphitheatre, the epitome of Lake District scenery. As we climb onto the craggy confusion of Hay Stacks, there is Innominate Tarn mirroring Pillar. Here is the rich and sombre colouring of a mature eighteenth-century landscape painting, with the dark heather, the patches of rich, green bilberry, the still, black waters of the tarns, and the rocky, olive-tinted tors. It is a landscape in which figures are soon lost, and where time has a new and different significance. Fine mountains are close about us, and we can look down on the marshalled forest of Ennerdale, up to Great Gable at the dale's head, and to the noble masses of Kirk Fell and Pillar.

From the summit of Hay Stacks, at about 1,750ft. we descend steeply to Scarth Gap at 1,425ft., and then ascend a worn scree slope to Seat. Before us rises the cone of High Crag, with long, narrow fans of scree, the ascent of which can be tedious. Once we have gained the summit, the ridge before us running to High Stile and Red Pike is the climax of the day's expedition. This is a splendid, elevated walk in a primitive terrain, giving sweeping views of earth and sky. We are at the craggy edge of the great hollow of Burtness Combe, and go on to the day's highest peak, High Stile, 2,644ft. Beyond, another great bowl

opens on our right, in which lies, black as a bottomless hole, Blaeberry Tarn. The cone of Red Pike is the last of the day's peaks. From it, the descent by Blaeberry Tarn is steep, and in the main strewn with loose boulders, but the views of the lake far beyond, and its surrounding mountains, are magnificent and change continuously as the path takes its zig-zag course. A longer and less steep descent by Lingcove Edge and Scale Force is, I think, to be preferred. I like the protracted enjoyment of prolonged descents, and although this one finishes on the usually very wet path by Crummock Water, Buttermere's white buildings are then beckoning across the level pastures.

Above: The view north to Saddleback from Hindscarth, over the ridges and valleys of the Derwent Fells and the shoulder of Maiden Moor. *Photo: E. A. Shepherd*

Overleaf: The main peaks on the southern side of the Buttermere Horseshoe from halfway up the Honister Pass. High Crag and Burtness Combe to the left of the main peak – High Stile, with Red Pike beyond. *Photo: E. A. Shepherd*

32   Great Gable

by Tony Greenbank

Maps O.S. 1:50,000 Sheet 90; O.S. 1:63,360 Tourist Map of the Lake District; O.S. 1:25,000 Outdoor Leisure Map – The English Lake District N.W. Start and finish at Seathwaite (ref. 235122).
Grading This walk is not for the inexperienced. It involves a considerable amount of rock scrambling and a rope should be carried.
Time 4–5 hours.
Distance 6 miles.
Escape Routes From the S side of Great Gable easy slopes lead down to Lingmell Beck and Wasdale Head.
Telephones Seathwaite and Wasdale Head.
Transport Railway Stations at Penrith, Workington and Carlisle. Keswick–Seatoller bus service.
Accommodation A great variety of accommodation is available in Borrowdale. Youth Hostels at Derwentwater, Longthwaite and Honister Hause.
Guidebooks *The Western Fells* by A. Wainwright (The Westmorland Gazette); *The Lakeland Peaks* by W. A. Poucher (Constable).

Right: A rock-climber making an ascent of the Napes Needle, one of the most celebrated rock features in the British Isles. The Climbers' Path comes through the gap and descends the cracks just right of the sunlit face. The first ascent of Napes Needle was made in 1886 by W. P. Haskett-Smith, climbing alone and with no nearby support; an achievement regarded as one of the landmarks of British climbing.
Photo: Phil Ideson

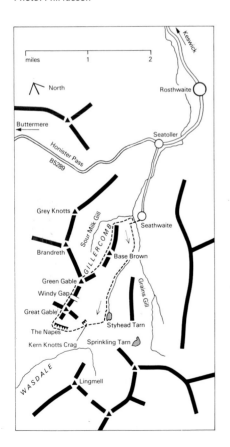

Approaching the head of Borrowdale, you will see two great hanging valleys dominating the view through the windscreen. The one on the right is Gillercomb, the one on the left Styhead. Encompassed by splendid sugarloaves and spilling silvery cascades down their mountainsides, they look a world apart. Beyond them lies Great Gable.

Seathwaite, starting point of this walk, and a short drive from Seatoller, is supposedly the wettest inhabited spot in England. It probably is. The rain gauges near Joe Edmondson's 'Raingauge Cottage' are too well-placed to be topped up overmuch by the passing hordes who, on seeing their funnels, invariably wish to add their own contribution. So it really is the rain which fills them, and which can flood this tiny community under the three hanging valleys so amazingly quickly. Consequently, expect a wet day's walk, but if you are blessed with good weather instead, what a bonus!

The virtue of Great Gable's classic climbers' tour from Seathwaite, in mist and rain, is worthwhile waterfall-at-full-throttle scenery. The atmosphere increases the apparent stature of the mountains tenfold, and there is continuous interest underfoot. To make this trip, you should have some experience of rock-climbing or exposed scrambling, for certain sections can be tricky. If uncomfortable in wet weather and exposed places, you shouldn't attempt this rather sporting route up Gable.

If you tempted Providence by washing the car, and it rains on arrival, remember: these are still good conditions. Splash through the farmyard, but not too far. The popular Sty Head route, directly ahead, can be crowded and is most certainly badly eroded. There's a better start, and you cut between the barns on the right to take it. There, framed between the weathered stones, Sour Milk Gill tumbles from the Gillercomb bowl overhead. Approach it down the lane, cross the bridge, and turn left through the first gate. Back to the waterfalls later; you should leave them now for the track across the stepping stones and past a small plantation. The stepping stones continue across swampy wastes, and into the mist beyond. These are the flanks of Base Brown, and on the return you will be coming the opposite way along

the crest above. If a ceiling of cloud obscures the view up there, the end of that ridge dive-bombing into Gillercomb might still be seen. It looks just about believable. Now you are *en route* for the top of Sty Head Pass, just as surely as those also heading that way among the caravan of walkers on the far side of the beck. Only they will be turning off right over Stockley Bridge, and you are already on the 'right' side of the water in more ways than one.

Travellers over Sty Head proper miss the best view of Taylor Gill Force (to Sty Head what Sour Milk Gill is to Gillercomb). You won't. Rounding the edge of a crag on which is perched, of all things, a gate, you see through the raindrops one of Lakeland's sights. Or at least in flood you do. A thundering mare's tail. And missed by most, for the regular track up Sty Head is screened from the waterfall at close-range. Your path, however, continues up rocks, across scree, and through trees on a knoll above the lip of the cataract. Presently it is joined by the Sty Head trade route, which crosses a small footbridge below Sty Head tarn. The paths now merge, and lead to the stretcher box on the Sty Head col. Branching upwards to the right from here, cross a grassy plateau, and Kern Knotts Crag will loom out of the raininess to face you head-on. By this time the track is all rock, devoid of even a blade of grass. You are on course for the Napes via the Climbers' Path.

It's worth a prowl around this crag. Kern Knotts Crack (the one with a sentry box), Innominate Crack, and what remains of Sepulchre (alas, in 1980 blitzed by an earthquake that sheared its bottom part smooth), have featured on so many postcards over the years; here is a chance to see them at first hand. Just round the corner, the tenuous track crosses rock and boulder, shale and scree, to the Napes, somewhere up there to the right. It passes a little cave bubbling with drinking water. It also divides in one or two places, but keep high and you will eventually ford a river of red stones – Great Hell Gate screes – and sense, if you haven't actually seen it yet, the presence of millions of tons of naked rock poised immediately above. Given a window in the mist, the view is awesome enough to make people overbalance. The

Top left: Great Gable from Lingmell with the line of the Climbers' Path marked. The Napes cliffs are in the centre, between the scree-filled couloirs of Little Hell Gate (left) and Great Hell Gate. *Photo: E. A. Shepherd*

Bottom left: Walkers congregate at the summit of Great Gable, one of the busiest mountains in the Lake District. *Photo: Tom Parker*

most gigantic (in the mist at any rate) sheet of rock rears overhead, so impending that it will often be dry in rain, save for a smudge or two of damp on this overlap or that slab. Tophet Wall is its name, and it is even more remarkable because the climb of that name which pierces its blankness is nowhere near as desperate as it looks.

By now the track will nearly touch the rock. Once past this point, and leaving Tophet Wall behind, yet more crag slides into view: the Napes Ridges. Within minutes you should see Napes Needle poised above, but not like the popular view photographed from the Dress Circle. It looks like a Stone Age club from down here, set on end, jutting in mid-air, as if waiting for some ghostly giant to grasp it. At this point the real traversing begins, unless you intend walking the whole way – in which case continue along the track to the screes of Little Hell Gate, and climb them by the right-hand edge.

The real scrambling starts with one of the big moments in the British mountains, when, after working up to the base of the Needle, then climbing an obvious groove with your back to the way you have come, you look clean through a narrow gap between the Needle, to your left, and the Needle Ridge to your right. The view springs suddenly at you, quite different from anything before. Below Kirkfell's magnificent slopes lie the peaceful fields of Wasdale Head. Straight across from you, black and bold against the sky, is the Sphinx Rock. It is one of the most powerful mountain views in the British Isles. The Needle and the Sphinx are two book-ends, packing between them volumes of perfect rock. To reach the Sphinx, you work your way along the rim of the bookshelf, descending here, climbing there, squeezing through gaps. As you wander through the pinnacles, buttresses, and ridges, spare a thought for the pioneers who developed Gable as a rock-climbing playground.

In the little gap between Sphinx Rock and Sphinx Ridge, and before you descend a short pitch to continue your traverse, look back behind you towards the Needle – yet another marvellous mountain view, and in a couple of feet it is gone.

Overlooking Little Hell Gate is a broken ridge, a good way up to the neck of the

mountain, where Great and Little Hell Gate screes meet the knife-edge. And one which you must now tread towards the summit.

Directly above, the broken mass of Westmorland Crags block the way and force a detour to their left. And still some way above, the summit of Great Gable (2,949ft.) has its poignant touch: the war memorial tablet of the Fell and Rock Climbing Club, with the remains of poppies and wreaths from the last Remembrance Day on the rock below. This memorial is a fine-relief map of the surrounding valleys and magnificent ridges. By such a sky-line you return: down into Windy Gap via shattered rock and scree, then up to Green Gable. A little further beyond this summit, descend easily by a rocky pasture to the Base Brown crest. Following this to the end, negotiate its final swoop into Gillercomb with care. A crag cuts off the descent with dangerous suddenness. There are also hazardous rocks under the Gillercomb side of this end of the ridge. To be safe, leave the ridge to the right, and then only when you are well down its blade and almost above Seathwaite. A good track across the mountainside is reached. Follow this back round into Gillercomb – under the dangerous crag. Just when you think you are wasting your time in going the wrong way, an obvious slope leads gently back to the lip of Sour Milk Gill. Follow this down by the footpath on its right, over the biggest stile in the world and back to where you began, through Stanley Edmondson's barns. In mist or bad conditions it is safer to take the well marked track from the col between Green Gable and Base Brown, which leads easily down into Gillercomb.

Right: The Sphinx Rock – a natural sculpture bearing an uncanny human resemblance. From the other side it looks more like a cat. Both profiles can only be fully appreciated by those taking the Climbers' Path which crosses the notch behind the Sphinx. Although the Sphinx is something of a postcard commonplace, the oblique sunlight in this photo fully reveals a surface subtlety not always appreciated. *Photo: E. A. Shepherd*

33 Helvellyn by Striding Edge

by A. Wainwright

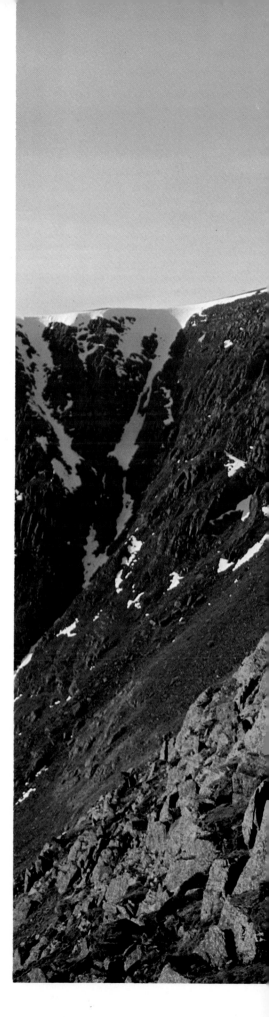

Maps O.S. 1:50,000 Sheet 90; O.S. 1:63,360 Tourist Map of the Lake District; O.S. 1:25,000 Outdoor Leisure Map – The English Lake District N.E. Start and finish at Patterdale (ref. 390161).
Grading A tough mountain walk involving some airy ridge scrambling. A serious route in winter conditions.
Time 5–6 hours.
Distance 8 miles.
Escape Routes From Helvellyn summit proceed N towards Raise, where easy slopes lead down to Glenridding.
Telephones Patterdale; Glenridding.
Transport Railway Stations at Penrith and Windermere. Bus Penrith–Patterdale. Mountain Goat bus service Glenridding–Windermere–Ambleside.
Accommodation Hotels, Guest Houses and Bed and Breakfast establishments abound. Youth Hostels at Grasmere (2), Greenside and Patterdale.
Guidebooks *The Lakeland Peaks* by W. A. Poucher (Constable); *Guide to the Eastern Fells* by A. Wainwright (The Westmorland Gazette).

Right: Looking along Striding Edge towards the Helvellyn plateau and summit. The top of Swirral Edge is profiled on the right.
Photo: Tom Parker

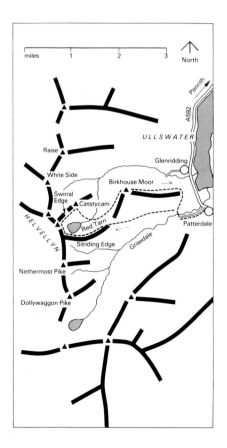

Helvellyn is the most frequented mountain in the Lake District. Its height, commanding position, easy accessibility, and reputation for sunrise effects, make it an obvious target, attracting thousands of walkers each year. Further, its lovely name, and the legends and poetry associated with it bestow an aura of romance, while a scattering of monuments adds unusual interest. For many visitors, it is a place of regular pilgrimage.

Steep but easy slopes form the western flank, along the base of which runs the busy Ambleside to Keswick road, giving access to well-worn paths that lead unerringly to the top. Much more rewarding and exciting is the less well-known eastern approach, from Patterdale. Park your car in Glenridding or Patterdale and take the narrow lane into Grisedale. The path crosses Grisedale Beck at a bridge, and then mounts the large, walled enclosure of Birkhouse Moor. Connoisseurs follow in the steps of the pioneers on the old grass path, and spare their feet unnecessary torture. The long climb to the upper wall-corner, where all paths and variations meet, is relieved by lovely retrospective views of the Ullswater area.

Through the wall-corner, it is the immediate prospect in front that arrests the attention. The path goes forward, ascending gradually, with the deep gulf of Grisedale far below on the left and the horseshoe of Helvellyn's edges and cliffs coming starkly into view ahead. A prominent, pinnacled tower, standing sentinel over Striding Edge, is soon reached. Beyond it, Striding Edge is suddenly revealed as a narrow ridge of naked rock poised high above a deep abyss on the left, and the stony basin of Red Tarn down to the right. This knife-edge is the best thing on the mountain for adventurous spirits. It is a tightrope in a dramatic setting, but without danger for walkers who keep to the path which soon runs alongside and just below the edge. Those who follow the crest strictly (recommended only in calm weather) will savour the best of the situation and note, as they pass along, the Dixon Memorial of 1855, the first of Helvellyn's monuments, and a grim reminder of the perils of a false step. The Edge ends abruptly in about 300 yards with an awkward descent of a short

Above: Two views looking down on Striding Edge. Cloud inversion isolates its jagged crest (upper photo). Lingering snow and low winter light accentuate the fine lines of the ridge (lower photo). *Photos: Van Greaves and Tom Parker*

chimney, and ahead is the final slope to the top of the mountain, the path here being submerged in unpleasant, loose scree. The top is reached at another monument: the Gough Memorial, erected 1890, commemorates an incident in 1805 in which a faithful dog guarded the remains of his fallen master for three months, before being found by a shepherd. (Helvellyn was obviously less popular in those days!) This inspired poems by Wordsworth and Scott. On the level top, keep along the rim of the cliffs above Red Tarn, passing the often-crowded summit and another monument, half-buried in stones, marking the spot where an aeroplane landed in 1926. Ignoring all other paths, turn down a rocky stairway when the steep cliffs ease. This is Swirral Edge, identifiable by the shapely peak of Catstycam ahead. It is less fearsome than Striding Edge, but needs care in places where it is eroded and slippery. At the foot of Swirral Edge, where the ground rises ahead to Catstycam (it is worth a detour to this lovely peak), follow a path slanting down to the outlet of Red Tarn, and ascending beyond to the wall-corner, where the route of ascent is joined and can be reversed to the car. Or instead, the top wall may be followed over Birkhouse Moor and down to Keldas, for a beautiful view of Ullswater before returning to the car. For walkers who have no car to dictate their steps, there is an alternative way down from Red Tarn, descending with the stream into the interesting valley of Greenside and Glenridding.

34   The Coniston Fells

by Harry Griffin

The compact group of the Coniston fells, a knuckled fist of craggy country in the south-west corner of Lakeland, provides a superb but undemanding round of the heights that, for variety, extensive views, and dramatic scenery, can hardly be surpassed. For much of the way you are stepping above great crags, peeping down on some of the finest mountain tarns in the district, or looking across deep-cut dales to the Scafells, the Yorkshire hills and, reaching out to the horizon, the Irish Sea. And at the end of the day, as you trot down through the bracken to Coniston, there is often the sunset on the sea, lengthening shadows across the turf, and the song of the larks. I have known these fells, especially Dow Crag, for 55 years, and must have made the round, with many variations, dozens of times, but, although I know each corner so intimately and can be there in less than an hour from my home, there is still a little sadness every time I leave all this quiet beauty, with its old memories.

Often the round has been done in winter, crunching along the heights on crisp, sunlit snows, and I remember one occasion, in a blizzard, when Low Water, heaped with ice-floes, looked like the Antarctic, and the wind-shelter cairn on Coniston Old Man was completely hidden in some of the deepest snow I have seen in the fells. Perhaps my most exciting round was an October anti-clockwise traverse during a remarkable thunder and lightning cloudburst, when several inches of rain fell within hours, new ravines were carved out of the fellsides, and hailstones the size of moth-balls pelted me on Swirl How, and rolled like a white, moving carpet down the slopes.

The round, from and back to Coniston, encompasses about 14 miles and if you go over all the tops, including the outliers, you will have collected 12 by the end of your walk. One autumn traverse, a few years ago, is especially remembered because of the perfect sunny weather and the exceptional distant views. The colours in the Yewdale woods were almost at their best, the bracken on the fells was turning to gold, and bright sunlight was chasing the cloud shadows across the fells. This was a roughly clockwise round; the reverse round is equally enjoyable, but the walk northwards along the ramparts

of Dow Crag, with the bold line of the Scafells straight ahead, is the perfect morning appetiser. You take the Walna Scar road from the village, up the steepish hill above the former railway station, and continue to the head of the pass, past reed-choked Boo Tarn, with the ugly scar of Bursting Stone quarry high up on the right. Not far away to the left is the Banniside Stone Circle, where human bones and fragments of pottery and cloth have been found. And it was near here that two schoolboys photographed what was claimed to be a flying saucer in 1954. I still have a copy of their remarkable untouched photograph.

The rough track to the summit of Walna Scar steepens beyond Cove Bridge, from where there is a first view of the splendid precipice of Dow Crag. As you trudge the zig-zags you might be surprised – or even infuriated – to learn that an MG sports car was once driven over the pass. Turn right at the pass for your first summit, Brown Pike, although a more rewarding route may be taken by following an old quarry track, where the pass veers to the left, that leads to a belvedere just above the black pool of Blind Tarn – blind, because it has no visible outlet. Here you may watch the fish rising before you scramble steeply to the summit cairn.

From Brown Pike, on this remembered autumn day, there was a clear sighting of the Isle of Man, looking almost within swimming distance across the sunlit waters. So clear was the island, I could pick out the sculpturing of Snaefell. To the north-west the highest land in England, the Scafells, was patterned in changing cloud shadows, blue against the sunlit greens and browns, with every detail of the crags, seven miles away, razor-sharp. Due west, the long, wooded length of Dunnerdale reached out to the sea while, further round the horizon, Morecambe could be seen across the bay and, 35 miles away as the raven flies, the unmistakeable flat top of Ingleborough.

After passing over Buck Pike the craggy battlements of Dow Crag – to me, the most familiar part of Lakeland – were traversed. There were climbers on Trident, an old favourite, and on all the buttress climbs – I could see the coloured blobs of their helmets as they crept up the sunlit walls far below

Maps O.S. 1:25,000 Outdoor Leisure Map – The English Lake District S.W; O.S. 1:63,360 Tourist Map of the Lake District; O.S. 1:50,000 Sheet 97. Start and finish at Coniston (ref. 302975).
Grading A fine mountain walk that should give no difficulty in good conditions. Care is needed in mist.
Time 7 hours.
Distance 14 miles.
Escape Routes From Goat's Hause, Levers Hause and Swirl Hause there are easy descents to Coniston. Tracked route from Wetherlam summit to Tilberthwaite.
Telephones Coniston;   Torver   and   Little Langdale.
Transport A regular bus service from Ambleside and Ulverston to Coniston.
Accommodation Hotels, Guest Houses and Bed and Breakfasts in Coniston. Coniston boasts two Youth Hostels, at Coppermines House and Holly How.
Guidebooks *The Southern Fells* by A. Wainwright (The Westmorland Gazette); *The Lakeland Peaks* by W. A. Poucher; *Freeman of the Hills* by A. H. Griffin (Hale).

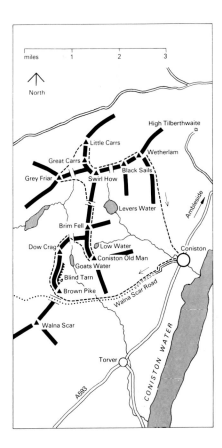

Above: The summit slopes of Coniston Old Man, looking north-west over Grey Friar to the Scafell Group. *Photo: E. A. Shepherd*

and, now and again, hear their voices. Goats Water, 1,000ft. below, looked smooth and dark as an ink blot, and tiny, matchstick figures on the Old Man, across the combe, showed I was not alone on the tops. The summit, reached from the shoulder of Goats Hause, was almost as crowded as Bowness in summer so I left hurriedly for the magnificent upland promenade along Brim Fell and Great How Crags to Swirl How. A more direct route to Swirl How from Goats Hause, avoiding the often overcrowded Old Man, traverses just above the crags of Swarth Brow, high above Seathwaite Tarn, Barrow's reservoir, emerging on the main ridge at Levers Hause. This track, rather difficult to find at first, was worked out many years ago

by an old climbing friend of mine.

From the Brim Fell ridge, the Coppermines Valley looked colourful and attractive in the sunlight, for the old workings and spoil heaps have become accepted features over a lifetime. 25 years ago, a hydro-electric scheme was proposed for this valley, with a reservoir drowning the spoil heaps – the only suggested reservoir scheme I have ever supported – but nothing came of it. Instead, Levers Water has become an important water supply for the High Furness area, with many new scars created. From Great How Crags there was the easy stroll to the outlying fell of Grey Friar – a beautiful little mountain and a beautiful name, with its splendid views of the Scafell range, seen across the gulf of

Above: The summit of Brown Pike, the first peak of the walk, with Dow Crag and Coniston Old Man in the background. *Photo: Bert Jenkins*

Wrynose Bottom. The Scafells now looked shadowed and remote, but the sun still glinted on the sea, while the chimneys of Windscale belched white smoke on the shore – the only sign of man, and a sinister one at that, in the whole, vast landscape.

Little Carrs and Great Carrs came next, and the sight, not far below the crags, of the pitiable remains of a crashed aircraft. The plane narrowly failed to top the ridge, disintegrating on the crags, with part of the wreckage lying where it struck and the remainder tumbling hundreds of feet to the bottom of Broad Slack. Then, on to the fine peak of Swirl How, down the rock staircase of Prison Band to Swirl Hause and the 500ft. ascent, first to Black Sails and, finally, to Wetherlam. Wetherlam, the mountain of a hundred holes, pitted by quarries and mines, is still a very lovely mountain. Nothing of its dereliction can be seen from the summit, and the views, especially of the Brathay countryside, with mountains, woodlands, and sparkling waters in the late sunlight of an October afternoon, were quite perfect. Herdwick sheep quietly grazed among the rocks, and there was not a breath of wind. Coming down the long south ridge, I could just pick out the goose-bield below Great How Crags, and one of the biggest boulders in Lakeland, the Pudding Stone. Down in the pub at Coniston, they were lighting the first fire of the winter. Going easily, the round had taken rather less than six hours.

121

35   Ward's Stone, Forest of Bowland

by Walt Unsworth

Maps O.S. 1:50,000 Sheets 97 and 102. Start and finish at Tarnbrook (ref. 587556).
Grading Easy under good conditions. In mist the route, which under landowner's instructions must be strictly adhered to, could be difficult to follow.
Time 4½ miles.
Distance 11 miles
Escape Routes In emergency the S side of the fells may be descended easily to the road.
Telephones Grizedale Bridge.
Transport Bus from Lancaster to Abbeystead, three miles from Tarnbrook.
Accommodation Inn at Bay Horse. Bed and Breakfast at Dolphinholme. Youth Hostel at Slaidburn.
Guidebooks *Bowland and Pendle Hill* by W. R. Mitchell (Dalesman); *A Bowland Sketchbook* by A. Wainwright (Westmorland Gazette).

Opposite page:

Top: The track from Tarnbrook to the Ward's Stone plateau.

Centre left: At the summit of Ward's Stone.

Centre right: The view to the Trough of Bowland from Tarnbrook Fell.

Bottom: Approaching Clougha Pike across Hare Appletree Fell.
Photos: John Gillham

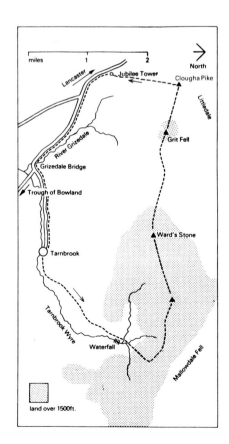

land over 1500ft.

A driver travelling north along the M6 notices that the hills begin to crowd in on his right shoulder as he approaches Lancaster. They are bold and bald, yet not without shape, and obviously hills of some consequence. They are in fact the Bowland Fells; the western edge of the ancient Forest of Bowland, 310 square miles of wilderness and one of the last wild regions of England.

Bowland has always been a secret place, curiously difficult of access despite its nearness to Lancashire's teeming cities. There are no large villages, no obvious tourist attractions, and most of the high fells – some 62 square miles – are kept strictly private and not available to the likes of you and me. The sad fact is, you will see more 'Keep Out' notices in Bowland than in any comparable area of Britain. It took 16 years of frustrating negotiation to create the limited access areas around Fair Snape Fell in the south of the region, and Clougha Pike in the north. These, and a few well-defined linear access routes, are all that the walker has won from this grouse-dominated wilderness. Apart from the access routes, a walker needs to be one, to quote Sean Jennett, 'who can march on undaunted by conscience or the fear of dire consequences'.* Ironically, the keepering of these moors has preserved them marvellously. No worn tracks here, no litter – this is what the Lakes must have been like 50 years ago!

The most interesting part of this wilderness is the great horseshoe of fells which encompasses Wyresdale – a tough and mainly private (restricted) route of some 18 miles from Parlick (1,416ft.) in the south to Grit Fell (1,531ft.) in the north, crossing *en route* the famous Trough of Bowland, the pass and road by which the Lancashire witches were transported to their fate in Lancaster Castle in 1612. Highest of these fells is Ward's Stone (1,836ft.), on the northern arm of the horseshoe. It is a walk for a clear day because the final panorama is quite outstanding.

The starting point for the walk is the hamlet of Tarnbrook, reached by a very narrow lane along the upper reaches of the Wyre. An obvious gate gives access onto Tarnbrook Fell, where a very good track makes a fairly gradual ascent to a small but picturesque waterfall (612 576). From here, the trick is to reach the watershed, and the way ahead looks bleak and daunting. Gradually the track peters out and is replaced by waymarks, usually wooden poles but sometimes painted rocks, the purpose of which is not so much to help the walker as to keep him on the straight and narrow, and prevent him wandering onto the grouse moors. Grouse whirr up by your feet occasionally, but a greater impact is made on the senses by the incredible flocks of seagulls – thousands of them everywhere, raucous and menacing, like a scene from Hitchcock's film, *The Birds*.

A stone wall guides you along the watershed, then there is a gap, and another stone wall. The going is fairly rough at this point, and the turn off from the second wall not at all obvious in bad weather. On a clear day, however, the cluster of rocks marking Ward's Stone can be seen on the skyline, and as you approach them the going underfoot changes from peat to hidden boulders of the ankle-twisting, catch-you-out variety. The rocks prove to be the first summit: the second, and higher one is half a mile further.

What an incredible view there is from Ward's Stone! Near at hand the wastelands of Bowland are laid out in their stark simplicity and beyond them tower Ingleborough and the Pennines. To the north-west are the blue remembered hills of Lakeland, but perhaps the most startling revelation is the nearness of Morecambe Bay, laid out maplike at your feet. It is a view of contrasts, exhilarating, unique.

From the summit rocks, plunge down westwards into a shallow bowl, thickly grown with heather, separating Ward's Stone from Grit Fell (1,531ft.). It is possible to quit the plateau at this point and descend to the road at Jubilee Tower (542 573) from where narrow lanes lead back to Tarnbrook. A better alternative is to continue along the ridge to the northern outlier, Clougha Pike, whose rocky flanks are a pleasant contrast to the more gentle contours of its neighbours.

A well-defined path southward from the summit sets the direction for the track across Hare Appletree Fell to the Jubilee Tower.

*Editor's note: It is perhaps worth noting that trespass is not a criminal offence, so long as no damage is caused, but a civil wrong. The aggrieved party, therefore, (in this case the landowners are the Duke of Westminster and the North West Water Board) cannot involve the police, and can only bring a civil action against the trespasser.

36   Snaefell and the Manx Hills

by Michael Hoy and Tim Wilson

Maps O.S. 1:50,000 Sheet 95. Start from the Hibernian (ref. 459912). Finish at Port Erin (ref. 196691).
Grading A long but easy walk, mainly over grassy or heather-clad hills.
Time 14 hours.
Distance 27 miles.
Escape Routes Numerous. The route is never more than 2 miles from a road.
Telephones St. John's; Port Erin.
Transport The Hibernian is served by the regular Douglas to Ramsey bus and (May to Sept only) by electric tram to Ballaglass Glen. Port Erin is connected to Castletown and Douglas by regular bus service and (May to Sept) by railway.
Accommodation Hotels, Guest Houses and Bed and Breakfast establishments abound. Youth Hostel at Laxey.
Guidebooks *Manx Hill Walks* (Manx Conservation Council); *A Fell Walking and Climbing Guide to the Isle of Man* by the Manx Fell and Rock Club (Cade); *The Naturalist in the Isle of Man* by L. S. Garrad (David and Charles).

This spectacular walk follows the Isle of Man's natural spine of old slate hills. In the north, rounded summits rise above rolling moorland cut by steep-sided valleys and wooded glens leading out to the coast, while south of the Neb, the narrowing escarpment offers an unrivalled ridge walk high above the sea. Gentle gradients, grass and heather underfoot, and few walls and fences, make this ideal walking country, largely undiscovered, and you will share the hills with wandering sheep, the curlew, and the mountain hare, but avoid the TT and Grand Prix race weeks, when the northern uplands echo to the whine of motor cycles.

The walk starts at the Hibernian, and follows the Gooseneck lane to Ballagilley, where a gated field leads onto the shoulder of North Barrule. A sharp climb threads up through rocky outcrops, easing to a gentler gradient towards the summit OS pillar at 1,854ft. the second highest on the Island. A clear path, with stiles over sheep-walls, leads south-west along the grassy ridge, edged on the left by an abrupt fall into Corrany valley, while the gentler western slope gives way to the wide fells of Lezayre and Michael. The traverse rides over two intermediate cairned heights before reaching Clagh Ouyr, where the ridge falls easily to the col at Black Hut.

Compared with the ascent of North Barrule, the walk up Snaefell (2,036ft.) is unspectacular, but there is a fine view down the Laxey Valley, once the Island's most productive mining area, and the site of *Lady Isabella*, the largest water-wheel in Europe. Shortly before the summit, you will cross the electric tramway, a unique survival from Victorian days which in summer offers easy access from Laxey. A much-worn path leads down to the Bungalow. At Brandywell, the highest point on the TT course, strike west up Beinn-y-Phott. From this cairned hill the route falls to cross a tussocky heath, with Carraghan rising to the left, and converges

with the B10 at a cattle grid. Bear left on to the track leading down towards Injebreck reservoir, but after 300 yards strike west over heather-clad Injebreck Hill to the B22.

The next challenge is Colden, a featureless dome which only comes to life when the heather blooms. Aim west above the small plantation to a shallow, damp col. A slow climb through deep heather now leads up to the cairn on Colden. From here, the route southwards crosses one of the bleakest parts of the Manx uplands. Over the Bishop's Way, in the windy gap below Lhargee Ruy, the patchy grass fails and splintered slate litters the dreary peat. It is a relief to return

Left: The Manx Hills from near Douglas. The mountains in view are Slieau Ruy, Colden, Carraghan, Beinn-y-Phott, and Snaefell on the extreme right. *Photo: Picturefolio, Isle of Man*

Top: North Barrule from the south. The walker sits on distinctive black slate rocks of the Manx Hills. *Photo: Michael Hoy*

Bottom: The tramway on Snaefell, looking towards North Barrule. *Photo: Steve Poulton*

Below: 'Lady Isabella' near Laxey, which is reputed to be the largest water wheel in Europe.
Photo: Picturefolio, Isle of Man

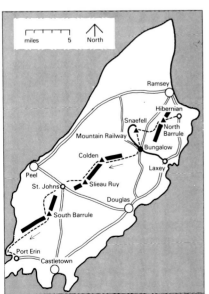

place of the Vikings. Opposite the gate of Tynwald Hill, in the roadside wall, is one of the Island's many Bronze Age burial cists.

The southern part of the walk starts up Gleneedle lane, where Slieau Whallian rises abruptly, less forbidding today in its plantation cover than when it was the traditional site of witchcraft trials by ordeal. At the end of the plantation, bear right up the track, and then strike straight for the ridge, which opens up new views of Peel and the Island's west coast. The ground cover deteriorates here, and it is an awkward walk along the ridge through gorse clumps to reach the lane at Arrasy, which leads onto a desolate waste known locally as Snuff-the-Wind, where a tall chimney and winding house, relics of the Island's mining past, loom over the ore-stained slag. Across the main road, a gentle walk through springy heather rises to the summit of South Barrule, at 1,586ft. the highest point in the south of the Island. Just before the OS pillar you pass over a low mound which encircles the hill-top, the remains of an Iron Age hill fort.

From South Barrule, descend by the well-marked path to Round Table cross-roads, contour south-west across the heath, and then take the wide track from the A36 up onto Cronk ny Arrey Laa, the Hill of the Day Watch. A few yards beyond the OS pillar the summit is marked by a large early Bronze Age burial cairn.

The remaining five miles of the route follow closely the Island's west coast. From Cronk ny Arrey Laa, keep well up on the seaward edge of the escarpment for the best views. After half a mile the shoulder swings close to the sea, and steep, grassy cliffs plunge 1,000ft. to the rocky shore. A rocky bluff falls to the Sloc gap, with its cluster of ancient hut circles, followed by a quick rise onto the plateau of Lhiattee ny Beinnee. The shoulder now drops towards Fleshwick, eventually skirting walled fields to dive down a steep *broogh* to the cove. The final challenge is Bradda Hill. From the tower on Bradda Head, descend to the well-made-up path which leads through the fuchsia and pine of Bradda Glen to Port Erin.

to heather again as you leave Slieau Ruy, where mountain hares abound and sheep burrow through the tussocks. Descend from the ridge in a sweeping curve westwards, skirting Beary Mountain to reach Dowse, an ancient meeting-point of high moorland paths. Here an old drovers' track winds between dry slate walls and eventually falls through tangled gorse to reach the Neb valley at Ballig. Follow the lane, past Tynwald Mills, now a centre for traditional Manx crafts, into St. John's. St. John's, which offers a convenient break in the route, is the historic centre of the Island. The stepped grass mound adjacent to the church is Tynwald Hill, symbol of 1,000 years of parliamentary government, where each year on July 5 a colourful open-air assembly of the Manx Parliament is held, at the meeting

37   Great Whernside and Buckden Pike

by Richard Gilbert

From my home village in the Howardian Hills, north of York, the view west is filled by the massive bulk of the Pennines. On many a winter morning, whilst driving to work, my spirits have been lifted by the sight of Penhill and Great Whernside sparkling white with snow. Great Whernside, a long whale-back rising high above Pateley Bridge in Nidderdale, dominates the eastern Pennines. It is a fell neglected by the hordes, yet it can offer a day which combines vigorous exercise with the charms of the Yorkshire Dales.

The obvious delights of the Dales, which bring tourists flocking in thousands, are the grey stone houses and barns in an upland setting, with green pastures, well-groomed sheep, drystone walls, and clear rivers. The startlingly white Carboniferous limestone which thrusts out of the hillsides, forming escarpments and boulder fields, not only provides the unique flavour of the Dales' scene, but also increases the alkalinity of the soil, encouraging good grasslands and grazing. The hill-walker experiences an abrupt change of landscape as he climbs out of the dales and up the fells. At about the 1,200ft. level the limestone is overlaid by gritstone and impervious clays, thus the high ground becomes acid and waterlogged and coarse grass, peat, and bilberry predominate.

My selected walk is in the heart of the Dales, in Upper Wharfedale, where the characteristic features I have just described are well exemplified. You start from the hamlet of Conistone, three miles up Wharfedale from Grassington. Across the dale is the huge, overhanging Kilnsey Crag, which was

Maps O.S. 1:50,000 Sheet 98. Start from Conistone (ref. 982675). Finish at Buckden (ref. 942772).
Grading A mainly easy walk over high fells. Certain stretches have coarse tussocky grass, others can be boggy.
Time 6–7 hours.
Distance 15 miles.
Escape Routes The route crosses the Kettlewell–Coverdale road, otherwise the fells may be descended easily in almost any direction.
Telephones Conistone; Kettlewell; Cray; Buckden.
Transport Buckden–Kettlewell–Kilnsey–Grassington–Skipton bus service daily (except Mon).
Accommodation Hotels at Buckden, Kettlewell, Kilnsey and Grassington. Bed and Breakfasts locally. Youth Hostels at Aysgarth, Kettlewell, Linton and Malham.
Guidebooks *The Yorkshire Dales* by Geoffrey Wright (David and Charles); *Exploring the Yorkshire Dales* by Edward Gower (Dalesman).

Above: Looking down Buckden Beck from the slopes of Buckden Pike. *Photo: E. A. Shepherd*

scoured out by glacial ice. Its great overhang was ascended by climbers, using artificial aids, as long ago as 1957.

You take the narrow lane past Conistone church and then branch right up a Land-Rover track, which serves a new TV booster aerial, not marked on the map. The track continues for three miles up Mossdale, a wide and open valley leading into the heart of Great Whernside. The gentle limestone landscape is left behind and you enter the world of cotton grass and curlews, skylarks, peewits, rabbits, and old mine workings. As you enjoy this lonely scene, reflect that you are barely an hour's drive from the conurbations of Leeds and Bradford.

Just before you reach the uninhabited stone house at Mossdale-head, ford the beck and strike up through some old spoil heaps to the broad south-east ridge of Great Whernside. Watch out for some severely eroded gullies, some 30ft. deep with steep sides like elephant traps. The high ridge is trackless, and you must fight your way across the peat hags and through the heather and bilberry. A boundary fence is your guide, a rather unsightly but inevitable alternative to the standing gritstones of the nineteenth century. Set in the peat at regular intervals, these weathered and rounded stones are entirely in keeping with the environment. Several are engraved WH 1863.

The three miles to Great Whernside's summit are, for me, the finest of the walk. It

is certainly the toughest and roughest section, but it is a walk in the best traditions of British fell country. Open views, expansive skies, coarse moorland, the croaking of grouse and calling of plovers, and a stiff breeze in your hair. It is a walk reminiscent of the high Cheviots or the hills of Peebles. Approaching the summit plateau, the view east suddenly unfolds and below lie the reservoirs of Nidderdale. Pieces of crashed aeroplane litter the ground, and various struts and spars have been incorporated into the boundary fence. Finally you surmount a low gritstone outcrop and the huge pile of stones marking the summit of Great Whernside at 2,310ft. can be seen ahead. This vast cairn dwarfs the OS pillar.

The plateau is bleak and inhospitable so, without lingering, walk on another half-mile to the northern top and then drop down the western slopes. You will soon pick up a good path, leading to the road between Wharfedale and Coverdale, at a line of Iron Age fortifications. Buckden Pike, which rises ahead to 2,302ft., is altogether a much easier proposition than Great Whernside. The peat is better-drained, the grass is less coarse, and there is a path of sorts beside a stone wall to aid navigation. High up on the summit ridge you pass a white stone cross, erected in memory of five Polish airmen who perished here in a crash in January 1942. Pieces of wreckage from their Wellington bomber still protrude through the peat.

It is a gentle descent down into Wharfedale, and you will welcome the re-emergence of the limestone. Make for the village of Cray and, as you approach the road, look out for a well-signed footpath which leads you round the hillside, down through the leafy Rakes Wood, and into Buckden village.

My last walk over Buckden Pike was on a perfect day in high summer. It was 1981, the year of appalling spring blizzards, and on the slopes of the Pike I commiserated with a hill farmer who was loading onto a trailer the carcasses of ewes killed by the storms ten weeks previously. From the summit ridge I descended the green hillsides, close-cropped by fell-ponies, their foals, and Jacob's sheep. The ground was a kaleidoscope of colour, with tormentil, thyme, and heath bedstraw. In the meadows above the river, the hay had been cut and an old woman with a pitchfork was turning it over to dry in the hot sun. Another colourful scene met me on the Buckden village green. A party of Swedish students, in national costume, were folk-dancing to a small band. I sat on the grass and watched for a few minutes before crossing the road to the Buck Inn for a large pot of tea and a plate of home-made scones with cream and strawberry jam. Here, in the peace of Upper Wharfedale, life seemed unreal and, heightened perhaps by the contrast with the bleak fell tops, I wallowed in nostalgia.

Top left: On the boulder-strewn summit plateau of Great Whernside. *Photo: Gordon Gadsby*

Bottom left: The jutting profile of Kilnsey Crag. *Photo: E. A. Shepherd*

Above: Buckden Pike from the west. *Photo: Bertram Unne (Courtesy of North Yorkshire County Library)*

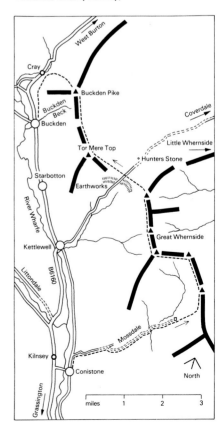

Two photographs illustrating the following chapter

Left: The spectacular cleft of Gordale Scar.
Photo: E. A. Shepherd

Right: Malham Cove, an impressive 300ft. wall of sheer limestone. The River Aire once poured over it, but now finds a subterranean course through limestone bedding planes to emerge at the foot of the cliff.
Photo: E. A. Shepherd

38   Malham Cove and Gordale Scar – a Botanists Paradise

by Oliver Gilbert

Maps O.S. 1:50,000 Sheet 98; O.S. 1:25,000 Outdoor Leisure Map – Malham and Upper Wharfedale. Start and finish at the National Park Information Centre (ref. 900628).
Grading An easy walk through spectacular limestone scenery. The scramble through Gordale could be tricky in wet weather when the beck is in spate.
Time 5 hours.
Distance 7 miles.
Escape Routes Numerous.
Telephones Malham village.
Transport Regular bus service between Skipton, Gargrave and Malham (Pennine Motors). Railway Stations at Settle, Skipton and Gargrave.
Accommodation Hotels and Bed and Breakfasts in Malham. Youth Hostels in Malham, Linton and Kettlewell.
Guidebooks *Walks in Limestone Country* by A. Wainwright (The Westmorland Gazette); *Malham and Malham Moor* by A. Raistrick (Dalesman); *Malham, A Practical Guide* (Dalesman).

You will have to choose whether to do this extremely popular walk out of season, when the landscape is reasonably free from people, or in summer, when the flowers are at their best. My personal choice is for spring, when the combination of white limestone, green grass, blue sky, lambs, and a show of early flowers is hard to beat. Though not a long expedition, it should be allotted a full day, as so many dramatic and compelling features will be encountered.

The walk starts in Malham village, where there is a large car-park and information centre. At the south end of the village, you cross the beck by a footbridge next to the smithy and follow the path downstream through hay meadows. After a quarter of a mile, turn left by a fine stone barn; way-marking, signposts, and footpath-surfacing will ensure that you do not miss the route. After a while, the path traverses a limestone gorge containing sycamore woodland with an abundance of spring flowers, including luxuriant growths of white-flowered ramsons; the garlicky smell of its bruised leaves often fills the air, and its triangular stems are edible. The head of this small gorge is closed by a waterfall, Janet's Foss, which flows down a moss-covered tufa screen; a more delightful spot is difficult to imagine. It is no wonder that earlier generations believed fairies lived here.

Passing to the left of the fall, a metalled road is reached, and followed for 100 yards before turning left again to follow the beck across the fields to Gordale Scar. Geographers are still arguing as to how this incomparable piece of limestone scenery came into existence but it is almost certainly not a collapsed cavern. From near the entrance, look up to see the yew trees clinging to the cliff face, appearing magnificently dark against the white limestone. Cliffs are one of their few natural habitats in Britain. Curiously, there are no yews on the precipice of Malham Cove only a mile away; instead, it supports many fine examples of the delicate, silvery-leaved, rock whitebeam, a rather rare tree almost wholly confined to limestone crags. Continuing into the gorge, which has an almost cathedral-like quality, a corner is rounded and you are confronted with a 30ft. waterfall which has to

be climbed. This is usually little more than a scramble, calling for only moderate agility, but if the beck is swollen you could be in for a drenching, or even turned back. Plans to construct a staircase up the fall could deprive many of an unforgettable experience. At the top of the fall, a scree gully on the left is ascended, and it eventually leads to the plateau. The path, now level, follows a shallow valley flanked by limestone pavement. These large areas of bare limestone, criss-crossed by deep fissures (grykes), are a botanist's paradise, as the surface of the pavement carries areas of fescue turf containing countless wild flowers such as violets, birdsfoot-trefoil, thyme, bed-straws and fairy flax. In the grykes, protected from both sun and grazing, a surprising mixture of woodland and cliff-face species exist, including wood sorrel, dog's mercury, herb robert, and at least a dozen ferns. Also, if you are lucky, the northern speciality baneberry can be found.

The next two miles across the plateau enjoy wide views. After climbing a stile in the drystone wall at Street Gate, on the ancient drove road of Mastiles Lane, there is a choice of routes to Malham Tarn, which appears suddenly on your left. The public has access to 300 yards of shore-line near the outflow; after stormy weather a wide variety of pond-weeds can be found washed up here. It is a privilege to visit this spot, which not long ago was described by an eminent ecologist as 'one of the most important sites for nature conservation in Europe'. The area is managed as a nature reserve by the Field Studies Council, who occupy the impressive house on the far shore. Skin divers have reported that the tarn is fed mainly by springs which well up in the middle. Behind it, the dark ridge of Fountains Fell rises to 2,000ft., completing a dramatic scene.

The outflow stream is followed, crossed where it flows under a road, then followed again till it disappears underground at a spot called Water Sinks. A patch of lead-contaminated ground near here provides, in June, a fine show of spring sandwort. Continue down the dry valley, which the stream still occupies briefly in exceptionally wet weather, making a detour right to avoid a dry waterfall at Comb Scar. This cliff, which is

inaccessible to grazing animals, carries open woodland, demonstrating that formerly all the limestone hills were covered by trees or scrub. The continuation of the dry valley below Comb Scar is straight as it follows a fault line to the Cove. This 360ft. high limestone amphitheatre, over which the stream once tumbled, holds a botanical mystery. In the 1860s, several well known botanists claimed to have discovered the rare hoary rock-rose on ledges near the top, adding that 'reaching it was risky for all but the cool-headed'. However, despite a number of daring searches, the plant still eludes the modern generation.

The popularity of the Cove is such that path construction has taken place to prevent erosion of the slopes. You will probably want to spend at least an hour in this spectacular spot. On clear days the view from the top includes Pendle Hill in Lancashire. It is well worth visiting the bottom, to see the young River Aire welling up from the base of the cliff, and to admire the tall blue flowers of Jacob's ladder, which clothe the scree slope on the east-side. Though abundant here, it is rare nationally, so should not be picked or trampled. It is over 300 years since John Ray, the 'father of British botany', discovered it here. You can afford to linger in this beautiful spot, as there are only a few fields to cross before the village is reached.

39   Wharfedale—a Taste of the Dales Way

by Colin Speakman

Maps O.S. 1:50,000 Sheets 98 and 104; O.S. 1:25,000 Outdoor Leisure Map – Malham and Upper Wharfedale (covers the northern section of the walk). Start from Ilkley (ref. 110482). Finish at Kettlewell (ref. 972723).
Grading An easy riverside walk, mainly on footpaths.
Time 8–9 hours.
Distance 24 miles.
Escape Routes Numerous. The walk can conveniently be terminated at Grassington after 17 miles.
Telephones Ilkley; Bolton Bridge; Gamsworth; Appletreewick; Burnsall; Grassington; Kilnsey; Kettlewell.
Transport Excellent rail and bus services from Leeds to Ilkley. Kettlewell–Ilkley and Kettlewell–Skipton bus services. Bargain *Dalesrider* or *Parklink* tickets available from many Yorkshire towns as far as Kettlewell.
Accommodation Hotels, Inns and Bed and Breakfasts at Ilkley, Grassington and Kettlewell. Youth Hostels at Kettlewell and Linton.
Guidebooks *The Dales Way* by C. Speakman (Dalesman); *Across Northern Hills* by Geoffrey Berry (Westmorland Gazette); *The Peak and Pennines* by W. A. Poucher (Constable); *Yorkshire the Dales* by M. Colbeck (Batsford).

Only just beyond the boundary of West Yorkshire, near the great conurbations of Leeds and Bradford and not too far from the smoke of industrial Lancashire, lies Wharfedale, perhaps the most majestic and romantic of the Yorkshire Dales. Wharfedale is astonishing for the quality of its landscape, from high gritstone outcrops and heather moorland to limestone crags, woodlands and meadows, and an almost infinite choice of walks along a network of interlinking paths. Little wonder that Wharfedale has been known, loved, and walked by generations of ramblers.

The focal point of Wharfedale is the Wharfe itself, mysterious, beautiful, dramatic, and there can be no better introduction to the Dales than to take the riverside path up the Wharfe into the heartland of the National Park. The official start of the Dales Way is at the seventeenth-century Ilkley Bridge, which is easily reached upstream from the riverside park. The track leads past allotments and sports grounds and crosses low fields and the old road to Addingham. It continues through the old mill and its cottages to Addingham Church, and along the river to Addingham High Mill, followed by a superb piece of riverside path, overlooked by the huge dome of Beamsley. By now it is clear why they say the Wharfe is the most beautiful river in England.

A half-mile of unpleasant road walking can be avoided by tracing the path past Lobwood House Farm and descending into Lob Wood, passing under a viaduct, before meeting a riverside path to Bolton Bridge. Once across the A59, the path enters the Yorkshire Dales National Park and swings around a gentle bend to Bolton Priory, the most sublime of riverside abbeys, beloved by Turner and Ruskin, Wordsworth and Landseer. Cross the wooden bridge and enter Bolton Woods, the high-level path giving superb views back across to the Priory, and forward through a landscape of unsurpassed beauty. Ford the beck, and keep beside the river to the Cavendish Pavilion, an oasis of tea, snacks, and ham and eggs at almost any time of the year.

The Dales Way follows the east side of the river, back across the wooden bridge, but if you have never walked through Strid Woods, enter the Nature Trail (small charge payable), and pick the high-level route, with majestic and romantic views down the wooded gorge. The Strid itself, reached by whatever path you follow, is a deeply-incised gorge, little over six feet wide at its narrowest point, carrying the full weight of the River Wharfe, its name a grisly reminder of the many people who have leapt to their death trying to cross the narrow gap.

Beyond the Strid the river opens out into a broad, pastoral landscape, soon reaching Barden Bridge, an elegant seventeenth-century structure. Immediately above the bridge is the half-ruined Barden Tower, a former hunting lodge and home of the legendary Shepherd Lord, the fifteenth-century scholar and soldier who, as a child, was brought up amongst Cumberland shepherds to escape detection by his father's political opponents. Beyond Barden, the Dales Way hugs the riverside meadows to Howgill, skirting the white, foaming rapids behind Appletreewick village, and passes under the shadow of the curious limestone reef-knolls, (river-washed tree-roots), before turning, at Woodhouse Farm, to Burnsall.

Burnsall, in a bowl of dark fells, has one of the finest settings of any village in England. This is the real limestone country, and beyond Loup Scar, and the little swing bridge at Hebden which was made by the village blacksmith, you saunter by tall chestnut trees, the river clear and limpid, trout flicking the surface. Linton Church, Craven's ancient place of worship, can be seen across the river just before you reach Linton Falls and Tin Bridge. A narrow, enclosed path, right, takes you to Grassington, a charming village surrounding a cobbled square, with shops, cafes, a bus station and no less than three pubs.

You can, of course, end your walk here, but the extra distance to Kettlewell offers a fitting climax. High-level walking now, from Grassington Town Head, up beyond the Iron Age fields and ancient woods, to those high, limestone pastures, picking your way with care onto the rocky terraces and finding the stiles in the drystone walls. Above Conistone, and the crag known as Conistone

land over 1000ft.   miles 1   2   3

Pie, the path follows a superb limestone terrace with panoramic views along the whole length of Wharfedale, across to Old Cote Moor and Kilnsey Crag, and down into Littondale. Great Whernside sweeps up behind you. A track to the side of Scar Gill brings you to the lane, and a riverside path into Kettlewell. And once again shops, cafes, pubs and a variety of accommodation tempt you away from that last bus down the valley.

Above: Wharfedale below the village of Burnsall.
Photo: Geoffrey Wright

Right: The Strid – the narrow defile that funnels the River Wharfe near Bolton Abbey. Although, at its narrowest point, only some six feet wide, to jump the gap is much more difficult than it appears, the gritstone being slippery and deeply undercut below the surface of the water, and one side higher than the other. The most recent of the many drownings here occurred in 1980. The cataract also featured in Wordsworth's fatalistic poem, 'The Force of Prayer'.
Photo: English Countryside Ltd.

40   Black Hambleton by the Drove Road

by Richard Gilbert

Maps O.S. 1:63,360 Tourist Map The North York Moors; O.S. 1:50,000 Sheet 100. Start from White Horse car park Kilburn (ref. 515812). Finish at Osmotherley (ref. 456973).
Grading An easy walk along a good path but the route follows a high moorland escarpment which is exposed to the elements.
Time 5–6 hours.
Distance 14 miles.
Escape Routes Numerous. Metalled roads cross the route at Sutton Bank, Sneck Yate Bank, Kepwick and Oak Dale.
Telephones Sutton Bank; Osmotherley and (in emergency) at the farms which nestle below the woods on the west facing flanks of the moors.
Transport The regular (United) bus service between Ripon and Scarborough passes through Kilburn. Osmotherley is on the Northallerton–Teesside route (United) and on the long distance Liverpool, Manchester, Leeds to Middlesbrough route.
Accommodation Hotels and Bed and Breakfasts in Kilburn and Osmotherley. Youth Hostel at Helmsley.
Guidebooks *North York Moors National Park Guide* (H.M.S.O.); *The Cleveland Way* by Alan Falconer published by The Countryside Commission (H.M.S.O.); *Guide to the Cleveland Way* by M. Boyes (Constable); *Walking on the North York Moors* (Dalesman); *Across Northern Hills* by Geoffrey Berry (Westmorland Gazette).

Stand beside the indicator on Sutton Bank, and look west across the Vale of Mowbray to the Pennine Chain. Then turn to the south, and gaze beyond the crumbling yellow limestone of Roulston Scar to the Vale of York, merging into the flatlands of the East Midlands. Looking south from the abrupt escarpment of the Hambleton hills, York Minster is the dominant feature and, on a clear day, Lincoln Cathedral, a pimple on the horizon, has been identified, 75 miles distant as the crow flies. Wordsworth watched the sun go down from this spot on his wedding day, and James Herriot claims the view to be the finest in England.

It is not difficult to imagine the scene 12,000 years ago. The patterned fields, now viewed from our perch, would have been covered with grey rivers of ice, hundreds of feet thick. For two million years, successive ice-ages formed the landscape which we now see. Vast tongues of ice, originating from the Scottish Highlands, the Lake District, and Scandinavia met in the vicinity of the North York Moors, the glaciers scouring out valleys and smoothing the plains. Yet the high ground on which we stand was not covered by the ice. This was the home of the mammoth, bison, woolly rhinoceros, and man.

The west-facing escarpment of the North York Moors extends for 14 miles, and provides us with a walk giving a variety of interest, breathtaking views, and a feeling of absolute freedom and space. Having completed the walk, I hope you will return to explore the area more thoroughly. Close at hand exists a wealth of lovely abbeys, churches, castles, and villages as well as a host of other historical sites and stimuli for the geologist, botanist, and natural historian.

Starting from the car park at the base of the Kilburn White Horse, you climb the steep path on the right to gain the crest of the hill. The White Horse has no great antiquity, being cut in 1857 by the village schoolmaster and helpers at the suggestion of Thomas Taylor. You follow the path which hugs the cliff edge above the crumbling Jurassic limestone of Roulston Scar. The cliffs funnel the west winds into strong up-currents, and you may see gliders soaring above. The airfield on the right is the home of the Yorkshire

Gliding Club. At Sutton Bank find a few minutes to browse in the National Park Information Centre and to inspect their exhibitions. Refreshments are available.

The coach parties and crowds are left behind as soon as you leave Sutton Bank and strike north along the narrow path through the heather. You will find no problems with the route, because it follows the Cleveland Way, with its acorn signs on gates and stiles. In less than a mile, the path skirts the top of Whitestone Cliff, a superb rock face giving steep routes of over 100ft., including The Night Watch, one of the great classic rock climbs of North Yorkshire. Below the rocks is Garbutt Wood Nature Reserve and the mysterious dark lake of Gormire. Gormire is one of only three natural lakes in Yorkshire (the others being Malham Tarn and Semmerwater). It was formed by the blocking of a meltwater channel by a landslip, and is reputed to be bottomless.

We continue north along the west-facing escarpment, our path overlooking wooded and sheltered valleys running up to the high moors. The tiny villages of Sutton, Cowesby, Thirlby, Boltby and Kepwick nestle below, the suffix '-by' is of Danish origin meaning settlement. On my last visit, in mid-May, the gullies of Boltby Scar were still packed with old snow, remnants of a late spring blizzard, yet the grassy platform below the cliffs was carpeted with primroses, cowslips, violets, and forget-me-nots, whilst wild honeysuckle tangled over the rocks. At High Barn (a gaunt ruin) we pass through a copse of twisted and bent trees, deformed by the prevailing westerlies, and emerge onto high open pasture grazed by sheep and fell ponies. This leads to Sneck Yate Bank, where the Boltby road crosses our path.

During this first section of the walk, we have been following a path just west of the Hambleton Drove Road, but one mile beyond Sneck Yate Bank we meet the drove road proper, and follow it for the next five miles. A road over the Hambleton hills has been in existence since time immemorial. It was used by Neolithic and Bronze Age people, by the Romans, and, until the coming of the railways, by cattle drovers from Scotland. The Hambleton road was popular with the Scottish drovers because

Above: The view south to the Vale of York from near the top of Whitestone Cliff on Sutton Bank. *Photo: Bertram Unne (Courtesy of North Yorkshire County Library)*

they thus avoided tolls on the main turnpikes as they drove their large herds of cattle south to be sold at the lucrative Michaelmas and Martinmas fairs at York and Malton. Drovers were accommodated at inns on the high moors: the Chequers, Limekiln House, Dialstone House, and the Hambleton Hotel. The latter, beside the A170 near Sutton Bank, is the only inn still in business. The Chequers Inn is said to have had a peat fire burning for 200 years. The building still stands on Osmotherley Moor, but it is now a farmhouse.

The drove road takes us through forestry plantations above Boltby reservoir, and then out onto bleak, open moorland. This scenery is typical of so much of upland Britain, and it is manna to the fellsman. The smell of damp peat and moss, the cries of the curlew, peewit and plover, the pull of heather and bilberry on the boots, and the sight of clouds racing overhead; these sensations stir memories of countless carefree days.

We cross the rough road leading down to Kepwick, and continue north along the broad track. A drystone wall accompanies us on the left, but on the right the moors roll away to the horizon, with only the occasional shooting butt, boundary stone, or tumulus to interrupt the view. Just before the track drops down steeply to Thimbleby Moor, it is worth making a 200-yard detour through the heather to visit the OS pillar marking the 1,309ft. summit of Black Hambleton. To the north you can see the line of the Cleveland hills, with Urra Moor (1,490ft.) the highest point on the North York Moors. These hills are crossed by the challenging 40 mile Lyke Wake Walk.

Having descended from Black Hambleton by a horribly eroded path, where the peat has been worn away to expose sticky yellow clay, we leave the drove road at the junction with the metalled road from Hawnby. Our path, clearly signposted, branches left and plunges down through the bracken to Oak Dale. It skirts the reservoir, crosses some meadows, and leads us to the peaceful old village of Osmotherley. If you have the time, take a walk around. Admire the stone cottages, and the slab table from which John Wesley preached. Visit the nearby Carthusian Priory of Mount Grace and, as the sun sinks, down a pint at one of the three old inns in the village centre. A fitting end to one of Yorkshire's great walks.

41   The Eastern Edges of the Peak

by Roger Redfern

Maps O.S. 1:50,000 Sheets 110 and 119; O.S. 1:25,000 Outdoor Leisure Map – The Dark Peak (for northern part of route only); O.S. 1:63,360 Tourist Map of the Peak District. Start from Flouch Inn (ref. 197016). Finish at Robin Hood Inn, Baslow (ref. 279721).
Grading A long walk over moorland and gritstone edges, much of it above 1,000ft.
Time 10 hours.
Distance 25 miles.
Escape Routes By Cut Gate path W to Slippery Stones. At Ladybower. From Ringinglow road E to Ringinglow or W to Hathersage. Down Burbage Brook to Padley. W from Curbar Gap to Curbar.
Telephones Flouch Inn; Fox House Inn; Baslow.
Transport Bus from Barnsley and Huddersfield to Flouch Inn. Bus service between Bakewell, Baslow and Chesterfield. Railway Station at Matlock.
Accommodation Hotel at Baslow. Hotels and Guest Houses at Bakewell and Matlock (4 miles S.E. of Rowsley). Youth Hostels at Langsett, Hathersage, Eyam and Bakewell.
Guidebooks High Peak by Byne and Sutton (Secker and Warburg 1966); Peakland Days by R. A. Redfern (Hale 1965); The Peak and Pennines by W. A. Poucher (Constable); The Peak District Companion by Rex Bellamy (David and Charles); Freedom to Roam by Howard Hill (Moorland Publishing Co.).

The king of ramblers, G. H. B. Ward, described the Flouch Inn as 'formerly a dingy-looking public house, but now of clean appearance and sinned against by advertisements'.* This convenient hostelry stands at almost 950ft. above sea level, three miles west of Penistone, on a busy crossroads where the Sheffield–Manchester road enters the bleak moorlands of the Woodhead district. It makes a convenient starting point for this route, which follows the crest of the gritstone escarpment east of the Derwent Valley to the sheltered village of Baslow, near Chatsworth Park. Much of the walk follows a level course well above 1,000ft., and attains 1,793ft. at Margery Hill, first summit of the day, four miles south of the Flouch Inn.

The footpath leaves the Manchester trunk road and descends along the western edge of a coniferous plantation, crosses the Porter or Little Don River on Brook House Bridge, and ascends gently along the side of Hingcliff Hill (1,151ft.). This is an area of ancient farms, long-deserted since the large reservoirs were built downstream. The path slants upwards, high above the deep, landslip ravine of Mickleden Clough, and a mile further reaches the watershed at over 1,700ft. Until the beginning of the century this track –the Cut Gate track–was kept in good repair so that farmers from the upper Derwent and Ashop valleys could ride to Penistone market. It is now a derelict, but still obvious, route; here on the ridge-top is a sudden broad view westwards across Bleaklow, as wild a prospect as any in England.

Leaving the Cut Gate, we turn to the south and soon reach the OS pillar on Margery Hill. Besides being the highest point of this walk, it is the highest summit in South Yorkshire. In early summer the moorlands here are decorated with blooms of the beautiful cloudberry, and a little later, acres of the nodding heads of cotton grass enliven the scene. A mile beyond Margery Hill, the ill-defined top of Featherbed Moss is crossed; tussocky terrain which is often boggy and always tiresome. To avoid a steep drop into the Abbey Brook clough it is advisable to swing round to the east now, aiming for the remains of the old shooting cabins in Sheepfold Clough, near the head of Abbey Brook.

*In the 1939 edition of *Across the Derbyshire Moors*.

A steady ascent over bogland soon brings us to the conspicuous, tor-topped Back Tor (1,765ft.). To the south, Derwent Edge sweeps away above the wooded declivities of Derwent Dale, now dammed and a reservoir.

Rights of way to the south of Dovestone Tor are disputed, so it is best to follow the route suggested in Chapter 40 of *The Big Walks* – south-eastwards across featureless Strines Edge to the Strines road at spot height 1,161, then along it to the A57 and east for half a mile before striking southwards again, aiming for Stanage Edge. The

Above: Looking north from the Salt Cellar on Derwent Edge, past Dovestone Tor to Back Tor. The challenge set out by wind-eroded features such as the Salt Cellar, so common on the gritstone moors and edges, has led many young hill-walkers into the sport of rock-climbing. The ascent of this rounded, bulging rock is by no means easy. *Photo: Roger Redfern*

going on top of this famous gritstone escarpment is easy and obvious. The weathered rocks make a fine foreground for photographs of the chequerboard lowlands of the Derwent Valley, far below. Halfway along the Stanage crest, we cross the route of the ancient packhorse trail between the Derwent and Don valleys. In the eighteenth century it was paved, and used to convey the millstones from quarries on Stanage to the new factories in Sheffield. Many of the unused millstones still lie in the bracken at the foot of the escarpment.

Crossing the Ringinglow–Hathersage road at 1,320ft. marks the halfway distance, but the hardest terrain is behind. Now the route follows the crest of Burbage Edge, high above Burbage Brook, 'a stream near a fortification'. The fortification here being the prehistoric Carl Wark, seen here beyond the brook and well described as 'a natural fortress improved by art'. Its larger brother-plateau is Higgar Tor, seen on the right of Carl Wark from Burbage Edge.

A short walk up the Sheffield road (A625), then right along the Grindleford road

Above: Looking north along Stanage Edge to High Neb in the distance. *Photo: Ken Wilson*

(B6521) for 100 yards, brings you to the drive to Longshaw Lodge, a former seat of the Dukes of Rutland. Easy going now leads to the B6054 which is followed, past the Grouse Inn, until a track on the left leads off to Froggatt Edge. This is the next great gritstone escarpment, best known for classic post-war routes like Valkyrie and Brown's Eliminate. Continue along its level crest where the walking is easy. In less than a mile Froggatt Edge becomes Curbar Edge, which dominates the woodlands and pasture fields above Curbar and Calver. Crossing the little col at Curbar Gap, where the lane plunges towards the Derwent, we reach Baslow Edge. The track here lies back a little from the brink and passes the conspicuous tor called the Eagle Stone, where Baslow lads used to prove their manhood by climbing to its flat top. Ahead is Wellington's Monu-

ment, from whence there is a clear view to the south over Chatsworth Park.

Turning eastwards, so as to maintain height, we soon reach the crossroads at the confluence of the Bar Brook and Blake Brook, and climb the stile due south again, aiming for the OS pillar at 1,014ft. on Birchen Edge. Here stands Nelson's Monument, long since devoid of its topmost gritstone ball. Close by are the Battleship Boulders, each with its carved name. In another half-mile we get down across the moor to the Robin Hood Inn. The pretty village of Baslow, at the edge of Chatsworth Park, is only one and a half miles away, down the A619 road to the west of the Robin Hood. There are bus services to Chesterfield and Bakewell from the Robin Hood, and to Sheffield and Bakewell from Baslow.

140

42   The Round of Kinder Scout from Edale

by Roger Redfern

The majority of walkers leave Edale village by way of Grindsbrook, along the Pennine Way highway. Another path, though, winds up the steep, smooth slope of Grindslow Knoll to enter the boundary of open country at the 1,200ft. contour. In winter conditions this hillside is probably the most popular ski slope in the Peak District.

Once upon the conical summit of Grindslow Knoll (1,850ft.), the levels of the Kinder Scout plateau dominate the horizon to east, west, and north. It is a brown, grey, and black plain in winter, often under a glowering cover of dark cloud. Sometimes, though, the winter sky smiles and the sharp outline of the white-crusted surface is highlighted against the pale and frosty firmament. In early summer, too, this upland and its steep perimeter edges come alive with colour, as bilberry, cloudberry, and heather brighten the 'islands' between chocolate groughs of peat.

From Grindslow Knoll's top, the Pennine Way highway can be seen coming up the rocky cleft of Grindsbrook Clough, immediately to the north. Our route, however, lies to the north-west, joining the highway near the head of Crowden Clough. Dominating this steep-sided tributary valley is the gritstone outcrop of Crowden Tower, the next objective, at 2,000ft. That jumbled, tor-dotted area immediately to the south-west of Crowden Tower is called 'Wool Packs' on large-scale OS maps but it is better known as 'The Mushroom Garden' or 'Whipsnade'. In misty weather, the gritstone tors here take on the countenance of wild animals. It is a unique corner of High Peakland. Our route now proceeds westwards, keeping to the 2,000ft. contour above Edale Head, then gently uphill to the 2,077ft. OS pillar on Kinder Low. This is the highest such pillar in the southern Pennines, for this upland's highest part (half a mile to the north-east) is unmarked. It is, incidentally, the highest top in England south of Fountains Fell.

Here, on the peaty waste of Kinder Low, there are extensive views to the west, out over that grand hill-and-valley country around Hayfield, Chinley, and New Mills. From Kinder Low we follow the edge of the plateau northwards, along the Pennine Way alternative to Peakland's most famous waterfall.

Kinder Downfall is the nick point where the Kinder River pours over a corner in the escarpment near the Great Buttress, one of the finest-situated of all gritstone cliffs. In harsh weather, the frozen fall presents a fantastic sight, of long icicles and blades of water locked in mid-air by the frost. When a south-westerly gale roars up the ravine below the Downfall, the water is blown back in great sheets across the plateau's edge; it is reminiscent of a storm on some rocky shore.

Proceeding to the north-west we come, in a mile, to the place where the Pennine Way descends steeply to Ashop Head and Mill Hill. Our route, though, turns back to the east, along Kinder Scout's northern escarpment – The Edge. This bold perimeter overlooks the west–east trough of Ashop Clough, and in clear conditions you can look out to the north, across the endless undulations of Bleaklow, a far wilder and finer upland than Kinder Scout. Half-way along The Edge stand the Boxing Gloves, a rough gritstone tor-group offering the photographer an impressive foreground. At the sharp prow of Fairbrook Naze we turn south, keeping to the edge of the plateau, and soon turn along the top of Seal Edge, where the Chinese Wall is the best outcrop on this part of Kinder, offering routes up to 35ft. in length.

A beaten track winds about the head of Blackden Clough – literally 'Black Valley' – and on by Blackden Edge, gently losing altitude all the way to the 1,710ft. summit of

Maps O.S. 1:50,000 Sheet 110; O.S. 1:63,360 Tourist Map of the Peak District; O.S. 1:25,000 Outdoor Leisure Map – The Dark Peak. Start and finish at Edale (ref. 123857).
Grading A tough moorland walk; very exposed in bad weather conditions.
Time 6–7 hours.
Distance 16 miles.
Escape Routes Numerous. The plateau is criss-crossed with paths leading down to lower ground.
Telephones Edale; Hayfield; Snake Inn; Hagg Farm; Ashopton.
Transport Railway Station at Edale for Sheffield and Manchester.
Accommodation Hotels and Bed and Breakfasts in Edale. Youth Hostels at Edale and Hagg Farm.
Guidebooks *The Peak and Pennines* by W. A. Poucher (Constable); *High Peak* by Byne and Sutton (Secker and Warburg 1966); *South Pennine Country* by R. A. Redfern (Hale); *The Peak District Companion* by Rex Bellamy (David and Charles); *Freedom to Roam* by Howard Hill (Moorland Publishing Co.).

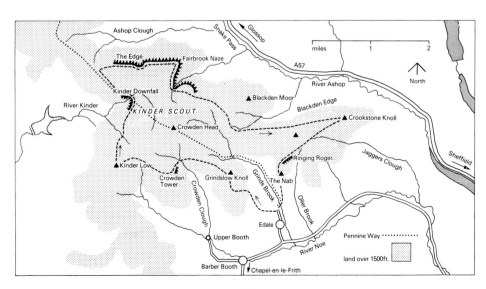

A series of photographs on the Kinder plateau

Above: The Woolpacks (top) and the barren ground at Kinder Low.

Top right: At the start of the route described, looking from Grindslow Knoll to Kinder Low. The wind-eroded rocks in the foreground, reminiscent of Henry Moore sculptures, have been defaced by graffiti.

Near right: Rockscape near Grindslow Knoll.

Far right: A view towards Grindslow Knoll from south of Kinder Low. *Photos: Shelagh Gregory*

Crookstone Knoll. Here we are at the far end of the plateau, looking out towards Bleaklow, up the mysterious trough of Alport Dale to the north, and to the great barrier whaleback of Derwent Edge in the east. On we go now towards the south-west, the route going back across the top of Jagger's Clough, vaguely on along the 1,900ft. contour to look down the length of Ollerbrook Clough to Edale.

Aiming south-west for a quarter of a mile beyond the top of Ollerbrook Clough, we arrive at the rocky top of the sharp arête called Ringing Roger (maybe an 'echoing rocher' or crag), and then go down it to the spur called The Nab. In 1659 it was 'Oaken Nab' – a wooded spur – trees then reaching higher up the valley sides than now. Cross out of the open country and down to the Pennine Way track near Grindslow House.

43   Dovedale from Axe Edge

by Phil Cooper

Maps O.S. 1:50,000 Sheet 119; O.S. 1:63,360 Tourist Map of the Peak District; O.S. 1:25,000 Outdoor Leisure Map – The White Peak. Start from Dove Head Cottages beside the A53 (ref. 031683). Finish at the Izaak Walton Hotel (ref. 144508).
Grading A long but easy walk.
Time 7–8 hours.
Distance 18 miles.
Escape Routes The walk may be conveniently cut short at Hartington which is connected to Buxton and Ilam by the Peak Pathfinder Bus Service in the summer months.
Telephones Glutton Bridge; Crowdcote; Hartington; Milldale; Thorpe; Ilam.
Transport Railway Station at Buxton. Buxton–Leek bus service runs along Axe Edge to the start. Ilam–Ashourne bus service on Tues, Thurs, Sat and Sun. Regular Ashbourne–Buxton bus service.
Accommodation Hotels and Guest Houses at Buxton and Ilam. Bed and Breakfasts locally. Youth Hostels at Buxton, Hartington and Ilam Hall.
Guidebooks *The Peak and Pennines* by W. A. Poucher (Constable); *The Dove and Manifold Valleys* by B. Spencer and L. Porter (Moorland Publishing Co.); *The Peak District Company* by Rex Bellamy (David and Charles); *Dovedale Guide* by K. Mantell (Derbyshire Countryside Ltd.).

Top right: Chrome Hill from Parkhouse Hill in Upper Dovedale. *Photo: Shelagh Gregory*
Near right: The Stepping Stones below Thorpe Cloud. *Photo: Phil Cooper*
Far right: Looking north up Wolfscote Dale near its junction with Biggin Dale. *Photo: John Allen*

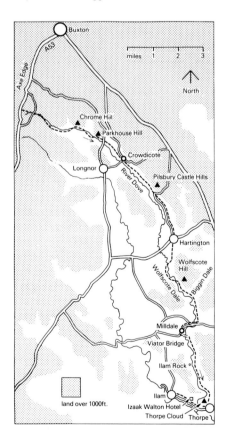

'Was you ever in Dovedale? I assure you there are things in Derbyshire as noble as in Greece or Switzerland.' Thus noted Lord Byron; a fair tribute from a Nottinghamshire man who died while he was fighting for Greece.

The walker in the gritstone Dark Peak finds many of his joys up aloft on the high moors and edges, but in the limestone White Peak it is the Dales which offer the finest scenes. Three miles of Dovedale from Milldale to Thorpe are very popular, but the walk described is 17 miles, from Dove Head to Thorpe. The river is closely linked with two famous anglers, Izaak Walton and Charles Cotton, who spent much time fishing here. Walton described their exploits in *The Compleat Angler*, first published in 1653.

The duo sought to pinpoint the source of their beloved river, and the spring is marked by a stone slab bearing the carved, intertwined initials of I.W. and C.C., now rather eroded. It is located a few yards from the A53 Leek–Buxton road, which contours round the moorlands of Axe Edge. Opposite Dove Head Cottages, at the Derbyshire/Staffordshire border, is a gate, and the stile immediately to the left gives access to the spring. The walk starts from the roadside 150 yards south, where a public footpath, marked by a stile, enters the upper valley and follows a track which in one place is carved out of the hillside. After half a mile this rejoins the tiny stream, close to a minor road bridge. Around the uppermost Dove, the rock is gritstone, and for several miles the infant river follows a valley which is rather narrow close to the stream, but broadens into rural hill-slopes for some hundreds of yards either side as the valley winds round Colshaw Hill and Brand Top. Washgate Bridge is a charming slender stone packhorse bridge with steep approaches, which is possibly medieval. These upper reaches of the Dove are quite undisturbed, unvisited, and largely unknown. Opposite Hollinsclough, the dale broadens, and up on the left are the serrations of Chrome Hill, which, with Parkhouse Hill, forms the gateway to Dowel Dale. This delightful pair are reef knolls, remains of coral reefs in the shallow tropical sea of the Carboniferous era, 330 million years ago, and their ascents, taking only

ten or fifteen minutes each, are highly recommended. The views are a delight, and Parkhouse taken by the west ridge is an amusing scramble.

A farm track leads from Glutton Bridge to Crowdicote, passing beneath Hitter Hill, Aldery Cliff, and High Wheeldon. You continue through pleasant pastureland past inquisitive cattle on Derbyshire limestone, but on the opposite bank Staffordshire is still gritstone. Pilsbury Castle Hills is a fascinating place; here is an earthwork with all the features of an early Norman motte and bailey fort, but with no apparent reason for its presence. A quiet narrow lane leads the walker to Hartington, a beautiful village and one of the best centres for an exploration of Dovedale. Hartington Hall, dating from 1611, is a Youth Hostel.

A Peak and Northern Counties Footpaths Society sign marks the start to the Beresford Dale path. You pass through several fields, and, on entering the woodland, there is a wet path down to the river bank. Cotton's and Walton's Fishing Temple, built in 1674, is visible through the trees, with the intertwined initials above its doorway.

A narrow footbridge leads you into Staffordshire, and here is Pike Pool, where the river flows slowly and deeply. A limestone monolith stands in the pool. On a knoll above here, on the Staffordshire side, are the remains of Beresford Hall, where Charles Cotton was born to be a country gentleman in 1630. He subsequently fell into debt, and the cave where he hid from his creditors is a little further down, on the Derbyshire side. Beresford Dale is enclosed, and everywhere thick with trees, bushes, and colourful flowers. Crossing back into Derbyshire over a second narrow bridge, there is a quaint stile, rather like the end of a clothes-peg.

Wolfscote Dale is more open, and characterised by limestone scree slopes, some small crags, and scattered trees. Wolfscote Hill is above, and soon Biggin Dale joins the main valley, its tiny stream giving its share to the Dove, which grows and passes over successions of weirs. Lode Mill and Dove Cottage, with its colourful garden, mark the end of Wolfscote Dale, and half a mile of tarmac leads to the charming hamlet of Milldale, where starts the tourists' Dovedale.

Above: The southern end of Wolfscote Dale from just below the junction with Biggin Dale. *Photo: Phil Cooper*

Top right: In the narrow part of Dovedale, with Pickering Tor on the left and Ilam Tower on the right. *Photo: Derbyshire Countryside Ltd.*

Bottom right: The footbridge at the northern end of Wolfscote Dale. *Photo: Derbyshire Countryside Ltd.*

Here is Viator's bridge, a functional stone structure of packhorse character. 'Viator', in Cotton's addition to *The Compleat Angler* tackled Hanson Toot, the steep grass slope ahead of the bridge, and found it hard going: 'Farewell Hanson Toot, I'll no more on thee!'

Those who do not already know the classic Dovedale down to Thorpe will revel in the discovery of a steep limestone gorge with precipitous crags and pinnacles, woodlands, abundant wild life, and the silver thread of the Dove winding its way over falls and weirs down the narrow dale. A weekday in late spring or in autumn, while the flowers are in bloom and the trees are thick with foliage, is the best time to go.

There are two cavernous openings at Dove Holes, where Nabs Dale joins. Close by a footbridge is the spectacular pinnacle of Ilam Rock, once ivy-clad, and opposite is Pickering Tor, on the Derbyshire side. The famous Lion's Head Rock, just above the path, is unmistakable. The dale here is extremely narrow and wooden duckboards have been installed to facilitate progress alongside the clear stream. A digression up the bank to Reynard's Cave is worthwhile; you pass through a natural arch just before the cave, and the knife-edge traverse over the top of the arch, with its sensational exposure, is a good diversion. The limestone pinnacles of Tissington Spires on the left are opposite

Jacob's Ladder, shortly before the path ascends to Lover's Leap, where it is customary to pause to view the grandeur whilst regaining your breath. You should include the short, sharp ascent of Thorpe Cloud, before finishing the walk at the Izaak Walton Hotel, near Ilam. The River Manifold joins the Dove close by, and the Dove continues serenely to join the Trent at Newton Solney, near Burton. A return walk north from Ilam up Manifold Dale is a superb sequel.

I leave you with Ruskin, who found Dovedale 'an alluring first lesson in all that is admirable and beautiful'.

44   The Western Peak by the Gritstone Trail

by Rex Bellamy

Maps O.S. 1:50,000 Sheets 109, 110, 118 and 119; 1:25,000 Outdoor Leisure Map – The White Peak; O.S. 1:63,360 Tourist Map of the Peak District. Start and finish at the Errwood Reservoir (ref. 010748). For Shutlingsloe start and finish at the Cat and Fiddle (ref. 001719).
Grading A long walk over high and often bleak moorlands.
Time 11 hours.
Distance 21 miles for the described circular walk including Shutlingsloe.
Escape Routes Numerous.
Telephones Fernilee; Taxal; Kettleshulme; The Cat and Fiddle Inn; Bottom of the Oven; Wildboarclough.
Transport Railway Stations at Buxton, Whaley Bridge, Disley and New Mills/Newtown. Regular bus services between Buxton and Whaley Bridge and an infrequent Buxton to Macclesfield service via The Cat and Fiddle.
Accommodation Buxton is probably the best centre but Inns and Bed and Breakfasts abound in the area. Youth Hostels at Buxton and Windgather.
Guidebooks The Peak and Pennines by W. A. Poucher (Constable); South Pennine Country by R. A. Redfern (Hale); The Peak District Companion by Rex Bellamy (David and Charles).

Top right: Looking south to the escarpment south of the Cat and Fiddle (left) and Shutlingsloe (right) from above Brookhouse. *Photo: Ken Wilson*

Bottom left: On the descent to the Goyt Valley, near Errwood Hall. *Photo: Cecil Davies*

Bottom right: Shutlingsloe from Tagsclough Hill. *Photo: Roger Redfern*

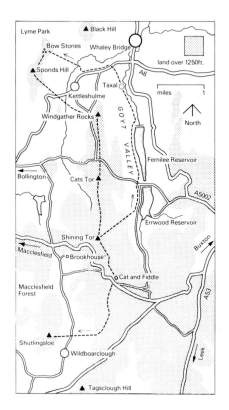

The affection inspired by a popular walk is not to be measured solely by the distance covered, the height climbed, nor the nature and span of the views. True, these are important components. So are diversity and difficulty – contrasts in terrain and scenery, and enough sustained exertion to leave an ache in the legs and a glow of satisfaction in the mind at the end of the day. On the western, less fashionable flank of the Peak District's gritstone 'horseshoe' is a walk that meets all these criteria. Essentially it is a ridge walk along hills that separate limestone dales from the plain of Cheshire, and it is loosely known as the Gritstone Trail, though many think of it as the Forest 1,500's, because of its historic associations and the 1,500ft. tors that punctuate its course.

There are several ways of tackling the walk, but all must incorporate primal views of Lyme Park, medial mileage via Bow Stones, Sponds Hill, Windgather Rocks, and Shining Tor, and a terminal view of Macclesfield Forest from the top of Shutlingsloe. You can do all that in a steady 12-hour day, or break it into two 'round' walks – parking the car at Lyme Park, Tegg's Nose, the Cat and Fiddle, or the Goyt Valley.

In the December before this book was published my brother and I drove to the southernmost Goyt Valley car park and did the longer 'round' walk. The sun, rising weakly, cast a pinkish blush over reservoirs that once drowned a farming community. There is a pretty grandeur about the Goyt Valley. The only sound came from sheep, filing gravely along what used to be the track of that remarkable engineering feat, the Cromford and High Peak Railway. We walked through woods and fields on the western shore, savoured the serenity of Taxal, resisted the beckoning bulk of Black Hill, swung down a lane past the remnants of Kettleshulme's candlewick mill, and then climbed from Handley Fold Farm to Bow Stones and the exhilarating Gritstone Trail.

The two Bow Stones, protectively enclosed near an isolated farm, could be chunks of eleventh-century crosses that served (not at their present location) to mark the boundary of Macclesfield Forest. The hollows on top once contained vinegar to disinfect coins left there in payment for provisions during the Plague years. They stand on the high south-eastern extremity of the National Trust country park that contains Lyme Hall, the 'Chatsworth' of the western Peak. The terrain plunges east and west of this airy, ancient road. After crossing Sponds Hill we cut east through fields, across Todd Brook, and up to the jagged skyline of Windgather Rocks.

It was here that, six hours out, we made our first assault on a flask of sherry that had intruded into the rucksack. This was the fuel needed for the last lap of a strenuous upper-and-downer that was now to cover a long stretch of bog-trotting over sucking muck. The track from Pym Chair to Oldgate Nick, Cats Tor, and Shining Tor is, as racing men say, 'soft going'. But the expansive views can be breathtaking when not shrouded in mist.

Divergent tracks lead to the Cat and Fiddle, the second highest pub in England and the only one on our route, or north-east down Shooter's Clough back to the Goyt Valley. We took the latter and enjoyed the big finish every tough walk needs if it is to find a warm place in the memory. A lovely diversity of scenery – moors, woodland, and water – opened before us, as if curtains had parted. The haunting ruins of Errwood Hall, secluded among steep slopes of rhododendrons, are well worth the signposted deviation.

Two days later, alone, I walked the last leg of the Forest 1,500's: from the lonely, sturdy Cat and Fiddle, in its landscape of sepia and tired green, down to Cumberland Brook and then, via Bank Top, up to the rocky summit of Shutlingsloe. Anyone completing the full walk from Lyme Park will realize, over the last half-mile, the way a tennis player feels when it's five-all in the fifth set at Wimbledon. But Shutlingsloe is a little marvel; a hill masquerading as a mountain, with dramatic contours and wide views to every point of the compass. The viewfinder repays examination. There is a choice of routes back to the Cat and Fiddle, or around the north-eastern perimeter of Macclesfield Forest to Tegg's Nose. All the way from Lyme Park to Shutlingsloe, the Forest 1,500's offer options. Only the enchantment is constant.

45   The Long Mynd and Stiperstones

by Chris Collier

As long ago as 1860, the author of a guide to the then newly opened Hereford to Shrewsbury railway wrote that if the scenery of the Church Stretton area were more widely known, it 'might render it one of the most attractive localities in England'. The same is still true today. Part of the appeal of the Long Mynd, and of the serrated ridge of Stiperstones to the north-west, where our walk ends, is that they are relatively little known.

The Long Mynd is a remarkable mountain, roughly nine miles long by four at its widest. Its rocks are some of Britain's oldest, Pre-Cambrian, and form a plateau of heather, bracken, and bilberry. The valleys which cut into its southern and eastern slopes, especially Callow Hollow and Ashes Hollow, are enclosed and isolated, and every ridge seems to carry an old track marking the route the drovers once took to the summer pastures of the Long Mynd. The Minton ridge is a fine example.

The Callow Hollow path, where we begin our walk, leads up from the Little Stretton to Minton road. Walk down the road from Little Stretton, and a little way beyond a ford take a track off to the right, through a small forestry plantation. This opens into a small, secluded hollow, at which point turn sharply right uphill along the north side of the wood, until suddenly Callow Hollow opens up beneath you. The path then descends steeply to the valley floor – the sense of isolation is remarkable – and continues by way of a pretty waterfall and through an abundance of hawthorn until, after about half an hour's walking, a fine valley comes into view on the right. This leads by way of an intriguing earthwork, marking the line of an old and now long-disused track, over to Ashes Hollow. Continue up the main valley, past a rocky outcrop, take the left fork as you near the top, and a short marshy stretch takes you to the road which runs along the Long Mynd summit. The road at this point follows the line of the Port Way, a Bronze Age track which runs the length of the plateau. Tumuli, not easily discernible, mark its line, and remind you that the Long Mynd summit has not always been the wilderness we see today.

After Pole Cottage, it is difficult to follow the Port Way's line. The road bends to the right, and you should take an ill-defined track off to the left, crossing the Port Way, which is barely traceable at this point, though it becomes a clear track again some distance further north. The track climbs gently to the Long Mynd's highest point, Pole Bank (1,695ft.). The views from here on a clear day can take in the Malverns, Brecon Beacons, Cader Idris, and Snowdon. Closer at hand, and looking east, the upper slopes of Caer Caradoc rise impressively above the plateau, and to the west lie Clun Forest, Corndon Hill, and the jagged ridge of our destination, Stiperstones. Nearby lie the valleys of Cardingmill and Townbrook. Between them, a ridge carries the Burway road down to Church Stretton. A short walk along the road is repaid by a spectacular view. A clearly-marked Iron Age fort (Bodbury Ring) rises above a high-level golf course, whilst beyond lies the Church Stretton valley, barely visible, and rising abruptly above the valley, the shapely peaks of Caer Caradoc and Linley Hill. Another short detour takes you north-east from Boiling Well to Lightspout Hollow and its delightful waterfall. But don't venture too far; the Cardingmill Valley, into which Lightspout Hollow runs, is very much the preserve of the car these days.

Descending from Pole Bank, the track crosses the bridleway to Medlicott, and drops down to the Ratlinghope road. It now continues through the heather to rejoin the line of the Port Way, and a little further on takes in the Mott Road path from the Cardingmill Valley. This is true Long Mynd country, lonely and wild, the haunt of curlew, grouse, and skylark; a flat and featureless plateau maybe, but never monotonous. The descent to Ratlinghope is best achieved either by the Ratlinghope road, or by the track to Duckley Nap, where it joins the All Stretton road, then north-west, by way of a track which takes you down past the ruined Marsh Farm, to the Darnford road.

Once in Ratlinghope, the temptation to head down to the pub at Bridges may prove to be too great. The Squilver road then allows easy access to the Stiperstones ridge. But there is a far more interesting route, which gives you a chance to explore the beautiful upper valley of the East Onny, and which all but avoids the roads. An old green

Walk   The Long Mynd and Stiperstones.
Maps   O.S. 1:50,000 Sheets 137 and 126. Start from Little Stretton (ref. 433911). Finish at Stiperstones Inn (ref. 363005).
Grading   Easy.
Time   5 hours.
Distance   12 miles.
Escape Routes   Numerous. The Stiperstones may be omitted by finishing the walk at Ratlinghope.
Telephones   Little Stretton; Ratlinghope; Stiperstones village.
Transport   Railway Station at Church Stretton (2 miles) on the Shrewsbury–Ludlow line. Regular bus service Church Stretton–Little Stretton.
Accommodation   Inns at Little Stretton and Stiperstones. Hotels at Church Stretton. Youth Hostels at Bridges (near Ratlinghope) and Wilderhope.
Guidebooks   *Shropshire Hill Country* by Vincent Waite (Dent); *Out and About, Travels in and Around Shropshire and the Welsh Borders* (Shropshire Journal); Information leaflets on the area can be obtained from the Information Centre, Church Road, Church Stretton, Salop.

Top left: A view up Ashes Hollow past the shoulder of Long Synalds to the Long Mynd plateau. *Photo: Van Greaves*

Bottom left: On the Stiperstones moors, looking north-east from below the Devil's Chair towards Scattered Rock. *Photo: Ken Wilson*

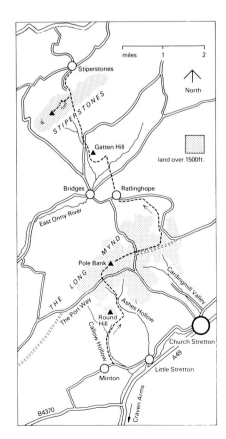

Top left: Blossom decorates the trees of the Long Mynd in this springtime view of Callow Hollow and Round Hill from Packetstone Hill. The route follows the valley, then cuts up the small subsidiary valley to the right to gain Ashes Hollow.

Bottom left: The Devil's Chair – the most distinctive of several sharp quartzite tors on the Stiperstones ridge.
Photos: Leonard and Marjorie Gayton

track leads up from above the turreted Ratlinghope church, crosses Ratlinghope Hill in great style, and leads on across the fields with a short stretch of tarred road, to Near Gatten Farm. The shorter route then takes you through the farm and over the top of Gatten Hill. The more beautiful leads off to the left, and round the hill. Watch out, amongst the trees, for warblers, wagtails, and a glimpse of a goldfinch if you're lucky. Both tracks lead to Far Gatten, then continue to The Hollies farm. Just after the farm, take a right turn, then angle sharply up to the left, over a stile and by way of rough and sometimes marshy ground, where you're likely to disturb a hare or two, on to the Stiperstones ridge itself.

The ridge, well worth walking in its entirety, marks an outcrop of hard quartzite rock, much younger than the Mynd's Pre-Cambrian, and providing a marked contrast to the rounded contours of its neighbour. It has been heavily eroded along its summit into a series of small tors, strongly reminiscent of Dartmoor. The Devil's Chair is the best known. When the wind's from the west and the mist comes down, 'the devil's on his throne'. The mist will, of course, also deny the walker the magnificent view. There is the tempting volcanic mound of Corndon in the foreground, with Offa's Dyke and the Welsh hills beyond, Linley Hill and Black Rhadley Hill to the south, and the long, sweeping ridge of the Long Mynd itself to the east. It is a peaceful landscape over which the walker casts his eye. Housman wrote of the area as 'the quietest under the sun'. As for the Long Mynd and Stiperstones, they are hardly easy, but they are off the beaten track, and, with one notable exception, so little written about* (the gentle Wenlock Edge caught Housman's imagination, not the Long Mynd) that the visitor comes with few preconceptions. He is likely to be more than agreeably surprised.

The final stage of the walk takes in the stretch of Stiperstones from the Devil's Chair to the point where a track leads down to the north-west, joining the road at the Stiperstones Inn.

*Mary Webb's novels, particulary *The Golden Arrow*, much of which takes place on the Stiperstones.

46   High Dyke

by Lord Hunt of Llanfair Waterdine

After many years of work and negotiations, which are a tribute to Tom Stephenson and Frank Noble as well as to enthusiastic members of the Ramblers' and Youth Hostels Associations, Offa's Dyke was formally designated as a National Footpath and declared open for enjoyment of the public in July 1971. For myself, having had the privilege of performing the opening ceremony, it holds pride of place among long-distance footpath walks south of the Scottish border. I have walked the footpath northwards and southwards and, from those experiences as well as from love born of long association, I claim that the finest stretch of the entire 168-mile length between the estuaries of Severn and Dee, is along the 16 miles between Knighton and the point where the Dyke descends into the plain of Montgomery.

But first a word about the Dyke itself. It was built at the behest of the Saxon King Offa, who ruled over Mercia during the second half of the eighth century. His general intention appears to have been to demarcate the border beyond which the Roman and Saxon invaders had driven the early Britons, and across which they were to be strongly discouraged from venturing forth. The resulting earthwork consisted of a high bank flanking a deep ditch on the west (or Welsh) side, beyond which a lesser bank of spoil can still be discerned in places. While some stretches of the obstacle have been destroyed by the ravages of climate and by man, long sections remain remarkably preserved over the span of more than 12 centuries; certain areas appear never to have been completed.

The whole length of the Welsh-English border along which the Dyke runs is rich in romantic legend, as well as brutal historical events. The Romans failed to penetrate beyond this frontier into the mountainous retreat of the Ordovices, Silures, and other early British tribes, whose Bronze Age forts still bear witness to their resistance. The Norman barons fought Welsh chieftains along the Marches over a period of 200 years; the ebb and flow of battle being traced by the salients, characteristic of the present national border, in which, in southern Shropshire, many Welsh place and personal names are still in use.

So let us meet at the Information and

Heritage Centre at Knighton. Parts of the town, with its steep little main street and clock tower, are medieval, and it is worth walking up the Narrows to savour that period of its history. The Offa's Dyke path descends from the Heritage Centre through a small park to the banks of the Teme, which it crosses to the English side at Panpwnton Farm and climbs up the northern flank of the valley to a hill of that name. We are now at about 1,300ft. and long views begin to open up. At the next rise, Cwm-sanaham Hill, it is worth pausing to admire the long, winding valley down which the Teme descends from its source in the distant Kerry hills. Just opposite, on the Welsh side, we see a side valley bridged by a high, stone viaduct, which carries a minor railway connecting Shrewsbury with Swansea. When my wife and I first came to live here* it was no rare occurrence to see three steam locomotives, one at each end and one in the middle, puffing and panting their noisy way up the incline of the Heyope valley.

Beside the viaduct stands a green hill, with clear evidence of earthworks on its crest, and with much history buried beneath the turf which now covers this ancient fortification. Knucklas Castle was the site of a Bronze Age fort. According to the Llanstephan manuscript, this was the home of Gwenhwyfar, daughter of a giant named Gogyrfan, and it was here that she was married to King Arthur. Some credence is given to this romantic legend by the discovery during the nineteenth century, in the burial mound beneath the castle, of a tomb containing five skeletons, two of them of unusual size. Much later, in 1954, a princely sword and two gold bracelets were unearthed during ploughing behind the castle.

But we must move on, for there is still a long way to go. We follow the modest bank which is all that remains of the Dyke, downwards to a lane connecting the valleys of Teme and Clun. A steep climb now leads up to a line of larches and Llanfair Hill (1,418ft.), the highest point along the entire length of the actual Dyke.† Beneath this

*Editor's note: The author lived in the Llanfair Waterdine area from 1944 to 1950, and subsequently maintained a small holiday cottage there. On assuming the Peerage in 1966 he incorporated the name in his title.

†There are several higher points on the official Offa's Dyke long-distance footpath.

Maps O.S. 1:50,000 Sheets 137 and 148. Start from Knighton (ref. 285725). Finish at the Blue Bell Inn on the A489 3 miles south of Montgomery (ref. 248932).
Grading A long and undulating walk over rolling uplands. There is a well-marked path along the entire route.
Time 8–9 hours.
Distance 16 miles.
Escape Routes Numerous. The walk can conveniently be left at the village of Newcastle near the crossing point of the river Clun, this is about the half-way mark.
Telephones Knighton; Llanfair Waterdine; Newcastle; Mainstone; Blue Bell Inn.
Transport Railway Stations at Knighton, Newtown and Welshpool (Shrewsbury–Swansea line). Bus services from Newtown and Welshpool to Montgomery.
Accommodation Hotels, Guest Houses and Bed and Breakfasts in Knighton and Montgomery. The Blue Bell Inn. Youth Hostels at Clun and Ludlow. Several farmhouses and cottages passed on the route of Offa's Dyke offer accommodation.
Guidebooks Offa's Dyke by C. J. Wright (Constable); Walks Along Offa's Dyke by E. and K. Kay (Spur); Through Welsh Border Country by Mark Richards (Thornhill Press); Offa's Dyke Path by the Countryside Commission (H.M.S.O.).

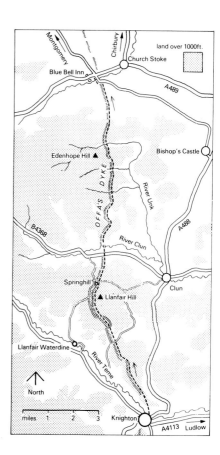

Above: The ditch and bank of Offa's Dyke, at a point north of Springhill and a mile and a half west of Clun. *Photo: Leonard and Marjorie Gayton*

Top right: Looking across the valley of the River Unk to Nutwood and Edenhope Hill. The Dyke descends Edenhope Hill on the left. *Photo: Rod Smith*

Bottom right: The Dyke at the top of Llanfair Hill, highest point on this ancient earthwork. *Photo: Van Greaves*

point, but out of sight, lies the hamlet of Llanfair Waterdine, an apt combination of Welsh and English nomenclature on the border between the two nations. In clear weather the view is stupendous. To the north-east runs the high ridge of Long Mynd, above Church Stretton; to the north, a striking summit is Corndon Hill, above Montgomery: to the west and south-west are the high moors of Kerry and Beguildy, which enclose the valley of the Teme: southwards we see the lowering bulk of Radnor Forest, and beyond, the massif of the Black Mountains above the Severn valley. Faintly in the distance we can identify the twin

peaks of the Brecon Beacons. Many times, standing here, I have felt a sense of timelessness, of a link with dimly perceived past ages, when the valleys below were filled with forest and on this high country, centuries before Offa built his Dyke, a small, dark people began to grow corn on the uplands and hunted boar and deer in the forest.

Since reaching the strip of larches we have been walking on the best preserved stretch of the earthwork, and we will remain with it for many miles yet. It leads us to the crest of the ridge, dividing the Teme from the Clun, along which runs a minor road tracing an ancient track for traders, including those carrying flint artifacts from the English chalklands. We descend steeply to another farm, Lower Spoad, in the Clun valley, where Mrs. Davies dispenses splendid teas and provides accommodation. We cross two more lanes before climbing again through bracken and scrubland to reach the remains of a cottage (Hergan) where a clear spring of piped water will be welcome on a hot day; for we have come 11 miles since leaving Knighton.

Crossing another minor road, we notice a curious aberration in the construction of the Dyke; one length runs straight ahead for 50 yards before ending abruptly, while the main line turns downhill to the left. It may be conjectured that two gangs of diggers, working without the oversight of surveyors, found their labours out of alignment at this point. After passing the isolated farm, Middle Knuck, the Dyke plunges down to the wooded glen of Cwm Ffrydd, where there are two derelict cottages and a tiny church, somewhat grandiosely styled Churchtown. The path continues to pursue its switchback course, making scant allowance for the uncompromising steepness of the land. Over Edenhope Hill and down into the valley of the river Unk, but now the traveller will be thankful to know that there remains just one more ascent, the slanting line up the far slope of the valley. The descent to the plain follows a well-preserved piece of the Dyke, and then a lane leading to the farms of Cwm and Lower Cwm. The latter offers accommodation and is superbly situated, with long views northwards over the flatlands between the towns of Montgomery and Chirbury.

After so long a stretch of high-level walking, with such a sense of space, I have found it disappointing to end the day in the trees flanking the caravan site of Mellington Hall. But there is comfort in the fact that we end the long journey a little farther on, at the Blue Bell Inn on the A489. It was here that my wife and I spent the first night of our journey along the Dyke after the opening ceremony in 1971. The day had been excessively hot and I recall how thankful we felt on coming to rest here, to receive a warm welcome and an excellent supper, and to enjoy the good Border beer!

47   The Malvern Hills

by Richard Gilbert

Maps   O.S. 1:50,000 Sheet 150. Start from the Winter Gardens in Great Malvern (ref. 776459). Finish at Rye Court (ref. 776357).
Grading   A very easy hill walk along good paths.
Time   5 hours.
Distance   11 miles.
Escape Routes   Main roads cross the hills at Wyche, Wynds Point and Hollybush.
Telephones   Great Malvern; Wyche; Malvern Hills Hotel; Hollybush.
Transport   Railway Station at Malvern. Bus service (Midland Red) to Worcester, Birmingham, Bristol and Gloucester.
Accommodation   A wide variety of accommodation is available in Malvern. Youth Hostels at Malvern Wells and Rushall near Ledbury.
Guidebooks   *Malvern Country* by Vincent Waite (Dent); *A History of Malvern* by Brian S. Smith (The Malvern Bookshop); Information leaflets on the Malverns available at the Information Office, Great Malvern.

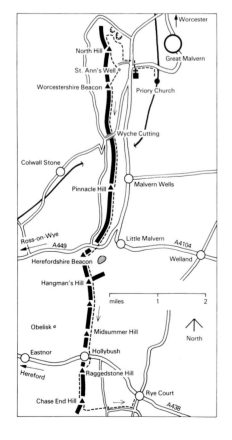

'The most beautiful silhouette in England' is how Stanley Baldwin described the Malvern hills. Wilfrid Noyce, after climbing the Worcestershire Beacon on a misty November's afternoon, wrote that for him the Beacon is both higher and lovelier than a 20,000ft. Tibetan lump (*Climbers' Club Journal* 1949). These opinions are shared by the thousands of people who live under the shadow of the hills in the county of Hereford and Worcester. They, and the motorists who speed past the eastern slopes on the M5, grow to love the gentle contours of the Malverns, and their colours, ever changing with the seasons. The Malverns not only inspired Sir Edward Elgar, who lived within sight of the hills for much of his life and loved to walk over them with his friends, but also provided the background to some of John Masefield's verse, and the fourteenth-century poem, Langland's *Vision of Piers Plowman.*

You can forget the alarm clock and the dawn start for the Malverns walk, because a delightful leisurely and relaxing day lies ahead. The Winter Gardens in Great Malvern make a convenient starting point. Alas, no longer can you sip your morning coffee to the strains of Campoli playing Dvorak's *Humoresque*; I had to make do with the town band's rendering of *Orpheus in the Underworld*, but in many ways Malvern has changed little since its development as a Victorian spa. As I walked up the hill past the Priory Church, built of mellowed stone and dating from the fourteenth century, the bells were ringing, and I was struck by an air of tranquility which remained with me all day. I left the town by St. Ann's Road, and then branched right along one of the dozens of well-contoured paths which zig-zag all over the hills. I made my way towards North Hill, enjoying the most gentle ascent imaginable through the bracken, gorse, foxgloves, and rose-bay willow-herb. A few mild, rocky bluffs appeared, of rock which is the most ancient in all England (at least 650 million years old). Had fatigue set in, I could have rested on one of many wooden seats placed at intervals along the path. I crossed the broad track known as the de Walden Drive, cut as a carriageway for Lady Howard de Walden in the nineteenth century, and soon after reached the broad top of North Hill.

The Malverns stretch south for seven-and-a-half miles to Chase End Hill, but the view is blocked by the highest hill, the Worcestershire Beacon, which is the next objective. I trotted down to the col and made a ten-minute detour to St. Ann's Well, where pure water gushes through a dolphin spout into a marble bowl. I was disappointed, for the water was flat and tasteless, like a mountain stream without the tang of peat. Malvern water is undoubtedly pure (so is distilled water), yet belief in its therapeutic powers was held tenaciously for generations.

The windswept summit of the Worcestershire Beacon, at 1,395ft. belies its modest height. As a view point, it can have few rivals in England, and looking due east, there is no higher ground until the Urals. I was fortunate to pick a day of clear air and high fleecy clouds, and I enjoyed identifying the

major features of the landscape with the help of the toposcope mounted near the cairn. Wenlock Edge, Long Mynd, Brecon Beacons and the Mendips were clearly visible. The Beacon was the site of one of the Armada warning bonfires, which blazed out across Britain in 1588, and the most recent bonfire was to celebrate the Royal Wedding in July 1981.

Proceeding south, the ridge narrows and descends to Wyche Cutting and the site of a disused gold mine. I found it a most extraordinary experience to be walking along a mountain ridge in a civilised suburban setting. Below the ridge were grand Victorian houses, with sharp gables and Gothic features, many with large gardens and tennis courts. The avenues were wide and lined with exotic trees. From most mountain ridges you see miles of bog, lonely

lakes, and perhaps a remote shepherd's cottage. But this juxtaposition to civilisation of the Malverns makes them unique in Britain.

The spaciousness which so characterises Malvern is due to the foresight of the land-owners at the time of the expansion of the town as a thriving spa, for they insisted that the builders observed aesthetically pleasing standards of layout for houses and roads, together with imaginative tree planting. Even Malvern's industry reflects good taste and tradition for, operating here, is the Morgan Car Company, turning out hand-built thoroughbred sports cars of traditional design. The inhabitants of Malvern are determined to preserve the character of the hills, and a body called the Malvern Hills Conservators has been highly successful in its activities. Erosion has been checked, car

Above: Heading south along the Malvern Ridge after descending Worcestershire Beacon. Pinnacle Hill is in the middle distance, with the terraced profile of the British Camp on Herefordshire Beacon beyond.
Photo: Marion Teal

Top: The northern end of the Malvern Hills seen from the earthworks of the British Camp.
Photo: Michael Saunders

Bottom: The Herefordshire Beacon and Hangman's Hill from near the obelisk at the southern, more rural, end of the Malvern Hills.
Photo: Richard Gibbens

parks provided, fences maintained, and encroaching urbanisation kept back.

The next prominent hill to the south is the Herefordshire Beacon, with its spectacular British Camp. The terraced earthworks can be seen from afar, and as you approach the Beacon, the details of the ramparts and ditches become clear. The Iron Age Fort was constructed in the fourth century BC. I crossed the main A449 Worcester–Ross road at the Malvern Hills Hotel and entered Herefordshire. As I began my climb up to the 1,114ft. summit of the Herefordshire Beacon,

I passed a plaque supposedly commemorating the place where William Langland 'slombred in a sleping' and dreamt his *Vision of Piers Plowman*. Just south of the Herefordshire Beacon, on another earthwork (thirteenth-century this time), known as Red Earl's Dyke, I stopped for a late lunch. The town of Malvern was behind me, and I felt more at ease in a predominantly rural setting. Woods, chequered fields, and hillocks spread away west across Herefordshire towards the Wye, contrasting with the flat Severn plain in Worcestershire to the east.

A short detour into the grounds of Eastnor Park will take you to a 90ft. stone obelisk built in 1812 to the memory of John Somers, but I pressed on over Midsummer Hill (another Iron Age Fort), to the A438 at Hollybush. Two more hills to go now, and the path up the first of them, Raggedstone Hill, starts a short distance down the Tewkesbury road near a phone box. On the south side of Raggedstone Hill, I was surprised to find a tiny hamlet, of half-timbered seventeenth-century houses, known as Whiteleaved Oak. A sunken lane then led me up onto Chase End Hill, and the OS pillar at 625ft. marking the southern extremity of the Malvern hills. Two miles further south, traffic snarled along the M50, but on my perch, overlooking the best of English pastoral scenery, I was oblivious to the roar and fumes. Reluctantly I descended the eastern slopes of Chase End Hill and walked through the lanes to the Rye Court cross-roads, where there is a three-hourly weekday bus service to Malvern. From the Winter Gardens I had enjoyed a fascinating five-hour walk over the unique and magnificent Malvern Hills.

Above: Pinnacle Hill from the south, seen here ringed with roads and houses and criss-crossed by footpaths – making them virtually a municipal park, and a unique aspect of these small mountains only rivalled in the British Isles by the considerably lower hills in Edinburgh. *Photo: Marian Teal*

48   The Wye Valley and the Forest of Dean

by Maurice and Marion Teal

Maps   O.S. 1:50,000 Sheet 162; O.S. 1:25,000 Outdoor Leisure Map – The Wye Valley and Forest of Dean. Start from Monmouth (ref. 508130). Finish at Welsh Bicknor Youth Hostel (ref. 591177).
Grading   Easy walking along forest and riverside paths.
Time   5–6 hours.
Distance   12 miles.
Escape Routes   Numerous.
Telephones   Monmouth; Redbrook; Yat Rock car park.
Transport   The Ross-on-Wye to Coleford bus service (National Welsh) passes through Lydbrook (2 miles from Welsh Bicknor Y.H.), not Sun. Regular Ross–Monmouth bus service.
Accommodation   Hotels at Monmouth and Symonds Yat. Guest Houses and Bed and Breakfasts at Monmouth. Youth Hostels at Monmouth and Welsh Bicknor.
Guidebooks   Forestry Commission Guide *Dean Forest and the Wye Valley* (H.M.S.O.); *Exploring the Wye Valley and the Forest of Dean* by R. Jones (Barton); *The Wye Valley*, Red Guide (Ward Lock); *Portrait of the Wye Valley* by H. L. V. Fletcher (Hale).

Top right: At Near Hearkening Rocks in the Forest of Dean. *Photo: Marion Teal*

Far right: The River Wye from Yat Rock. *Photo: Chris Barber*

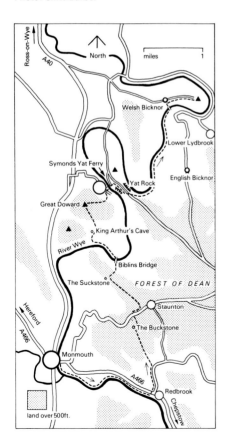

Although a scenic river for most of its course, the Wye is at its best between Ross and Monmouth. Here the waterway has formed a serpentine route through hills thrusting up towards the 1,000ft. contour; hills clothed with trees of the ancient Forest of Dean. The combination of river, hills, and forest gives rise to fine scenery, unique in this country, and the walk described below contrives to take in the best of it. The route, sometimes at river level, sometimes on the hilltops, includes the paradox of the walker following the Wye downstream over two sections, but finishing miles up-river.

Although completely different from the ridges that feature extensively in this volume, this route contains a great deal of ascent and descent. This, plus the rock features that are encountered along the way, helps to give it a whiff of the mountain atmosphere. Though it may be done by stationing private transport at each end, or by using public transport, the original concept was as a hostel to hostel route; that is, from Monmouth to Welsh Bicknor.

Whether leaving the Youth Hostel or the roomy car park at Monmouth, the walker should head for the Wye bridge on the south-east side of town. You can negotiate the busy A40 by means of an underpass, then cross the bridge to look for a footpath some yards beyond, on the right-hand side of the road. Starting down a driveway, the right of way soon becomes a path that approaches and follows the riverside as the Wye bends to the left under a disused railway viaduct. Level walking past meadowland alternates with undulating sections where the riverbank steepens. Just short of Redbrook, the footpath gives on to the A466, which hereabouts follows a course near to the river. Walk along the road and turn left by the Bush Inn to ascend a lane, steep at first, passing the place where the Offa's Dyke path goes left. The path you seek is signposted the Buckstone, but even so is not easily seen. It is a narrow track slanting up on the left-hand side of the lane, beyond a right-hand bend. Thereafter the route is waymarked and ascends through thick woodland of the Forest of Dean. Watch out for a section where the way goes right then left in quick succession.

At the top of the hill the Buckstone can be seen just below to the left. This unusually shaped rock was once a rocking stone but is now cemented in position. The path descends to Staunton where, during opening hours, you may well be diverted a few yards right to the White Horse. Those who do not succumb to such temptation should cross the A4136 to a narrow entrance between walls. This soon becomes a pleasant pathway through woodland, contouring the slopes high on the side of the Wye Valley, with delightful views towards the distant Black Mountains. Eventually the path descends to give on to a wider track and, following this to the right, the Suckstone can soon be seen above and to the right. The route climbs to pass to the right of this huge mass of sand-stone conglomerate estimated (at 12,000 tons) to be one of the largest boulders in the country.

You continue to climb in the same line until confronted by overhanging sandstone cliffs known as the Near Hearkening Rocks. Here you should turn left and follow the base of the crags, before climbing again briefly. Although the route is waymarked, extra care must now be exercised. You turn left along a broad forest track, only to leave it again almost immediately to the right. A little further, as the route descends through wood-land, another broad track is crossed at an angle. The way steepens until the walker finds himself on level ground by the river Wye. A few steps leftward now bring you to Biblins bridge, a well-known Forest land-mark. You cross the river by means of the bridge, a suspended walkway of wire mesh erected by the Forestry Commission in 1958, and turn left to walk once more down-river. Ahead the Seven Sisters can now be seen, a series of limestone pillars that rise from the steep flank of the valley. Ten minutes from the bridge, turn right and climb steeply through the trees. When confronted by a cliff-face, the track bends left and follows the base of the rocks until a breach in the defences allows you to scramble up to higher ground. As the slope eases, follow the yellow arrows round to the left.

There are a couple of places where you may venture to the edge of the cliffs to enjoy the magnificent views up and down the river. Afterwards, leave the rocks behind and walk

through the forest until the track bears right and passes near to King Arthur's Cave. The entrance can be seen to the left in a small outcropping rock face. Although not an extensive cavern it is of interest by virtue of its connections with Paleolithic man.

The waymarked track continues over Great Doward, alternately traversing broad-leaved forest and young pines, before descending to the riverside at Symonds Yat. Prospecting to the left along a narrow lane, you soon discover the ferry. It is a one man-power affair, propulsion being by means of a rope slung between the river banks. The fare is 20p (children 15p), but the ferry runs all the year, day in day out, except when flood conditions prevail. Disembarking, go right along a path, but turn sharp left after passing the Forest View Hotel. A path snakes up through woods that are predominantly beech, to the hilltop near the Yat Rock. The top of the rock is a well-known viewpoint and generally populous, but the views are worth seeing.

Afterwards, walk down the public road for perhaps 150 yards to where a path goes right near two disused kilns. The path becomes a narrow track through woodland, levelling out before descending eventually to a broad riverside track. Walk upstream past a series of gates, but, following a wooden barrier, turn left to a double stile at the water's edge. The route now keeps close to the river until a disused railway bridge is reached. Welsh Bicknor Youth Hostel is then a quarter of a mile along the north bank, and the road and public transport away to the right.

49   The Ancient Footpaths of the Chilterns

by Christopher Hall

Low, lovely, beech-hung, and made of chalk, the Chiltern Hills lie within day-trip range of London. Most of them are in Buckinghamshire, but this walk, though starting in that county, is mostly set in Oxfordshire, which contains the remotest Chiltern countryside remaining. This is a countryside of small fields, and narrow valleys with oddly-shaped woodlands reaching down into them. The hills – an official 'Area of Outstanding Natural Beauty' – are exceptionally rich in public paths, with more than four miles of them to every square mile, more than twice the national average density. The paths are mostly signposted, and very often they have been waymarked by the busy volunteers of the Chiltern Society, who have done much over the last decade and a half to get the paths properly walked and cared for. Here you will find more paths across fields restored after ploughing than in any other part of Britain. And the waymarks – white arrows painted on trees and stiles – are a reassuring aid even to those familiar to the area.

We start in the centre of Stokenchurch, a big, straggling village on the A40, which, though not very beautiful, is very Chiltern. Essentially it is a thin line of houses, thickened by modern developments, around a large green, like many other settlements hereabouts. The Chilterns were relatively poor land before agricultural techniques improved; consequently, they have a high proportion of commons and greens. This village still has two small factories making furniture parts – remnants of an industry originally drawing its raw material from the surrounding beech woods, and now centred on High Wycombe, although today the timber is mostly imported.

From the bus-stop, our way is west across the green, the cricket field, and the footbridge over the motorway, to cross the Ibstone road at 753963. The facing track takes us downhill across a field. We bear left into the first wood, and the path plunges precipitously to the 'bottom', as the sharp

Top left: The route from Cowleaze Wood, past Bald Hill, to the Icknield Way. *Photo: Raymond Lea*

Bottom left: The path leads under mature trees in Stonor Park. *Photo: Raymond Lea*

Chiltern valleys are called. Immediately, we are going uphill again, across a field to the corner of the wood opposite. Please don't go round the edge, even if there is a crop. The farmer is breaking the law in not restoring the path, and we must not let him get away with it. Inside the wood, the path takes us over a low ridge and straight ahead at a clearly waymarked crossing path, and we are descending into the next bottom. Out of the wood we skirt the back of Lower Vicar's Farm (a farm no more), go up beside the hedge, and left for 20 yards along a track; then right again and uphill across a biggish field to the edge of the wood. Pause here and look back on the Wormsley Valley. It is the finest unspoiled Chiltern valley left. At any time of the year the view of its intricate mosaic of field and wood is rewarding, especially so in the autumn.

We leave Buckinghamshire now and go straight ahead through the Forestry Commission woodland, emerging on the Christmas Common road in the picnic area of Cowleaze Wood. Cross the road at 725954 and follow the path slanting down the hill. At first it clings, as do the old tracks, to the easiest gradient. The right-angled turns (clearly marked) halfway down are the result of a modern diversion. Never mind; a pleasant walk along the slope of Bald Hill (part of the Aston Rowant National Nature Reserve) remains. We go obliquely through a small wood (719962), and across a field to the wide, grassy Icknield Way – now part of the Countryside Commission's official Ridgeway Path.

Avert your eyes from the crass sweep of the M40, slicing through the hills to the right, and turn left. We follow the ancient green way for about a mile and a quarter as it winds along the base of the Chiltern spurs. At 703946 we turn left onto the bridleway up Pyrton Hill. This is part of the Oxfordshire Way, another long-distance path devised by the Oxfordshire Council for the Protection of Rural England to link the Chilterns and the Cotswolds. This part of it (known locally as the driftway because it was used for driving sheep and cattle) is a medieval route.

At the top, we are back on the edge of the Chiltern escarpment for the best panorama of the day. To the south-west is the line of the

Maps   O.S. 1:50,000 Sheets 165 and 175. Start from Stokenchurch (ref. 759964). Finish at Nettlebed (ref. 702870).
Grading   Easy.
Time   4 hours.
Distance   12 miles.
Telephones   Stokenchurch; Christmas Common; Stonor; Nettlebed.
Transport   Stokenchurch is on the London (Victoria) to Oxford bus route, operated jointly by Oxford South Midland and Green Line. Buses every 2 hours 7 days a week. Nettlebed is connected to Oxford and London by a daily bus service operated by Oxford South Midland.
Accommodation   Hotels and Bed and Breakfasts in Stokenchurch. Nettlebed has two Inns. Youth Hostels at Henley on Thames, Bradenham and Oxford.
Guidebooks   *Along the Chiltern Way* by G. R. Crosher (Cassell); *Walks for Motorists, Chilterns South* by N. Moon (Warne); Numerous maps and guides produced by the Chiltern Society (Shire Publications, Princes Risborough).

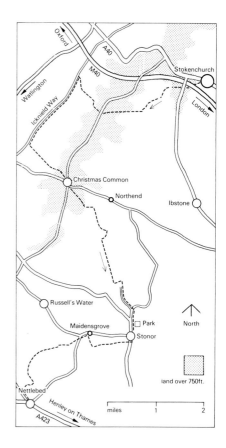

Berkshire Downs; west are the Cotswolds and, in the middle distance, a glimpse of Oxford's tower blocks. Brill lifts its solitary 600ft. hill on the county border to the north-north-west. On the road (715 936) turn right. The scatter of houses here is Christmas Common, a hamlet named after the seasonal truce signed here by Parliamentarians and Royalists in 1643. The Fox and Hounds is a good pub. Now take the minor road (716 932), and when the metalling ends, take the path left into the wood and stay with it to the county boundary. Here, turn right uphill through the wood, across a field, and so to the unsurfaced lane by Hollandridge Farm. Note the magnificent, deep-roofed barn, and follow the track downhill. Turn left onto a path along a field edge at 730 902, and down to the bottom, then right until you reach the road just above Stonor. This village has Stonor House, dating from the thirteenth century (open certain days April–September) and owned by the Stonors, who still live there.

Our last lap takes us by the path leaving the road at 738 887, up across a field, and into the wood and across another field. So to the airy upland of Russell's Water Common at Maidensgrove. Our route is by a series of switchbacking hills and fields, leaving the common on a track at 718 887, bearing right along the top edge of a wood (part of the Warburg Nature Reserve), and down to the junction of tracks at 709 884. Make for Westwood Farm, but turn left into the wood just before you reach it. Follow a shallow valley upwards on the far side of the wood, and take the path just left of the new house facing you. This brings you through our last Chiltern wood onto Nettlebed Common – another superb village open space, mostly wooded this time. Nettlebed itself is an old brick-making settlement (observe the kiln) on the A423, and it marks the end of our walk.

Above left: The lush, pastoral landscape of the Chilterns is well seen in this view of Watlington Hill. *Photo: Raymond Lea*

Left: Heavily-laden hikers on the Icknield Way near Chinnor. *Photo: Raymond Lea*

164

50   A Cotswold Classic

by Mark Richards

Unlike mountain areas, the Cotswolds do not possess classic walks as such, rather classic locations, often fragmented snippets of sheer delight amid an agrarian landscape. The one distinction that most enshrines its charm is the oolitic limestone upon which it is founded. Mellowed by time, conveying an enduring sense of serenity, its amiability is reflected in even the humblest dwelling or barn. In common with mountains, however, it is only when the relief of the land breaks away into deep valleys and proud escarpments that the whole landscape incites active admiration. The quality of walking is epitomised by the Cotswold Way, which clings tenaciously to the main north-west facing escarpment, discovering the intimate,

and often dramatic, details throughout its course between Bath and Chipping Campden; thereby affording walkers frequent opportunities to gaze across the breezy wolds resplendent with waving corn, and verdant sheep pastures bound by grey drystone walls. They can also revel in far-ranging views across the spreading Severn and Evesham Vales. The walk featured here, selected as typifying the most admired characteristics of Cotswold country, is a fascinating circular excursion of eleven miles. The designation of the Cotswolds as an 'Area of Outstanding Natural Beauty', was never intended to imply that here was a region prepared for, and requiring, visitors *en masse*. The designation was purely conservational

Maps O.S. 1:50,000 Sheet 150. Start and finish at Fish Hill quarry (ref. 120369).
Grading Easy.
Time 4–5 hours.
Distance 11 miles.
Telephones Fish Inn; Broadway; Stanton; Stanway; Snowshill.
Transport Railway Stations at Evesham and Moreton-in-Marsh. Regular bus services to Broadway from Stow-on-the-Wold, Stratford, Evesham and Moreton-in-Marsh.
Accommodation Hotels, Guest Houses and Bed and Breakfasts in Broadway. Youth Hostels at Cleeve Hill and Stow-on-the-Wold.
Guidebooks *The Cotswold Way* by Mark Richards (Thornhill Press); *A Guide to the Cotswold Way* by Dick Sale (Constable); *Cotswolds Walks for Motorists* (Warne Gerrard); *Walking in the Cotswolds* by H. Drury (Hale).

Above: Climbing the Cotswold escarpment to Broadway Tower. This striking edifice dates from the great age of folly building, and commands a sumptuous view.
Photo: Steve Poulton

Above: A group of buildings, built of the delightful, honey-coloured local stone, in the small and characteristic Cotswold town of Broadway. Photo: Raymond Lea

Top right: Looking south from the outskirts of Broadway along the Cotswold Way. Photo: Marion Teal

in conception. In consequence only a limited number of official picnic areas have been laid out, one such, the work of Worcestershire County Council, is in a shallow quarry located at the top of Fish Hill. This provides a convenient start for the described walk.

The memorial topograph, the focal point of the site, may be deemed the starting point. It is an example of good local craftsmanship and design which compensates for the somewhat restricted panorama. A nature trail leads off through an overgrown quarry and down a short section of the original Fish Hill coaching road to the minor road running under the beech-embowered Campden Hole scarp. At the entrance to Farncombe House, diverge down the pastures to enter Broadway High Street by Pike Cottage. On the other side of the road stands Court Farm, a magnificent example of Cotswold domestic vernacular architecture. Entering Broadway in this manner affords a delightful preamble along this justly famous village street. There is much to admire in the street, frequently cited as typifying the virtues of Cotswold and traditional English village charm. Whilst

elsewhere on this walk the pride of Cotswold masons blooms just as fair, Broadway will always claim pre-eminence as an attraction for visitors. At the Green the route, now in company with the Cotswold Way, turns left along the Snowshill road. Contrary to appearances, this is the original 'broad way', climbing the Cotswold scarp on an easier gradient than the Fish Hill turnpike. Crossing the fields to West End, our route follows the footpath to Buckland-beneath-Burhill and is punctuated with pleasant views across the fertile vale to Bredon and Dumbleton Hills. On entry into the delightful environs of Buckland, the rectory, reputedly the oldest parsonage in England, is on the left. Further up the lane, sited on rising ground, is the manor house and church – the latter a notable example of pre-Reformation Perpendicular. Returning to the route, we go right and join a well-graded bridleway to Laverton, which rather charmingly means 'farmstead frequented by larks'. This dependency of Buckland is composed of a variety of well-ordered seventeenth-century houses and cottages. By field paths now we proceed to Stanton, entering the most secretive of passage-ways into the churchyard. The church and adjacent Court confirms the genius of Cotswold proportion. Entering the main street by the medieval cross, the serenity and peculiar unity of this almost model village becomes apparent. Wending the way up the lane to the Mount Inn for refreshment, you are conscious of a rare beauty imposed by the honey-golden Coscombe stone. Despite obvious charm and accessibility, Stanton displays a commendable disregard for any form of commercialism and an endearing dignity pervades.

Beyond Stanton, the route again coincides with the Cotswold Way, and leads through ridge and furrow pastures and parkland to Stanway. Properly known as Church Stanway, the name embodies a clear reference to the ancient stone surfaced way, sometime salt way, up the escarpment. This is a community dominated by the large house, a fine Elizabethan mansion well seen from the churchyard, wherein is buried Dr. Thomas Dover. His curious claim to fame was his rescue of Alexander Selkirk from the island of Juan Fernandez in 1708. This

man's strange existence formed the basis of the story of *Robinson Crusoe*. There are several buildings of interest, including the Gatehouse and Tithe Barn, but do not neglect the war memorial, for it is a remarkable bronze figure of Saint George slaying the dragon, set on a limestone plinth. Passing the Old Bakehouse (teas), the route approaches the escarpment, adhering to the Stanway Estate waymarks, up the Lidcombe Wood re-entrant. At the head of the re-entrant, waymarks momentarily disappear, but a footpath does exist, running from the dutch barn at Parks Farm to Shenberrow, a tiny hill-fort overlooking Stanton. The name is said to mean bright or beautiful fortified hill; whilst not wishing to deny the quality of the setting today, the allusion is not obvious. Stretching back from the Edge is the high sweeping wold associated with that Saxon 'Cod' whose name has also endured in the nearby village name Cutsdean. 'Cot's Wold' (Cotswold) has over the years been broadened in meaning, and today it is applied to the whole stone belt, from Chipping Campden through Cirencester to Bath in the Avon Valley.

At this point it would be practical to divert from the main route to visit Snowshill, a small, grey, upland village sheltering just beneath the crest of the Edge. Snowshill Manor is the star attraction, a splendid Cotswold house in the care of the National Trust, containing a treasured collection of bygones. The Cotswold Way leads you down through Broadway Coppice to West End once more, where it is necessary to follow the minor road to St. Eadburgh's, a fine old church long since taken from communal service. Here turn up Coneygree Lane, at the top of which branch left to rejoin the Cotswold Way on its direct ascent to Broadway Tower. Built as a folly landmark in 1800 by the Earl of Coventry, today its blessings as a prospect tower are the delight of the many visitors to the Country Park, wherein it now stands. It forms a fitting finale to this memorable walk, particularly with the setting sun to highlight the limits of the western horizon. The Cotswold Way leads unerringly back past the old Fish Inn, a hostelry from earliest coaching days, to the topograph to conclude the walk.

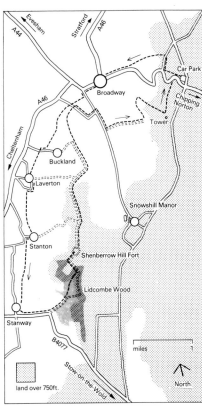

ENGLAND   Berkshire

51   The Ridgeway over the Berkshire Downs

by Janet Wedgwood

Maps   O.S. 1:50,000 Sheet 174. Start from the Ridgeway S of Ashbury (ref. 273844). Finish at Gore Hill (ref. 491835).
Grading   An easy walk maintaining a fairly constant height.
Time   5 hours.
Distance   16 miles.
Escape Routes   Numerous.
Telephones   None passed on route but diversions could easily be made to villages or farms in an emergency.
Transport   Railway Stations at Swindon, Didcot and Newbury. Swindon to Ashbury bus service (Bristol Omnibus Co.). From Gore Hill walk to either Chilton or East Ilsley which are on the Oxford–Newbury bus route.
Accommodation   Inns at Ashbury, Compton and West Ilsley. Bed and Breakfast available locally. Youth Hostel at Streatley.
Guidebooks   *Discovering the Ridgeway* by Vera Burden (Shire Publications); *The Oldest Road, An Exploration of the Ridgeway* by J. R. L. Anderson and Fay Godwin (Wildwood House); *The Ridgeway Path* by Sean Jennett (H.M.S.O.); *Walks Along the Ridgeway* by Elizabeth Cull (Spur).

There is something satisfying about a route which follows a natural line, whether on a rock climb, a mountain ascent or simply a cross-country walk. This is certainly true of most sections of the ancient Ridgeway, which follows the escarpment of the chalk downs that run through Berkshire, Oxfordshire, and Wiltshire. It is a prehistoric trackway which links with the Icknield Way at the Goring/Streatley crossing of the Thames and climbs straight up onto the downs from there. After the first few miles of gradual ascent, it generally maintains a height of between 600ft. and 700ft. as it runs along the north edge of the downs almost to Swindon, then swings south to Overton Hill a mile or

so from Avebury. Many prehistoric sites, such as hill forts, burial mounds, and flint workings, are dotted along its length of more than 40 miles. On this basis it has been assumed that Neolithic Man preferred to live and to travel on chalk uplands, whose sparse vegetation made them safer than the thick forests and swamps of lower ground. An alternative view, supported by aerial photography, is that in fact there were quite as many settlements and trackways in the valleys, but these have since been obliterated by arable farming. In contrast, the Ridgeway tracks and adjacent prehistoric sites have survived particularly well because the land has always been used as pasture.

Top left: Here, on the slopes of White Horse Hill, Uffington, arable farming and the deeply-incised chalk escarpment are juxtaposed, forming a surreal pattern in the landscape. *Photo: Raymond Lea*

Above: Walkers head east along the Ridgeway above Kingston Lisle. *Photo: Marion Teal*

But whatever the truth of the matter, whether the Ridgeway was a major highway in prehistoric times or merely part of a complicated trackway system, you cannot walk along it without recognising that it must always have provided an excellent route across the country for the long distance traveller, if only because he could see quite clearly where he was going.

A section of the Ridgeway which is highly recommended for a day's walk lies between the B4000 out of Ashbury, and the A34 at Gore Hill (16 miles), to which the energetic might add the seven mile stretch to the Thames at Streatley. Guide books normally take the traveller from west to east, one of them making the sensible observation that the prevailing wind will then be at your back. Certainly we were very glad to be travelling in that direction when we first walked along the route, on a blowy March day. There is another advantage for those walkers who wish to visit two of the best prehistoric sites of the Ridgeway: Wayland's Smithy and White Horse Hill, Uffington. These both lie within three miles of the start, and it is pleasant to visit them first thing in the morning, when they may be deserted, and when you are fresh enough to enjoy a mile or so of detour around the White Horse and the hill fort at Uffington.

It is easy to find the start of the walk, for

where the Ridgeway crosses the Ashbury–Lambourne road, less than a mile south-east of Ashbury, it is running along the watershed in its typical way. Nearly a mile along the track there is, on the left, a conspicuous clump of beech trees which stand in a circle around the Neolithic long barrow known as Wayland's Smithy. This is constructed of the same huge sarsen stones as those found at Avebury, and is just the sort of place to inspire a legend. The smith-god Wayland is supposed to shoe a horse here during the night for the price of a silver coin, providing that no human remains to watch.

A mile after Wayland's Smithy, the track makes a fairly steep ascent to White Horse Hill. For those who want to explore this fascinating area, a stile gives access to the turf ramparts of Uffington Castle, an eight-acre Iron Age hill fort with a very commanding position. The famous White Horse, which is cut on the northern flank of the hill, has its origins shrouded in mystery but is usually considered to be at least 2,000 years old. It is quite remarkable that it has remained free of weeds throughout this time.

From White Horse Hill the Ridgeway continues in its general easterly direction without complication, crossing several minor roads and passing above the deep fold in the downs known as the Devil's Punchbowl. Here a photographer may feel strangely inadequate, as it is not easy to do justice to the subtle sculpturing of these slopes. The view beyond is spectacular, but many people do not approve of the increasing tendency of the Didcot Power Station cooling towers to dominate the landscape as you move east.

Perhaps this opinion results mainly from a strong association of ideas, for in fact the towers are rather fine structures and one cannot help thinking that the Megalithic builders of Avebury might have appreciated them. Equally, they might be admired as historic monuments by a future civilisation.

Another hill fort site lies by the Ridgeway on Segsbury Down, and shortly after this the route encounters its only complications. A right turn has to be made along the A338 for 30 yards before continuing east on a gravelled lane. Another right turn re-establishes the route on a typically wide and grassy track, and as long as you keep left at the fork a few hundred yards further on, the rest of the way is straightforward. A stone monument standing beside a clump of dogwood provides a useful landmark, for below the Ridgeway at this point lie sections of Grim's Ditch. This prehistoric earthwork was probably dug either as a territorial boundary or for defensive purposes, and runs approximately parallel with the route from here on across the Hendred and Chilton Downs.

After passing the turn to East Hendred, the final stretch to Gore Hill is particularly wide and open, a reminder of centuries of use as a drove road. Below sprawls the untidy complex of buildings that makes up the Atomic Energy Research Establishment at Harwell. To most of us it has little visual appeal, but we all have different ideas as to what makes an interesting landscape. One summer day we walked here when the air resonated with the songs of skylarks, when meadow browns, orange tips and marbled whites surrounded us with a continuous flutter of movement, when poppies lined the route and the aromatic scent of melilot accompanied us along the way. Unimpressed by any of this, one member of the party observed, 'This must be a unique view. From here you can see two nuclear reactors, a proton synchrotron, and a 1,200 Megawatt coal-fired power station.'

The walk ends as it began, at a point where its watershed route is intersected by a metalled road, in this case the A34. But really we should not call this an end, simply a convenient stopping place, for the path continues on to the Thames and beyond, and does not end until it reaches Norfolk.

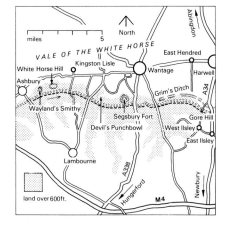

52   The Wiltshire Downs

by Geoffrey Wright

Paradoxically, man's roots appear to lie deepest where the soil is most shallow. Nowhere is this more apparent than on the chalklands of Wiltshire, where prehistoric man has left more legacies than almost anywhere else in Britain. Avebury is a focus for Neolithic sites, earthworks and ancient trackways, and forms an appropriate start and finish point for a perambulation through prehistory spanning 4,000 years in a dozen miles.

Nowhere is the scenery either spectacular or grand. Downland has calm, wide horizons with smoothly sensuous lines and gentle slopes, darkened only occasionally by beech clumps or the shadows of blue-massing clouds. Walking is best on the chalk in late spring or early summer, with hedgerows white-frothed and the turf gay with wild flowers. September and October have their own colourful rewards, but I find winter walking on the chalk the least pleasant of all.

A large car park on the southern edge of Avebury village is a good starting-point both for the walk and for a brief visit to the great stone circle, perhaps to absorb its atmosphere of brooding mystery engendered by the massive megaliths of standing sarsen stones. Leaving Avebury to the south by a footpath signposted 'Silbury', a track keeps to the edge of a succession of fields, crosses stiles, and soon brings Silbury Hill into view. If you wish to climb Europe's largest prehistoric mound (a mere 130ft. high, covering five acres, and formerly having a 20ft. ditch surrounding it), you need to detour a quarter of a mile westwards along the A4, pondering, perhaps, the sheer logistics of constructing it 4,000 years ago, a task estimated to have taken at least 500 men about ten years to complete. The view from the top in the arc to the south and west embraces the walk ahead.

Across the A4 a path is signposted 'West Kennett Long Barrow'. This soon crosses the infant River Kennett by a small bridge – impassable if the river is in flood, which occasionally happens in winter. Beyond the bridge, a track heads eastward to East Kennett village, but if you wish to see the remarkable Long Barrow you need another quarter mile detour up the downland slope to the south. In East Kennett, follow the metalled road right through the village, and

where the houses end and the road bears left, keep right, through the gate of East Kennett Manor Farm, along the route of the Ridgeway. The official Long Distance Footpath starts a mile to the north, on Overton Hill by the main Bath road, but our walk picks up its southward continuation, and, 200 yards beyond the farm buildings, by sarsen stones in the hedgerow, climbs a chalk bank onto open fields, with widening views northwards across a dry valley to swelling downland and the distant skyline accent of the Lansdown Column.

In rather less than a mile, the Ridgeway passes through a metal gate and enters a small copse, which soon becomes a narrow but very tangled belt of woodland, with oak, elder, and blackthorn. Here, in many Septembers, I have picked some of the fattest, juiciest blackberries anywhere. The jungle ends suddenly at open downland again, with views ahead to Adam's Grave, a prominent long barrow on Walker's Hill. To the immediate right (west) is the line of the Wansdyke, a linear defence work built probably in the sixth century, and running almost 60 miles across country from east of Marlborough to the Bristol Channel. Our way follows it westward for five miles to the A361, and a short way beyond to Morgan's Hill.

Route-finding is no problem. Path-finding is a little more difficult, for only sketchy tracks run along the grass-grown ramparts, first on one side, then the other. The deep ditch between is often heavily overgrown

Maps   O.S. 1:50,000 Sheet 173. Start and finish at Avebury (ref. 102699).
Grading   Generally easy walking, no steep gradients, but overgrown in some places.
Time   5–6 hours.
Distance   12–14 miles depending on whether small optional detours (Silbury Hill, West Kennett Long Barrow, Windmill Hill) are included.
Escape Routes   Numerous.
Telephones   Avebury; East Kennett.
Transport   Railway Station at Swindon. The Swindon–Devizes bus service passes through Avebury.
Accommodation   Hotels and Bed and Breakfasts at Avebury and surrounding villages.
Guidebooks   *Prehistoric Avebury* by A. Burl (Yale U.P.); *Exploring Prehistoric England* by P. J. Helm (Hale); *The Ridgeway Path* by Sean Jennett (H.M.S.O.)

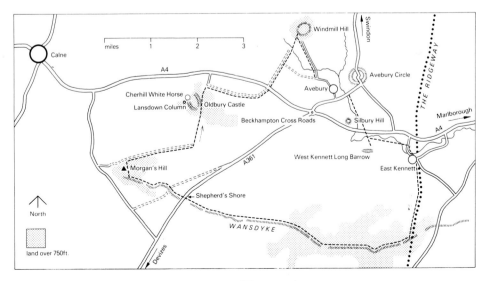

Left: Oldbury Hill Fort (upper photo) and approaching Silbury Hill (lower photo). *Photos: Van Greaves*

Top right: The racy figure of the Cherhill White Horse is a feature of relatively modern origin.
Photos: Van Greaves

Bottom right: Rocks of the Avebury Stone Circle – one of the finest Neolithic sites in Britain. *Photo: Richard Pearce*

with nettles or shrubs, and in any case is too enclosed to afford pleasant walking. At one stage the Wansdyke forms the northern boundary of the Pewsey Down National Nature Reserve, designated in 1977 to conserve its outstanding chalk down flora. Beyond this, it is best to keep to the south side of the earthwork, forsaking it in favour of a long, steady pull up the gentle slope of an enormous field to the highest part of the walk, where the Wansdyke crosses the northern shoulder of Tan Hill at about 900ft. Good tracks lead off north and north-east to Beckhampton and East Kennett, each about three miles away, and this is roughly the halfway stage of this walk. Ahead, the Wansdyke continues its writhing undulations westwards towards the A361, crossing it at Shepherd's Shore, where a wooden stile adjoining the northern end of farm buildings is optimistically waymarked 'Morgan's Hill'.

There is little evidence to indicate that the track is much used, but by keeping to the right-hand side of the Wansdyke, a chalk lane is eventually reached, crossed, and the left-hand rampart then sought and followed to the top of the hill, where two telecommunications masts are an aiming point. Avoid taking an apparent short-cut which passes close to them, but instead go through a wooden gate labelled 'Morgan's Hill Nature Reserve', keep the masts on your right (north), and continue along a good track until you meet another one coming up from the south. Turn right, descend a field to another wooden 'Nature Reserve' gate, and, with a small wood below you to the north, head eastwards along the well-defined line of the Roman Road from London to Bath. This is a good track, offering easier walking for one and a half miles.

On reaching a plantation of young trees on the right, turn left (north) through a small gate and follow a track curving gently upwards to the ramparts of Oldbury Castle, an Iron Age hill fort, with the now very prominent Lansdown Column (erected in 1845) on its eastern crest. This is the last climb of the walk, on to Cherhill Down (National Trust), about 850ft. Detour if you wish to see the huge monument close up, and also for a view of the Cherhill White Horse, a

130ft. long chalk figure cut into the turf of a north-facing combe in 1730. Descending northwards from Cherhill Down by a chalk lane, turn right (east) after passing some new waterworks, and follow an old track, now very overgrown with grass, running parallel to, but about 150ft. higher than, the busy A4. In a mile descend to a beech clump by the roadside, cross over, and take the metalled lane signposted 'Windmill Hill'.

In another half-mile a lane leads off to the right to Avebury, returning you to the western end of the village in a couple of miles. Alternatively, and if you are prepared to fight another jungle battle through a very dense thicket of elder, hawthorn and other bushes – another little-used public right-of-way – you can round off the prehistory with a visit to the geographically insignificant Windmill Hill, a low breast of open downland crowned by a number of disc barrows, with spacious, timeless views. Return to Avebury by a track leading from its south-west corner.

53   The Mendip Hills

by Robin Atthill

The great rolling mass of Mendip is now the frontier between Somerset and Avon: the range climbs slowly westwards from Frome to form the plateau which culminates in Black Down, before breaking up as it approaches the Bristol Channel. It is full of history, and ringed with beautiful villages that are studded with splendid houses and magnificent churches. The walk I recommend strikes southward straight across the range to the top of Cheddar Gorge, and then takes in the highest point of Black Down (1,065ft.) with the whole of the West Country spread out beneath your feet, and away across the Severn the great mountains of Wales.

Strike south from Bristol, over Dundry and past the Chew Valley Lake, to Compton Martin, lying under the rampart of Mendip. Between the pub and the church – a splendid church, full of solid Norman work – a lane runs up the hill into the combe, the cottages peter out, and you find yourself in an abandoned quarry. Swinging to the right and climbing steeply, you are in Compton Wood, and if you come in the spring you will be overwhelmed by the sheets of bluebells that seem to flood the hillside as you climb higher and higher. The wood ends just below Hazel Farm: turn and look at the view across the Chew Valley Lake, at the tumbled hills that carry your eye across to the Cotswolds beyond Bath, and further east the the White Horse above Westbury.

Beyond the farm you come to a lane along which you turn south. The lane becomes a drive that once swept round the field to Hazel Manor. Enlarged as a nineteenth-century shooting lodge, and gutted by fire in 1929, it gradually crumbled into ruin until the ruin was finally demolished and replaced by modern farm buildings. The walled garden which became a pig-run, the bothies and the gardener's cottage – these alone survived, reminders of one of the only large houses on Mendip.

On down the drive, past the little lodge, and out along the only stretch of road that you will be walking all day. This is real Mendip terrain, with its grey stone walls and its scattered, lonely farms, and the sense of remoteness and isolation which has survived since the enclosures were made, late in the

eighteenth century. At the Stirrup Cup – which is not a pub, and I'm afraid this is a very dry walk – follow the lane which skirts the grounds of what was once Nordrach Sanatorium, though the name has now disappeared from the map. When the lane swings left, you must climb a stile onto a track that brings you down into a wood. Here beside the track are the horizontal lead-flues that have miraculously survived from the middle of the nineteenth century – an industrial archaeologist's Mecca. In fact a classical archaeologist's Mecca too, for across the reedy lake, beyond the tumbled piles of lead-slag that survived the smelting, is the grid plan of a Roman settlement, and higher up the hill there is even a little amphitheatre.

Down the valley, now a nature reserve, you pass the desolate remains of old smelting sites. It is a dry valley now, for the water-course plunges underground below the limestone, though in 1968 tremendous summer storms built up the water level above ground and swept away both the causeways across the valley. On the high ground to the left is the site of Bleak House, where the manager of the mines kept watch, and behind that are huge clefts and pockets in the rock where the lead ore was dug out over three hundred years ago. Carry on down Velvet Bottom, which gouges its way deeper into the landscape, through spoil-heaps that mark more mine-workings, past the old buddles, shallow circular pits used for dressing the lead before smelting, past a series of dams built in

Maps O.S. 1:50,000 Sheet 182. Start and finish at Compton Martin (ref. 545571).
Grading Easy.
Time 6 hours.
Distance 15 miles.
Telephones Compton Martin; Cheddar; Charterhouse Outdoor Activities Centre.
Transport Bus from Bristol to Compton Martin (Bristol Omnibus Company). The Bath–Weston-super-Mare service also passes through the village.
Accommodation Hotel in West Harptree. Bed and Breakfast locally. Youth Hostel at Cheddar.
Guidebooks Mendip Walks by Tom Elkin (Mendip Publishing); Mendips – Caves and View from the Hills by Barrington and Stanton (Cheddar Valley Press).

Facing page: Collapsed cavern or the abandoned gorge of a once-powerful river? The precipitous splendour of Cheddar Gorge, can be appreciated from an alternative perspective by walkers who take the airy paths along its rim, instead of mingling with the sightseers who below. *Photo: West Air Photography*

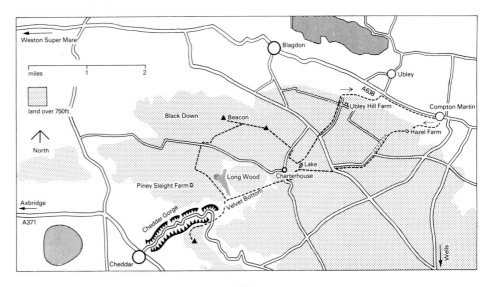

the last century to retain the water, wending your way down until you reach Black Rock Gate – and Cheddar Gorge.

Straight across the road, a path climbs the wooded escarpment on the far side: it is rough and steep, but gradually you come out into the open, and the gradient eases. The path climbs over a little ridge, and there before you stretches almost the whole of Somerset. The Bristol Channel reaches from Brean Down through Bridgwater Bay to Countisbury Foreland; Exmoor, the Quantocks, the Blackdowns, and the Dorset Heights lie away across the moors; close below you is Cheddar Reservoir, dotted perhaps with tiny sailing craft; and immediately below, on your right, is a 400ft. drop down the cliffs, almost perpendicular, into the gorge.

When you have feasted your eyes on this classic landscape you must turn, reluctantly, and make your way down to Black Rock Gate again, and start back up the valley towards Charterhouse. But when the track forks, you must turn up the left-hand valley, and when you come to Long Wood, keep outside the wood on the west side, and climb the track that brings you out across the fields until you reach the rough road from Piney Sleight. Turn right along it, across the metalled road from Charterhouse, and take the path that leads up to the nick in the skyline.

This is Black Down, the highest point on Mendip, and smothered in glorious heather if you're here in August. It's worth digressing to the summit to get the stupendous view to the north and west, from Dundry right across the Bristol Channel to the Brecon Beacons and the Black Mountains. Then you must turn away eastwards along the drove road, which brings you down off Black Down, past the Roman settlement, back to the minery.

Don't go back to Nordrach unless you are pressed for time, but take the path beside the lake that goes up across the fields along the parish boundary to the Blagdon road, at a point where the map marks a boundary stone. Go straight on up the lane, and on the crest beyond Ubley Hill Farm you will get your last great panorama – Blagdon Lake, girdled by its hills – and then it's all downhill until you reach the road above Ubley, about a mile and a half from where you started in Compton Martin – and if you're lucky, there may even be a bus.

Above left: A superb spiral pillar in Compton Martin Church – a rare feature in English Romanesque architecture, and similar to the famous chevron columns of Durham Cathedral. *Photo: Mike Bate*

Below left: At Black Down summit, highest point in the Mendips. *Photo: Dick Sale*

Above: Velvet Bottom, the dry limestone valley which provides a delicate prelude to the grandeur of Cheddar Gorge. *Photo: Leonard and Marjorie Gayton*

54   The Dunkery Circuit

by Brian Chugg

Maps O.S. 1:50,000 Sheet 181; O.S. 1:63,360 Tourist Map – Exmoor. Start and finish at Horner (ref. 898455).
Grading A high and exposed moorland walk. Not recommended to inexperienced parties in bad conditions.
Time 6 hours.
Distance 11 miles.
Escape Routes The walk crosses minor roads near Lang Combe Head and Thurley Combe. Each offers a direct return to Horner or Porlock.
Telephones Private telephones (for emergency use only) at Horner, Cloutsham, Wilmersham and Lucott.
Transport Porlock, 1½ miles from Horner, is served by buses from Minehead and (in summer) Lynmouth.
Accommodation Hotels and Bed and Breakfasts at Porlock. Youth Hostels at Exford and Minehead.
Guidebooks *National Park Guide No. 8 Exmoor* (H.M.S.O.); *Waymarked Walks No. 2* (Exmoor National Park); *Exmoor* by S. H. Burton (Hodder and Stoughton); *Portrait of Exmoor* by J. H. B. Peel (Hale).

Top right: Dunkery Beacon (1,705ft.), the highest point on Exmoor, is a popular venue with all kinds of outdoor enthusiasts.
Photo: Geoffrey Wright

Bottom right: Bridlepaths bisect the tangled, heathery plateau of Exmoor; fortunately, for the heather itself is rough going.
Photo: Brian Chugg

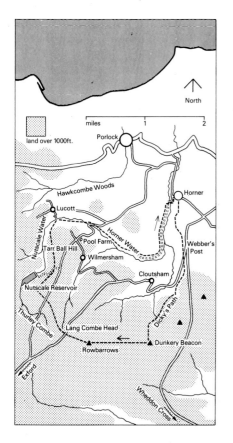

To the south of Porlock, near the Somersetshire coast, lies some magnificent scenery which attracted the attention of such of the romantic poets as Coleridge and Southey, and appeals increasingly to the modern cross-country walker. A spectacular system of wooded valleys is guarded by the 'triple-crown' of Dunkery Hill, 1,705ft. No other part of the Exmoor National Park rises as high; few wooded valleys in the South West approach the depth of these and, arguably, no other hill country in southern England as a whole is so grandly proportioned. The exceptional views from the top remind me that this is the boundary between the productive farmlands of the southern counties and the acid soils and harsher climate of our western moors.

On this walk field naturalists will discover two of the characteristic types of habitat to be found on Exmoor: open heather moor and ancient, semi-natural woodland. The contrast between the high moor with its sparse ground-cover and the woodland paths in the valleys, hidden during the summer under the lush leaf-canopy, is indeed striking.

Between the fourteenth and the mid-seventeenth century, Dunkery was a signal station, and some of the paths by which the beacon may be approached today felt the tread of purposeful feet in earlier times. The woodland rides also were probably sketched out when this was part of a Royal Forest and Cloutsham was a hunting lodge. So, from the points of view of scenic excellence, ecological interest and a long tradition of human use, there is no hesitation in describing this walk as classic.

From the starting place – the hamlet of Horner – Dunkery Hill is visible beyond the valley to the south. I trust that Dunkery will not be obscured by cloud or mist on the day chosen for a first visit. The walk is a pleasure in any season, but visitors should not assume that the southerly latitude is a guarantee of mild weather. When snow or heavy rain is forecast the walk should not be attempted, because serious hazards develop rapidly.

Leave Horner Green by walking eastwards. Soon after passing the mill on the south side of the lane a sign-post indicates the path to Webber's Post. Between the trees on the left there will be glimpses of Selworthy church on the opposite side of Porlock Vale. Keep to the centre of the incline in order to reach, by the shortest route, the saddle of land known as Webber's Post. The central section of the circuit now spreads out before you. At some places combes where hawthorn, rowan, and alders struggle and whortleberry thrives, reach up from the valleys into the heather-covered moors which dominate the skyline. Most of what can be seen was presented to the National Trust by the former owners, Sir Richard Ackland and Colonel W. Wiggin.

The road from Horner to Wheddon Cross can be seen ascending the hill immediately to the south of Webber's Post. Find a path on the west of this road. This involves crossing a side road which goes to Cloutsham. Then, if the day is fine, there is no problem, because the summit will be visible and a westward-leading path can be selected. The most gradual climb is produced by taking a section of Dicky's Path, which commences just below the 1,000ft. contour where it meets the Horner–Wheddon Cross road. In just under a mile, a north–south path from Cloutsham is reached; here, turn south. A steep, half-mile climb then brings us near the top, but the cairn itself will not come into view until the last minute. From this point a vast panorama is visible on clear days. Two Bronze Age barrows lie on the near western horizon, in a stretch of moor where the red grouse or the black grouse are sometimes put up by walkers. A path leads directly to these barrows, Little and Great Rowbarrow.

At the barrows, turning north-west, follow the well-trodden path – it is downhill almost all the way from this point! Go across the road at Lang Combe Head and continue in a north-westerly direction. Cross the Exford–Pool Farm road, then head towards Nutscale reservoir, which supplies Minehead. This is the only part of the route where there is no obvious trail. Walk over the heather moor to bring the reservoir into view. The aim of the walker should then be to reach the banks of Nutscale Water at Lucott ford, approximately one mile beyond the reservoir.

Walkers will have noticed that in some localities hedged fields, which support a large population of sheep, have been established between the woods and the moors.

The fields of Pool Farm and Wilmersham, which are being skirted, illustrate the fact that although Exmoor is a National Park, it is also a place of work for those who live there.

To return to the hillside above the reservoir: follow the track which passes along the contour until it connects with the path that crosses Tarr Ball Hill. After about three-quarters of a mile, join the narrow, surfaced road for a short distance. At the hairpin bend, continue ahead in the direction of Lucott. Height is gradually being lost and, joining a stony lane, the stream is reached.

At this stage walkers who would like to extend the walk can go through Lucott and return to Horner through Hawkcombe woods and, possibly, Porlock. But the last few miles beside Horner Water may be among the most interesting of the circuit, especially for ornithologists. Many of this country's woodland birds and migrants frequent the area. Following the cascading stream, we proceed through attractive oak woods. Here too, there may be a glimpse of the wild red deer.

55   The Quantocks

by David Clemson

Maps   O.S. 1:50,000 Sheet 181. Start and finish at Holford (ref. 157411).
Grading   Easy.
Time   5–6 hours.
Distance   12 miles.
Escape Routes   Descents from high ground may be easily made to the villages of Nether Stowey, Crowcombe, Bicknoller and West Quantoxhead.
Telephones   Holford; Crowcombe; Bicknoller.
Transport   Railway Stations at Taunton and Bridgwater. The Bridgwater–Minehead bus service (Western National) passes through Holford. The Taunton–Minehead service passes through Crowcombe.
Accommodation   Numerous Hotels, Inns and Bed and Breakfasts in the surrounding villages. Youth Hostels at Holford and Crowcombe.
Guidebooks   *Discovering the Quantocks* by Berta Lawrence (Shire Publications); *Portrait of the Quantocks* by V. Waite (Hale).

The Quantock Hills of Somerset are often regarded as a mere backdrop to the north Somerset coast, lying as they do between the Mendips to the north-east and Exmoor to the west. But for the discerning walker who appreciates fine views and also enjoys a great variety of flora and fauna, then the Quantocks must rate highly. For the 'mountain peak collector' or the 'route marcher', the view of the Quantocks from the Black Mountains of Wales, across the Bristol Channel, will probably suffice, but for the classic walker the vista from the Somerset side must be experienced. The Quantock Hills have a quiet dignity and majesty, despite the incursions of man throughout history, upon the slopes, amongst the combes, and along the ridges. Here can be found hamlets, drove roads, tumuli, ancient camps, and the Forestry Commission. Here can also be found deer, solitude, free-roaming ponies, and a multitude of flowers.

Variety of flora and fauna depends not only upon climate and afforestation by man, but also, fundamentally, on the geological strata underlying the landscape. The Quantocks have three main foundations. At the northern end we have the oldest rock, the Hangman grits, which underlie the highest point of the hills, rising to 1,261ft. at Will's Neck. Then come the Ilfracombe beds, a mixture of sandstones, slates, and limestones in which fossils can be found. Finally, in the southern section, we find the youngest rocks, the Morte slates.

I have chosen a circular route as, for me, this represents a convenient and satisfying pattern for walking and, in the environs of the Quantocks, also permits a wide variety of changing landscapes to be sampled. The starting and finishing point for the walk is the village of Holford on the north-eastern corner of the hills, about two miles from the coast and on the main A39 Bridgwater to Minehead road. Although a circular route, it is possible to reach the route via off-shoot spurs at a number of points. These include Nether Stowey, Kilve, West Quantoxhead, Bicknoller and Crowcombe.

Holford is a picturesque village and is a popular stopping-off point not only for its charm but also for its connections with Wordsworth. Nearby Alfoxton is where

Wordsworth wrote a number of his poems, and Dorothy kept her journal. Whilst you may move west or south out of Holford on this walk, I have chosen to move south, as the latter stages of the walk are then in the direction of the sea. On precious fine days it sometimes feels as though you could step straight across the Bristol Channel.

Moving south from the centre of the village, you enter Holford Combe and follow the small, delightful stream up a gentle gradient for about a mile, crossing the water as the path dictates. Here I have seen, at different times, the fairy-story toadstool fly agaric which, after drying, helped the Vikings to while away their long sea voyages with its hallucinogenic effect (not to be recommended; it can be fatal!), and magnificent fritillaries basking in the warmth of the sun. To your left you will see Dowsborough, the site of an Iron Age camp, standing at 1,000ft., and the steeper gradient on its south-western slopes represents the first pause for breath. Just after the climb, and almost directly south of Dowsborough, you will meet a narrow road and, turning right, you should follow it south for about half a mile to a junction with the Crowcombe–Nether Stowey road. Nether Stowey is famous for its connection with Samuel Taylor Coleridge, for it was here that he wrote 'The Rime of the Ancient Mariner' and 'Kubla Khan'. Coleridge's cottage in the village, maintained by the National Trust, is worth a visit.

Almost directly opposite the road junction there is a pull-in for cars, and a broad trackway leading south towards the adjacent Quantock Forest. This trackway is known as Dead Woman's Ditch, and stories abound about its origins. Walk down the Ditch and enter the forest. Following the contour tracks to the right and then to the left will bring you down into Rams Combe, and a stream, which you follow eastwards until it is joined

Top right: The mudflats of the Bristol Channel, stretching away to the north, lend the Quantocks a sense of distance and wide horizons out of all proportion to their height, as in this view from their western end near Beacon Hill *Photo: Van Greaves*

Bottom right: The drove road between Triscombe and Crowcombe Park Gate runs through an avenue of gnarled beeches. *Photo: David Clemson*

Above: Autumn in the Quantocks – a rider heads south from Crowcombe Park Gate.
Photo: Dick Sale

by the Quantock Combe stream. These woodlands are good places for a sight of the deer which abound on the Quantocks, and also for the huge wood ants' nests which are composed of pine needles and can be as large as five feet high and fifteen feet across! Turn right into Quantock Combe and follow it upstream for about half a mile, when a path to the south will lead you up through Great Wood and, again after about half a mile, to the metalled road to Triscombe Stone. Take this road uphill until you reach the car park.

You have now reached the southernmost point of the walk, and are adjacent to the Ilfracombe beds. You are also on the Drove Road which runs north-west to Crowcombe Park Gate between grand beeches, and which marks your path for the next mile and a half. As you progress along the route it is possible to view the Brendon Hills and, beyond and to the west, Exmoor. In the valley below runs the A358 and the old railway line from Taunton to Minehead, which is now run by the West Somerset Railway Company.

When you reach Crowcombe Park Gate

(there isn't a gate), the exposed ridge opens up atop the grits, and the track to be taken unfolds itself before you as a pale, dusty strip to the north-west. Here you move into a moorland habitat, with stunted trees, heathers, and whortleberry. Crossing the Crowcombe road, you step out along the ridge and towards the sea. To left and right over the next two to three miles, you will see tumuli, skylarks and, perhaps, the Quantock ponies, which are rounded up each year, some for sale and some to return. The furthermost point north of the route is the triangulation point on Beacon Hill, a good spot at which to lean your back and gaze out over West and East Quantoxhead and across the Channel, in which the islands of Flatholm and Steepholm can be seen. It is necessary to retrace your steps now for about half a mile and then, bearing east, turn towards the woods of Hodder's Combe beneath Lady's Edge. Hodder's Combe leads back to Holford village, our starting and finishing combes being two of the most beautiful in the Quantock Hills.

56   A Visit to Cranmere Pool

by Hugh Westacott

Dartmoor is often described as the last wilderness in southern England. This is an apt description, but it has encouraged the idea, sedulously fostered in Conan Doyle's *Hound of the Baskervilles*, that the whole of the Moor is one vast, heaving, primeval swamp, into which men and animals alike sink without trace. This, of course, is nonsense. Like all hill areas, Dartmoor must be treated with respect, but Conan Doyle's dreaded Grimpen Mires are totally fictitious; the mires, fens, and feather-beds are easily recognised, and even if blundered into by accident during a mist, are unlikely to give the walker anything worse than wet feet.

The fascination of Dartmoor lies not so much in its scenery, which is wild but not nearly so spectacular as other National Parks, or indeed some parts of the Devon coastline, but for its peculiar, brooding atmosphere and for the many archaeological remains and the evidence of the more recent mining and quarrying activities which litter the Moor. This walk is 17 miles, and it includes some of the wildest parts of Dartmoor and a visit to Cranmere Pool which, until the construction of the military road, was in the most remote and inaccessible part of the Moor.

The walk starts from the car park in Postbridge, on the B3212 (small shop, pub which serves bar snacks, Lydgate House Hotel which serves lunches and cream teas). Walk downhill to the East Dart river, turn downstream past the medieval clapper bridge, and then walk towards the forest edge. Cross the road and walk through some fields to the Lych Way, an ancient trackway which linked this part of the Moor with the parish church of Lydgate on the western edge of Dartmoor. Turn right and head westward through the forest, cross the B3212, and make for the chimney of Powder Mills, where gunpowder was manufactured. Cross the clapper bridge, turn right, and then bear left to reach a hunting gate in the wall between Littaford Tors and Longford Tor, and climb to the top of the ridge.

Below is the valley of the West Dart and the stunted oaks of Wistman's Wood. Skirt the northern edge of the wood, descend into the valley, cross the river (difficult if in flood), and follow the left-hand side of a stone wall to pass close to Lydford Tor to reach the Cowsic river at Traveller's Ford. At this point, leave the track and head north along the west bank of the Cowsic until you reach its headwaters.

From now on the going becomes rough, as there is no clear path and the terrain is broken. Take a compass bearing and make for the slight dip between Fur Tor and Cut Hill, and then continue to Black Hill, skirting the edge of Cut Combe Water. From the top of the aptly-named Black Hill continue due north for about three-quarters of a mile to Cranmere Pool. Despite its name, there is hardly ever any water in it these days and it is no more than a large hollow of quaking bog and peat.

Many years ago, when Dartmoor was first being discovered by tourists, a famous Dartmoor guide, James Perrott, used to take visitors to the Pool which in those days always contained water. In 1854 he left a large screw-top jar at Cranmere Pool in which postcards were left to be collected and mailed by the next party. Nowadays there is a brick-built letterbox maintained by the National Park Department containing a visitor's book and a rubber stamp in which to record your visit. There is an interesting legend connected with Cranmere Pool. It is supposed to be haunted by the ghost of Benjamin Gayer (Benjie Gear), who appears as a dwarf and can sometimes be heard sobbing as he pursues his endless task of constructing dykes to prevent the water of Cranmere Pool draining away. His spirit was set this task after he died of remorse for appropriating ransom money intended to release prisoners of the Turks.

Leave Cranmere Pool by heading southwest to East Dart Head, which lies in an extensive area of bog. Keep to the western edge of the bog and walk down the valley. Gradually the stream becomes more definite in shape as it increases in volume, and it will be necessary to cross over from time to time to find the best route. At Sandy Hole Pass the East Dart passes through a gorge, and here there is evidence of the banks being narrowed and built up by tin miners in the last century. Nearly a mile later, the river sweeps round to the north and then turns south, and it is important to get onto the eastern bank before it gets too wide and deep. Cross a

Maps   O.S. 1:63,360 Tourist Map of Dartmoor; O.S. 1:50,000 Sheet 191. Start and finish at Postbridge (ref. 645790).
Grading   A long and rough walk over wild and remote moorland. Can be serious in bad conditions. Part of the route passes through firing ranges and it is essential to check that these are open by by telephoning the Range Officer at Okehampton 2939 before leaving Postbridge.
Time   7 hours.
Distance   17 miles.
Escape Routes   The military road 1 mile N of Cranmere Pool.
Telephones   Postbridge; Bellever.
Transport   Postbridge is on the Plymouth to Moretonhampstead bus route. This infrequent service operates at weekends and Bank holidays from mid-June to the end of September with an additional service on Wed from the third week in July to the third week in August.
Accommodation   Hotel at Postbridge. Youth Hostel at Bellever.
Guidebooks   *Guide to Dartmoor* by William Crossing, edited by Brian Le Messurier (David and Charles); *The Penguin Guide to Dartmoor* by H. D. Westacott (Penguin); *Walks and Rides on Dartmoor* by H. D. Westacott (Footpath Publications); *Exploring Dartmoor* by F. H. Starkey (published by the author, High Orchard, Haytor Vale, Newton Abbot).

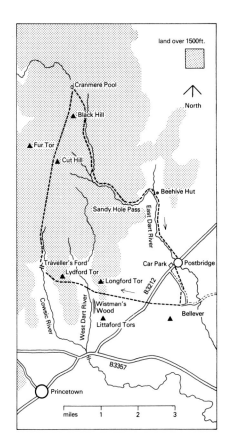

tributary stream and follow the east bank of the main river past the famous Beehive Hut. Nobody knows how old this hut is, but it undoubtedly represents an age-old tradition in hut building and the many ancient huts still to be seen on the Moor, but which are rarely more than one stone high, must have looked like this one in their heyday. A path heads due north towards Fenworthy Forest, and if this is followed for about a mile, you will come upon a fine double circle of standing stones. This is unquestionably of prehistoric origin, although it cannot be dated precisely.

Continue following the river until you reach a large house on the left, hidden in a belt of trees. Turn left along the edge of the field beyond the house, and then right at the end of the field. On reaching the road, turn right, and walk back to the car park.

Above: Grey Wethers Stone Circle, just north of the Beehive Hut. *Photo: Don Sargeant*

Above left: The East Dart River at Postbridge. *Photo: Andy Hosking*

Far left: A Dartmoor pony picks its way across typical Dartmoor terrain. *Photo: Dave Matthews*

Near left: At Cranmere Pool. *Photo: Peter Wild*

57   Lamorna Cove to Pendeen Watch

by Dave Cook

Maps O.S. 1:50,000 Sheet 203. Start from Lamorna Cove (ref. 450243). Finish at Pendeen (ref. 382344) or Zennor (ref. 454385).

Grading A long and varied walk which follows a waymarked path hugging the edge of a rugged and fascinating stretch of coastline.

Time Allow at least 2 days to derive maximum enjoyment from this magnificent walk.

Distance 21 miles to Pendeen (the described route) or 26 miles to Zennor.

Escape Routes Numerous.

Telephones Widely distributed in the villages along the coast or just inland.

Transport Railway Stations at Penzance and St. Ives. Regular weekday bus services from Penzance to Lamorna, Penzance to St. Just and St. Just to St. Ives via Pendeen and Zennor.

Accommodation Hotels, Inns, Guest Houses and Bed and Breakfasts abound. Youth Hostels at Penzance, Land's End and Hayle (near St. Ives).

Guidebooks *Cornwall Coast Path* by the Countryside Commission (H.M.S.O.); *Walking the North Cornwall Coastal Footpath* by Mark Richards (Thornhill Press); *Cornwall's Coastal Footpaths* by W. V. Hunter (Tor Mark Press); *Cornwall's Structure and Scenery* by R. M. Barton (Tor Mark Press).

Top right: Botallack Mine. The ruins of mines stand all along the North Cornish Coast in gaunt witness to a once-important industry now almost extinct. Their workings frequently run far out beneath the Atlantic in search of precious lodes of metal. In the eighteenth and nineteenth centuries the Cornish miners were regarded as the master-craftsmen of the mining industry, and carried their expertise throughout the world. *Photo: Tom Parker*

Bottom right: Ruined mine buildings near Pendeen. *Photo: Derek Forss*

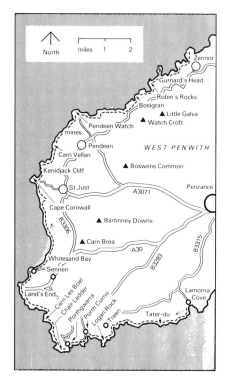

A wave starting from North America has a 3,000 mile run at Cornwall. Usually when the sea hits our land, in the long run it's no contest. South coast cliffs slither stealthily downhill, and regular injections of concrete are needed to prevent large chunks of East Anglia, like Atlantis, disappearing beneath the waves. In Land's End, and the granite fortress from which it projects, the Atlantic has a worthy opponent. More than anywhere on England's coastline, here we have a contest. Which makes the walk from Lamorna, round the tip of Britain's south-west mainland extremity to Pendeen light-house not only a circuit of majestic beauty, but also a unique grandstand for watching this timeless duel. A decade ago, when the requirements of politics and work meant a move with heavy heart from towns with the Pennines on the skyline, I felt that nothing south of Derby could compensate for the cliffs and moorlands of my youth. However, over the years this iron-clad coast has come to provide a backdrop to walking and climbing that is in every way as satisfying as northern hills.

This walk round Land's End divides neatly into three parts; twelve miles along the sunny south side; then nine going north to Pendeen Watch; with the possible hard man's extension of a further five, doubling back eastwards to Gurnard's Head and Zennor. We did the trip over two afternoons at the beginning of January, but an early start and a couple of lunchtime pints at the 'Old Success' in Sennen Cove, should see a stout walker round in a day.

The toytown cove of Lamorna sparkled like a diamond as we climbed onto the switchback of mud and gorse, neatly sign-posted with little acorns, that forms what the OS map calls with remarkable inexactness the 'Cornwall North Coast Pathway'. Being right at the very end of England, there may be some excuse for confusing left and right, but in Cornwall there most definitely is a north and south!

Evenly spaced and gently graded head-lands took us to the day's first lighthouse, Tater-du's squat and gleaming tower. Then to a unique feature in West Penwith, woods beside the sea, gnarled and festooned with moss, grotesquely out of place in this land where every tree is forced to grow sideways rather than high. We skirted the foreshore, mingling with the polystyrene beside the waves.

Logan Rock now filled the horizon, pointing like a giant howitzer at America and the darkening sky. Penberth's cluster of houses and fishing boats nestled on its leeward side, its sheltering gulls startled by our clattering heels. From here on the coastline begins to crumble, jagged fingers squeezing little bays of tawny sand. Some, like Porth Curno, are dressed for the part, with car parks, an open-air theatre, and deserted tea-rooms. Others, like Pednvounder, are secluded and usually deserted, magic strips of paradise hammered out of the rocky walls.

We dropped down to the sea again at Porthgwarra's tiny cove, amazed to see a sign giving details of the harbour master. With room for a couple of boats and no more, this man must be a candidate for the 'Guinness Book of Records'. The next three miles is rock-climbing coast and looks it. Proud pillars of marmalade-coloured granite cream out of the thumping sea. Great caverns testify to the awesome power of those thumps. With darkness gathering, we sped over the dry moorland turf into Land's End's deserted car parks. Strange islands of white-ringed rock, the Armed Knight, Kettle's Bottom, the Peal, and the Irish Lady, thundered eerily in the gloom. Last lap, and we spiralled steeply down into Sennen Cove, where ghostly wet-suited figures were pulling their frozen surf-boards from the foam.

Next day, the flail of Atlantic rain forbade departure until early afternoon. Cold, damp monochrome and slatey seas would frame our horizons today. From Sennen we galumphed through the sand, into an even lovelier miniature extension a mile round the bay. Here, in summer, nudists now play, although not without also exposing Cornwall's split personality on these things. Local residents, pressing for a ban, dis-covered that holiday brochures advertised their beach as a naturists' haven to the World, even as they petitioned their Council. Today, only wet dogs ran on the sand as the west wind drove us back onto the cliffs, as if

we had idled too long in this land of cream teas. Cape Cornwall seemed very near, but a steep-sided narrow valley, its flanks honey-combed with old mine workings, was an unexpected obstacle. A similar feature defended the Cape on the north side, this time with its river barely jumpable because of winter rains.

A steep climb to Kenidjack Castle signalled a dramatic change in the atmosphere of the walk. A mining graveyard lay before us, with chimneys and wheelhouses looming gauntly out of the mist. Unlike many West Riding valleys, where much of the industrial debris has been vanquished by nature's counter-attack, here the old buildings, blasted clean by onshore gales, are built of stone so hard they will stand for ever. The result is a landscape of overwhelming melancholy.

It is easy to miss the great rock features with which this section of coastline bristles, because the old mine trackways which the

Top: The coastal path above Tater-du, west of Lamorna, is at its best in spring, when the cliff tops are covered with wild daffodils.
Photo: Richard Wilson

Above: The Mynack Theatre – situated in a splendid position above the granite cliffs opposite Logan Rock. *Photo: Richard Wilson*

Centre: The ruined buildings of the Botallack Mine at St Just, showing their spectacular position above the cliffs. *Photo: Tom Parker*

path joins were built with other things in mind than sightseeing. Carn Vellan in particular juts menacingly above the sea, but few will see its intimidating profile. However, no-one can miss the amazing sequence of mine-workings, that at one point stride down towards the waves, as if, in a collective suicide pact, the tin industry, unable to bear Bolivia any longer, decided to return from whence it came.

Suddenly, at Boscaswell, industrialisation's last outriders fade away. Pendeen Watch

loomed bold and white out of the rain, a beacon for us on the cliff-top path as well as for the ships beyond. We looked at the lowering sky, and thinking of the long miles that lay between Gurnard's Head and ourselves, scuttled fast into the cosy warmth of 'The Radjel'.

We didn't finish the walk ourselves on this short and stormy winter's day, though a strong walker with more time on his hands might easily have done so. A pity, for the five miles from Pendeen Watch to Zennor are as

spectacular as any on the walk. The Whirl Pool; the crossing of the top of Commando Ridge, a rock-climb of serrated, easy magnificence, a sinewy spine of rock stretching from the ocean to the bouldery moors, carrying a plaque to the Marine Commandos who trained here in the war years; Porthmoina Cove, with its basking shark of an island and the gleaming wonder-cliff of Bosigran Face beyond; Robin's Rocks, above which is a mind-blowing passage through a cleft crag; Zawn Duel, deep,

green, dripping, and evil; Gurnard's Head, a crescendo, a vicious club of promontory battering back at the sea; all these before you heave up the valley-reach to Zennor, and your numbed senses gratefully ease out across the purples and browns which cloak the granite-studded backbone of West Penwith. We knew it well, but it was not for us on this winter's evening. We left it out there, still waging its unceasing, elemental warfare, as we settled down by the fire in Pendeen's favourite pub.

Above: Typical Cornish granite cliff scenery at Logan Rock, with the fine beach of Porth Curno visible at lower left. *Photo: Phil Ideson*

58   The Dorset Coast and the Purbeck Hills

by Eric Newby

Maps   O.S. 1:50,000 Sheets 194 and 195; O.S. 1:25,000 Outdoor Leisure Map – Purbeck. Start from Corfe Castle (ref. 959824). Finish at Hardy Monument (ref. 613877).
Grading   A long but easy walk.
Time   8–9 hours.
Distance   27 miles.
Escape Routes   Numerous.
Telephones   Corfe Castle; East Creech; West Lulworth; Portesham; Martinstown.
Transport   Railway Stations at Poole and Wareham. Daily bus service Poole–Wareham–Corfe Castle–Swanage.
Accommodation   Hotels, Inns and Bed and Breakfasts abound in the area. Youth Hostels at Swanage and Litton Cheney.
Guidebooks   *The Dorset Coast* by R. J. W. Hammond (Ward Lock). *Days Out in Dorset* by Joy Parsons (Thornhill Press).

Top right: Dorset boasts some of the finest sections of English coastal scenery, abounding in marvellous natural features – elegant beaches, rolling hills and chalk cliffs, tide-eroded pinnacles and arches. The walkers in this picture are heading east past Durdle Door.
Photo: Andy Hosking

Bottom right: Lulworth Cove.
Photo: Leonard and Marjorie Gayton

From Corfe Castle to the Hardy Monument on Black Down is a longish day's walk. I make it 29 miles, including those to the nearest passing-out points where there are pubs. In winter this can be a very cold walk. If the wind and rain are strong from the west, start at the Monument; if easterly, which can be bitter, start at Corfe. In winter expect lots of mud and in summer lots of pollen.

Note that the walk will be impossible if there is firing on the Lulworth ranges. Walks through the ranges are normally open for about six weekends a year, three weeks around Christmas, a week at Easter, at the beginning of June and from the end of July until mid-September. Check with the Range Officer at Bindon Abbey 462721.

And so to the walk. Leave Corfe Castle. Cross the Corfe River where it goes under the road to Church Knowle and climb West Hill onto the downs. Then head west (it is impossible to get lost) along the whaleback of chalk and grass over Knowle Hill.

Pass Creech Barrow, enormous tump on right, from which in clear weather, and if you can spare the energy for the detour, you can see your destination, the Monument, beyond Dorchester.

Grange Arch. The magnificent facade of the manor house can be seen by looking down a cutting in the wood to the north of it. Shortly after this you enter the Lulworth Firing Range Area which extends six miles to the west and the next two miles is on road, but with wide views opening up now to the south-east over St. Aldhelm's Head.

At Povington Hill car park, 623ft. up, turn left off the road along the range walk. Inland are the tank ranges, dotted with burnt-out tanks and, miles away, the North Dorset Downs.

Flower's Barrow, a magnificent Iron Age hill fort on Rings Hill, part of which has fallen away into Worbarrow Bay, more than 500ft. below. The view west over Arish Mell, the offshore Mupe Rocks, and westwards towards Weymouth is one of the greatest land/seascapes in southern England.

Now descend, past a tumulus miraculously preserved from the shell-fire which has pitted the surrounding chalk hills, to Arish Mell, a minute cove sealed off with barbed wire. Then climb the near-vertical slopes of Bindon Hill, from whose high cliffs a detour can be made to Mupe Bay and a remarkable forest of fossilised trees.

Lulworth Cove and West Lulworth, with an enormous car park, just what one has come on this walk to avoid, which destroys the feeling, that may now have built up, that the world belongs to you alone.

The Dorset Coast Path now follows one of the most spectacular sections of its entire length, an astonishing switchback over Dungy Head, Durdle Door, Bat's Head, and along to Burning Cliff above Ringstead Bay. If you are not familiar with this superb stretch of cliff, with its arches and pinnacles of white limestone, you should follow the cliff-top path. However, today I have my sights set on the Monument and so I take an alternative route, parallel to the Coast Path but a little way inland, rejoining the designated path near Ringstead Bay.

From Hambury House I take a path along the north side of Hambury Tout, then beside one of the more unfortunately positioned caravan sites in this part of England to Newlands Farm. Here I pick up a fine, unfrequented ridgeway, very muddy in winter, with wide views inland and seawards.

Pass a tall obelisk, a beacon or seamark, and then a stone with an inscription to the memory of Llewelyn Powys, the Dorset novelist and essayist, on which I sit for a moment.

Plod on to South Down, a stretch of

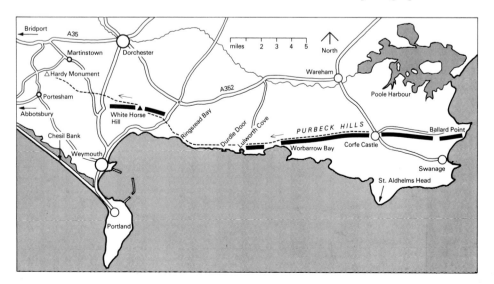

Top: A view to the west along the beach and cliffs by Durdle Door – a beautiful coastline unfortunately still utilized for military purposes.
Photo: Tom Parker

National Trust green downland above Ringstead Bay, with Weymouth and Portland quite close now. And from here a mile or so, mostly by road, down to Upton.

Now up the slopes of White Horse Hill, catching a fleeting glimpse of George III on horseback cut in the chalk. Continue along the ridgeway for two very muddy miles, passing prehistoric tumuli in ever-increasing numbers until reaching the corner of Came Wood. This wood concealed invasion forces in 1944, and nearby is a bank barrow 600ft. long with round barrows at either end and some bell barrows hidden away in the wood itself.

Follow the tarmac road west past a golf course, and a secret establishment buried deep in the chalk.

Cross the main Weymouth–Dorchester road and continue along the ridgeway which is now hemmed in on every side by huge tumuli, the biggest of which, at the crossing of the B3145 from Upwey to Martinstown, is an enormous disc barrow 80ft. in diameter, enclosed by a ditch and an outer bank.

Fine views now over the vast green bulk of Maiden Castle to Dorchester. I am on the last few miles, and among the greatest concentration of tumuli in Dorset. Climbing gently over Corton Down and along the ridge of Bronkham Hill, the tumuli are everywhere like giant mushrooms.

Reach the summit of Black Down, 777ft., the highest point of the entire walk, with the ugly monument to Admiral Sir Thomas Hardy, a sort of chimney with a bulging top, looming another 70ft. above it.

From the Monument the energetic can continue to Abbotsbury Castle, otherwise walk south down to Portesham or Abbotsbury or north to Winterbourne Abbas or Martinstown.

59   High Level from Guildford to Box Hill

by Christopher John Wright

Beyond the sprawl of London's southern suburbs rises the chalk escarpment of the North Downs. Its more gentle northern slopes are forested in parts, while its steep southern scarp slope is mostly bare, uncultivated common land. Running along the ridge is an exhilarating path, a high-level route right across Surrey and Kent; in places a prehistoric ridgeway and the supposed medieval Pilgrims' Way from Winchester to Canterbury.

Keeping close to the summit of the chalk ridge is the long-distance North Downs Way footpath, running from Farnham in Surrey to the cliffs above Dover. From the higher stretches of the ridge there are breathtaking views across the Weald. The section between Guildford and Box Hill is a good introduction to the delightful walking which can be had along the green tracks and paths, through the woodland, and along the airy slopes.

Guildford is strategically set on steep slopes either side of the River Wey, where it breaks through the chalk ridge on its way north to the Thames. In the centre of this ancient and delightful town, just south of the High Street, is the strong square keep of Henry II's castle. From its top is a view of the town and, to the south-east, the wooded slopes of Saint Martha's Hill, which is our first objective. Running south-east of the castle a road – the middle road of three where there is a junction – rises gradually for half a mile across the end of the rounded ridge to Pewley Down, where it becomes a bridleway. Where this forks, bear right and continue ahead towards Saint Martha's. This path runs along the edge of Chantries Wood,

crosses the Chilworth road, then climbs a sandy hill – we have just left the chalk and are now on the greensand or sandstone – through yew and beech to emerge on the top of Saint Martha's Hill, directly beside the church. Saint Martha's church was built in the Norman style in the 1840s on the site of a Norman church of similar plan. From it there is a broad panorama of rolling hills: to the south-east the woods of the Weald, with Leith Hill (965ft.), the highest hill in Surrey, eight miles away, while closer at hand the ridge of the Downs stretches away into the distance beyond Dorking.

The sandy path leading east off the hill is the North Downs Way, and it bears north to reach Guildford Lane at a corner. Follow the road uphill, and when it bends left, turn right to reach Newlands Corner, a notable viewpoint where the Guildford–Dorking road, the A25, crests the ridge. Reputedly giving one of the finest views of southern England, Newlands Corner has the South Downs as a backcloth and, close at hand, the greensand hills of St Martha's, Hascombe, Hindhead and Blackdown. It also has a vast car park for visitors.

Beyond Newlands Corner, our route follows the North Downs Way to Box Hill, a distance of ten miles. The bridleway forms part of the old drove road, or packhorse trail, whose origins go back to prehistoric times. The going would then have been dry and level, avoiding the difficulties of thick clay and impenetrable forest in the Weald below. Today the only difficulties are those created up here by horse-riders and trail motorcyclists.

The bridleway runs due east, passing

Maps   O.S. 1:50,000 Sheets 186 and 187. Start from Guildford (ref. 996493). Finish at Box Hill (ref. 179512).
Grading   Easy. The walking is mostly on paths.
Time   4 hours.
Distance   12 miles.
Escape Routes   Newlands Corner (A25) after 3 miles. Numerous minor paths lead S to the A25 and E towards Dorking.
Telephones   Guildford; Newlands Corner; Shere; Gomshall; Ranmore Common; West Humble; Dorking.
Transport   Railway Stations at Guildford and Dorking (Waterloo). Green Line bus services to Guildford and Dorking from Victoria Coach Station, Marble Arch and Kings Cross. Guildford–Dorking bus services Nos. 425 or 439.
Accommodation   Hotels, Inns and Guest Houses in Guildford, Dorking and surrounding villages. Youth Hostel at Tanners Hatch.
Guidebooks   *A Guide to the Pilgrims' Way and North Downs Way* by C. J. Wright (Constable); *Surrey Walks* by G. Hollis (Surrey Advertiser); *Walks in the Surrey Hills* by J. Spayne and A. Kryinski (Spur); *The Pilgrims' Way* by Sean Jennett (Cassell).

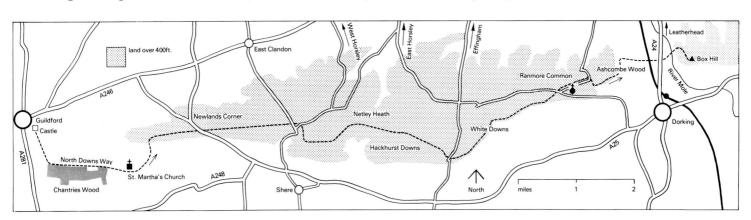

Above: The view south from Box Hill over Brockham. *Photo: Derek Forss*

Right: A light mist hangs over the River Mole, and its stepping stones, at the foot of Box Hill. *Photo: Derek Forss*

path crosses the Effingham road and leads out on to White Downs, where Ranmore Church and Box Hill become visible. The path contours round the thickly wooded coombe and then emerges at Ranmore Common. The spire of Saint Bartholomew's church is a landmark for miles around. It was designed by Sir George Gilbert Scott and built in 1859 for Lord Ashcombe, son of Thomas Cubitt. Cubitt, the founder of the family fortune, built the mansion of Polesden Lacey in 1824: it lies one mile north of the church. Cubitt also built for himself the Mansion Denbies in 1849, but it was demolished in 1954 and only the stables remain.

At a bend in the road beyond the church take at first the drive signposted 'Bridlepath to Dorking' but then turn east on the old road through Denbies park, along the edge of Ashcombe Wood and down a tree-lined track, under the railway line, under the Dorking–Leatherhead road, the A24, by a subway and so reach the River Mole.

Box Hill's wooded flank to the River Mole is very steep, and rather than a direct ascent, it is best to make a gradual zig-zag climb by the ridge which runs down north-west from the summit towards the Burford Bridge Hotel. Cross the stepping-stones – or the footbridge slightly downstream if the river is in flood – and continue straight ahead, uphill, and up some steps. At the top of these, turn left along a narrow path (blue waymarks) for half a mile, and then turn back right up the ridge to the top of the hill, passing the Labelliere Grave. A local eccentric was buried upside down here in 1800.

One of the most spectacular viewpoints on the North Downs and probably the most popular in the Home Counties, the 900 acres of Box Hill have been held by the National Trust and opened to the public for more than half a century. The panorama from the top, 563ft. above sea level, is not the most extensive of views, but it is breathtaking. Far beyond the blue-green haze is Ashdown Forest and the South Downs, while nearer at hand are the greensand hills and a patchwork of woods and fields, and at our feet is the valley, with the shining River Mole winding its way to the Thames.

through the car park at West Hangar and on to the Shere–East Clandon road, then around Combe Bottom by crossing the Shere–East Horsley road, south past Hollister Farm, then east again above Colekitchen Coombe to Netley Heath. There is a confusing series of tracks here, but you keep straight on to a point where the track forms a circle. Here you leave the drove road and cross the open slopes of Hackhurst Downs: a track coming up from the south brings the Pilgrims' Way route up to the Downs.

From the open Hackhurst Downs, the

60   The Seven Sisters and the Long Man of Wilmington

by Richard Gilbert

Maps   O.S. 1:50,000 Sheet 199. Start and finish at Duke's Drive, Eastbourne. (ref. 599971).
Grading   A long but easy walk over rolling downland.
Time   7–8 hours.
Distance   20 miles.
Escape Routes   Numerous.
Telephones   Eastbourne; Beachy Head; Birling Gap; Exceat; Litlington; Alfriston; Jevington.
Transport   Good rail service London to Eastbourne. Local buses from Eastbourne to Beachy Head, Birling Gap, Exceat, Seaford and Alfriston.
Accommodation   A wide range of accommodation available in Eastbourne and the surrounding villages. Youth Hostels at Beachy Head and Alfriston.
Guidebooks   *The South Downs Way* by Sean Jennett published by the Countryside Commission (H.M.S.O.); *The South Downs* by Ben Darby (Hale); *Along the South Downs* by D. Harrison (Cassell); *Along the South Downs Way* by the Eastbourne Rambling Club, printed by Sumfield and Day, Eastbourne; *Walks Along the South Downs Way* by Lord Teviot (Spur).

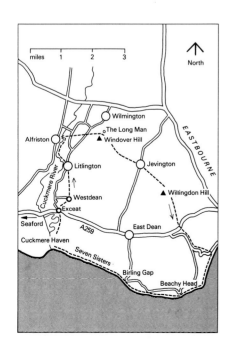

I have always maintained that it is the wide variety and contrast that makes walking in the British Isles such a satisfying pastime. Contrast may be experienced during a single day, when early morning rain moves away to give clear skies and sparkling air or, on the other hand, when the walker changes his environment. Thus my delight at walking over the short springy turf of the South Downs scarcely a week after a brief holiday in the grim confines of Coruisk, in the Cuillin of Skye. Coruisk had provided gales and rain, ragged clouds and sharp black peaks. White horses raced across Loch Scavaig and shearwaters skimmed through the troughs. Yet now off the coast of Sussex, below the chalk cliffs, the Channel was barely rippled and the sails of the yachts hung loosely.

By using a combination of footpaths and bridleways, the eastern section of the South Downs Way gives a circular walk which includes the finest stretch of coastal scenery in South East England and also some high, open downland offering a wealth of historic interest dating back to Neolithic times. The walking is easy, local transport is good, and you are never far from an attractive village with an ancient inn for refreshment. The entire area of the walk has justly been designated one of Outstanding Natural Beauty.

Start from the top of Duke's Drive, at the westernmost extremity of Eastbourne, and follow the cliff-top path towards Beachy Head. Immediately you are in another world. The Eastbourne traffic fades away behind you, the chalk cliffs gleam brilliant white in the sunshine and, walking on the even turf, you hardly notice the switchback course of the path. In summer the downs are bedecked with flowers like an alpine meadow. In mid-August I found centuary, thyme, viper's bugloss, yellow rattle, rest-harrow, eyebright, scabious, knapweed and betony, to name just a few. Earlier in the year several varieties of orchid can be found. The steeper slopes of the downs were vivid yellow with ragwort, growing to profusion amongst clumps of gorse and brambles. I found many ripe blackberries. Unusually for England these days, butterflies were common, particularly the chalkhill blue and the small skipper.

At Beachy Head the cliffs plunge vertically for 520ft. completely dwarfing the lighthouse, a mere 142ft., which is built on a plinth a short way out from the shore. Layers of flint can be seen protruding from the chalk, and holes and ledges provide homes for rock pipits and jackdaws. A museum of natural history is sited near the cliff-top. Buy an information leaflet and you will be amazed at the extent of historic sites that abound in the Beachy Head area. Iron Age enclosures, Neolithic and Bronze Age tumuli, Roman and Medieval settlements and trackways.

Passing the stump of the old Belle Tout lighthouse, built in 1831, you descend to sea-level at Birling Gap, where there is a large car park, toilets, refreshment kiosks, and the inevitable litter. The next two miles, over the seven rounded chalk cliffs known as the Seven Sisters, are the highlight of the walk. The East Sussex County Council have turned much of the area into a Country Park, and they have done an excellent job of preservation. There is complete absence of development, caravan sites, or ugly public amenities. Apart from well-maintained stiles and some fencing, the cliff-tops are left in a wonderfully wild and natural state.

In the same way that the mountaineer enjoys seeing snowy peaks outlined against a blue sky, so the walker on the Seven Sisters enjoys the wide vista of bottle-green sea set against the beetling chalk cliffs of the downs. I sat on the cliff-edge of the seventh sister (Haven Brow), overlooking Cuckmere Haven, and ate my sandwiches to the sound of wheeling gulls and waves grinding the shingle beach below the cliffs. At Cuckmere Haven, walk north along the river bank to the car park and Seven Sisters Information Centre at Exceat. The Cuckmere river meanders slowly inland, and its shallow waters provide habitat for a great variety of wading birds.

Beyond Exceat the character of the walk changes. As you turn inland, the seascape is replaced by woods, downs, dry valleys, and picturesque villages of the Sussex Weald.

Top right: A view to the west from Windover Hill towards Firle Beacon. *Photo: David Harvey*

Right and overleaf: The South Downs meet the coast at the impressive line of chalk cliffs known as the Seven Sisters. *Photos: Andy Hosking and David Harvey*

Above: Well-defined pathways slant eastwards across typical South Downs scenery on Windover Hill. *Photo: David Harvey*

First you follow the acorn waymarks through Friston Forest, passing the secluded 'olde worlde' village of Westdean, then you emerge into cornfields and pastures until you descend to Litlington. A good path now leads along the banks of the Cuckmere river to Alfriston, whose church spire, rising above the trees, beckons you across the water meadows.

You may wish to break the walk at Alfriston, at one of several inns (smugglers' haunts in the last century) in that delightful and ancient East Sussex village; in which case take the white-painted footbridge over the river. Otherwise turn right at the bridge and climb slowly up the path to Windover Hill and the Long Man of Wilmington. Once above the cornfields, follow a wide chalk bridleway for half a mile but then branch left onto a narrow path which traverses the north side of the hill, overlooking the Long Man of Wilmington. This giant figure, cut out of the turf, is 226ft. long and is something of a mystery to historians, but it is thought to be Romano-British in origin.

Back on Windover Hill you pass a long barrow (a Neolithic burial chamber) and then you stride out freely over the high ground guided by South Downs Way indicators set on low concrete pedestals. On my recent walk, owing to a late start, the sun was sinking as I descended the downs towards Jevington, turning the stubble fields to a burnished gold. Jevington church (dating from Saxon times), built of flint and with a tiled roof, heralded my arrival in the village, where there is a welcoming inn.

A leafy lane leads out of Jevington up Willingdon Hill, 660ft., and then, quite suddenly, you find yourself back in civilisation. The town of Eastbourne sprawls below and, although you still have four miles to go to the finish of the walk, somehow the magic has gone. The bridleway passes through a golf course, crosses the main A259 Seaford to Eastbourne road, and then meets the zig-zag road of Upper Dukes Drive. The street lights were on when I returned to my car at 8.30 p.m., feeling elated that my small section of the South Downs Way had provided such a perfect walk through the best of English coastal and downland scenery.

61 The Clwydian Hills

by Peter and Muriel Wild

The main tops of the Clwydian Hills lie between Bodfari and Llandegla, a walk of about 12 miles, which is clearly waymarked, as it is part of the Offa's Dyke Path. For our walk, the path starts in Bodfari, on the A541 directly opposite the village shop, and we rise steeply for a mile and a half to Moel y Parc, whose summit, with its TV mast, is still marked on the map as 'Danger Area'. It was used for training in the last war. On this section, the Offa's Dyke Path does not keep to the line of the Dyke. From the Dee Valley to Prestatyn it follows a scenic route which keeps to the high ground as much as possible. Below Moel y Parc, to the south, a road which crosses the hills is known locally as the Cheese Road, because farmers' wives used it to take their cheeses to Caerwys market.

Iron Age man had hill forts on the Clwydian Hills 500 years before the Romans came to Britain. Our next top is Penycloddiau, the largest of the three hill forts we shall cross on this walk. It covers over 50 acres and from it, as from all these hills, there are splendid views; westward across the Denbigh moors to Snowdonia; northward to the sea at Rhyl; southward to the Llantysilio Mountains; and eastward to Liverpool and the Lancashire plain. Below us, to the north-west, we can see the square tower of St. Asaph Cathedral, the smallest and arguably the oldest cathedral in Britain. When Cunedda swept down from Strathclyde and conquered North Wales, in the sixth century, he was accompanied by Bishop Kentigern, who established a Celtic Christian settlement there in 560AD.

From Penycloddiau we drop to the road, where the Clwyd Country Park begins, and then we climb Moel Arthur. Erosion is a problem on this steep slope, and the path is changed at times and marked by stakes to allow the grass to recover. The ramparts of this, the second hill fort, are high enough to be impressive, and the line of the path is designed to protect them from erosion. Almost due west we can see Denbigh, whose Norman castle stands proudly on its crag. Built by Edward I to subdue the Welsh, it was held by loyal Welshmen for Charles I, and was one of the last castles to surrender to Cromwell.

From Moel Arthur we descend to a road,

and then climb again, first over Moel Llys-y-Coed and Moel Dywyll, and then to Moel Fammau, the highest of the Clwydians. Here we are crossing open, heather-covered country, interspersed with sheep pastures where we may disturb grouse, see wheatears in spring, fieldfares in autumn, stonechats, meadow pipits, and larks in summer. Kestrels, buzzards, and peregrines may often be seen overhead, but because the base rock is Silurian, there are few flowers. The National Trust has covenants with landowners protecting 3,125 acres in this area.

As we approach Moel Fammau, the square remains of the summit tower dominate the view. Built to celebrate the jubilee of George III in 1810, the tower originally had a square base, topped by a slender spire, but this was shattered in a violent storm in 1862. The ruins of the tower had become a dreadful eyesore, but in 1970, to mark European Conservation Year, a grand, voluntary clearing operation was organized, and as their contribution, the apprentices of Shotton Iron Works made four indicators of the finest steel to name the mountains to be seen from the tower. On the right day, in addition to those named, you will also see the Berwyns, the Arenigs, and the South Pennine Moorlands.

Descending gently to the south, you come to Bwlch Pen Barras, the site of a huge car park, whence hundreds of family parties climb the hill to enjoy the views. Below us lies Ruthin, another Edwardian stronghold seven miles south of Denbigh, though little now remains of the Norman castle. We continue south over Foel Fenlli, the third hill fort, and follow the path to the inn at Clwyd Gate, where the A494 begins its steep descent to the Vale of Clwyd. From here the path skirts the west flanks of Moel Gyw and Moel Llanfair, crosses Moel y Plas, overlooking Llyn Gweryd, where colonies of black-headed gulls nest in the spring, and drops to the meeting of several ways at 171543. Here there are alternative routes. We may follow the Offa's Dyke Path, which drops from Tyddyn-tlodion to the River Alun, continuing by fields to Llandegla village, or we may take the unpaved bridle road to the south-west and include the tops of Moel y Waun and Moel yr Accre, keeping to the east of the latter and dropping to the lane

Maps O.S. 1:50,000 Sheets 116 and 117. Start from Bodfari (ref. 093701). Finish at Llandegla (ref. 196525) or Llangollen (ref. 215419).
Grading An easy walk along a waymarked path over mainly grassy hills.
Time 5 hours to Llandegla; 8 hours to Llangollen.
Distance 16 miles to Llandegla; 24 miles to Llangollen.
Escape Routes Numerous.
Telephones Bodfari; Llangynhafal; A494 at Bwlch-y-parc; Llandegla.
Transport No public transport to Llandegla. A limited bus service between Mold and Denbigh serves Bodfari. Enquire from Crosville Motor Services Ltd., Crane Wharf, Chester. Llangollen is well-connected by bus to Chester, Oswestry, Corwen, Wrexham and Ruabon (Railway Station).
Accommodation Hotels, Inns and Bed and Breakfasts in Bodfari, Llandegla and Llangollen. Youth Hostels at Llangollen and Maeshafn.
Guidebooks *Offa's Dyke Path* by the Countryside Commission (H.M.S.O.); *Offa's Dyke* by C. J. Wright (Constable); *Walks Along Offa's Dyke* by Ernest and Katherine Kay (Spur); *Walks in Clwyd* by J. Baker (Spread Eagle); *Clwyd and the Vale of Ruthin* by F. Maxwell (Spread Eagle).

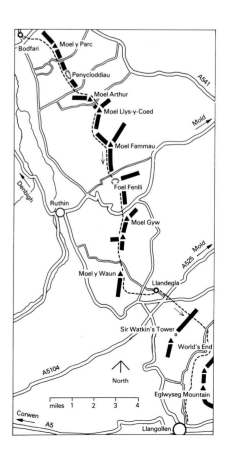

Top left: The Clwydian ridge stretches south, with Moel Fammau's Jubilee Tower prominent in the distance.
Photo: Peter Wild

Bottom left: The Clwydian range gives pleasant walking along well-trodden paths over grass, bilberry, and heather-clad hills.
Photo: C. Douglas Milner

Right: To the south of the Clwydian Hills, the limestone bastions of Eglwyseg Mountain tower over the pines of the Eglwyseg Valley, north of Llangollen.
Photo: C. Douglas Milner

Above: The view to the south-west from Eglwyseg Mountain, across the Vale of Llangollen to the foothills of the Berwyns. *Photo: Leonard and Marjorie Gayton*

Left: Foel Fenlli's hill fort, seen from the slopes of Moel Fammau. *Photo: John Woodhouse*

at Bryniau, and so to the road a mile or more west of Llandegla.

Should this walk seem too short, we can go on by the Offa's Dyke Path to Llangollen, a further eight miles. From the A525 in Llandegla, the path goes by Hafod Bilston and thence is marked by stakes leading south-east to the road across the moor. Turning right along the road we reach World's End, and the splendid limestone escarpment of the Eglwyseg Rocks. Below the rocks, there are limestone flowers in abundance, and small woodland birds. Above, on the moor we may see kestrels and peregrines. Standing aloof on its conical hill, just above Llangollen, is Castell Dinas Bran – Crow Castle in English – once the stronghold of the princes of northern Powys.

62   The Carnedds by the Cwm Eigiau Horseshoe

by Rob Collister

A grey mid-November day. I picked my way up a steep, wooded hillside above Dolgarrog, over crackling, freshly-fallen leaves of oak and beech, eschewing the road by which you can drive to Cwm Eigiau. The hillside I climbed is the first redoubt of the Carneddau, five miles away, and the unmistakable boundary of the old, hard, mountain rocks. On the other side of the Conwy a neat patchwork of green fields betokens different rocks and a more amenable soil and climate. For Wales, this is a long approach to the hills, but to walk from a tidal river is to appreciate fully the height of a mountain second only to Snowdon; and to start from a valley is to feel more keenly the bleakness of a plateau where freeze-thaw activity is still sorting loose stones into stripes and polygons.

Above the wooded hillside, the angle eases. Trees give way to bracken. The hills are dotted with ruins, whose former occupants gave up the unequal struggle with wind, rain, and poor soil, and departed for the cities or the colonies. No-one actually lives here now. 'You cannot live in the present, at least not in Wales', wrote R. S. Thomas. In this lonely upland, which is possibly emptier now than it has been for 4,000 years, you can understand what he meant.

Our walk proper starts by the Cwm Eigiau dam, with its jagged rent,* and leaves the stony track at Hafod-y-rhiw to climb onto the broad spur to the south, which gives a long, rough haul up towards Pen Llithrig-y-wrach. As I climbed on this November day, a falcon passed overhead, flying fast and determined towards the cliffs of Creigiau Gleision. Miles away to the south, a lake on Moel Siabod glittered in the grey landscape. Clouds were gathering in the west, the wind was stronger, and cold. Rain could not be far away. But on the Great Orme the sun, as usual, was shining.

I ran down the grassy slope to Bwlch Trimarchog, the pass of the three horsemen,

where three parish boundaries meet. Easy to imagine three dignitaries, back in history, leading their horses to this spot, perhaps to settle a dispute, and giving the place a name for evermore. Less easy, though, to find a source for Pen Llithrig-y-wrach, the slippery slope of the witch.

A short, steep climb leads to the top of Pen yr Helgi Du. It is a spacious summit, but a few steps northward bring a dramatic change. Abruptly the ridge narrows to a knife-edge, revealing for the first time the dark waters of Ffynnon Llugwy on the one hand, and the ruins of the Cwm Eigiau slate quarries, derelict since 1890, far below on the other. Almost simultaneously the ridge plunges downwards, confronting you with the huge, craggy profile of Craig yr Ysfa, and though it soon becomes apparent that the descent is a short one, it is steep and hands are needed in places. A zig-zag path up loose scree from the lake joins in at the col. Since the CEGB, with arrogant disregard of democratic process, and the purpose and meaning of a National Park, built a tarmac road up to the lake, this path has become a popular route, and the Carnedds more frequented.

A short scramble up a rock slab from the col leads to Craig yr Ysfa, really a shoulder of Carnedd Llewelyn rather than a top. Three of the classic rock climbs of Snowdonia emerge hereabouts – Amphitheatre Buttress, Pinnacle Wall, and Great Gully. There were three climbers on the upper arête of the former, their small figures adding scale to the

Maps O.S. 1:50,000 Sheet 115. Start and finish at the Cwm Eigiau roadhead (732662).
Grading A tough mountain walk which includes the ascent of the second highest peak in Wales.
Time 5 hours.
Distance 9 miles.
Escape Routes From Bwlch Trimarchog descend S to the A5 in the Ogwen Valley. From Pen yr Helgi Du descend to the good path beside Ffynnon Llugwy Reservoir.
Telephones Dolgarrog; Pont Rhyd-goch in Ogwen Valley. (The M.R. telephone at Eigiau Dam, shown on the map, is no longer there).
Transport Railway Station at Dolgarrog served from Betws-y-Coed and Llandudno Junction. Bus service from Llanrwst.
Accommodation Hotels in Betws-y-Coed and Llanrwst. Bed and Breakfast in Dolgarrog and Tal-y-Bont. Youth Hostels at Ro Wen, Oaklands and Capel Curig.
Guidebooks The Welsh Peaks by W. A. Poucher (Constable); Hill Walking in Snowdonia by E. G. Rowland (Cicerone Press); The Carneddau by Tony Moulam (Gaston/West Col).

*In November 1925, just after the completion of a complex system of leats, tunnels, and dams designed to provide power for the aluminium works at Dolgarrog, the Eigiau dam burst. Water poured down the broad, open valley for two miles before being funnelled into the Dolgarrog gorge. This funnelling restricted the extent of the damage but sixteen people, most of them at chapel, were killed and a number of houses destroyed. Close examination of the ruined dam will reveal the cause of the failure – one of the classic mistakes of civil engineering. The dam had been built on top of moraine debris, causing it to move under pressure as the water backed up behind it.

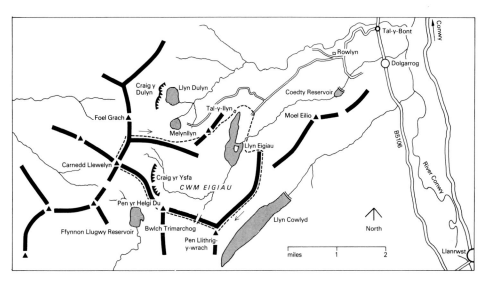

Top left: The ridge above
Craig yr Ysfa.
Photo: Peter Wells

Above: The eastern
slopes of Foel Grach, with
Carnedd Llewelyn in the
background.
Photo: Peter Wild

Lower left: Llyn Dulyn,
east of Foel Grach,
reaches a depth of over
fifty feet within three feet
of the shore in places.
Photo: Ken Vickers

Near left: Pen Llithrig-y-
wrach (left) and Pen yr
Helgi Du (right) from the
slopes of Foel Grach.
*Photomontage:
Peter Wild*

surrounding rock, but their echoing cries effectively dispelled the dark drama of the place. It was tempting, but unfair, to resent their noise. How many times had I uttered the same calls myself? Solitude and silence are a bonus in Wales, not a right.

Four wild ponies were grazing the grass slopes beneath Llewelyn. A few feet short of the summit I peered over the edge on my right, where scree-slopes drop to Ffynnon Llyffant, a little tarn that is rarely visited since there is no easy way up from it to Llewelyn. In the hard winter of '78 I had stood in this selfsame spot, pondering on the 'lonely impulse of delight' that had brought me here on ski, before I found myself almost without thinking launching down into the first turn. Today, Snowdon was buried in cloud and the wind was biting. Hands thrust deep in pockets, I passed quickly over the summit to a new view – Anglesey, Puffin Island, and a wide expanse of sunlit sea that made me think of Coigach. Just before the grassy plateau between Llewelyn and Foel Grach, I turned aside to investigate the small rock tower that is a conspicuous feature from the east. All round it are loose stones originally piled up by men, and on its top the remains of a circular burial cairn. Legend has it that this was the burial place of the Tristan or Tristram of the Arthurian stories, but it was probably old before Arthur's time, dating, like the many other hilltop cairns in the Carnedds, from the Bronze Age.

From the plateau, I turned away down the ridge that runs south-east to a region of eroding peat bogs overlooking the deep, dark lakes of Dulyn and Melynllyn. These are dramatic cwms with wet, vegetated crags rising directly from deep water, well worth the detour. Downstream of Dulyn, the walled enclosures of the Bronze Age settlement stood out clearly. Behind me, wraiths of cloud were swirling about Llewelyn and, suddenly, the steep, glaciated faces I had just traversed became an inky black, the pale, grassy flank of Pen Llithrig-y-wrach standing out like snow by contrast.

Turning, I ran the length of the ridge to the ruined farm of Tal-y-llyn, drops of rain chasing me down the wind, and as the light was fading, arrived at the Eigiau roadhead.

63   The Glyders from Pen-y-Gwryd

by Showell Styles

This walk approaches and then crosses the summits of Glyder Fach (3,262ft.) and Glyder Fawr (3,279ft.) by way of the southern flanks of the mountains. Here the terrain is less steep and rocky than on the north or Ogwen side, and consequently less interesting in detail; but the views of Snowdonia are grander and more extensive than from the northern approach. Ideally, therefore, a clear day, with the tops free from mist, is needed to get full value from the walk.

The route starts and finishes close to the Pen-y-Gwryd Hotel. A lay-by 300 yards east of the hotel on the A4086 is handily placed, almost opposite a ladder-stile giving access to the old Miners' Track that crosses the Glyder ridge, and there is usually room for a car here. Crossing the stile, you set foot on the Miners' Track, once the route taken every week by hardy Welsh quarrymen

crossing from their homes in Bethesda to the ill-fated Snowdon mines, and today a popular and very well-marked path. The labours of National Park wardens and volunteer workers have made it possible to walk dry-shod over the first marshy section, where the Nantygwryd stream is crossed by a footbridge. Soon the path mounts more steeply, rough and rocky, passing a conspicuous and massive boulder, whence there is one of the best of all views of the Snowdon group. It climbs at last to a wide saddle of moorland, usually wet going, where the sharp cone of Tryfan thrusts dramatically above the rim ahead. At the rim, the old path begins its descent to cross Bwlch Tryfan, and we turn left – west – to follow the broad, stony ridge. The ascent to this point will have taken an hour or more and there are a further 800ft. to climb to the top of Glyder Fach.

Above: The Miners' Track over the Glyders ascends easy slopes from Pen-y-Gwryd but offers splendid views across the Snowdon massif. *Photo: Gordon Gadsby*

Maps O.S. 1:50,000 Sheet 115; O.S. 1:25,000 Outdoor Leisure Map – Snowdonia National Park (Snowdonia). Start and finish at Pen-y-Gwryd Hotel (ref. 660559).
Grading A rough mountain walk which is straightforward in good conditions.
Time 5 hours.
Distance 6 miles.
Escape Routes The southern slopes of the Glyders, although steep and rocky in places, may, with care, be descended almost anywhere.
Telephones Pen-y-Pass; Pen-y-Gwryd.
Transport Railway Stations at Bangor and Betws-y-Coed. Bus services (not Sun.) Caernarfon to Pen-y-Gwryd and Beddgelert to Pen-y-Gwryd (Porthmadog–Llanrwst route). Snowdon Sherpa buses run in the summer.
Accommodation Pen-y-Gwryd Hotel. Other Hotels, Guest Houses and Bed and Breakfasts in Capel Curig, Llanberis and Beddgelert. Youth Hostels at Pen-y-Pass, Llanberis and Capel Curig.
Guidebooks The Welsh Peaks by W. A. Poucher (Constable); Hill Walking in Snowdonia by E. G. Rowland (Cicerone Press); The Glyder Range by Showell Styles (Gaston/West Col).

Bristly Ridge shows its serrated outline on your right, and a bouldery clamber soon lands you on less steep terrain close to the cock's-comb of Bristly's abutment. Heading up leftward, you pass close to the jutting Cantilever (so often used as a stance for photographic subjects) and come, just beyond it, to Glyder Fach's remarkable summit, which can only be reached by a hand-and-foot scramble. From it you can see ahead the Gothic pinnacles of Castell y Gwynt, Castle of the Winds. An energetic walker might clamber over and down

between the pinnacles, but the path – sufficiently rocky – goes round to the left of the Castell, to the notch of Bwlch y Ddwy Glyder under its western face.

From this Bwlch a walker wishing to descend to Ogwen by the Gribin Ridge would go up north-westerly on a little path to the big cairn that marks the start of the Gribin, and after clambering down the ridge (airy but quite easy) to Llyn Bochlwyd, strike the path that goes down from the lake's northern end to Ogwen Cottage. To complete the Glyder traverse the lower and much plainer

Above left: The track crosses the eastern spur of Glyder Fach by Llyn Caseg-fraith, where there is a good view of the Bristly Ridge, a much tougher line of ascent to Glyder Fach from the north. The Pen-y-Gwryd approach gains the summit by the slopes on the left.
Photo: Gordon Gadsby

Below left: On the Ogwen side of the Glyders, the Gribin Ridge provides an interesting descent. *Photo: Peter Wild*

Above: A good time to arrive on the Glyder plateau is late afternoon on a sunny day, when slanting westerly light emphasises the fine rock scenery hereabouts. In this view, Castell y Gwynt is silhouetted against the Snowdon group. *Photo: Barry Smith*

Above: Looking back to Glyder Fach and Castell y Gwynt from the top of the Gribin Ridge. *Photo: Peter Wild*

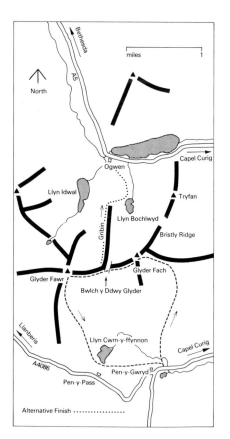

path across the slope is taken. This path brings you up to the broad, stony saddle from which, on the north, the rocky slopes of the Nameless Cwm drop 2,000ft. to Llyn Idwal. The dark, vertical face of Clogwyn Du hangs impressively above the depths, on your right front. Mounting a brief 'riser' in the ridge, the well-cairned path comes to the final, stony flat, where the odd stooks of rocks that mark the top of Glyder Fawr sit against the skyline.

As with Glyder Fach, there is no orthodox cairn to mark the highest point. The summit stook is identifiable by a massive slab, on edge, split widely into two. This is a superb viewpoint for almost every top in Snowdonia. The onward route from it is nowadays pretty plain, but in mist it is less so, and some care in starting it is necessary. From the stook of the summit go south-south-west on a little path that dips and rises to round the next stook. Keep slightly to the right (cairns) until in about 100 yards you strike red waymarks* and a path descending south-west. This is the route leading down to Pen-y-Pass Youth Hostel, and it is almost over-waymarked with cairns and red blobs on the rocks. Soon trending south, it comes down by rocky steps and grassy bays, with the most magnificent views of Snowdon above and the Llanberis Pass below, to a flat, boggy saddle nearly 2,000ft. below Glyder

Fawr's summit.

Here bear to the left, leaving the path, and go down eastward to the shore of Llyn Cwm-y-ffynnon, which can be seen just below. Follow the shore along to the south tip of the lake – boggy going – where there is a step-over place to cross a wire fence. Beyond, mount a faint path to get over the top of the rock bluff that drops into the lake at this point. Wide shelves of bog confront you and there is no path, but by keeping roughly at the same level you can skirt these gently-sloping moorlands until the small lake by the Pen-y-Gwryd Hotel ('Llyn Lockwood') is seen below. Now strike down the slope, heading for the footbridge over the river and the last 150 yards of path, which will bring you back to the stile and the lay-by. In mist, this last bit is best done by steering due east once you are clear of the rock bluff. But do choose a mist-free day if you can. As the old limerick (culled from the original visitors' book of Ogwen Cottage) cheerfully puts it:

Ye rash men who go up the Glyders
Not one of you ever considers
If you see a thick fog when
You start from Lake Ogwen
Your wives may be turned into widders!

Editor's note: This is, thankfully, a rare example of the continental practice of painted waymarking in our mountains. With luck, and vigilance, it will not proliferate.

64   Snowdon – Llanberis to Beddgelert

by Tony Moulam

Llanberis, at the foot of the well-known road pass which bears its name, is a relatively modern little town, sprawling along Llyn Padarn, and complete with a new by-pass. It is unfortunately overshadowed by the ugly terraces of the Dinorwic slate quarries, on the south-west flank of Elidir Fawr. In their heyday the quarries were worked by upwards of 2,000 men and boys, who made the fortune of the Duff family, which also acquired much of Snowdon. The decline of the industry left the excavations a disued eyesore, but the galleries now conceal the CEGB's pumped storage power scheme. In contrast, Beddgelert, at the confluence of the rivers Colwyn and Glaslyn, is a delightful village, perhaps the prettiest in Wales, with picturesque houses, cottages, and hotels. A magnificent walk links these two places and gives marvellous views of the mountains and hills surrounding Snowdon. On its way to the summit it passes along the top of the sombre cliffs of Clogwyn du'r Arddu. From the top of Snowdon, the relatively unfrequented south ridge is followed, and the fine and shapely little peak of Yr Aran can be taken in as a finale.

The route from Llanberis starts out up Capel Coch road, just west of the handsome church, passes the Youth Hostel, and comes out onto a horizontal track at about 700ft. The Snowdon track and the Snowdon Mountain Railway, which was opened in 1896, having been built in just over a year, can be seen ahead across the Afon Arddu. It offers a toil-free but expensive way of avoiding the first half of the walk, but it adds nothing to the beauty of the long spur it follows up the mountain.

The going gets a bit steeper after crossing the Afon Dwthwch, which continues down to form the famous Ceunant Bach falls, but the well-made and still easily graded track goes on beneath the heather-clad north spur of Foel-goch, which is a fine scene and sight in the early morning autumn sun. Soon we reach Tynyraelgerth, a last derelict and uninhabited cottage, which brings to mind the hard life the Welsh farmer led in former days. Narrower now, but still well-defined, the track runs parallel to the line of felled wooden electricity pylons on its left. It enters the defile leading up to Bwlch Maesgwm,

between Foel-goch and Moel Cynghorion, which was often called 'Telegraph Col' by English walkers.

From the col, a path continues south to Llyn Cwellyn, and gives imposing views ahead of Mynydd Mawr (Elephant Mountain) and, away to the left, Y Wyddfa rising sheer above Cwm Clogwyn. Y Garn, Moel Lefn, and Moel Hebog lurk across the Colwyn valley, rather like petrified and wooded prehistoric monsters, to provide an unspoilt alternative prospect. I was once lucky enough to see a kite, with its distinctive forked tail, rise lazily from the shale cliff on Foel-goch, above the pass, where a peculiarly shattered pinnacle stands guard like a derelict tank, threatening the path.

The track to the col provides an easy and logical start to this walk. The walker who wants to make the complete north–south traverse of these hills will not, however, want to miss the fine little summit of Moel Eilio, at the northern end of the chain. This is gained by its gentle, grassy north ridge from Bwlch-y-groes, on the old road over from Llanberis to Waen Fawr. An airy traverse of the subsidiary summits, Foel-gron and Foel-goch, gives splendid views over Cwm Brwynog with its abandoned farming community and cliff-bound head, then leads steeply down to Telegraph Col.

The ridge we want leaves the col and rises north-westward to Moel Cynghorion, along the top of a broken clifflet facing north. Beyond the summit, the rim of Clogwyn Llechwedd-llo forces the now faint path to turn south-east, and drop steeply to Bwlch Cwmbrwynog. From here the easiest continuation is found by crossing to the south side of the ridge to join the Snowdon Ranger Track as it zig-zags up the barren flank of the ridge. It is better aesthetically (if not for the feet) to keep as near to the edge as you dare, to enjoy the sight of Llyn Du'r Arddu cupped in its cwm. Although not a lot of the climbers' cliff can be seen, there is an aura of seriousness and inaccessibility about the place, and, except on the brightest of days, the aptness of the translation of its name, the black cliff of darkness,* is easily realised.

*The correct translation of a cliff often referred to as 'the black cliff of the dark hollow' and other versions.

Maps   O.S. 1:50,000 Sheet 115; O.S. 1:25,000 Outdoor Leisure Map – Snowdonia National Park (Snowdonia). Start from Llanberis (ref. 579600). Finish at Beddgelert (ref. 591481).
Grading   A high and exposed mountain traverse. In winter conditions it can be serious.
Time   6–7 hours.
Distance   12 miles.
Escape Routes   From Bwlch Cwmbrwynog take the Snowdon Ranger track to the Y.H. beside Llyn Cwellyn. From Snowdon summit the mountain railway track may easily be followed down to Llanberis.
Telephones   Llanberis; Snowdon Ranger Hostel; Beddgelert.
Transport   Railway Stations at Bangor and Betws-y-Coed. Bus services (not Sun.) Caernarfon–Beddgelert, Caernarfon–Llanberis, and Porthmadog–Beddgelert–Llanrwst. Snowdon Sherpa buses run in the summer.
Accommodation   Hotels, Guest Houses and Bed and Breakfast establishments abound. Youth Hostels at Llanberis, Snowdon Ranger, Capel Curig, Bryn Gwynant and Pen-y-Pass.
Guidebooks   *The Welsh Peaks* by W. A. Poucher (Constable); *Hill Walking in Snowdonia* by E. G. Rowland (Cicerone Press); *The Snowdon Range* by Showell Styles (Gaston/West Col.)

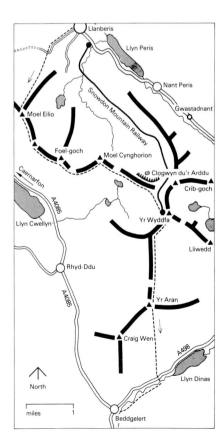

Above: The walk over Snowdon from Moel Eilio suddenly assumes a dramatic character when Clogwyn du'r Arddu comes into view after the crossing of Moel Cynghorion. In this winter view, the massif looks threatening and alpine, with a storm-cap of clouds swathing the summit of Snowdon.
Photo: Ken Wilson

Right: The col between Moel Cynghorion and the ridge above Clogwyn du'r Arddu (right). The walker is on the Snowdon Ranger path, which joins the described route just above the col.
Photo: Roger Redfern

Facing page: Mountaineers trudge up the southern ridge of Snowdon – the Bwlch Main ridge. This fine arête forms the southern section of the Llanberis to Beddgelert walk. The so-called 'hotel', a spartan blockhouse which provides refreshment throughout the summer months, is clearly visible.
Photo: Roger Redfern

Above: The final part of the walk descends the west slopes of Yr Aran towards Beddgelert. The peaks to the north of Moel Hebog are in the background. *Photo: Gordon Gadsby*

towards Point 3,026, which was for some reason never counted as a Welsh 3,000 and now, with metrication, its chance has gone. The views ahead again extend beyond the nearer hills to the Rhinogs, and even Cader Idris in the distance.

From Point 3,026 – it has no metric identification – the true south ridge begins, running into the midday sun. It traverses the top of Clogwyn Du, a remote cliff with a few unsatisfactory rock climbs. The great hollow on the left is Cwm Tregalan, and ruined quarry buildings can be seen amongst and about the huge moraine heaps which romantic writers have identified as the old city which was buried in revenge for Mordor's treachery and King Arthur's death. The cwm is closed in on the further side by the ridge between Bwlch y saethau and Bwlch Ciliau, and the back of Lliwedd. Lliwedd's great north face, glimpsed from Snowdon's summit, is reputed to hold the cave where the Knights of the Round Table sleep,† waiting to be woken by the greatest Briton, in the hour of his country's need.

Now back to reality, and a steep drop in the ridge, still with a good and well-marked path, bringing it down to Bwlch Maderin. Here a miners' track from the old workings in Cwm y llan crosses on its weekend way to Rhyd-Ddu. Ahead is the forbiddingly steep, broken face of Yr Aran, presenting the final challenge of the route. A way can be made up the shaly cliff, or on its eastern edge, to the top, where a pause would be welcome, with the excuse of a final backward look at Snowdon above its south ridge. Now a steep but grassy slope leads south-east into Cwm Bleiddiaid, and onto a (private) farm track from Hafod-y-Porth brings the route to the road.

Instead of following it meekly into Beddgelert, it is best to turn left and, in a few yards, enter the field opposite by a gate. The path turns left under a little knoll to disclose a footbridge, not marked on the 1:50 000 map. Cross it, and turn right along a pleasant path by the riverside, which leads gently into the village, and journey's end.

We now come out onto a sloping, stony plateau and, in season, the busy engines on the railway again obtrude. Philistines will take the track straight to the hotel, but it is better to avoid it and visit the summit cairn. The hotel is hidden from here, and the atmosphere and situation of Llyn Llydaw far below can be drunk in. The lake is enclosed by the two arms of the Horseshoe, with the exciting-looking ridges of Crib-goch to the north, and Lliwedd to the south, guarding the culminating point of the Snowdon massif, or indeed of England and Wales, and for that matter south of the Tay.

To descend the south ridge from the summit, first set off in a south-west direction

†This is generally identified as the cave at half-height in Lliwedd's Slanting Gully, which is known as Ogof Arthur. Slanting Gully, a rock-climb which is still graded Hard Very Difficult, was first ascended by Welsh miners, in search of Arthur's treasure or lodes of copper, in the 1860s – almost certainly the earliest rock climb on Lliwedd, or perhaps even in Wales.

65   Snowdon by the Miners' Track

by David Cox

Maps O.S. 1:50,000 Sheet 115; O.S. 1:25,000 Outdoor Leisure Map – Snowdonia National Park (Snowdonia). Start from Pen-y-Pass (ref. 646557). Finish at Beddgelert (ref. 591481).
Grading A high but straightforward mountain traverse. In winter, though, this walk can very quickly become much more serious.
Time 6 hours.
Distance 11 miles.
Escape Routes If severe conditions are encountered on Snowdon summit, the mountain railway track may be followed down to Llanberis.
Telephones Pen-y-Pass; Nantgwynant.
Transport Railway Stations at Bangor and Betws-y-Coed. Bus services (not Sun) Caernarfon–Beddgelert, Porthmadog–Beddgelert–Llanrwst, and Caernarfon–Pen-y-Pass. Snowdon Sherpa buses run in the summer.
Accommodation Hotels, Guest Houses and Bed and Breakfast establishments abound. Youth Hostels at Pen-y-Pass, Capel Curig, Bryn Gwynant.
Guidebooks *The Welsh Peaks* by W. A. Poucher (Constable); *Hill Walking in Snowdonia* by E. G. Rowland (Cicerone Press); *The Snowdon Range* by Showell Styles (Gaston/West Col).

I seem to remember that the ridges descending from Snowdon and its subsidiary summit, Crib-y-ddysgl, have been compared – as they appear on the map – to the arms (or are they legs?) of a starfish. We ought also to bear in mind that between each of them, and indeed between any subsidiary ones which may bifurcate lower down, there will be a cwm. So, although the famous Horseshoe, the circuit of Snowdon's two easterly ridges, is undoubtedly the finest walk on the mountain (if Crib-goch's knife-edge can strictly be called a walk), we should not forget that there are also two fine cwms on the easterly side of Snowdon, Cwm Dyli and Cwm y llan. Snowdon can equally well be traversed by going up one of these and down

the other. This walk covers two of Snowdon's best cwms, and makes a worthy complement to the Horseshoe itself.

The Miners' Track, on the Cwm Dyli side, and the Watkin Path have strongly contrasted histories. About 100 years ago, the benevolent owner of the south-east side of Snowdon, Sir Edward Watkin, laid out a path to enable visitors to reach the summit without dismounting from their ponies. Surviving prints, now rare, show that this feat was sometimes accomplished; but I wonder when anyone was last bold enough to perform it, the steep final section of the path having largely collapsed years ago. On the other side of the mountain, the Miners' Track was not then just another tourist path

Facing page: Snowdon dominates the scene above Llyn Llydaw which is rimmed by the Miners' Track and other remnants of an industrial past. *Photo: Van Greaves*

Below: On the Miners' Track by Glaslyn, looking back towards Lliwedd. The rocky ridge in the middle distance leads up to Bwlch y saethau and the Watkin Path. *Photo: Gordon Gadsby*

up Snowdon; as its name implies, only a handful of the people who used it can have wanted to go any higher than they needed to in order to earn minimal wages for doing a heavy, dangerous job. Much of their history is still visible as you walk up the track – a row of derelict cottages, like ruined barracks, down beside Llyn Teyrn; the crushing mill, equally derelict, half way along Llyn Llydaw; the numerous shafts and workings, then the centre of a large copper-mining industry, higher up; and the Miners' Track itself – once a cart road, up which Lockwood, landlord of Pen-y-Gwryd until the 1930s, claimed to have driven a motor car as far as Glaslyn.

The Miners' Track, or our section of it (for miners used to walk from Bethesda, crossing the Glyders from Ogwen to Pen-y-Gwryd), starts at Pen-y-Pass, now a Youth Hostel, but once a mountain hotel, associated for many years with the historic climbing parties presided over by Geoffrey Winthrop Young. The top of the pass is nearly 1,200ft., and if you have transport you are already one-third of the way up Snowdon before you start walking. Two well-known paths start from the car park, the Pyg Track, which initially keeps to the Llanberis Pass side of the ridge, and the Miners' Track, which goes south before winding around into upper Cwm Dyli. Nearly two miles of easy walking bring you to the edge of Llyn Llydaw and, assuming clear weather, to one of the classic views of North Wales; Snowdon seen across the foreground of the lake, with Lliwedd's great cliffs away to the left. Round on the right is the causeway, which crosses the lake at its narrowest point. The water level is controlled by the demands of the power station in lower Cwm Dyli, and if the causeway should be submerged, a tiresome detour has to be made round the end of the lake in order to rejoin the broad track on the northern side.

Half the map distance from Pen-y-Pass to the top of Snowdon is covered without gaining much height. The path only begins to climb seriously when it leaves Llydaw and strikes up the hill to bring you out eventually by Glaslyn, the little, dark lake magnificently placed beneath the huge eastern cliffs and screes of Y Wyddfa. From Glaslyn a stretch

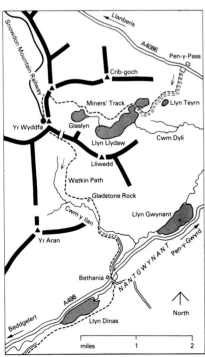

of steep, grassy hillside leads up until the path joins the Pyg Track, which has been contouring the southern slopes of Crib-goch. Soon afterwards you embark on the zig-zags, the strenuous, rocky, final section of the path as it climbs to the top of the cwm. At the ridge, you are suddenly looking into a different world: extensive panoramas to the north and west, always assuming they are not blotted out by mist, and a few yards away (not blotted out by anything) the Snowdon railway, and perhaps a crowded train puffing up or down it. The top is now a few minutes distant up to the left. It has to be visited, but when the trains are running it is not a place where you will want to linger – wonderful though it can sometimes be, especially under snow.

And so to the descent. In mist, it may not be easy to find the Watkin Path, which leaves the south-west ridge about 200 yards below the summit to strike across leftwards onto the southern face. In icy conditions, the next

section, which is steep and rocky, needs to be taken very seriously; but ordinarily it presents no technical problems, and the angle eases as you come down onto the saddle at the foot, Bwlch y saethau. The path continues on towards Lliwedd for some distance before turning down into the cwm on the right.

One great charm of this walk lies in the contrast between the wild crag and lake scenery of Cwm Dyli and the more peaceful beauties of Cwm y llan. The character of the going changes. There is still a lot of height to be lost and it is still some miles down to the road, but the route is now all downhill and straightforward. At first the path loses height steadily, making its way down the south-west slopes of Lliwedd towards the floor of the upper cwm. Then there is a pleasant stretch of almost level valley, the track keeping on hard ground, away from the stream. Presently you pass the Gladstone Rock, the extraordinary spot chosen by

Mr. Gladstone, then aged 83, to address the people of Wales on the subject of Welsh Church disestablishment. The path crosses the stream and descends into the lower cwm, where the river drops in an exciting series of cascades and deep pools, unlike anything else on Snowdon, until you come out onto open ground, and shortly down to the road.

Personally, at this stage I should hitch a lift. But you can of course walk the three and a half miles down the road to Beddgelert – or you can even get there by crossing the river at the bridge below Bethania cottages and using those nice-looking tracks shown on the map on the other side of Llyn Dinas.

Above left: The final bastions of Snowdon above Glaslyn.
Photo: Peter Wild

Above: The descent from the summit slants across the south-east slopes starting from the ridge on the left.
Photo: Gordon Gadsby

Right: The Watkin Path emerges from the narrows of Cwm y Llan, above the wooded valley of Nantgwynant.
Photo: Ken Wilson

66   Cnicht and the Moelwyns

by Showell Styles

Maps O.S. 1:50,000 Sheets 115 and 124; O.S. 1:25,000 Outdoor Leisure Map – Snowdonia National Park (Harlech). Start and finish at Croesor (ref. 635449).
Grading A rough walk over mixed terrain involving bogs, scree slopes and mild scrambling.
Time 7 hours.
Distance 14 miles.
Escape Routes From Llyn yr Adar an easy descent can be made S into upper Cwm Croesor. From the old quarry buildings at Bwlch Rhosydd paths lead S.W. into Cwm Croesor and E towards Blaenau Ffestiniog.
Telephones Croesor and Tanygrisiau.
Transport Railway Station at Blaenau Ffestiniog. Bus services Caernarfon–Beddgelert, Porthmadog – Maentwrog – Blaenau Ffestiniog, Porthmadog–Beddgelert (alight at Aberglaslyn).
Accommodation Hotels, and Bed and Breakfasts at Beddgelert, Maentwrog and Blaenau Ffestiniog. Youth Hostels at Ffestiniog and Bryn Gwynant.
Guidebooks *The Welsh Peaks* by W. A. Poucher (Constable); *Hill Walking in Snowdonia* by E. G. Rowland (Cicerone Press).

The mountain group of the Moelwyns, rising between Snowdon and the sea, provides the hill walker with a fine and varied round trip taking in all its tops over 2,000ft. At a generous estimate, the distance is no more than 14 miles, but seven or even eight hours could be taken over it by a party more interested in enjoyment of mountain scenery than in making records. The three main summits – Cnicht, Moelwyn Mawr, and Moelwyn Bach – stand conspicuously on its western rim, fronting the sea; but behind them, fringing a wild region of rock and lake, are the four lesser tops of Y Cyrniau, Moel Druman, Allt Fawr and Moel-yr-hydd, all worth a visit and commanding splendid

views. The start and finish of the walk is the little village of Croesor, reached from the A4085 road which links Beddgelert and Penrhyndeudraeth.

There's a car park at Croesor nowadays, for Cnicht – 2,265ft., and in full view from the village – is an increasingly popular little mountain. The uphill lane out of Croesor becomes a rough track, from which marker posts lead off to the right and guide you to the crest of the south-west ridge, easily followed to a saddle just below the summit. The steep rise that confronts you here is best climbed to the right, where an easy groove calls for the use of hands. School parties clamber up and down this regularly, and there is nothing

Above left: The route climbs onto the long ridge of Cnicht from Cwm Croesor. *Photo: Ken Wilson*

Above: A group of walkers on the south-west ridge of Cnicht. *Photo: Tom Dodd*

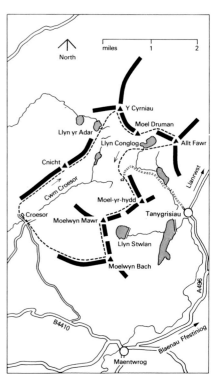

daunting about it.

On the rocky summit you can see that Cnicht's sharp top is in reality the end of a long ridge, and this ridge you follow for half a mile. It slants down eventually to Llyn yr Adar, Lake of the Birds. You head north by a boggy path above its eastern shore, and gain the small, craggy ridge rising north-east to Y Cyrniau (sometimes called on maps Creigiau'r Cwn) which raises splintery horns above the three tiny Lakes of the Dogs, Llynnau'r Cwn. The highest horn, 2,192ft., is immediately south of the most easterly lake, and from this lake you turn right-handed along the watershed ridge, south at first and then south-east and east. The

magnificent views of Snowdonia which have been with you so far are now astern, and on your left hand the land falls steeply away into deep, wild valleys beyond which hill and glen stretch right away to the English border.

Passing several little lakes, among them the charming Llyn Terfyn, you reach the massive knob of Moel Druman, 2,152ft., and cross it to descend and rise again across a moorland slope to the summit of Allt Fawr. This 'Big Height', 2,297ft., looks down on the slate region of Blaenau Ffestiniog and is the most easterly point of your route. From it you can see Llyn Conglog, half-a-mile to westward, a sizeable lake with a conspicuous promontory. The route goes down and along

Top right: The western slopes of Moelwyn Mawr and Moelwyn Bach from the road running south from Croesor. *Photo: Ken Wilson*

Bottom right: The relics of a former quarrying community – barracks, chapel, and houses – impart a melancholy atmosphere to Cwm Orthin. *Photo: Ian Reynolds*

Above: Abandoned quarry workings add interest to the landscape near Llyn Croesor. Cnicht lies behind. Note the collapsed wall in the foreground. *Photo: Richard Gibbens*

beyond a long saddle of rock and moor, and when the grassy shale of its steep dome has been surmounted to the OS cairn at 2,527ft., you have all North Wales in view. If the day is clear, you can look from Plynlimon and Cader Idris in the south to Snowdon, Tryfan, and the Carnedds in the north, and from the sea-coast to the inland ranges of Berwyn and the Arans.

The route keeps its best part to the last; and now the satisfying rocky ridge dropping due south over Craig Ysgafn, with shattered crags falling to Llyn Stwlan, below on the left, takes you down 600ft. to Bwlch Stwlan. From this narrow pass between Moelwyn Mawr and Moelwyn Bach, the seventh and final top is seen looming formidably overhead, a sheer and weirdly-shaped crag above steep screes. Alternative routes are available here; one by a small but obvious path mounting the scree to by-pass the summit crag on the left, the other a scramble straight up to the foot of the crag and a traverse to the right along its base. In hard winter conditions it is best to avoid both these and contour southwest from Bwlch Stwlan, so as to gain the ridge west of the summit. But in normal circumstances neither of the more direct routes presents difficulty, with ordinary care and attention to footing.

Moelwyn Bach, 193ft. lower than its big brother, which occupies most of the view northward, has an even finer view to the south. Beyond the woodlands of Tan-y-bwlch and the Vale of Ffestiniog, the frontier mountains of Mid-Wales rise far away, with the receding peaks of the Rhinogs framing the prospect, and the westering sun lighting the wide sea-plain between Harlech and the Lleyn Peninsula. Half the pleasure of this walk, in fact, is in the distance and variety of its changing views, and you would be well advised to pick a clear fine day for it if that is possible.

Moelwyn Bach is defended by crags on three of its sides, but the long west ridge by which you descend to Croesor is the easiest and pleasantest of walking. A stile and a corner of forestry at its foot lead onto the narrow hill road a mile from the village, and 20 minutes of downhill – the superb views enduring to the end – bring you back to the car park.

its southern shore, heading south-west at the lake's end down trackless moorland to Bwlch Rhosydd, the pass at the head of the Croesor valley, where there are ruined buildings and piles of slate debris.

A track starting from east of the largest ruin takes you out of the slate maze onto moorland, and soon you can slant up leftward to the easy ridge leading to the top of Moel-yr-hydd, 2,124ft., your fifth top. There's no cairn here, but a superb view. Moelwyn Mawr rises west-south-west

67   The Pennant Ridges – Moel Hebog Y Garn and Craig Cwm Silyn

by Jim Perrin

Maps O.S. 1:50,000 Sheet 115; O.S. 1:25,000 Outdoor Leisure Map – Snowdonia National Park (Snowdonia). Start and finish by the chapel in Cwm Pennant (ref. 531453).
Grading A fine mountain walk. Rough in places with some airy scrambling which, however, can be avoided.
Time 9 hours.
Distance 15 miles.
Escape Routes To Beddgelert or Pennant from Bwlch Meillionen or Bwlch Cwm Trwsgl. To Rhyd-Ddu from Bwlch-y-Ddwy-Elor.
Telephone Pennant chapel, at the start of the walk.
Transport The Caernarfon–Porthmadog bus service passes through Golan, 4 miles from the start of the walk. Less frequent service Caernarfon–Rhyd-Ddu–Beddgelert.
Accommodation Hotels, Guest Houses and Bed and Breakfasts in Tremadog and Beddgelert. Youth Hostels at Ffestiniog, Bryn Gwynant and Snowdon Ranger.
Guidebooks *The Welsh Peaks* by W. A. Poucher (Constable); *On Foot in North Wales* by Patrick Monkhouse (Maclehose 1934); *The Snowdonia National Park* by William Condry (Collins' New Naturalist); *Hill Walking in Snowdonia* by E. G. Rowland (Cicerone Press).

Right: A view to the north-east from Craig Cwm Silyn towards the Snowdon massif. The two peaks in the middle distance are Mynydd Tal-y-mignedd and Trum y Ddysgl. *Photo: Jim Perrin*

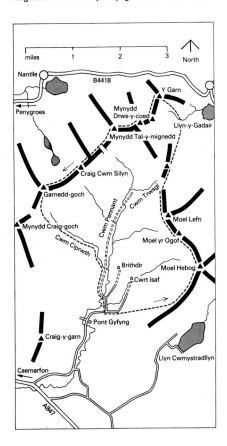

Time moves slowly in Cwm Pennant. Memories of the games men have played here linger in woods and at field corners. The houses and walls are rearrangements of the same stones which Bronze Age man used to build his hut circles and long houses. The only bustle about the place comes at the brief crises of the farmer's year, or to an eye telescoping time into the continuum of history. It is an exquisite place, and yet an anguished place also. In that flawless configuration of ridges about the valley head is more beauty than we can easily bear. There are certain evenings when it brings with it an aching sense of a fulfilment beyond man's attainments; something too vast, too perfect, for us to witness long and not despair.

To walk the hills which surround Cwm Pennant is a matter, depending on the route taken, of some 15 miles, and 6,000 or 7,000ft. of ascent. For the most part it is delightful going on short-cropped turf, and in places the ridge is exposed, rocky, and narrow. It seems best to start with Moel Hebog. The name means the hill of the hawk, but there is little of the hawk's predatory grace about this great, languid dome. In the general plan, its ascent from Pennant might seem long and tedious, but there are few hills so rich in outlook and detail as Hebog. You start from the chapel, and walk up the farm track towards Cwrt Isaf for perhaps a quarter of a mile, until a footpath branches off to the right to follow the south bank of the Ceunant y Ddol. It leads you up towards Braich y Gornel. This is a broad, open hillside, its turf richly textured in early summer with spotted heath and early purple orchids, and by lousewort and devilsbit scabious. Wheatears flick and skylarks lure you frantically away from their nests; buzzards wheel overhead as you gain height and foot by foot the view opens out to embrace two seas on either side of the Lleyn, and innumerable mountains stretching south and east. Braich y Gornel is a flat, grassy shoulder studded with the remains of Iron and Bronze Age man. The richest concentration of round and long huts in Wales is to be found on these southern and western slopes of Moel Hebog; a prehistoric city sprawling across the hillside, ruined, silent, defunct. You leave it behind as you mount a stile and pant up the final steep

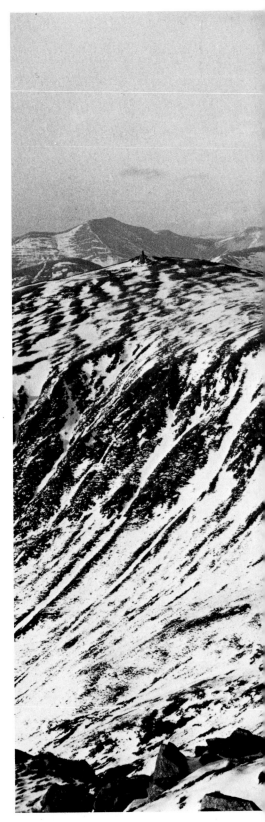

226

Top right: The eastern summits of Cwm Pennant – a view south from Moel Lefn to Moel Hebog (left).
Photo: Van Greaves

Below right: The prominent east ridge of Craig Cwm Silyn provides a pleasant scrambling route to the summit from Bwlch Dros Bern, a pass at the head of Cwm Pennant, linking it to the Nantlle Valley. *Photo: Van Greaves*

Above: The abandoned water wheel in Cwm Ciprwth, originally used to pump water from the copper mines hereabouts. The mountains in the background are Moel yr Ogof and Moel Lefn. *Photo: Jim Perrin*

slopes to the smooth, round summit. To my mind, the best views of Snowdonia are to be gained from its southern and western approaches. Ruskin asserted that mountains are better to look at than look from; a mountaineer would hold to the opposite. From the summit of Moel Hebog the two points of view happily coincide.

The descent from Hebog to Bwlch Meillionen is knee-jarringly uneventful, but the bwlch itself is a dramatic place. The rock type has changed to a rough, brown conglomerate, outcropping everywhere and abounding with plant life. This is the place to look for starry and mossy saxifrage, the burnet rose, or mountain everlasting. Mosses and ferns grow in profusion. On the cliff down and round to the right of the col, a nettle-infested and overhung ledge is the eponymous cave of Owain Glyndwr, a chieftain of the early fifteenth century who, after the acquisition of the Arthurian myth by the English throne, gave the Welsh a focal point for their heroic afflatus.

From the col, the path climbs steeply upwards through a dank, narrow cleft in the rock to emerge in a fantasy of little pinnacles and reed-grown lakelets aping the major peaks visible to the east. The rocky section of Moel yr Ogof now ahead can be skirted to the right, or taken direct by a pleasant scramble. The texture of the rock along the summit ridge between Moel yr Ogof and Moel Lefn is a source of infinite, unworn pleasure, yet even here fashion is beginning to take its toll, in the shape of an inanely proliferating irrelevance of cairns. To a man who enjoys the wildness of this country, they can be nothing other than an obscenity. After the descent from Moel Lefn, there is a complex area of bogs, bluffs, and heathery knolls between Bwlch Sais (the Englishman's Pass, which must surely be an ironic reflection by the Welsh on English travellers' habits, since it is compounded of steep scree and leads nowhere) and Bwlch Cwm Trwsgl. Care should be taken, when dropping down to the latter, not to drop inadvertently into the well-concealed hole of the Princess Quarry. Once at the bwlch, the path contours round to the left, to join the path up from Blaen Pennant by the men's barracks of the old Prince of Wales Quarry. It is a sad place, this abandoned slate mine in its high cwm, and lives were lost in the rockfall which closed it in 1882. There are hut circles in the cwm too, and a lake dimpled by rising trout. On the cliffs above, in a position of total inaccessibility, peregrines nest. Yet for all its attractions, this 'rough cwm' is an eery and oppressive place, an impression accentuated by the name of the pass you must now take – Bwlch-y-ddwy-elor – the pass of the two biers. From whence this name derives I cannot say. A possible explanation is that corpses were brought over from Rhyd-Ddu for burial at Llanfihangel y Pennant, and transferred from one bier to another on top of the pass. Whatever the derivation, the path is best followed down towards Rhyd-Ddu until clear of the forest, and then an easy rising ascent made across Cwm Marchnad, (another strange name – there was surely never a market here?) to the rock-strewn summit of Y Garn. Drws-y-coed lies hugely far below, Snowdon and Mynydd Mawr are just across their respective valleys. To the

Above: The summit rocks of Moel yr Ogof, the small peak just north of Moel Hebog.
Photo: Richard Gibbens

south and west lies one of the finest hill ridges in Britain, a sea on each side, the ridge swooping and rearing out to fade down into the long arm of the Lleyn, and the two differently enchanting valleys of Pennant and Dyffryn Nantlle at either hand. A short essay is no place to expand on themes, but if you want to seek out the atmosphere of this group of hills, then go, for folklore and legend, to the second and fourth branches of the *Mabinogion*, and for poetry, to the two best Welsh poets of this century, Robert Williams-Parry, and Sir T. H. Parry-Williams, cousins, born respectively at Talysarn and Rhyd-Ddu. The image of these hills resonates through their work. For them, as for any receptive visitor:

Mae lleisiau a drychiolaethau ar hyd y lle.
(There are voices and phantoms through-out the place.)

From Y Garn , the path mounts steeply over the impressive comb of Clogwyn Marchnad, before swinging round west to gain the broad crown of Mynydd Drws-y-coed. This is quite the airiest part of the whole walk, and those of more timid disposition will be well advised to skirt along the southern flank rather than keeping to the crest of the ridge. Between Mynydd Drws-y-coed and Mynydd Tal-y-mignedd, a trap for the unwary is the ridge which curves round to the south-east, and leads back to Bwlch-y-ddwy-elor. But in clear weather the huge summit cairn of Mynydd Tal-y-mignedd presents no problems of identification. It

is a tower some 20ft. high, built to commemorate Queen Victoria's Diamond Jubilee. 20 years ago, it was considerably higher than it is now, but of late it has begun to fall into disrepair.

Between us now and the summit of Craig Cwm Silyn, the ridge dips disconcertingly to the little-used pass of Bwlch Dros Bern, once a regular pathway between Nantlle and Pennant. Craig Cwm Silyn, with its fine cliffs to the north, is almost our last summit, and a stiffish climb up from the bwlch. A short stretch over Garnedd-goch, and thereafter the ridge meanders along, losing height, gradually toeing down into marshy ground above Garn Dolbenmaen. It is best to slip off back down into Pennant from Bwlch Cwmdulyn, dropping down through Cwm Ciprwth, a high, heathery little valley with its own particular oddity. For near the bottom, before the stream tips over into Pennant to join the Dwyfor, is a 24ft. water-wheel of cast iron, clearly inscribed with the name of its maker, 'Dingey and Son, Truro'. It was brought from Cornwall over a century ago to pump water from a copper mine here, which never came to much. It still creaks round, an inch or two at a time on its rusty axis, standing proud for a few years yet in its lonely stretch of moorland. Cwm Pennant lies a few hundred feet below. Your car will be a mile or so along the valley road. And so I leave you here, with this last emblem of man's making slowly being subsumed into a grander, more perfect, more infinitely considered scheme of creation.

68   Deepest Meirionydd: Arenig Fawr to Rhobell Fawr

by Jim Perrin

'Of all the hills which I saw in Wales, none made a greater impression on me,' was George Borrow's verdict on Arenig Fawr. We should let it stand. It is a fine and distinctive hill. You can see it from all quarters of Snowdonia, its twin-topped summit the only definite and recognisable feature on an endlessly brown and rolling horizon. Like Moel Siabod, to which it bears a curious resemblance, there is really only one satisfying way to climb it, and that is by the east ridge which runs up from the southern end of Llyn Arenig Fawr. You can approach this mountain lake, which has few equals in Wales, either from Rhyd-y-fen to the north, or more attractively, by a longer approach from the hamlet of Parc to the south, climbing gradually past the old stone cottage of Cefn-y-maes, with its beautiful beech trees, and across an open, squelchy heath to the lake. The east ridge loses itself on a broad, grassy shoulder at about the 2,000ft. contour, and half an hour should see you from here to the summit, at 2,801ft., where there is an OS pillar and a memorial to the dead of an American aeroplane. The latter seems curiously dissonant, as though pointing up a moral that mountains are not memorials for men. From the summit, the view is extraordinary, most of all for its sense of remoteness and distance. But Arenig Fawr is only the first objective on today's walk.

A mile due south along the backbone of the mountain, and you can descend from some tiny lakelets to the boggy saddle between Arenig and Moel Llyfnant, which latter is climbed by its steep eastern slopes. To the south now, ten miles of wonderfully complex and mirey moorland separate us from the deep valleys which converge on Dolgellau. It is undiscovered, rough, and trackless country, and there is nowhere else quite like it in Wales. Exploration and re-discovery are the keynotes. I say trackless, but in fact it is not; there is a tenuous interlacing of ancient pathways across a once-more-populous terrain. With de-population, they underwent a slow attenuation; over the last ten years, with afforestation, they have been largely destroyed. Many of the paths marked on the most recent maps as public rights-of-way have been ploughed up for new plantation, and this to grow a crop the

economics of harvesting which grow increasingly in doubt.

But to the walk. You descend from Moel Llyfnant, rather a shapely hill, to the west, and then down to Fotty, properly Hafodty, the summer-dwelling, clear evidence of transhumance in medieval Wales. A path from here runs down to Blaen-Lliw. There are two good itineraries from Blaen-Lliw to Rhobell Fawr. One is long, rough, and takes in Dduallt, a superb little peak like a smaller version of Tryfan. It leaves Pennant-Lliw by the spongy shoulder of Mynydd Bryn-llech called Cors y Gwartheg-llwydion, bog of the grey cattle, and climbs up onto the magnificent wide morass of Waunygriafolen, moor of the rowan trees, though you will look for them in vain these days, their remains lying deep in the peat. Thence by the shrinking, peat-girt pool of Llyn Crych-y-waen to Dduallt, climbed by its north ridge. Dduallt is an esoteric pearl of a hill, and has a resident tame fox, which keeps a curb on the localised and very numerous vole popu-lation. This route is distinctly for the fit and ardent bog-trotter, and passes through some of the best quagmires and most marginal land in Wales. For those who want a more reasonable day's walk, including the three main summits of Arenig, Llyfnant, and Rhobell, the second alternative is a safer bet.

From Blaen-Lliw, follow the Pen-y-Feidiog road west for half a mile or so to a sheep-pen on the right, opposite which a path marked on the map does not exist on the ground but heads south, skirting forestry to the west, over Banciau'r Eisteddfod. After a short mile it creeps into forestry, and along a wide forestry track. Patrick Monkhouse, in his classic book *On Foot in North Wales*, describes walking this way in the early 1930s, and coming across the farm of Twr y Maen. 'Twr y Maen,' he wrote, 'Is one of those remote Welsh farms which pick up an inconceivable living under circumstances which would drive the average Englishman crazy in a month.' The farmer who owned it, a pleasant chap to judge from Monkhouse's account, was bought out, died, or left, and the name and position of his farm have disappeared from the map. You can still find its ruins at 793 309, if you search assiduously amongst the conifers. Shortly after here, watch out for

Maps O.S. 1:50,000 sheet 124; O.S. 1:25,000 Outdoor Leisure Map–Snowdonia National Park (Bala). Start at Parc (ref. 875338) or Pont Rhyd-y-fen (ref. 822393). Finish at Llanfachreth (ref. 754225).
Grading A long and rough walk over remote and desolate hills.
Time 11 hours.
Distance 20 miles.
Escape Routes To Llanuwchllyn from Blaen-Lliw. To Pont Aber-geirw from Cwm yr Allt-lwyd. To Rhydymain from Ty-newydd-y-mynydd.
Telephones Pont Rhyd-y-fen; Pont Aber-geirw.
Transport Railway Stations at Barmouth and Blaenau Ffestiniog. Crosville bus services to Bala, Llanuwchllyn and, infrequently, to Llanfachreth from Dolgellau.
Accommodation Hotels at Bala and Dolgellau. Bed and Breakfasts at Llanuwchllyn. Youth Hostels at Bala Ffestiniog and Dolgellau.
Guidebooks *On Foot in North Wales* by Patrick Monkhouse (Maclehose 1934); *The Snowdonia National Park* by William Condry (Collins New Naturalist).

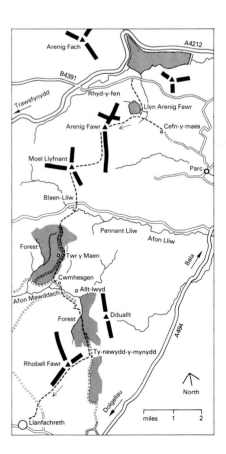

Above: The eastern flank of Arenig Fawr, seen from the moorland by Cefn-y-maes. The described walk traverses the skyline from right to left. *Photo: Barry Smith*

a path which branches off left through the trees at 789306, and leads to Cwmhesgen. Descending a firebreak to leave the forest, it gives the best view of our objective and my favourite Welsh hill, the rugged and lonely dome of Rhobell Fawr.

The valley below, Cwm yr Allt-lwyd, valley of the grey height, is astonishingly desolate. Of all the houses in this long valley, two remain inhabited, one a working farm, the other a second home. The rest are ruins, their roof-trees stark against the sky.

The last time I climbed Rhobell Fawr, our party followed the right-of-way marked as climbing over the moor between Rhobell-y-big and Foel Gron. It is all now being planted and the paths have quite gone. In a

few years it will be hopeless to attempt to follow it. I wonder at the legality of this process. The direct path we were taking on this day is, after the first half-mile, a bog-trot in the best Bleaklow tradition, but it is direct, and it somehow gives the original, undespoiled flavour of this odd and isolated hill. As an approach, it feels to be longer than it is, as it dips in and out of splashy hollows and rounds tiny, splintery hummocks before climbing the broad back of the hill. There is a massive feel to the summit dome, a swelling symmetry whose detail is etched in rough, granular rock. And it is remote, with scarcely any trace of a path on its shaggy slopes. It stands as the perfect type of a Welsh landscape.

The easiest way to Rhobell Fawr is to follow the Nant yr Helyg, which joins into the Mawddach just downstream of an impressive gorge, until, a hundred yards past a ruined hafod, you cross the stream and follow firebreaks through the forest to Ty-newydd-y-mynydd, where the Waunygriafolen route comes in. The ascent of Rhobell Fawr is now a simple matter of crossing a boggy depression and climbing its eastern slope to the spikey summit. Rather than stop here, I would recommend descending a little to the south-west top of the mountain. And then there is the view, miraculously beautiful, an intricacy of little wooded hills and lapidary pools and lakes in the foreground, then the Mawddach estuary, framed between Cader to the south

and the Rhinogs northerly. I cannot resist quoting Monkhouse again: 'With the evening light behind it, the Rhinog range seems strangely spacious and celestial, as if its sins had been forgiven it.' Of Cader Idris, what can you say other than that it is the most beautiful of Welsh hills. But the most beautiful of Welsh views is this from Rhobell, out beyond these immaculate mountain forms to the western sea. It brings a peace beyond the power of words to describe.

The descent is easy: keep the estuary in front and head for the lane-end at Cors-y-garnedd. Thence, long miles along lovely lanes lead to Llanfachreth and Dolgellau.

Top: A view along the summit ridge of Arenig Fawr. *Photo: Peter Wild*

Bottom: Looking back north to the summit ridge of Arenig Fawr from the small lake above Craig y Bychan. *Photo: Dave Matthews*

69   The Migneint and Arenig Fach

by Harold Drasdo

Maps O.S. 1:50,000 Sheets 124 and 125; O.S. 1:25,000 Outdoor Leisure Map – Snowdonia National Park (Bala). Start and finish near Pont ar Gonwy on the B4407 between Pentrefoelas and Ffestiniog (ref. 776443).
Grading A rather rough and boggy walk over high and desolate moorland.
Time 5 hours.
Distance 11 miles.
Escape Routes From the summit of Arenig Fach and from Carnedd Iago easy slopes lead S to the B4391 road.
Telephones Maes-y-tail beside Llyn Celyn; Ysbyty Ifan.
Transport Railway Station at Blaenau Ffestiniog. Infrequent bus service (Thurs only) from Bala to Arenig hamlet.
Accommodation Hotels at Betws-y-Coed and Ffestiniog. Bed and Breakfast at Ysbyty Ifan. Youth Hostels at Ffestiniog and Plas Rhiwaedog (near Bala).
Guidebooks *The Welsh Peaks* by W. A. Poucher (Constable); *Hill Walking in Snowdonia* by E. G. Rowland (Cicerone Press).

Once I met a man on the Migneint. The shock to each of us was almost disabling. Then he changed course and made haste to intercept me. I went forward with mixed feelings since I could see at a distance that he was a shepherd, and the area is a National Trust restricted access estate. But he greeted me warmly, telling me that he'd been out there every day for six weeks and hadn't seen a soul. It wasn't easy to get away.

East of Ffestiniog two roads diverge, enclosing a triangle of high moorland. Just inside and just above these roads a gentle ridge sweeps round, nearly encircling a shallow desolate depression, a secret place, the Migneint. This is a landscape insistent on a single theme. Long miles of heather, spacious stream systems, bottomless sphagnum bogs, a couple of tiny lakes, *juncus* marshes. Neither roads nor paths may be seen in any direction. A solitary feature dominates the waste. From the east Arenig Fach looks into it: a little hill which, with a powdering of snow and nothing to lend it scale, sometimes assumes an aspect of indefinite distance and colossal bulk.

There's nothing theatrical about the Migneint, and in fact it's sensed as much as seen. A first crossing ought really to be made by compass in thick cloud, and the ability to walk fairly long shots to precise locations would be helpful. The experience, though memorable, would not appeal to everyone. But if it tempts you, follow me. Firstly, pull on your wellingtons, then start from 776 443,

where you may or may not find a milestone. A bearing on Llechwedd-mawr will take you straight into peat hags. Work through or round these and find the spot height. Then make your way to Llyn Serw and down to the stream to the west. Soon you will come upon a lost little cliff on the bank.

Take a break at this mysterious place while I explain what's so good about this walk. In a fair number of excursions, I've discovered less than a dozen positive features on the Migneint. There's the small cliff you are sitting by; the tiny lakes of Serw and Dywarchen; an ancient slate mine, its approach route now swallowed by the swamps; a crude shelter high up the Arenig. And there is Cefngarw, a lonely habitation now used only for sheep-gathering. When I first entered it, a few outlandish Welsh names were scribbled on the plaster and the signatures, get ready, of two Germans. A life-size ram was drawn in meticulous detail on one wall and a short verse was written on another: 'Look after all the kettles / Be careful with the wood / We leave the door unbolted / As long as you'll be good.' It feels like the last place on earth but once a postman walked here twice a week if occasion demanded. Lately some fencing has reached up the valley to this area. A new generation makes its doomed but courageous attempt to subdue the sodden moor. Now when, after a half-hour of driving rain or mist, you suddenly stumble on one of these landmarks you experience what I can only describe as a sense of encounter. There is a curious atmosphere, preternatural though by no means hostile. You tend to loiter for longer than there is good reason. The faculties, dazed by the endless jewelled particularity of vegetation, pool and stream, suddenly regroup in some sort of force field.

To continue. Make your way to the top of Arenig Fach. If, after a few days of heavy rain, you visit Cefngarw and then head for spot height 1,507 you may find the trivial Afon Serw slightly awkward to cross. From the summit the most appropriate route of return is to follow the long procession of boundary stones on the ridge west and north. You will take in Carnedd Iago. (From the south-west, forestry plantation threatens the Migneint skyline.) You can visit Dywarchen.

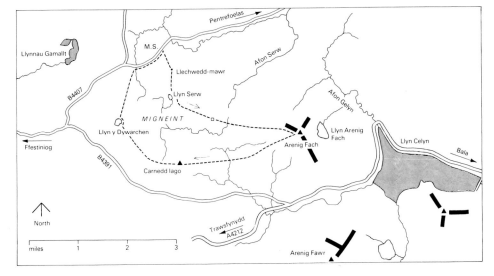

Above: A walker sets out across the desolate marshland of Migneint towards Arenig Fach. *Photo: Showell Styles*

And you can strike out for the road early or late according to inclination. If time presses, a shorter route would use the Nant y Gangen and Nant Llwyni-howel.

By now I can fancy murmurs of protest. The party has been marched up the wrong side of the mountain and then sent back home the same way. The east face with its fine lake and shapely structure has been deliberately concealed from view. The point is this: there are plenty of mountains around here but only one Migneint. The route described makes the most of it, permitting no early overview. If you can fix the transport, you could work out your own descent to the Llyn Celyn road. The going is difficult over most of this ground but in fine conditions a strong walker would make nothing of it. It is, after all, a quite small piece of land. So for those with support and with no objection to crossing a metalled road the logical extensions may be worth noting.

Arenig Fach is matched to the south by Arenig Fawr. The match is perfect. And the Migneint develops more scenically to the north-west, around the Llynnau Gamallt. This is a beautiful complex of lakes and crags offering excellent short walks, but it would be wrong to single out just one of these.

There remains the big Arenig and this time, I suppose, we take the popular route: up to the lake; easily round the east and south shores or, more daringly, nearer climbers' territory, by the west, and up the Bryn y Dyfrgi. On approaching the top of this admirable hill you cross a rock-strewn plateau. Here you will see a scatter of aircraft wreckage, the remains of a Flying Fortress, and close by a memorial to the eight Americans who died here on August 4, 1943. The names slide off the memory but the states of origin are added and strike a strange resonance: Idaho, Wyoming, and the rest. The huge machine, its crew at ease maybe, pounding steadily through the cloud so many years ago, to meet the very summit of the immovable Arenig.

Left: Cwm Cau, to the south of the summit of Cader Idris, is one of the most dramatic of Welsh mountain cwms. The main feature of the cliff at its head is the Pencoed Pillar on the left, which throws a large shadow onto the grassy cliffs behind.
Photo: Peter Wild

70   Cader Idris from the South

by John Neill

Maps   O.S. 1:50,000 sheet 124; O.S. 1:25,000 Outdoor Leisure Map–Snowdonia National Park (Cader Idris). Start and finish at Minffordd (ref. 733116).
Grading   An easy, but rough, walk over one of Wales' finest peaks.
Time   4 hours.
Distance   6 miles.
Escape Routes   From Bwlch Cau down the stone shoot into Cwm Cau. From the slight col N.E. of Penygadair down Fox's Path to Gwernan Lake. From the col near Twr Du, descend S into Cwm Cau.
Telephones   Minffordd; Tal-y-llyn; Ty'n-y-ceunant.
Transport   Railway Station at Machynlleth. Tal-y-llyn narrow gauge railway to Abergynolwyn. Bus service Machynlleth to Dolgellau.
Accommodation   Hotels at Tal-y-llyn and Cross Foxes. Youth Hostels at Corris and Kings.
Guidebooks   *The Welsh Peaks* by W. A. Poucher (Constable); *Hill Walking in Snowdonia* by E. G. Rowland (Cicerone Press).

Top right: A view along the northern edge of the Cader Idris ridge, looking west from Mynydd Moel to the main summit, Penygadair, and beyond to the Mawddach estuary.
Photo: Maurice Teal

Bottom right: The prominent stratification of the northern cliffs of Cader Idris is particularly apparent when the sunlight is at the correct angle. *Photo: Leonard and Marjorie Gayton*

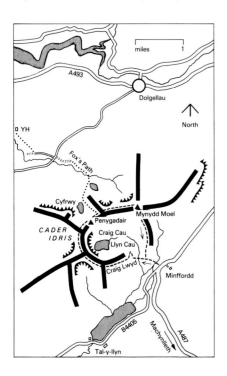

Cader Idris, though not the highest mountain in Wales outside the Snowdon group (the Arans are higher), is certainly the finest. An almost continuous line of cliffs guards the northern side of the long east–west ridge which forms the main mass of the mountain. These cliffs are those which give rise to the popular saying that the walls of Dolgellau, the town lying beneath them to the north, are a mile high.

The southern flanks of the ridge also are very rocky, with a succession of cliff-encircled cwms. The finest of these, Cwm Cau, is one of the wildest in Wales, and its circuit gives a magnificent walk, taking in the principal summit of the mountain.

This walk is best taken in a clockwise direction, starting and finishing at Minffordd on the A487 Dolgellau–Machynlleth road. Adjacent to a Nature Conservancy notice, a footpath leads away through trees to a footbridge near some ruined buildings. The path then ascends steep slopes to the left of the rocky bed of Nant Cau. The walker is now in the Cader Idris National Nature Reserve and he will find he is confined, by the Nature Conservancy Council, to a single-track path in a bid to control heavy erosion.

The path leaves the trees to swing left into the middle section of Cwm Cau, and then it slants up to a line of cairns below broken rocks forming the beginning of the cliffs lining the cwm. At this point, at last, the uppermost section of the cwm comes into view, its floor occupied by the dark waters of Llyn Cau. A better view of the cwm may be obtained by forsaking the path and following the stream to the outlet of the lake. From this point the entire cliffs encircling the cwm may be seen, with their succession of gullies and buttresses, with, in the middle, the massive Pencoed Pillar, and to its right grassy terraces stepping up towards the skyline. These cliffs are some of those on which the great climber of the 1890s, O. G. Jones, taught himself to climb, by solitary scrambles inspired by his readings of Alpine literature. Later he made his name in the Lake District before returning to Wales for much pioneering, mostly with the Abraham brothers.

The ordinary path, heavily eroded, ascends to the rocky crest of the ridge bounding Cwm Cau to the south, then turns west to a shoulder and narrow section giving fine views down over Craig Cwm Amarch to Tal-y-llyn Lake, and across Cwm Cau to the cliffs of Penygadair. An ascent past the heads of various gullies and by the top of Pencoed Pillar leads to the subsidiary summit of Craig Cau.

The route now descends to the north, to the ridge forming the col of Bwlch Cau, from which a stone-shoot descends into the cwm to give one of the few easy lines through the cliffs. On ascending again up the breast of the main mountain, a point is reached on its east–west ridge overlooking the northern cliffs. Over on the left will be seen the summit of Cyfrwy, with cliffs descending to Llyn y Gadair. Turn east along the rocky main ridge to reach the true summit, Penygadair, 2,927ft. This splendid viewpoint, from which nearly all the mountains of North and Central Wales may be seen, is crowned by a large cairn, and near it is a refuge built from the summit boulders. This latter is the modern successor to a rough shelter which once harboured an old woman who sold refreshments to walkers visiting the summit. The Mawddach estuary, and its gleaming sandflats beyond Barmouth, lie far below. The nearness of the sea brings to Cader an impression of enormous height and isolation. Walk a few yards in any direction from the summit, and the finely-sculpted nature of the mountain becomes apparent, as deeply-gouged cwms fine down its massive features into graceful, curving forms. It is little wonder that Cader was a favourite with Romantic painters such as Richard Wilson.*

After a flat shoulder, the slopes descend further to a broad col, with the cliffs of Twr Du falling away on the north side. It is possible to descend into Cwm Cau from here by a boggy, scrambling route beside a stream, running south between the cliffs of Penygadair and those of Mynydd Moel. A better expedition, however, is to continue along the broad ridge to the summit of Mynydd Moel then turn down south-east to reach the junction of two walls. From there, take a diagonal route back into lower Cwm Cau to re-join the path of ascent.

*Richard Wilson's best-known painting of Cader Idris hangs in the Tate Gallery.

71 The North Pembroke Coast: St. David's Head to St. Non's Bay

by Jan Morris

A blustery, brooding, volatile sort of day is what you need for the Pembrokeshire coast path, because even a snatch of this intermittently terrific walk can be as much an imaginative as a physical experience: so elemental are the prospects, so bold the winds off the sea, so inescapable the wild creatures, and above all so ancient the evocations of the place. To get the right snatch, I suggest a walk around the head of the St David's peninsula – southward from Penmaen Dewi, St David's Head, around the shore of Ramsey Sound to St Non's Bay: for in this brief but exhilarating excursion not only will you sense the power, almost the shock, of the fierce landscape and the island-studded sea, but you will also constantly feel, somewhere over your left shoulder, the presence of the little city of Tyddewi, St David's itself, the shrine and burial place of the saint who made this promontory holy long ago, and who haunts it gently still.

It is a moody walk. It starts boisterously, for St David's Head, the westernmost point of Wales, is open to the grand blast of the Atlantic, and if the day is right the wind whips the moorland grasses flat over the ground, and sends the spray flying high over the cliffs to lie in fizzy white blobs among the gorse. Through the weird rock-holes and caverns of the shore below, the surf tumultuously throws itself at, and fringes in white, all the islands out at sea – Carreg Rhoson, Daufraich, and away to the south-west the tall and lonely lighthouse rock of Em-sger, South Bishop.

South of the headland called Pencarnan the feeling shifts, for then the offshore mass of Ynys Dewi, Ramsey Island, shelters you from the western ocean, subduing the wind, calming the sea a little, and casting a sort of hush upon the moorland all around. And when you turn the southern point of the peninsula, to find yourself walking eastwards along the high bluffs, then there is another sensation again, a sensation of calm grandeur this time: for now as you scramble up and down the undulating path, around the necks of coves and narrow inlets, you are looking out always across the vast sheltered expanse of St Bride's Bay. The line of the shore runs off in a long, flat curve to peter out in the low hump of Skomer Island, and far,

far away the smoke of the Milford oil refineries streams southward with the wind.

The character of the coastline changes too, almost mile by mile. Up by Penmaen Dewi, where the queer outcrops of the peninsula stand like huge piles of rubble above the stony fields, everything is bare, blown-about and gusty; but in the sheltered stretches to the south, crops grow almost to the cliff-edge, wild flowers blossom even in December, and the very grass is lusher to the foot. One minute the herring-gulls are shrieking above us, riding the wind like drunks, while the dapper oyster-catchers parade upon their sandy foreshore; the next minute, it may be a raven croaking his way deliberately towards Tyddewi, or a couple of buzzards, or a wren hopping and scuttling through the shrub.

There is always life around, but life so varied, in so short a space, as to seem almost illusory. Those birds are like so many vivacious spirits. The rabbits who cross your path leap light as air itself. When I was walking over Pencarnan one day I saw a little red-breasted robin sitting still and silent as an idol in a crevice in the rocks: and all along the cliff-top path, on the edge of the gorse, small mammals have made tentative burrows in the turf – not holes exactly, only scoops, or earth-nibbles, as though they are leaving signs for us.

In summer you may meet scores of other walkers, in winter hardly any, but anyway this is not a lonely expedition, for everywhere man has left his traces. At one extreme of antiquity are the Neolithic enclosures whose blurred outlines you may still detect on the slopes above your track: at the other, the St David's lifeboat waits high in its stilted boathouse above the sea-cleft of Porth-clais, the crackled murmur of its radio watch just reaching you above the tide. Here are old lime-kilns by the shore; here the lobster pots are tidily stacked; above the lifeboat station stands the noble medieval chapel of St Justinian – no more than a ruin now, inhabited by a pony from the next-door farm, but still tremendous in site and stately in proportion. And away out at sea, disappearing sometimes behind Ynys Dewi, now re-appearing in St Bride's Bay or beyond St David's Head, the tankers sail by for Milford Haven, or the Cork ferry steals

Maps O.S. 1:50,000 Sheet 157. Start and finish at St. David's (ref. 752252).
Grading Easy.
Time 5 hours.
Distance 12 miles.
Escape Routes Numerous.
Telephones St. David's; Whitesand Bay.
Transport Railway Stations at Fishguard and Haverfordwest. Bus services to both these towns from St. David's.
Accommodation Hotels, Guest Houses and Bed and Breakfasts in St. David's. Youth Hostel at Llaethdy on St. David's Head.
Guidebooks *Pembrokeshire Coast*, National Park Guide by Dillwyn Miles (H.M.S.O.); *Walking the Pembrokeshire Coast Path* by P. Stark (Tenby Press); *The Pembrokeshire Coast Path* by J. H. Barrett (H.M.S.O.); *Pembrokeshire* by Brian John (David and Charles).

Top left: The coastline of Pembroke is rich in prehistoric monuments, such as this impressive cromlech near St. David's Head.
Photo: Ken Bryan

Bottom left: Whitesand Bay nestles close under St. David's Head, protected from the south-westerly gales by the bird sanctuary of Ramsey Island. *Photo: Bruce Atkins*

Penllechwen
St. David's Head (Penmaen Dewi)
▲ Carnllidi
Whitesand Bay
Pencarnan
St. David's (Tyddewi)
St. Justinian's Chapel
St. Non's Chapel
Porth-clais
Ramsey Island
A.487

miles 1 North

Above: The coastline to the west of Porth-clais harbour, one of many tiny, rocky inlets between St. David's Head and Newgale Sands, its entrance indicated by these conical towers.
Photo: Ian Reynolds

like a ghost all white out of the Irish Sea.

Mostly, all the same, they are allusions or suggestions that you will feel – emanations I suppose, of all the men of God who landed on these shores in the early years of Christendom, or who sailed away in their coracles to take the faith to Ireland, or settled here to meditate in cave or hermit's cell. This is a very holy walk: and when at the end of your day you leave the track along the cliffs,

and set off inland from St Non's Bay, just beyond the ridge you will find, half-buried in its hollow, snug against the wind but wheeled all about by squabbling rooks, the old cathedral of St David himself, Dewi Sant of Wales – whose presence here, in death as in life, has given solace to so many generations of pious pilgrims, and cast an incidental blessing too, I think it safe to say, upon pagans walking by.

72 The South Pembroke Coast: Stackpole Quay to Freshwater West

by Jim Perrin

Stackpole Quay marks the transition between the old red sandstone and the Carboniferous limestone. To the east for several miles the cliffs crumble and slither; westwardly they jut and glow, great sheets of marbled stone sculpted and scoured by waves unimpeded across 3,000 miles of ocean. But the path from the National Trust car park at the quay is gentle enough. It climbs onto typical Pembrokeshire cliff-top terrain. Inland, woods and fields, cultivated, green country-side, whilst all along the broad cliff-path there are odd-looking hollows, booming chasms, linking with long caves at sea-level. Half a mile from Stackpole Quay you come to Barafundle, a quarter-mile across, no road to it, its containing walls a delicate frieze of white limestone, its sand steeply shelving into blue-green water. Beyond it, the twin promontories of Stackpole Head and Mowing Word. Ploughed fields reach almost to the cliff-edge. The land is quite flat, the cliffs suddenly dropping with startling verticality into deep water. Auks nest here; peregrines too; the turf is tapestried with bugloss, thrift, and tiny mushrooms. To the south you may see the outline of Lundy, 40 miles away in the Bristol Channel. Continually, it is sea-level which attracts your craning interest. It is a labyrinth – arches, blow-holes, stacks – every cliff feature imaginable and more besides – neither land nor sea-scape but the flux between the two, occupied and invaded on a turn and turn-about basis as tide and rock work through their cycles of savage onslaught and obdurate resistance.

Where the sea wins it is generous, pays back a sort of tribute in the bays. A mile or so past Stackpole is Broad Haven. A detour here along the north-east shore of the lily-ponds, lovely, trout-rich pools ringed with woods carpeted in rose-of-Sharon, brings us to Bosherston, and its cafe, actually called 'Olde Worlde', where Mrs. Weston's good tea will fortify you against the conflict to come, and where information can be had about activity on the tank-ranges of the next section. A mile south along the road from Bosherston is St. Govan's Chapel, an exquisitely-situated Celtic Christian site through which there is easy access to fascinating sea-level scenery. West again, the hinterland is now a virtual scrapyard, all churned-up grass, shell-fragments, and rusting tanks. As if in compensation or anguish, the scenery grows more dramatic – great clefts such as Stennis Ford or the narrower Huntsman's Leap tease at a raw, vertiginous compulsion to jump. If you are unlucky, as I once was, you may be accosted by a military type who will tell you that climbing or walking here have four things to count against them: that the cliffs are dangerous, that you may scare the sea-birds, or damage the archaeological remains. When I pointed out that that only made three, he blustered that he couldn't remember the fourth, but it was a damned good reason anyway.*

It is about three miles along to the roadhead at Elegug Stacks. A broad track across open ground with superb cliff scenery to look back on, and potent, wide horizons of wind and water which ultimately will win the ground on which we walk. The Stack Rocks themselves, first climbed in 1970, are impressive enough, theatrical grand gestures in shattered stone, climactic, but the two startling features hereabouts are the Cauldron, a vast blow-hole which makes Flimston Head into virtually a hollow rock, and the superb flying buttress known as the Green Bridge of Wales. This stands at the boundary of Range West, into which there is no entry. You are confronted by a sign which unequivocally forbids access at all times. Live shells litter the land; shattered houses and churches stud the horizon; the designated coastal path shrinks off miles inland by road to wander amongst oil-refineries. If you were to ignore the notice and go into the tank range, taking care not to step on any of the hideously ornate instruments of human destruction scattered around, after another four miles of close-cropped turf and wide-skied, easy walking, you would fetch up at Freshwater West, a wild bay of reefs and rollers bearing the full brunt of Atlantic storms. On the way, you would pass Pen-y-holt Bay, the most exciting geological site in Wales, where the very rock itself seems in perpetual motion, an extra-ordinary swirl of strata across the floor of the bay. The prohibitions are a national scandal, but the path remains closed . . .

*The fourth is that you might blow yourself up on an unexploded bomb.

Maps O.S. 1:50,000 Sheet 158. Start at Stackpole Quay (ref. 993958). Finish at Freshwater West (ref. 885995).
Grading An easy walk along level cliff-top paths, with considerable objective dangers. Access to long sections of the walk may at times be difficult or impossible.
Time 6 hours.
Distance 12 miles.
Escape Routes To Pembroke from Stack Rocks or Bosherston.
Telephones Bosherston.
Transport Railway Stations at Lamphey and Pembroke.
Accommodation Hotels and Bed and Breakfast at Pembroke, Bosherston, Freshwater East, and Lamphey.
Guidebooks *Pembrokeshire Coast*, National Park Guide by Dillwyn Miles (H.M.S.O.); *Walking the Pembrokeshire Coast Path* by P. Stark (Tenby Press); *The Pembrokeshire Coast Path* by J. H. Barrett (H.M.S.O.); *Pembrokeshire* by Brian John (David and Charles).

Overleaf: The magnificent coastal scenery of South Pembrokeshire is typified by features such as this vast flying buttress of wave-ravaged limestone, the 'Green Bridge of Wales'. Beyond it, cliffs run eastwards in an unbroken line to St. Govan's Head. *Photo: Phil Ideson*

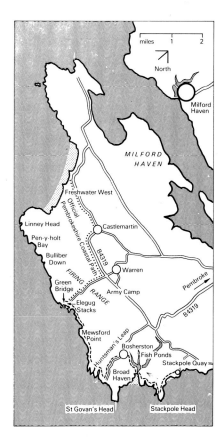

73   The Presely Hills

by Wynford Vaughan-Thomas

Maps O.S. 1:50,000 Sheet 145. Start from Newport (ref. 058390). Finish at Crymmych (ref. 183338).
Grading A long but easy walk across gently rolling hills.
Time 8–9 hours.
Distance 21 miles including the detour to Freni-fawr.
Escape Routes Numerous. The B4329 from Eglwyswrw to Haverfordwest conveniently divides the route into two sections.
Transport Railway Station at Fishguard. Bus service Fishguard to Newport. Crymmych has a thrice-daily bus service to Cardigan which is well connected to Newport.
Accommodation Hotels and Bed and Breakfast at Newport. Inn, the Crymmych Arms, at Crymmych. Youth Hostels at Pwll Deri and Trevine.
Guidebooks *Preseli Hills* by B. S. John (Greencroft); *Pembrokeshire Landscape* by R. Evans and J. B. Stephen (Five Arches); *Pembrokeshire* by R. M. Lockley (Hale); *Pembrokeshire* by B. S. John (David and Charles).

The Presely Hills, tucked away in the north-west corner of what used to be the old county of Pembrokeshire in the far west of South Wales, have always been hills of mystery. This long ridge of open moorland has always had a lost, out-of-the-way look about it. It has never, thank Heavens, been on the popular tourist map. Even the spelling of the name is curiously uncertain. Is it Prescely or Preselau or Preselli? Or the new form which appears on the rate demands of the local council – Preseli? Welsh scholars seem now to have agreed that we ought to spell it Presely. But whichever way you spell their name, these hills have a compelling charm to those fortunate to know them.

They form a high rampart lying south of the River Teifi in its lower course, and, like the Mountains of Mourne, they sweep down to the sea between the little port of Fishguard and Newport. The coastline here is thus a very splendid affair of high cliffs and secret bays, but the hills roll back gently from it at first, leaving a graceful outlier in the 1,000ft. high cone of Mynydd Carningli. The main range now stretches away to the east for about ten miles in a series of summits, the highest of which is Foel-cwmcerwyn.

The hard summit rocks have weathered out into strange rock outcrops, rather like the tors of Dartmoor, although, of course, they are not granite. These outcrops give the eastern skyline of the Preselys the outline of an angry porcupine with quills erect. Naturally, legends have gathered around them. The old folk-tales claim that King Arthur himself is buried on the ridge and that, past these wild outcrops, he and his knights hunted the dangerous and magical wild boar, the Twrch Trwyth. When the mists drift in from the sea, as they often do, you feel compelled to believe all the stories and legends tell.

The Preselys are indeed a magical place. They are littered with cromlechs, stone circles and lonely rock-piled barrows. Pentre Ifan, the largest cromlech in Wales, lies on the lower slopes. Two giant Iron Age forts mark the western and eastern ends of the range. A trackway runs over the main part of the ridge. As you walk it, you are treading in the footsteps of the men who first made it, over 5,000 years ago. The traverse of the Preselys, from the sea to the final uplift of Freni-fawr beyond Crymmych, takes you on a romantic tour back through our mysterious pre-history.

Good walkers, experienced in tramping the hills, will find no serious problems on the Preselys. There are no dangers comparable with those on the Snowdon Horseshoe. True there is a quarried cliff tucked under the summit of Foel-cwmcerwyn, but you would have to excercise considerable ingenuity to fall over it. This is English-speaking country. Some 800 years ago the Normans put their iron grip on the whole of the southern section of the county and imported settlers on a big scale from Somerset and Devon. The Welsh were driven back into the southern foothills of the Preselys and the range acted as a barrier to further Anglo-Norman advance. A sharp line, known in recent times as the Landsker still divides English and Welsh-speaking Pembrokeshire. The Presely Hills, as all the place names show, is firmly in the Welsh-speaking part.

As you approach the very Welsh summits you may be lucky. You may have struck one of those remarkable days of crystal clarity that occur about three times a year – usually in winter, when light snow has washed the air clean. First, you look westwards and there, rising over the far horizon, are the summits of the Wicklow Hills. They are so surprising a sight on the far skyline that it is no wonder that the old Welsh poets and bards pictured them as the mysterious Tir

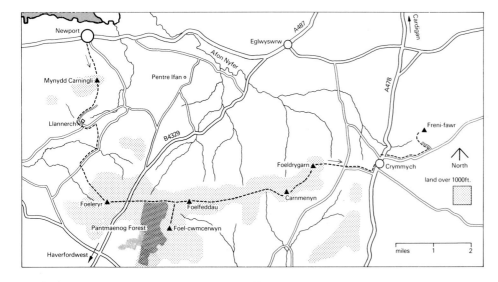

nanog, the land of perpetual youth to which the elect are transported after a noble death.

The northern skyline is even more astonishing. The whole snow-clad range of mountains, from Snowdon itself, down through the sharp peaks of Lleyn peninsula to the lone hill of Bardsey island, stand boldly up over the sea. On such days, when the moorlands of Plynlimon, between Presely top and Snowdonia come astonishingly close, you walk through into a new, bright, private world.

We begin our walk from the church in Newport and follow a lane alongside a small stream that leads out onto the open hillside. A path through the heather takes you to the ridge and beyond to the summit of Mynydd Carningli — a fine tumble of rocks crowned with the ruined stone walls of an Iron Age fort.

The track now goes swiftly downhill through the bracken to meet a rough road and the valley floor of the Gwaun River at Llannerch. You now have to face a 1,400ft. ascent to the main Presely ridge at Foeleryr, but a delightful lane takes you pleasantly upwards through a dingle, alive with the sound of the tumbling Gwaun stream and carpeted with bluebells and daffodils in spring. Again you reach a road, along which you turn right for about three-quarters of a mile until you meet the heather and bracken-clad hillside, which provides an easy climb to the top of Foeleryr. Foeleryr is the Peak of the Eagle, but these noble birds have long since faded from these high places.

The Haverfordwest road crosses the range at the Bwlch, which is directly below you, and the route ahead is plain. You skirt the edge of the big fir plantation west of Foel-cwmcerwyn and hit the prehistoric trackway which will now guide you forward over the range until you reach the road to Crymmych. The summit of Foel-cwmcerwyn lies off the trackway and you must cross a high stile to reach it. But this short detour will allow you to pay tribute to the High Place of the Preselys (1,760ft.) a splendid viewpoint.

Returning to the trackway, you have the whole range before you, a series of gentle ups-and-downs, with the surprise of continually coming across lonely standing stones and circles and the remarkable rocky outcrops which are the charm of the Preselys.

Above: The Presely bluestone, a rare type of dolerite rock, litters the summit of Carnmenyn. Stones from here were used to build Stonehenge. *Photo: Derry Brabbs*

The most remarkable of them all are clustered around Carnmenyn. It was from here that the bluestones for the inner circle of Stonehenge were dragged down to the shores of Milford Haven, then placed on rafts and floated up the Bristol Channel to the mouth of the Avon. A final long haul over the chalk of Salisbury Plain brought them to their distant destination. These rocks are of the rare spotted dolerite formation and must have been very important and holy indeed to our prehistoric ancestors, to inspire them to such efforts.

You still sense their mystery as you follow the trackway onwards towards Foeldrygarn, well worth the detour through the heather to see the ramparts of the Iron Age fort. Thence it is all downhill to the modest fleshpots of Crymmych. The keen walker, however, may feel compelled to take in the last uplift of the range, Freni-fawr. This is an easy stroll, first along the road east from Crymmych and then up the track through heather and stunted oak onto the summit.

You look westward and the whole range is spread before you, from Carningli and the sea, past Presely top to the rocky tors of Carnmenyn and the fort on Foeldrygarn. When the bracken is dying to gold on the lower slopes, and the heather tinges the summit with purple, and the buzzard soars effortlessly overhead on outstretched wings, surely the secrets of the Preselys will be revealed to you.

74   The Aghla–Errigal Horseshoe

by Denis Rankin

The two features which typify the Donegal Highlands north of the Derryveagh Mountains are quartzite screes and dryness; on one November day, after the wettest autumn on record, I returned dryshod, and nowhere else throughout the Donegal Highlands would this be possible, in any season.

The Errigal–Aghla group of hills which are encompassed by the road through Falcarragh, Gweedore, Dunlewy, and the Muckish Gap, are usually approached from Letterkenny, to the south-east. By the time you have successfully negotiated the tortuous mountain road to Dunlewy, immediately below the quartzite cone of Errigal, all the major peaks have been shown to advantage, but for the visitor to the area I recommend

continuing round the coast road and making an approach from the north. As you approach the start of the walk, the whole horseshoe is seen to offer a particularly attractive circuit and both Muckish and Crocknalaragagh, which are not included in the horseshoe, are also visible. If a different starting or finishing point is chosen, the walk can be lengthened at either end by including Muckish and Crocknalaragagh at the start, or by continuing into the Derryveagh Mountains at the end.

One dark Saturday night in November I dug myself out of my Fermanagh weekend retreat and drove 90 sleepy miles, practically the whole length of County Donegal, to the Youth Hostel at Errigal. I escaped from its

Above: The quartzite screes of Errigal shine in the evening sun and reflect in the waters of Lough Nacung. *Photo: Phil Cooper*

Maps O.S. 1:50,000 Sheet 1. Start and finish at the Tullaghobegley river bridge (ref. 935260).
Grading A straightforward mountain walk. Errigal has a fine, sharp summit ridge.
Time 5–6 hours.
Distance 12 miles.
Escape Routes It is possible to descend S from anywhere on the horseshoe to the Creeslough–Bunbeg road.
Telephones Gweedore, Errigal Y.H. (Dunlewy), Falcarragh.
Transport Rail link Belfast to Derry. Express bus service Dublin to Letterkenny. Twice daily service (not Sun) Derry to Letterkenny and on to Falcarragh.
Accommodation Hotels and Guest Houses at Falcarragh and Bunbeg. Bed and Breakfast and Youth Hostel at Dunlewy.
Guidebooks Irish Walk Guide Vol. 3 *The North West, Donegal–Sligo* by Patrick Simms and Gerard Foley (Gill and Macmillan), *Irish Peaks* by Joss Lynam (Constable).

249

Top right: A view into the Poisoned Glen, from the summit of Errigal. Photo: P. Simms

Bottom right: Errigal and Aghla Mor from the south ridge of Aghla Beg. Photo: P. Simms

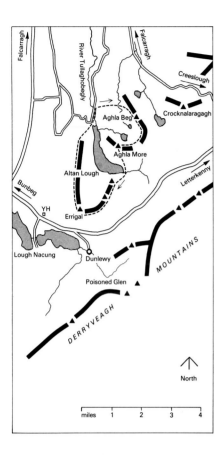

warmth into a watery moonlight on Sunday morning. By the time I had reached the start, at the north end of Altan Lough, a grey November morning had dawned, mostly clear though windy. Errigal had already put its cap on, which promised rain for the afternoon. A track 50 yards north of the river crossing led across pasture land, past a single-roomed cottage, and within a short distance, to the heathery moor. The heather, which was short and bone-dry, eventually gave way to scree, before a fence led to the massive cairn on Aghla Beg. The second summit, which is not immediately apparent from below, is higher, and from it the vista is dominated by scree. The November wind beckoned haste, over quartz and more heather in a sweeping curve to the summit of Aghla More, which appears as a prominent cone from below. Aghla More just misses the 2,000ft. contour, and provides a steep descent of 1,400ft. on superb, springy turf to the shore at the head of Altan Lough.

Ascending from Altan Lough, I crossed the two unmarked ring contours of Beaghy and Mackoght; the incompleteness of many Irish maps is one of the great joys of Irish hill-walking, and contrasts with the precise photogrammetry of the Ordnance Survey – surely a contradiction in terms for wilderness areas. Do not be tempted to circumnavigate Mackoght, the summit before Errigal; its topography is similar to that of Errigal, and the view from its summit, down Altan Lough to the Atlantic beyond, is well worth the extra effort involved. On tackling Errigal (Aireagál, an oratory) itself, I became aware of the fine outline of the Derryveagh Mountains. An altogether more desolate panorama than that to the north, the circuit from Dooish to Slieve Snaght is well worthwhile, but be warned, the ground between the many granite slabs holds much surface water. On introducing a Cairngorm-based climber to the Poisoned Glen, his comment was that it had not occurred to him that flippers and wet suit were essential equipment for the Irish hills. The Poisoned Glen is indeed a floating bog, and good views are obtained from Errigal of its massive granite crags. Once the mecca of the Irish rock climber, the exploratory nature of the long routes no longer fits into the modern ethos.

On reaching the summit ridge, I observed a substantial, square-shaped cairn. This is a memorial to Joey Glover, who had been assassinated five years ago almost to the day. Joey, from Londonderry, had been for many years an inspiration behind the North West Mountaineering Club, which is based in that county, and had trod the summit of Errigal more times than I would care to remember. He had a ferocious appetite for the hills, both in Ireland and elsewhere, and many are the stories of the Club ploughing through bogs in pursuit of the resolute Joey. In his memory, his Club have inaugurated the 'Glover Marathon', an organised walk which takes place annually on the second Saturday in September, and takes in all the peaks in this horseshoe, with the addition of Muckish and Crocknalaragagh at the start.

I was soon in the mist and on Errigal's 2,466ft. summit; there are two tops 25 yards apart, neither large enough to support a cairn, and separated by a wafer-thin arête. From this arête, a red scar indicates the start of a scree run which descends to Dunlewy, and is the equal of any to be found on Skye or Liathach. It is so steep that few have the audacity to run, but this preserves it, and it will be some years before it becomes bald – an excellent venue for a fell race. I have yet to witness the extensive view, which, it is reported, includes landmarks of all Ulster's nine counties as well as Tory Island, the Donegal coastline, and the Sligo mountains.

On leaving the summit, the navigation is straightforward because the arête is so thin, and by keeping to the ridge which encompasses Altan Lough, I was confronted with some scrambling amongst the troll-like precipices, and finally some scree, before reaching the heather below. Errigal's scree is not stable, a gust of wind not only precipitated me into an involuntary bumslide, but also dislodged a brick-sized piece of quartz which hurtled past my ear. Once on *terra firma*, uncharacteristic peat hags led me to a track with a U-bend. The right-hand prong of the U led back to the start, and all the time my exhilaration was enhanced by a fine view of the elevated Horn Head. Horn Head is like the prow of some great ship, proudly butting the Atlantic gales, and I too had a feeling of pride after completing a very fine horseshoe.

75   The Benbulbin Group

by Gerry Foley

Maps   O.S. 1:50,000 Sheet 16. Start and finish at the car park by Glencar Waterfall (ref. 761435).
Grading   A long but simple mountain walk. Good route finding is needed in misty conditions.
Time   6–7 hours.
Distance   15 miles.
Escape Routes   From Truskmore take the T.V. Station access road down to Gleniff. Benbulbin may be descended safely S at ref. 690450 and N.E. at ref. 700450.
Telephones   Drumcliff; Grange; Ballaghnatrillick.
Transport   Railway Station at Sligo. The Sligo–Cluainin bus service passes Glencar Lake.
Accommodation   Hotels in Sligo, Bed and Breakfast available locally. Youth Hostel (An Oige) at Garrison.
Guidebooks   Irish Walk Guide Vol. 3 *The North West, Donegal–Sligo* by Patrick Simms and Gerard Foley (Gill and Macmillan), *Irish Peaks* by Joss Lynam (Constable).

The magnetic charm of the Benbulbin (Beann Gulbin; peak of Gulba) escarpment lies in the beauty of its massive blue limestone walls, rocky spires, and deep gullies. The vantage point of this huge Carboniferous table-mountain provides, on a clear day, a panorama that is unique to the Sligo-Leitrim counties. The plateau rises majestically above the lowlands, six miles north of Sligo town. Our journey, which should prove to be both physically demanding and emotionally inspiring, is a circular walk around the escarpment, starting and finishing at Glencar waterfall, where there is a small car park.

From the car park, follow the surfaced road west along the lake shore for approximately 400 yards, and turn right up the unsurfaced road that climbs onto the escarpment. This road is called the Bog Road, and is used to gain access to the turf (peat) banks on top of the mountain. The walk up the road provides some interesting views of Glencar Lake, and winds up through mixed woodlands and steep limestone crags.

The road levels out as it emerges from the trees at the top of the escarpment. Here we leave it and turn west, to continue our walk by skirting the edges of the cliffs.

From here on we get an excellent view of the Castel Gal ridge which dominates the skyline to the south of the lake. Immediately below us is a small but exquisite valley, created by erosion and landslip, which is known locally as the Swiss Valley. Continuing, we cross a stream called Sruth in Aghaidh an Airde (Stream Against the Height), which falls down the steep crags. On a windy day, depending on the direction of the winds, the spray from the stream, as it flows over the cliff, is blown back and gives the impression that the stream is blowing against the height.

As we continue, we pass above the reef limestone cliffs of Tormore. These crags provide the only reliable climbing rock in the Benbulbin range, and many excellent climbs have been put up here. Further on we pass under the remains of an old cable and bucket overhead transport system that was used to convey the barytes (barium sulphate) from the mines, much higher up, down to the mill on the lake shore. The ore vein which runs north–south in direction, has been worked, on and off, since the beginning of the century.

Following the escarpment edge, we observe that the valley widens out into a flat plain, which gives way to the glimmering waters of Sligo Bay. The next interesting feature which we meet is a large, hanging valley known as King's Gully. This is the only safe and easy escape route between the Bog Road and here. Skirting the gully, we scramble onto the table-like formation called Finn McCumhail's Table. Finn was a mythological giant who was reputed to have hunted wild boar in these hills. Indeed, many colourful legends are told about the adventures of Finn and his band of men. From Finn's Table the view is quite extensive, taking in the Castel Gal ridge, the metamorphic Ox mountains, Sligo town, the ancient hill of Knocknarea with its burial mound, and Drumcliff, where the poet W. B. Yeats is buried.

We now turn north-west along the wide ridge that leads to Benbulbin, 1,730ft. The south slopes of the ridge are gentle, and a quick descent can be made if circumstances compel. Benbulbin Head is enclosed on three sides by very steep and dangerous cliffs. On no account should an attempt be made to descend any of the gullies that cleave these unstable crags. The view from here extends to take in Inishmurray, Donegal Bay, and the hills of Donegal. On a clear day, looking west from here, you should be able to see the Nephin range of mountains in Mayo.

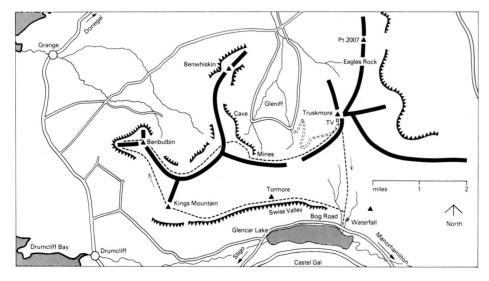

We now retrace our steps along the ridge, keeping to the northern edge, and continue until we are adjacent to Finn's Table. Our direction changes to north-east and we follow the high ground, which ends suddenly at the steep cliffs which fall dramatically into the Gleniff valley. To the north, the Benwhiskin ridge extends like a long finger, and to the south the ground falls away towards the barytes mines. The Benwhiskin ridge provides an interesting walk, which should be included if time is available, or otherwise as an alternative to visiting Truskmore. Be careful at the mines as there are a number of open pits. The first recorded operations here were in 1858 and the last in the late 1970s.

The next leg of our journey takes us to the highest point on the plateau, Truskmore

Above: The view from Benbulbin to Benwhiskin showing clearly the crumbling cliffs that rim the massif. *Photo: Phil Cooper*

Right: Glencar Lake from the cliffs near Kings Mountain. *Photo: Phil Cooper*

Top: The extraordinary profile of Benwhiskin.
Photo: Gerry Foley

Above: A view of Benbulbin from the west.
Photo: Phil Cooper

(2,120ft.). The summit is composed of a 100ft. layer of Yordale sandstone, and is the highest of the Carboniferous successions on the plateau. Looking west, we get an excel-

lent view of the steep reef limestone cliffs which block that end of the Gleniff valley. If we observe carefully, we should notice the dark entrance to a very large cave, high up in the cliffs on the flank of the Benwhiskin ridge. The cave, which has the enchanting name of Diarmaid and Grainne's cave, gives access to three large caverns, the biggest of which could hold two large houses. Geologists believe that it was part of a huge underground water course. The mythological associations with the cave are worth recounting. Finn McCumhail had a wife named Grainne who ran away with a fellow called Diarmaid. Diarmaid and Grainne, pursued by Finn, hid in the cave, but eventually Finn caught up with them and put the pair to death.

From Truskmore we turn south, and our journey from here is downhill all the way, back to the Bog Road and Glencar. On the way, we can keep an eye open for rare alpine flowers that can be found on this fascinating plateau.

76 Mweelrea

by Tony Whilde

The January cloud lifted momentarily as I struggled forward against a biting wind. I stopped, transfixed, disbelieving. Just three feet to my right was the icy rim of a near-vertical 1,000ft. drop to Doo Lough, the black lake – aptly named in the circumstances.

Such was my introduction to Mweelrea, on a cold, snowy day well over a decade ago. And it was the first of many surprises that the 'bald grey mountain' (or 'an maol riabhach' in Irish) was to spring on me over the years. But that was before the Ordnance Survey got round to indicating, on their half-inch maps, the presence of the cliffs on the north face of the approach ridge from Delphi.

With composure regained, my companion and I continued to the summit with suspect map, compass – and great care. But the cloud refused to lift again and my first ascent of the highest summit in the western provinces of Connacht remains memorable only for the near-calamity at the cliffs. Mweelrea still hadn't finished playing tricks with us, for by the time we had descended to the Owennaglogh valley, the clouds had evaporated, the wind had blown itself out, and bright, wintry sunshine silhouetted the peak which had eluded us all day. First round to Mweelrea!

The next round brought revenge, but not without some discomfort from a most unusual quarter. A journey across Killary Harbour in a leaking rubber canoe, on an otherwise perfect February day, left us soaking wet before we had even started climbing. However, the almost direct ascent from the old famine village of Uggool, on the north shore of Killary Harbour, soon warmed us.

Mweelrea is not only the highest (2,688ft.) and most impressive peak in the west of Ireland, it is unique for its blend of evocative scenery and variety of challenging approaches. To the west, a long, grassy slope sweeps down to one of the finest beaches in these islands, protected from the ever-restless Atlantic by a myriad of islands and treacherous, partly-submerged rocks. To the east, in stark contrast, vertical cliffs tumble into a still, almost lifeless, ocean of bog, broken only by small streams fed by two corrie loughs below the summit. In the distance are the rounded Sheeffry Hills and

the flat-topped Maumtrasna Mountains. To the north-east stands the lone peak of Croagh Patrick, its tiny summit chapel sometimes glinting in the sun. And to the north-west, rising from the sea, the hills of Clare Island and Achill. To the south, almost at your feet, is Killary Harbour, reputed by some to be Ireland's only fjord. It is nine miles long, and nowhere wider than about a quarter of a mile. Beyond Killary, your eyes are drawn immediately to the bare quartzite peaks of the Maum Turks and the Twelve Bens.

Unlike the inhospitable quartzites of the Maum Turks and the Bens, the rocks of Mweelrea produce at least moderately fertile soil and, where the slope and weather permit, you will find a healthy covering of vegetation – even on the somewhat unspectacular summit, where a thin layer of peat supports a spongy carpet of moss. Animal life is less in evidence, but the airy silence is often broken by the familiar croak of the raven.

The Mweelrea Horseshoe walk starts near a ruined building beside the Bundorragha River just upstream of Delphi Lodge. There is no bridge, and in winter this will probably mean an icy paddle, but any discomfort will soon be forgotten as you move almost immediately onto steep rocky ground. This brings you to the broad and undulating main ridge of Benlugmore and in good conditions navigation is easy. If the mist comes down, though, remember there are cliffs on the right; the cliffs which took me by surprise. Take care, too, not to drift onto the south-east spur of Benlugmore, for many a walker has found himself half-way down to the Owennaglogh valley before realising his mistake. You should continue over the summit of Benlugmore, and then descend to the col above the high-walled corner overlooking Doo Lough and Glencullin Lough.

It was here, on a winter descent, that Mweelrea nearly claimed an unsuspecting victim. Maire, a perky little climber from Kerry, was descending the scree when she started to slide. To the horror of all above her she didn't stop, but disappeared silently over the edge of the cliff. But, thankfully, Mweelrea was only issuing a warning and Maire landed unhurt in a snowdrift.

Your route now swings south-westwards, traversing below the minor summit of Ben-

Maps O.S. 1:50,000 Sheet 37. Start and finish at Delphi (ref. 846660).
Grading A magnificent mountain traverse. Mostly straightforward but rather steep on the descent from Mweelrea.
Time 5–6 hours.
Distance 9 miles.
Escape Routes From Pt. 2616ft. descend the easy S.E. ridge to the Owennaglogh Valley. From the Mweelrea summit descend W to the shore.
Telephones Leenaun.
Transport Railway Stations at Westport and Galway. Bus service Galway–Leenaun (not Sun).
Accommodation Hotel and Bed and Breakfast at Leenaun. Youth Hostel (An Oige) at Gubbadanbo on S shore of Killary Harbour.
Guidebooks Irish Walk Guide Vol. 2 *The West, Clare–Galway–Mayo* by Tony Whilde (Gill and Macmillan), *Irish Peaks* by Joss Lynam (Constable).

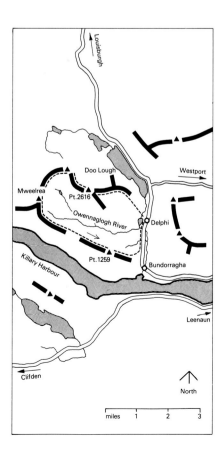

bury and then southwards to the col below the final approach to Mweelrea. For spectacular and contrasting views, you should follow the rim of the Mweelrea corries up to the summit. Take care in snow because cornices can develop here.

The descent, towards Killary Harbour, is steep, and can be slippery, and the angle doesn't ease for 1,000ft. Once on more level ground, you must make the choice between taking a high-level route over point 1,259ft. to the road, or descending to the valley and following the river to the road. Go for the former choice, particularly in wet conditions, although it does entail a longer road walk back to the finish. The valley route is hard going, and it is a poor finale to such a magnificent walk.

My last visit to Mweelrea was on a perfect August day. The party I was leading was in good spirits when we reached Bundorragha on the shore of Killary Harbour and we were all looking forward to a good meal before making our way to the pub. But life is never straightforward on Mweelrea, and we spent the evening searching for a party which had taken a different route. They were stranded on the shore near Bunnaglass and had to be rescued by boat, in the moonlight.

Mweelrea – a mountain of beauty, challenge, and endless surprises.

Top left: A view down the steep southern ridge of Mweelrea towards Killary Harbour.
Photo: Pat McMahon

Left: The Mweelrea massif from the south east.
Photo: Hamish Brown

Top right: A view across the massive cliffs of Mweelrea's eastern corrie. *Photo: Phil Cooper*

Right: Mweelrea from the east. *Photo: Hamish Brown*

77   The Glencoaghan Horseshoe of the Twelve Bens

by Joss Lynam

Maps   O.S. 1:50,000 Sheets 37 and 39. Start and finish at Benlettery Youth Hostel (ref. 771482).
Grading   A magnificent mountain walk over mainly rocky ridges. Not suitable for the inexperienced hill walker.
Time   7 hours with the Benbaun option.
Distance   11 miles.
Escape Routes   From Maumina or Maumnageeragh (between Bengower and Benbreen) descend easily down Glencoaghan.
Telephones   Recess, Clifden, Benlettery Y.H.
Transport   The Galway–Clifden bus service (daily) passes Benlettery Y.H. Railway Station at Galway.
Accommodation   Hotels and Bed and Breakfasts in Ballynahinch, Kylemore and Clifden. Youth Hostels (An Oige) at Benlettery and Killary.
Guidebooks   Irish Walk Guide Vol. 2 *The West, Clare–Galway–Mayo* by Tony Whilde (Gill and Macmillan), *Mountaineering in Ireland* by C. W. Wall (F.M.C.I.); *The Twelve Bens* by Joss Lynam (F.M.C.I.); *Irish Peaks* by Joss Lynam (Constable).

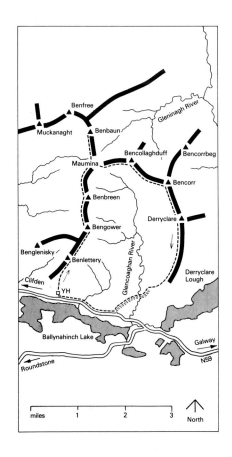

I first saw the Twelve Bens (or the Twelve Pins as the map wrongly calls them) nearly 50 years ago. The early years of my life were spent in London, but each summer the family moved to the West of Ireland for six weeks to stay in a rented house or with relations. One year, I think it was 1934, while staying with an uncle near Galway, we went by car through Oughterard to Kylemore, and I still have a vivid memory of driving through the Inagh valley, with what seemed like enormous rocky mountains looming over us on either side – the same impression as the valley had made on Bartlett 100 years earlier.

I did not see the Bens again until after the war, but since then, living in Ireland, I have walked them many times. They are hills of quartzite, gleaming white in the sun, rockier than any other Irish hills except their neighbours, the Maum Turks on the far side of Lough Inagh. Unlike the granite or the sandstone, these quartzite hills show rounded, ice-smoothed surfaces of bare rock, only occasionally steepening into real crags. But if crags are rare, rock is omnipresent, forming characteristically conical hills, separated by deep gaps. The walker cannot wander at will, as he can on so many Irish hills; he may follow the ridges, or the boggy valleys, but between valley and ridge he must pick his route with care. These hills exact respect, and it is perhaps this characteristic which makes them my favourites in Ireland.

In contrast to the long line of the Maum Turks, the Bens are a tangled knot of mountains centred on Maumina, a three-way pass between the Owenglin valley on the west, Gleninagh on the north-east, and Glencoaghan on the south. I know three good walks, all of which take the walker to Maumina, where he can see the summits rising steeply all around him. The shortest of these walks, the circuit of Gleninagh, collects the three highest summits, and gives fine views of the big crag on the north face of Bencorr. The longest, from Benlettery Hostel on the south to Kylemore on the north, is a magnificent walk crossing the whole group. Between these in length is the walk I have chosen to describe.

If you drive along the Galway–Clifden road, about two miles beyond Recess you will pass a small lake on your right, containing a tree-capped island. Stop and look, for this is the perfect viewpoint to see all your route, from Benlettery on your left, past Bencollaghduff closing the head of the valley, to Derryclare.

You can do the horseshoe in either direction; I have never made up my mind which I prefer. Going clockwise, the long stretch up to Bencorr is a killer late in the day; but the climbs up to Benbreen and Bengower are not much easier. Tony Whilde says go east to west so that you can descend straight into the youth hostel and brew up. On the other hand, if you start up Benlettery you will be up on the ridge more quickly. I will describe the route in a clockwise direction.

From the hostel head straight up the slopes towards Benlettery. There are few fences and walls to negotiate, and a lot of boggy ground which you may try (fruitlessly) to avoid, and then you climb dry heather and rock slopes, which will bring you in an hour or so to the top of Benlettery. There is still no view to the north, but you can look south across the lake-spotted plain to Errisbeg, rising solitarily behind Roundstone, and on across Galway Bay to the Aran Islands and the hills of the Burren of North Clare. I cannot promise you this view; the Bens are close to the Atlantic and get at least their fair share of the rain-clouds blowing in from the sea.

After the long pull up to Benlettery, a gentle descent and a not-too-strenuous ascent bring you to the rocky summit of Bengower (2,184ft., the Peak of the Goat). As you descend north to the next gap, Maumna-geeragh, keep to the left to avoid crags; even so, you will find a series of outcrops to circumvent. Beyond the gap, a steep climb of about 600ft., and a lot of scree (again keep slightly to the left) brings you to the summit of Benbreen (2,276ft., Peak of the Hostel) at the south end of a boomerang-shaped ridge.

Keep along the ridge, over the middle top, to the north top, which is a good spot to stop for some food and the view. You are over-

Top right: Bengower and Benbreen seen from Derryclare. The walk traverses the skyline ridge from left to right.
Photo: Hamish Brown

Bottom right: Looking back from Bencollaghduff to Bencullagh, Muckanaght and Benbaun.
Photo: Phil Cooper

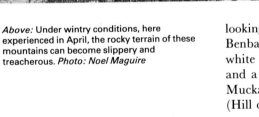

Above: Under wintry conditions, here experienced in April, the rocky terrain of these mountains can become slippery and treacherous. *Photo: Noel Maguire*

looking the nub of the Bens. To the north is Benbaun (2,395ft., the White Peak), its white screes falling from its blocky summit and a ridge running away west to Benfree, Muckanaght and Bencullagh. Muckanaght (Hill of the Pigs) stands out from the other summits by reason of its regular green slopes; unlike the other Bens, it is formed of schist, which decomposes easily to form a better soil than the hard quartzite. Looking east, you can see the rest of your route, and you can appreciate that once you pass Maumina, descent to Glencoaghan is not easy, except by way of the south ridge of Derryclare.

Descend now to Maumina. In mist, take a compass bearing, and remember to keep left of the ridge which bears right down into Glencoaghan (if you are going anti-

clockwise, remember when descending to Maumnageeragh that *that* end of the Benbreen ridge also curves away east into Glencoaghan). If you are feeling energetic, you can traverse across to the other Maumina col, and thence collect Benbaun, but it is a steep climb of 1,000ft. or so, and will add one and a half hours or more to your journey.

Back at Maumina, a fairly gentle 900ft. climb along a long ridge takes you to the top of Bencollaghduff, from which you can admire the screes of Benbaun dropping over 1,000ft. into upper Gleninagh. You can look across at the big crag which forms the north face of Bencorr, and on which are to be found the longest rock climbs in Ireland. The descent to the Devil's Col is gentle, and almost all on bare rock. This is perhaps the

Above: A view across Glencoaghan from Benbreen towards Bencorr and Derryclare, the final peaks of the horseshoe walk. This is a reverse view to the upper picture on page 258.
Photo: Hamish Brown

most desolate part of the Bens, a wide plateau of bare rock edged by crags both north and south. Water is scarce on this ridge, but you should find some at the col, and it is worth taking a drink before starting the long slog (600ft. or so) up the face of scree, rock, and heather onto the Bencorr ridge. You emerge just beside a subsidiary top (if going in reverse, remember to leave the ridge here), from which a 100ft. ascent along the rough, irregular ridge brings you to the summit (2,336ft.). You will probably be glad of a breather here, to look down the steep rocky coums facing Gleninagh, and beyond to the long line of the Maum Turks beginning away to the south-east, and marching north to Killary Harbour.

A short descent leads to a col, and then there is a mere 300ft. rise to the last summit, Derryclare (2,220ft., the Wood of the Plain). In spite of its name, it is one of the Twelve. Actually, there is no definite list, but apart from the six Bens on this horseshoe, I would include the four from Benbaun to Bencullagh, north of the Owenglin, and the isolated Benbrack, overlooking Kylemore, with the twelfth place tied between Benglenisky and the higher, but less individual, Bencorrbeg.

From Derryclare descend along the ridge over Lop Rock and pick up a footpath which leads round the nose of the ridge, whence you can cross the bog to the road up the east side of the Glen. If you started from the youth hostel, you now have over two miles of a road walk back to the hostel, and believe it or not, there is not even a pub on the way.

261

78   The Galty Ridgewalk

by Frank Martindale

Maps   O.S. 1:50,000 Sheets 73 and 74. Start from Baurnagurrahy (ref. 815222). Finish at Caher (ref. 048250).

Grading   A magnificent mountain walk along a high and, at times, narrow ridge. Straightforward under good conditions.

Time   7–8 hours.

Distance   17 miles.

Escape Routes   From Galtymore head due N down steep but safe slopes until the forest is reached. From Galtybeg descend S for ½ mile to locate turf cutter's track which can be followed down to the main road.

Telephones   Lisvarrinane and Rossadnehird in the Glen of Aherlow; Kilcoran and Caher.

Transport   No public transport to west end of ridge. Infrequent bus and train services to Caher from Waterford and Limerick junction.

Accommodation   Hotels, Guest Houses and Bed and Breakfasts in Caher, Glen of Aherlow and Tipperary. Youth Hostels (An Oige) at Ballydavid Wood and Mountain Lodge.

Guidebooks   Irish Walk Guide Vol. 6 *The South East, Tipperary–Waterford* by Frank Martindale (Gill and Macmillan); *Guide to Eire's 3000ft. Mountains* by H. Mulholland (Mulholland, School Avenue, Little Neston, Wirrall); *Irish Peaks* by Joss Lynam (Constable).

The Galty mountains (an Anglicization of Coillte, which is Irish for wooded, for at one time they were totally covered by forests) rise in splendid isolation from the fertile fields of Munster. My first impression, on seeing them, was that they had no right to be there. From the north, in particular, there are no foothills to suggest you are coming into mountainous country, and though the Slievenamuck hills run parallel to them, they are so close together as to be almost an entity.

This isolation would make the Galtees very noticeable mountains if they were only of modest height, but by the standards of these islands, this is not the case. Apart from boasting one of our few 3,000 footers, they maintain at their western end a height of over 2,500ft. for at least eight miles. Moreover, at the western end they form a true ridge; not knife-edged, as the Reeks, but still narrow enough to provide plunging views into narrow valleys on each side, without moving one's feet. This ridge makes for easy navigation and, whilst the eastern third of the range is more rounded, the reduced height over this stretch usually ensures better visibility.

The main ridge is about 16 miles long, runs roughly east/west and ends, or begins, at the historically attractive small town of Caher. There is no obvious reason for recommending that the walk should be tackled in one direction rather than the other, though I have always started at the western end. I prefer to get the steep ascent of Temple Hill

behind me early in the day, though this does result in covering the least interesting section of the walk in the evening.

Assuming a start from the west, room to park a car will be found close to the bridge where the stream flowing down the northwest slope of Temple Hill passes under the road. On the map, this is just north of Baurnagurrahy. After crossing a few fields (stay on the western bank of the stream at the request of the local farmer) you are faced by a long and steep, though straightforward, climb to the cairned summit of Temple Hill (2,579ft.). Now turn east, and immediately lose much of your hard-won height by descending into the valley which cuts Temple Hill off from the rest of the range. You can save much of this height by contouring south round the head of the valley but, if visibility is bad, take care not to stray too far onto the slopes of Knockaterriff.

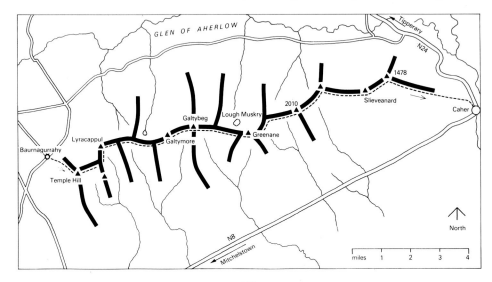

Above: A view to the west from Galtymore towards Slievecushnabinnia.
Photo: Hamish Brown

The climb out of the valley across old turf cuttings, of which there are many in this area, brings you to the summit of Lyracappul (2,712ft.) and the start of a truly superb stretch of hill-walking. A drystone wall runs from this point almost to Galtymore, and you are thus free to forget map and compass work and enjoy the beautiful views north into the Glen of Aherlow and south along a series of lovely valleys. The Glen has a long and colourful history, for its seclusion always attracted fugitives, particularly during its period of dense afforestation in the fifteenth and sixteenth centuries.

It was then that the Desmond Geraldines, using their local knowledge to advantage, attacked the Crown forces. Shortly afterwards the Glen became a haven for the noted scholar of Irish, Father Geoffrey Keating. Father Keating was being sought by a local landowner whose morals he had dared to criticize in a sermon, and he is reputed to have written his celebrated History of Ireland (*Foras Feaso ar Eirinn*) whilst living in a cave at the foot of the Galtees. I take leave to doubt the existence of an actual cave, but there is no doubt that he found sanctuary in the Glen, as have many others in more recent times.

After passing very close to the cliffs above Lough Curra, the wall ends just below the plateau summit of Galtymore (3,018ft.). This is the country's highest inland mountain and, due to its isolation, it enjoys majestic views in every direction. Lough Derg and the River Shannon are easily visible and, on a good day, I have picked out the sea, some 60 miles to the south. There has been a long tradition of cross-building on the summit, the current one having been erected in 1975 through the efforts of a group of local youngsters who made over 130 individual ascents

carrying up building materials.

The route now descends to the col above Lough Diheen before rising again to Galtybeg. A stop should be made to have a look down on Diheen, for this is the lake containing a serpent, banished there by St. Patrick for terrorizing the locals. Almost all Irish mountain ranges have lakes containing serpents, but Diheen is unique because its occupant re-appears every seventh Easter Monday morning, begging St. Patrick for mercy.

From Galtybeg the route descends to another shallow col, again with a lake below to the north, before crossing a plateau towards an outcrop of rock known locally as O'Loughnan's Castle. Below is the largest and most attractive of the lakes, Lough Muskry; take a peep, and then climb through peat hags crossing the Greenane plateau (2,636ft.) in a north-easterly direction. A ruined shelter at the far end of the plateau then leads to an ill-defined ditch, running east through a series of deep peat hags until you reach point 2,010ft.

Gorse and boulders now begin to appear, and navigation becomes more difficult, for the top of the ridge is less easy to define as it swings north, then south and then north again. The best advice I can give is to head generally east whilst ensuring that you do not lose too much height; in any case the ever-encroaching forestry plantations mean that if you go astray, it will not cause you too much inconvenience.

Slieveanard, though named on the half-inch OS map, is easily missed, for it is marked only by a small cairn adjoining a bulldozed forest perimeter track. The dominant peak at this end of the range is recorded as point 1,478ft. and, although it can be by-passed to the south, I feel it should be included as a logical final objective.

From your vantage point, you will see that your way off the Galtees must go through forestry. This can best be achieved by taking a bearing of 120° from Slieveanard and allowing yourself to be channelled by the fence into a narrow sheep-track, which will eventually lead you to the metalled road less than a mile from Caher.

79   Brandon Mountain

by Hamish Brown

Do you remember Brandon,
Our mountain in the west:
Brandon that looks on oceans
Brandon of the blessed?

I have been surprised to see how many people, past and present, have declared Brandon to be their favourite mountain. Winthrop Young wrote some memorable lines on Brandon; Collie loved this wild region; Praeger of *The Way that I Went* (Ireland's greatest hill book) gave it top place in his affections – so there is nothing original in my enthusiasm. Despite having faced more wet days on it than any other hill, I have been up a score of times. Its geographic position ensures it receives a fair share of precipitation. Locally they say you can see America on a clear day, which might be hard to disprove under the conditions. The wild and wet simply ensures you make further visits.

The sea-bitten south-west of Kerry contains much grand scenery. The Dingle Peninsula, with its backbone of the Slieve Mish Mountains, runs furthest west, and Brandon is the last big hill on its length. Both coastal roads west pass great, sweeping arcs of sandy bays; in the south, Inch Strand juts out for four miles, pointing across to the Reeks and Carrauntoohill – the only range in Ireland to top Brandon.

Brandon is a range rather than a solitary summit, running about seven miles from north to south, from the sea to the Conair Pass. The western slopes are comparatively tame but the eastern side has been gouged out to form 1,000ft. prows, with scalloped corries of sandstone. Every shelf in the rock has a sequin of water, and the rivers tumble down, forming tail-falls from one 'paternoster' lake to the next, Lough Nalacken and Lough Cruttia being the biggest. An eastern ridge sends the waters off in different directions, but the big lochs are held tight under the highest crags, and drain down to the bramble-edged fields of the Owenmore Valley. An approach up this route is the most interesting really, but most people still prefer to start at Faha, perhaps for the height which can be gained by car. Even the motorist is given a grandstand view into the eastern heart of Brandon, from the Conair Pass.

Above the pass is Ballysitteragh (2,050ft.), a hill in its own right, then a dip and a switchback to Brandon Peak (2,764ft.) and eventually Brandon Mountain (3,127ft.). Beyond it lies some odd, bold, windy country ending at Masatiompan (2,509ft.) where the contours vanish into the sea. No road wends round. On the south you can motor as far as Brandon Creek; on the north via friendly Cloghane as far as Brandon Point. Between, Brandon Head thrusts out to meet the surge and smash of the Atlantic.

The historic route up is the Saint's Road from Ballybrack. Any road soon peters out, but the ascent up the western slopes is uncomplicated. Saint Brendan (Brandon) built his oratory on the summit, and its ruins are still visible beside a well. On one occasion as many as 10,000 people came up this route to hear a great preacher during a pilgrimage.

The pilgrim route today comes up from the east. It must be quite a penance to the unathletic non-hillgoer. It is a fine route, marked, safe, and impressive. It starts in Faha, above Cloghane, and wends past a garden shrine to flank the east ridge into the great corrie in the very heart of the mountain. It then zig-zags an improbable course up to the rim of cliff, about ten minutes walking along and down from the summit. The route is marked by posts bearing 'road' signs declaring: 'Aire Cnoc-gear' which does not mean 'engage low gear' but simply warns to take care, dangerous hill. This might be described as the standard route up the hill and the descent can then be made to Ballybrack to complete the traverse.

The approach via Lough Cruttia and Lough Nalacken joins in with the Faha route. It is rough, untracked, and even finer scenically. The east ridge juts out in Suilven-like boldness, and for years I looked at its sharp jaggedness to conclude it could not be traversed without proper climbing. Then, one wet day, friends went off from Faha, and I used my 'already done it' excuse to stay behind, only that was boring, so I set off to 'look at' the east ridge. It gave some heady situations, and the greasy rock left no room for error – but it went. The really experienced hill-person would find it the best way of all. Good walking can be had by following the long eastern cliff-edge southwards, hold-

Maps O.S. 1:50,000 Sheet 70. Start from Faha (ref. 491125). Finish at Ballybrack (ref. 420090).
Grading A straightforward walk over a spectacular mountain.
Time 4 hours.
Distance 6 miles.
Escape Routes The route takes the easiest line. In difficulty simply turn back.
Telephone Cloghane.
Transport Dingle to Tralee bus service passes through Cloghane (not Sun).
Accommodation Hotel at Cloghane, several in Dingle. Bed and Breakfast available locally. Independent hostel at Dingle, but no Youth Hostel (An Oige) on the peninsula.
Guidebooks Irish Walk Guide Vol. 1 *The South West, Kerry–West Cork* by Sean O'Suilleabhain (Gill and Macmillan); *Guide to Eire's 3000ft. Mountains* by H. Mulholland (Mulholland, School Avenue, Little Neston, Wirrall); *Irish Peaks* by Joss Lynam (Constable).

Above left: Lough Cruttia lies underneath the towering walls of Brandon Peak.
Photo: Hamish Brown

Below left: A string of lakes, like rosary beads, drain down from the upper corries of Brandon into Lough Cruttia. *Photo: Phil Cooper*

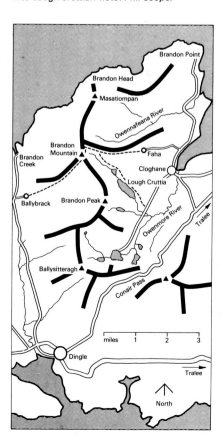

ing the heights won, to eventually tumble down to the lonely head of the Owenmore Valley (the lower slopes have a unique texture of gorse and boulders). Equally good walking northwards leads to Brandon Head and the sea, to stand on the frightening merging of alien worlds. You may not see America, but look out for fishing curraghs out on the swell.

One visit to Brandon would never do, which is why I have done more than just describe the one pop-classic traverse. By the time you have sewn together the possible variations, you might even have had a dry day. Wet or dry, you would return anyway, for Brandon, Brandon of the blessed.

Top: Brandon Mountain from Brandon Peak.
Photo: Sean Kelly

Left: The east ridge of Brandon, perhaps the best ascent of the mountain for the hill-walker who can contend with hard scrambling problems of up to 'Difficult' standard. The route traverses the skyline (right to left) to halfway along the slabby ridge, where it descends the far side to turn the steep lower step. The pilgrim route ascends the slope below the bands of cliffs.

Index

A'Choich, 79
Achtriochtan, Loch, 69
Aghla, 249
Aherlow, Glen of, 263
Alder, Ben, 63, 64, 76
Alligin, Beinn, 46
Alltchaorunn, 71
Am Bastier, 37
Am Buachaille, 10
A'Mhuing, 53
An Caisteal, 13
Andrew, Ken, 92
Angle Tarn, 100
Aonach Dubh, 70
Ardvorlich, 84
Ardvourlie, 26
Arenig Fach, 234
Arenig Fawr, 231
Arivurichardich, 85
Ashes Hollow, 151
Assynt, Loch, 19
Atthill, Robin, 175
Avebury, 168, 171, 173
Axe Edge, 144

Ba, Coireach a', 78
Bad Step, 39
Base Brown, 112, 115
Baslow, 140
Beachy Head, 196
Beacon Hill (Quantocks), 182
Beddgelert, 213, 221
Bellamy, Rex, 148
Benalder Cottage, 64
Benbulbin, 252
Benlugmore, 255
Bennan, 94
Bennet, Donald, 39, 69
Benwhiskin, 254
Benyellary, 94
Berkshire Downs, 168
Berry, Geoffrey, 108
Bhastier, Bealach a', 35
Bhatain, Sgor a', 13
Bhuiridh, Beinn a', 74
Bianasdail, Gleann, 43
Bidean nam Bian, 69, 71, 76
Biod an Fhithich, 53
Birchen Edge, 140
Birkhouse Moor, 118
Black Down, 175, 177
Black Hambleton, 136, 137
Black Hill, 89
Black Mount, 76
Blencathra, 104
Bodfari, 201
Bolton Priory, 134
Bonington, Chris, 104
Bosigran, 189
Bowland, Forest of, 122
Box Hill, 193
Braeleny Farm, 85
Braes of Foss, 63
Brandon, 267
Breabag, 18
Bridge of Gaur, 64
Bridge of Orchy, 64, 76
Broadway, 166

Brown Pike, 119
Buachaille Etive Mor, 71
Buchan Burn, 92
Buckden Pike, 127
Buckland, 166
Buckstone, The, 160
Burbage Edge, 139
Burnsall, 134
Buttermere, 108, 109
Buttermilk Burn, 81

Cader Idris, 238
Cailness Gorge, 86
Callow Hollow, 151
Camasunary, 39
Cape Wrath, 10
Carnedd Llewelyn, 205
Carnedds, The, 205
Carnmenyn, 247
Castlelaw Hill, 89
Cat and Fiddle, 148
Chaonasaid, Sgor, 13
Charlie, Bonny Prince, 60, 64, 66
Chase End Hill, 156, 159
Chearcaill, Beinn a', 29
Cheddar Gorge, 175
Chiltern Hills, 163
Chleirich, Sgor a', 13
Christmas Common, 164
Chrome Hill, 144
Chugg, Brian, 178
Clach Leathad, 76
Clemson, David, 180
Clisham, 26
Cluny's Cage, 64, 66
Clwydian Hills, 201
Cnicht, 222
Cobbler, The, 81
Collier, Chris, 151
Collister, Rob, 205
Compton Martin, 175, 177
Coniston Fells, 119
Coniston Old Man, 119
Conistone, 127
Conival, 16
Cook, Dave, 186
Cooper, Phil, 12, 144
Corfe Castle, 190
Cornish Coast Path, 186
Corrieyairack Pass, 60
Corrour Bothy, 58
Corrour Lodge, 66
Coruisk, Loch, 39
Cotswolds, The, 165
Cousins, Sandy, 43, 81
Cox, David, 218
Coylumbridge, 56
Crag Lough, 97
Craig Cwm Silyn, 226
Craignaw, 93
Cranmere Pool, 183
Creag Mo, 26
Creiche, Coire na, 40
Croe, Glen, 81
Croesor, 222, 224
Crowcombe Park Gate, 182
Cruachan, Ben, 74, 76
Cruinn a' Bheinn, 86

Crymmych, 246, 248
Cuillin of Skye, 33, 39, 49, 55
Curbar Edge, 140
Cwm Cau, 238
Cwm Eigiau, 205
Cwm-y-ffynnon, Llyn, 212

Dale Head, 108
Dales Way, 134
Dartmoor, 183
Derry Lodge, 58
Devil's Bowling Green, 93
Devil's Chair, 152
Devil's Point, 58
Dolgarrog, 205
Dorset Coast, 190
Dovedale, 144
Dow Crag, 119
Drasdo, Harold, 234
Drochaid Glas, 74
Druim nan Ramh, 35, 39
Dduallt, 231
Dubh, Gleann, 16
Dunkery Beacon, 178

Eastbourne, 196
Eastern Edges, Peak, 138
Edale, 141
Edenhope Hill, 155
Edge, The, 141
Edra, Beinn, 29
Eglwyseg Mountain, 204
Elgol, 39
Enoch, Loch, 92
Ericht, Loch, 64
Errigal, 249
Exmoor, 178

Fada, Lochan, 43
Faha, 267, 268
Fearna, Loch, 51
Fhada, Beinn, 70
Fhada, Gleann na Beinne, 79
Fhionnaich, Loch, 13
Fionn Choire, 37
Fish Hill, 166, 167
Flotterstone, 89
Flouch Inn, 138
Foley, Gerry, 253
Forcan Ridge, 53, 79
Forest of Dean, 160
Fort Augustus, 60, 67
Freshwater West, 243
Froggatt Edge, 140
Froswick, 102
Fuar-chathaidh, Beallach, 78

Gabhail, Coire, 70
Gairland Burn, 92
Galloway Hills, 92
Galty Mountains, 262, 263
Garvamore, 60
Gilbert, Oliver, 132
Gilbert, Richard, 10, 22, 64, 74, 76, 96,
  127, 136, 156, 196
Gillean, Sgurr nan, 33, 40
Gillercomb, 112, 115
Gillman, Peter, 16

Glencoaghan Horseshoe, 258
Glencorse, 89
Gleouraich, 51
Glyders, 209, 211, 212
Gordale Scar, 132
Gore Hill, 170
Gormire, 136
Goyt Valley, 148
Grassington, 127, 134
Great Gable, 112
Great Hellgate, 112
Great Malvern, 156
Great Whernside, 127, 128, 135
Green Gable, 115
Greenbank, Tony, 112
Greenwood, Stephen, 51
Grey Friar, 120
Griffin, Harry, 119
Grim's Ditch, 170
Grindslow Knoll, 141
Grit Fell, 122
Gritstone Trail, 148
Guildford, 193

Hadrian's Wall, 96
Hall, Christopher, 163
Harris, Isle of, 26, 49
Hay Stacks, 109
Helvellyn, 116
Herefordshire Beacon, 158
Hetherington, Alastair, 60
Hibernian, 124
High Crag, 109
High Stile, 109
High Street, 100
Hindscarth, 108
Holford, 180
Honister Pass, 108
Horner, 178
Horns of Alligin, 49
Housesteads Fort, 97
Hoy, Michael, 124
Hunt, Lord, 153

Icknield Way, 163
Ill Bell, 102
Ilam, 147
Ilkley Bridge, 134
Inchnadamph Hotel, 16
Irthing, River, 99
Isle of Man, 119, 124

Keal, Loch na, 79
Kettlewell, 134, 135
Kilburn White Horse, 136
Killary Harbour, 255
Kilmarie, 39
Kilnsey Crag, 127, 135
Kinder Low, 141
Kinder Scout, 141
Kingshouse Hotel, 76
Kinloch Rannoch, 63
Kinlochewe, 43
Knighton, 153
Knucklas Castle, 153
Kyle of Durness, 10, 12
Kyle of Tongue, 13

Lady Isabella, 125
Lairig Ghru, 56
Lamorna Cove, 186
Land's End, 186
Lanercost Priory, 99
Langaig, Loch, 32
Laogh, Coir'nan, 46
Leac nan Each, Sgurr, 55
Light, Jo, 53
Llanberis, 213
Llanfair Waterdine, 154
Lochan, Coire nan, 69
Lomond, Ben, 86
Long Man of Wilmington, 196
Long Mynd, 151, 154, 157
Lota Corrie, 33
Loyal, Ben, 13
Loyne, Glen, 51
Luibeg, 58
Lulworth Cove, 190
Lurgainn, Loch, 22
Lyme Park, 148
Lynam, Joss, 258

Maaruig River, 26
Maidensgrove, 164
Malham Cove, 132
Malvern Hills, 156
Margery Hill, 138
Martindale, Frank, 262
Maskelyne, Nevil, 63
Mather, Neil, 89
Maumina, 258
McNeish, Cameron, 63
Meall a' Bhuiridh, 76
Meall an Odhar, 53
Meall Cuanail, 74
Meall na h-Iolaire, 85
Mendips, 157, 175
Merrick, 94
Mhaim, Bealach a', 37, 40
Mhic Nobuil, Coire, 46
Mhor, Sgurr, 46
Migneint, 234
Milldale, 144
Milngavie, 88
Miners' Track, 218
Moel Fammau, 201
Moel Hebog, 226
Moel y Cynghorion, 213
Moelwyn Mawr, 224
Moelwyns, 222
Moffat, Gwen, 19
Monmouth, 160
Montgomery, 153
Mor, Sgurr, 29
More, Ben, (Mull), 79
More Assynt, Ben, 13, 16, 19
More Coigach, Ben, 24, 32
Morgan's Hill, 171, 172
Morris, Jan, 241
Moulam, Tony, 213
Mull, Isle of, 79
Mulla-fo-dheas, 26
Mullwharchar, 94
Mungrisdale, 104
Murray, W. H., 71

Mweelrea, 255
Mynydd Moel, 238

Nab, The, 142
Narnain Boulders, 81
Needle, The, 32
Neill, John, 238
Neldricken, Loch, 92
Nettlebed, 164
Newby, Eric, 190
Nicholson's Chimney, 37
North Barrule, 124
North Downs, 193
North Pembroke Coast, 241

Offa's Dyke, 153, 160, 201, 204
Oldbury Castle, 172
Oldshoremore, 10
Osmotherley, 137
Ossian, Loch, 66
Ossian's Cave, 70
Our, Ben, 85

Patterdale, 100, 116
Pen Llithrig-y-wrach, 205
Pen-y-Pass, 212, 219
Pen-y-Gwrd, 209, 212
Pendeen Watch, 186
Pennant, Cwm, 226
Pentlands, 89
Perrin, Jim, 226, 231, 243
Pilsbury Castle Hills, 144
Policeman, The, 35
Pools of Dee, 57
Port Erin, 126
Postbridge, 183
Poucher, W. A., 33
Presely Hills, 246
Price, Tom, 100
Purbeck Hills, 190

Quantocks, 180
Quinag, 16, 19, 22
Quirang, 29
Quoich, Loch, 51

Raggedstone Hill, 159
Rainigadale, 26
Rankin, Denis, 249
Rannoch, Loch, 63
Rannoch, Moor of, 63, 64, 71, 76
Ratlinghope, 151
Red Earl's Dyke, 158
Red Pike, 109
Red Tarn, 116
Redfern, Roger, 138, 141
Rhobell Fawr, 231
Riabhach, Coire, 33
Ribigill Farm, 13
Richards, Mark, 165
Ridgeway, The, 168, 171
Ringing Roger, 142
Robinson, 108
Rose, Charles, 46
Rowardennan, 88
Rubha Ban, 39

Saddle of Glen Shiel, 51, 53

Saddleback, 104
Sail Gharbh, 20
Sail Gorm, 20
Sandwood Bay, 11, 20
Sandy Hole Pass, 183
Scaladale River, 27
Scales, 104
Scavaig, Loch, 39
Schiehallion, 63, 71
Seaforth, Loch, 26
Seathwaite, 112, 115
Segsbury Down, 170
Sennen Cove, 186
Seven Sisters, 196
Sewing Shields, 96
Sharp Edge, 104
Shenberrow, 167
Shining Tor, 148
Showell Styles, 209, 222
Shutlingsloe, 148
Silbury, 171
Sinclair Hut, 57
Sionascaig, Loch, 22
Slieau Whallian, 126
Sligachan, 33, 39
Slioch, 43
Smith, Roger, 84
Snaefell, 119, 124
Snowdon, 213, 218
South Barrule, 126
South Pembroke Coast, 243
Sour Milk Gill, 112, 115
Speakman, Colin, 134
Spidean Coinich, 19
Spidean Dhomhuill Bhric, 53
Spidean Mialach, 51
Sron na Creise, 76
St. Ann's Well, 156
St. David's Head, 241
St. George's Bridge, 60
St. Non's Bay, 241
Stac Pollaidh, 22
Stackpole Quay, 243
Staffin, 29
Stanage Edge, 138
Stanway, 166
Stephen, Ian, 26
Steven, Campbell, 79
Stiperstones, 151
Stob Coire Sgreamhach, 70
Stob Dearg (Buachaille), 71
Stob Dearg (Cruachan), 74
Stob Diamh, 74
Stob Garbh, 75
Stob Ghabhar, 76
Stob na Broige, 72
Stokenchurch, 163
Stonor House, 164
Strid, 134
Striding Edge, 116
Stuc a' Chroin, 84
Sty Head, 112
Succoth, 81
Suilven, 16, 19, 22, 32
Sutton Bank, 136
Swirl How, 120, 121
Swirral Edge, 118
Symonds Yat, 161

Tairneilear, Coir' a', 40
Tarnbrook, 122
Taylor Gill Force, 112
Teal, Maurice and Marion, 160
Tempar, 63
Thornthwaite Crag, 101, 102
Toll a' Mhadaidh, 46
Tom na Gruagaich, 46
Tomnaval, 26
Torridon, 46
Traligill, River, 16
Trool, Glen, 92
Trotternish, 29, 35
Troutbeck, 103
Truskmore, 254
Tuill Bhain, Sgurr an, 43
Tulla, Loch, 78
Turnhouse Hill, 91
Twelve Bens, 258

Unsworth, Walt, 122

Vaughan-Thomas, Wynford, 246
Velvet Bottom, 175
Viator's Bridge, 144
Vorlich, Ben, 84

Wade, General, 60
Wainwright, A. 116
Walna Scar Road, 119
Walton, Izaak, 144
Wansdyke, 171, 172
Ward's Stone, 122
Watkin Path, 218, 220
Watson, Adam, 56
Wayland's Smithy, 169
Wedgwood, Janet, 168
Weir, Tom, 29, 86
Welsh Bicknor, 160
West Dart River, 183
West Highland Way, 76, 86
West Kennett Long Barrow, 171
West Kip, 90
Westacott, Hugh, 183
Westmorland Crags, 115
Wetherlam, 121
Wharfedale, 127, 134
Whilde, Tony, 255
White Horse Hill, Uffington, 169
Wild, Peter and Muriel, 201
Wilson, Tim, 124
Wiltshire Downs, 171
Windgather Rocks, 148
Windy Gap, 115
Wolfscote Dale, 144
Worcestershire Beacon, 156
Wright, C. J., 193
Wright, Geoffrey, 171
Wye Valley, 160
Wyresdale, 122

Y Garn (Pennant), 226
Yairack Burn, 60
Yr Aran, 216

Zennor, 186

Other Good Walks and Scrambles

Ross-shire	Cul Mor and Cul Beag from the Knockan geological trail car park. 11 miles.
Ross-shire	Ben More Coigach from Culnacraig near Achiltibuie. Traverse of main ridge, returning over Sgurr an Fhidhleir and Cona' Mheall. 8 miles.
Ross-shire	Ullapool to Bonar Bridge through Glens Achall, Douchary, Mor and Strath Carron. 40 miles.
Ross-shire	Beinn Dearg Forest. Circuit of Eididh nan Clach Geala, Meall nan Ceapraichean and Beinn Dearg from Inverlael Lodge. 14 miles.
Ross-shire	Achnashellach to Kinlochewe through the Coulin Pass. 11 miles.
Inverness-shire/Ross-shire	Traverse of Beinn Fhada from Croe Bridge to Cluanie Inn via Alltbeath. 16 miles.
Isle of Skye	Kilmarie to Sligachan over Bla Bheinn (Blaven) and Clach Glas. *For the experienced climber only.* 13 miles.
Inverness-shire	Cairngorms. Circuit from Coylumbridge including Gleann Einich, Sgoran Dubh Mor, Sgor Gaoith, Braeriach and the Lairig Ghru. 24 miles.
Inverness-shire/Aberdeenshire	Cairngorms. Clova to Braemar via Glen Doll, Jock's Road, Tolmount and Glen Callater. 18 miles.
Inverness-shire	Glen Finnan horseshoe walk over Streap, Sgurr Thuilm and Sgurr nan Coireachan. 16 miles.
Perthshire	A traverse of the Ochils between Glendevon and Dunblane. 16 miles.
The Isle of Jura	Round of the Paps of Jura, including Glas Bheinn and Dubh Bheinn, from Craighouse. 15 miles.
Selkirkshire	Melrose Abbey to Dryburgh Abbey over the Eildon Hills. 6 miles.
Dumfries and Galloway	Galloway Highlands. Cairnsmore of Carsphairn and Beninner from Carsphairn. 11 miles.
Cumbria	Northern Lakeland. Circuit of the fells west of Mungrisedale including Bowscale Fell, Bannerdale, Great Calva, Knott, the Caldbeck Fells and Carrock Fell. 18 miles.
Cumbria	Coledale Horseshoe from Braithwaite, including Causey Pike, Crag Hill, Eel Crag and Grisedale Pike. 9 miles.
Cumbria	Heron Pike, Rydal Fell, Fairfield, Hart Crag and High Pike from Rydal. 10 miles.
Northumberland	The Southern Cheviots. Circular walk from Ingram via Linhope Spout, Hedgehope and Threestoneburn House. 14 miles.
North Yorkshire.	Swaledale. Through the valley of the River Swale between Gunnerside and Keld. 6 miles.
North Yorkshire	North York Moors. Circuit of Farndale from Gillamoor via Rudland Rigg, Rosedale Railway, Church Houses and the beck. Especially recommended in April when Farndale is a mass of wild daffodils. 20 miles.
Lancashire	Ascent of Pendle Hill from Barley via Ogden Clough. 7 miles.
Humberside	One of the finest sections of the Wolds Way across the Yorkshire Wolds between North Ferriby and Arras. 20 miles.
Staffordshire	The White Peak. The valley of the Manifold River between Longnor and Ilam. 14 miles.
Cheshire	The Sandstone Trail from Delamere Forest to Duckington village. 32 miles.
Nottinghamshire	Across Sherwood Forest from Worksop to Rainworth via Clumber Park, Birklands and Clipstone Forest. 22 miles.
Gwynedd	Snowdonia. Traverse of Moel Siabod from Capel Curig to Pen-y-Gwryd. 7 miles.
Powys	Radnor Forest. New Radnor to Llandegley over Whimble, Black Mixen and Great Rhos. 9 miles.
Powys/Dyfed	Across the High Fanau (Fforest Fawr and Black Mountains) from Storey Arms to Brynamman including Fan Fawr, Fan Gihiryoh and Carmarthen Van. 24 miles.
Gloucestershire	The Cotswolds. The Winchcombe to Painswick section of the Cotswold Way. 26 miles.
West Glamorgan	The Gower Peninsula. Coastal path from Worms Head to the Mumbles. 19 miles.
Buckinghamshire/Hertfordshire	The Northern Chilterns. Wendover to Ivinghoe via Cock's Hill, Pitstone Hill and Ivinghoe Beacon. 14 miles.
Essex/Hertfordshire	The Three Forests Way from Loughton to Bishops Stortford via Epping Forest and Nazeing. 27 miles.
Kent	The Charing to Canterbury section of the Pilgrim's Way via Chilham Castle and Bigbury Camp. 15 miles.
Hampshire	The New Forest. Circular walk from Burley via Poundhill Heath, Lyndhurst, Minstead and Mark Ash Wood. 20 miles.
Cornwall	Across Bodmin Moor. Henwood to Camelford over Kilmar Tor, Smallacombe Downs, Brown Willy and Rough Tor. 15 miles.
Co. Wexford/Co. Carlow	Mount Leinster and the Blackstairs Ridge traverse from Bunclody to St. Mullins. 18 miles.
Co. Tipperary/Co. Waterford	Across the sandstone hills of the Knockmealdown Ridge from 152048 to Ballyporeen. 17 miles.
Co. Mayo	The Nephin Beg Ridge from Bangor Bridge to 923963. 22 miles.
Co. Tyrone/Co. Derry	The Sperrin Ridge (Sperrin Skyway) from 716997 to Butterlope Glen. 17 miles.

The Country Code

1 Guard against all risks of fire
2 Fasten all gates
3 Keep dogs under proper control
4 Keep to paths across farm land
5 Avoid damaging fences, hedges and walls
6 Leave no litter
7 Safeguard water supplies
8 Protect wildlife, plants and trees
9 Go carefully on country roads
10 Respect the life of the countryside

The Country Code is not a list of restrictions placed on the walker. It should be seen as a recipe for freedom. We must not forget that free access to the hills depends on continuing co-operation of farmers and landowners. No charge is levied for access to the hills and the least we, as walkers, can do in return is to scrupulously observe the Country Code.

It is morally indefensible to leave paper, polythene bags, tin cans and bottles on hillsides or in ditches. Such rubbish can be a serious hazard to livestock and in some cases can be a fire risk. Moreover unless we keep the hills clear of rubbish we will destroy the very reason for their attractiveness.

Another important point is the need to protect dry stone walls and fences. These should never be climbed. A gate or stile can usually be located and some walls have specially constructed steps. Nothing enrages a farmer more than to have to repeatedly repair walls and fences after thoughtless damage caused by walkers, and our relationship with the farming community can be seriously undermined by such incidents.

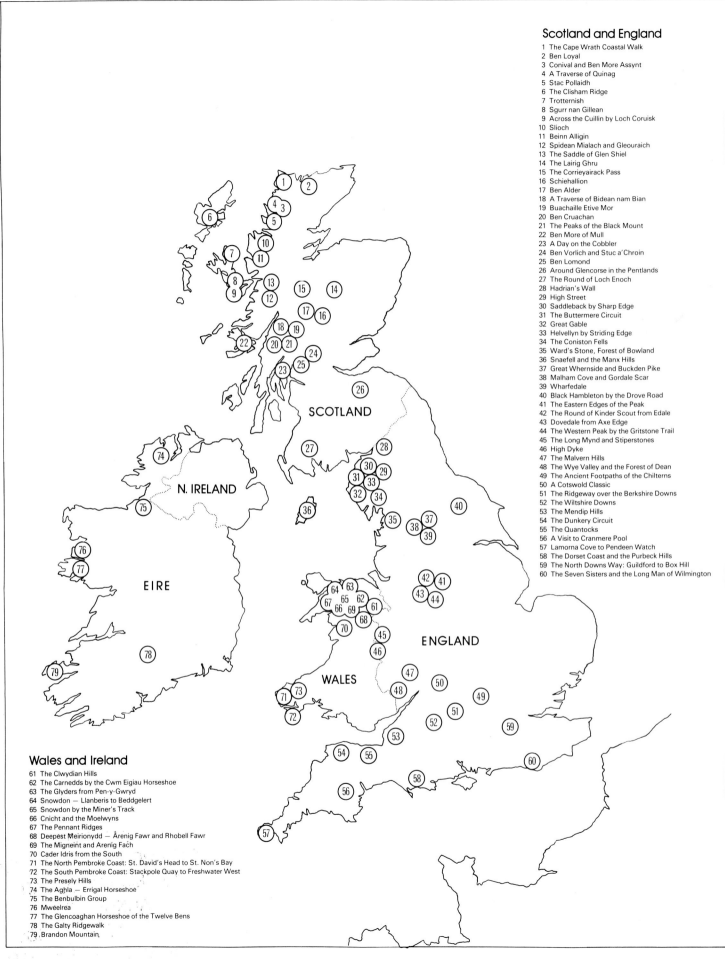

Scotland and England

1 The Cape Wrath Coastal Walk
2 Ben Loyal
3 Conival and Ben More Assynt
4 A Traverse of Quinag
5 Stac Pollaidh
6 The Clisham Ridge
7 Trotternish
8 Sgurr nan Gillean
9 Across the Cuillin by Loch Coruisk
10 Slioch
11 Beinn Alligin
12 Spidean Mialach and Gleouraich
13 The Saddle of Glen Shiel
14 The Lairig Ghru
15 The Corrieyairack Pass
16 Schiehallion
17 Ben Alder
18 A Traverse of Bidean nam Bian
19 Buachaille Etive Mor
20 Ben Cruachan
21 The Peaks of the Black Mount
22 Ben More of Mull
23 A Day on the Cobbler
24 Ben Vorlich and Stuc a'Chroin
25 Ben Lomond
26 Around Glencorse in the Pentlands
27 The Round of Loch Enoch
28 Hadrian's Wall
29 High Street
30 Saddleback by Sharp Edge
31 The Buttermere Circuit
32 Great Gable
33 Helvellyn by Striding Edge
34 The Coniston Fells
35 Ward's Stone, Forest of Bowland
36 Snaefell and the Manx Hills
37 Great Whernside and Buckden Pike
38 Malham Cove and Gordale Scar
39 Wharfedale
40 Black Hambleton by the Drove Road
41 The Eastern Edges of the Peak
42 The Round of Kinder Scout from Edale
43 Dovedale from Axe Edge
44 The Western Peak by the Gritstone Trail
45 The Long Mynd and Stiperstones
46 High Dyke
47 The Malvern Hills
48 The Wye Valley and the Forest of Dean
49 The Ancient Footpaths of the Chilterns
50 A Cotswold Classic
51 The Ridgeway over the Berkshire Downs
52 The Wiltshire Downs
53 The Mendip Hills
54 The Dunkery Circuit
55 The Quantocks
56 A Visit to Cranmere Pool
57 Lamorna Cove to Pendeen Watch
58 The Dorset Coast and the Purbeck Hills
59 The North Downs Way: Guildford to Box Hill
60 The Seven Sisters and the Long Man of Wilmington

Wales and Ireland

61 The Clwydian Hills
62 The Carnedds by the Cwm Eigiau Horseshoe
63 The Glyders from Pen-y-Gwryd
64 Snowdon — Llanberis to Beddgelert
65 Snowdon by the Miner's Track
66 Cnicht and the Moelwyns
67 The Pennant Ridges
68 Deepest Meirionydd — Arenig Fawr and Rhobell Fawr
69 The Migneint and Arenig Fach
70 Cader Idris from the South
71 The North Pembroke Coast: St. David's Head to St. Non's Bay
72 The South Pembroke Coast: Stackpole Quay to Freshwater West
73 The Presely Hills
74 The Aghla — Errigal Horseshoe
75 The Benbulbin Group
76 Mweelrea
77 The Glencoaghan Horseshoe of the Twelve Bens
78 The Galty Ridgewalk
79 Brandon Mountain